# THE WORLD GUIDE TO
# MODEL TRAINS

# THE WORLD GUIDE TO
# MODEL TRAINS

The Guide to International Railways and Ready-to-Run Models

Compiled by Peter McHoy; Consultant Editor: Chris Ellis

**GREENWICH HOUSE**
**Distributed by Crown Publishers, Inc.**
**New York**

# Acknowledgements

**Compiled by** Peter McHoy
**Consultant Editor** Chris Ellis
**Designer** Clive Sutherland
**House Editors** Isabel Clark, Jackie Fortey
**Editorial Assistants** Geraldine Carter, Tim Faulkner,
Paul MacNamara, Liz Orme
**Photographer** Gavin Cottrell
**Maps Compiled by** Kenneth Westcott-Jones
**Maps Illustrated by** Clive Sutherland

This book would not have been possible without the considerable help of manufacturers and individuals within the trade.

In particular we would like to thank the following manufacturers for their patience and help: K Arnold GmbH; Dick Redles, Bachmann Industries Inc; Bemo Modelleisenbahnen GmbH; Mr Klotsch, VEB Berliner-Bahnen; Bowser Manufacturing Co; Electrotren; P. Graham Farish, Grafar Ltd; Mr Setzer, Gebr. Fleischmann KG; Mr Ellis Green, Herkimer Tool and Model Works, Inc; Simon Kohler, Hornby Hobbies Ltd; Mr J. Monreal, Model-Iber (Ibertren); Kadee Quality Products Co; Dieter Bücherl and Mr J. Karasek, Liliput GmbH; Mr E. L. Rozsa, Liliput (UK) Ltd; Milvia Fanelli, Lima spa; Louis Gostinger, Fundimensions (Lionel); Stuart Jesson, The Palitoy Company; Bogdan Ercigoj, Mehanotehnika; Detlev Beyer, Gebr. Märklin & Cie GmbH; Mr S. C. Pritchard, Pritchard Patent Product Co Ltd (Peco); Mr Ploberger, Roco-Modellspielwaren GmbH; Mr Doerfler, Trix Mangold GmbH; Robert Rao and Richard Maston, Tyco Industries Inc; Walter Waibel AG; Mrs Wrenn, G & R Wrenn Ltd.

Our thanks also go to the following agents and model shops for their help: F. J. de Beraza (Delta Pacific Company), John Hills (M&R Model Railways Ltd), Graham Hubbard (Eastern Models), Gordon Imhoff (Mays Models), Mr Lawrence (United Sterling Corporation Ltd), Mr and Mrs Lee (Model & Tool Supplies), Tony Richards (A. M. Richards), Colin Sparrow (Beatties of London Ltd), and the staff of the Brighton and Kingston-upon-Thames branches.

David Lloyd (Continental Modeller) also helped to put us on the right lines.

Whilst every care is made to ensure that the information given in this book is correct at the time of going to press, the Publishers cannot guarantee that prices and measurements given have not been altered by manufacturers since that date.

First English edition published by Ward Lock Ltd 1983
This 1983 edition is published by Greenwich House, a division of Arlington House, Inc., distributed by Crown Publishers, Inc.

hgfedcba

Created, designed and produced by Ventura Publishing Limited.
44 Uxbridge Street, London W8 7TG

All correspondence concerned with the contents of this book should be addressed to Ventura Publishing Ltd., 44 Uxbridge Street, London W8 7TG

Library of Congress Cataloging in Publication Data
Main entry under title:
The World Guide to Model Trains

    Includes index
1. Railroads-Models. 1. McHoy, Peter.
TF197.W67    1983    625.1′9    83-5516
ISBN 0-517-41036-2

Typesetting by Peter McHoy and Wordsmiths, Somerset.
Colour origination by Photographic Design & Integrated Graphics, Herts.
Printed and bound in Belgium by Brepols N.V., Turnhout

# Contents

# Introduction

## Using the book

Railways have held a special fascination for generations of enthusiasts. The appeal has been much the same whether the locomotives have been steam, diesel, or electric, and it has mattered little whether the period has been the 1920s or the 1980s. Not surprisingly, each generation has its preferences – those who spent their youth watching steam trains are quite likely to have a slight contempt for diesel or electric locomotives; yet diesels and electrics have their own following. The youngster of today can become as excited by a modern high speed train, or a powerful diesel hauling a heavy freight train as his father or grandfather was enthralled by the sight, sound, and even smell, of the hissing and puffing steam monsters of their younger days.

Whether you are seven or seventy, it makes little difference – the appeal of railway modeling is much the same. It's the chance to create your own private piece of nostalgia, or to run a modern railway *your* way that is the real appeal. You build your own world, your own time capsule, your own bit of history.

## Deciding what you want

Railway modelers are as diverse as any other group of people. Different modelers look for different things in their railways and it is useful to decide what really interest *you* most if you are to buy wisely and build your railway sensibly.

Almost all railway modelers started with a model train-set, probably as a child, and from there they can 'graduate' in a number of different ways. To some of the most enthusiastic modelers, the interest lies in *making* the models, or even concentrating on scenery and track. However, probably the largest group of model railway enthusiasts are those who get their pleasure from *running* trains. The scenery is important of course, but the signal box and freight shed are likely to be bought ready-assembled or in kit form, the track will probably have been bought 'off the shelf', and most of the rolling stock is likely to have been bought ready-to-run. It is for this group of enthusiasts that *The World Guide to Model Trains* is intended. Whether you are a beginner or an experienced modeler, this book should help you to get more from your model railway.

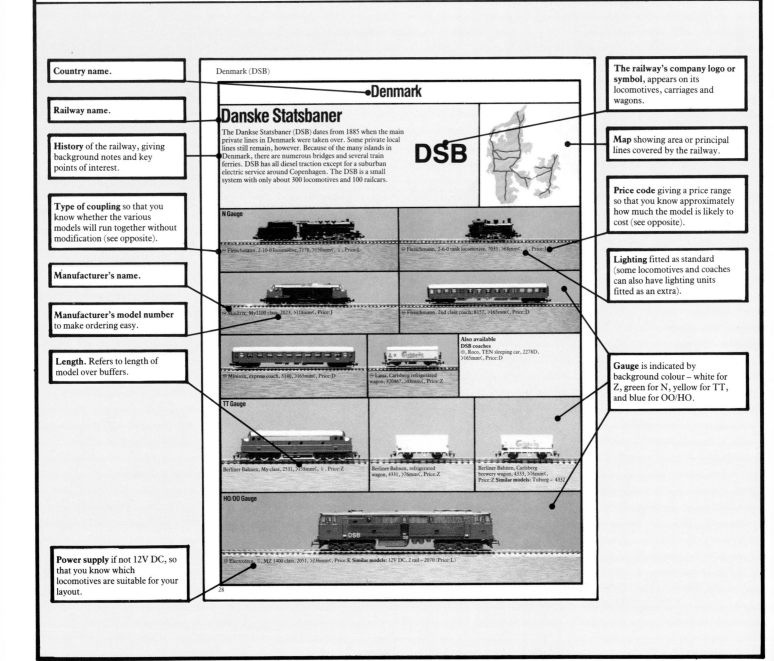

Country name.

Railway name.

History of the railway, giving background notes and key points of interest.

Type of coupling so that you know whether the various models will run together without modification (see opposite).

Manufacturer's name.

Manufacturer's model number to make ordering easy.

Length. Refers to length of model over buffers.

Power supply if not 12V DC, so that you know which locomotives are suitable for your layout.

The railway's company logo or symbol, appears on its locomotives, carriages and wagons.

Map showing area or principal lines covered by the railway.

Price code giving a price range so that you know approximately how much the model is likely to cost (see opposite).

Lighting fitted as standard (some locomotives and coaches can also have lighting units fitted as an extra).

Gauge is indicated by background colour – white for Z, green for N, yellow for TT, and blue for OO/HO.

Denmark (DSB)

### Denmark

## Danske Statsbaner

The Danske Statsbaner (DSB) dates from 1885 when the main private lines in Denmark were taken over. Some private local lines still remain, however. Because of the many islands in Denmark, there are numerous bridges and several train ferries. DSB has all diesel traction except for a suburban electric service around Copenhagen. The DSB is a small system with only about 300 locomotives and 100 railcars.

**DSB**

**N Gauge**

Fleischmann, 2-10-0 locomotive, 7178, >150mm<, Price:L

Fleischmann, 2-6-0 tank locomotive, 7031, >68mm<, Price:J

Minitrix, My1100 class, 2023, >118mm<, Price:J

Fleischmann, 2nd class coach, 8157, >165mm<, Price:D

Minitrix, express coach, 3140, >165mm<, Price:D

Lima, Carlsberg refrigerated wagon, 320467, >88mm<, Price:Z

**Also available**
**DSB coaches**
Roco, TEN sleeping car, 2278D, >165mm<, Price:D

**TT Gauge**

Berliner Bahnen, My class, 2531, >158mm<, Price:Z

Berliner Bahnen, refrigerated wagon, 4331, >76mm<, Price:Z

Berliner Bahnen, Carlsberg brewery wagon, 4333, >76mm<, Price:Z Similar models: Tuborg – 4332

**HO/OO Gauge**

Electrotren, MZ 1400 class, 2051, >236mm<, Price:K Similar models: 12V DC, 2 rail – 2070 (Price:L)

28

## How the book can help

The book has been arranged so that you can decide on a line or railway that you want to model, and then see at a glance which ready-to-run models are available.

Twenty, or even ten, years ago, the same model would be in production for a decade or more; now many models are produced in one-off runs. When these have been sold, they are likely to be replaced with new models. We received much cooperation from manufacturers, who allowed us to photograph new items before they were released, but inevitably some models may have appeared since this book was compiled.

If you have difficulty obtaining any of the models locally, consult the list of manufacturers on page 255. This gives addresses to write to and details of whether models can be ordered direct from the manufacturer. You will also be able to keep up-to-date on model changes by sending for catalogues that particularly interest you.

Bear in mind that you may find some retailers with stocks of old models no longer in production and not included in this book. You are most likely to track these down by reading the advertisements in model railway magazines.

This book contains details of most items of rolling stock that are available for the countries covered by the book. Where the variation in a model is only one of livery – the same model might be painted in different colors, or identical wagons might be painted with the individual markings of several private companies – we have usually illustrated one version and listed the others under 'similar models'.

Many European trains cross boundaries, and you may find the wagons of one country in the marshalling yards of another (this explains why in a few instances you can buy a few wagons or coaches of a particular country but no locomotives). In each case we have included the wagons under the owning country. Some famous trains that run through several countries have their own coaches and locomotives allocated, and they are painted in special colors. More than one country may contribute to the service, so you may have French and German TEE (Trans Europe Express) coaches. Again, you will find them listed under the country owning them. Often they will be listed as 'similar models', as it is likely that the locomotives and coaches are exactly the same as those used for other express services, but painted in special colors.

## Key to codes and symbols

The symbols used throughout the book have been kept to a minimum, to make them easier to remember.

## Gauge

The pages for the main part of the book are color-coded so that you can see at a glance which pages are for your gauge. (OO and HO run on the same track and have been grouped together; most British-outline models are OO, others are likely to be HO scale).

white: Z gauge
green: N gauge
yellow: TT gauge
blue: OO/HO gauge (including HOe and HOm)

## Couplings

It is vital to know which type of coupling a model is fitted with if you want to be able to run models of different manufacturers together without modification. The various couplings, and possible modifications, are explained in detail on page 10. To be able to run stock together without modification, keep to models with the same coupling symbol, which is the first one in each caption.

⊖ = N gauge standard
□ = N gauge Kadee magnetic
◎ = NEM A/B (Märklin type)
◉ = horn-hook
⊗ = tension-lock (Hornby type)
➁ = Trix Express
▣ = tension-lock (Fleischmann type)
▣ = Arnold Simplex coupling
⊞ = Z gauge standard

## Power supply

Most model railways run on 12-volt DC current through a transformer (or from batteries – see page 12). The vast majority of models are supplied from a two-rail system, but some use central studs between the rails, and several offer the option of catenary (overhead wire) operation for electric-outline locomotives. Exceptions to two-rail 12-volt systems are noted in the text or in the captions. The symbols used are:

≤ = 16V AC, third rail or stud contact
≃ = 16V AC, two-rail
≡ = 12V DC, third rail (OO/HO gauge)
≠ = 12V DC, third rail (N gauge)
= = 8V DC
⌢ = Working pantograph for catenary pick-up
⇼ = Dummy (non-working) pantograph

Where no symbols for voltage or collection appear, the model is supplied in the usual 12V DC two-rail version.

## Lighting

Some locomotives and coaches are fitted with working lights. This is indicated by ☼. You can also buy lighting kits separately for some coaches, but only integral lighting has been indicated.

## Smoke

Some locomotives will emit 'smoke' when a special oil is used in the chimney. These models have been indicated by ⬡.

## Model number

The manufacturer's model number has been given to make ordering easier. It is important to quote this accurately when ordering, otherwise you may be sent a model in the wrong livery. In a few instances the manufacturer provides several liveries or private-owner markings under the one model number – in these cases we have indicated that you will have to give details of the model required when you order.

## Price code

Models vary considerably in price – so to give you some guide we have given each model a price code. Prices change from year to year, and from country to country; they can also be affected at short notice by changes in exchange rates. You can also buy many models at a discount from companies that advertise in model railway magazines. To provide a guide to the relative cost, the following price codes have been used, based on the manufacturer's recommended retail price.

The prices quoted are based on those for Great Britain; we have used dollar conversions, based on the exchange rate at April 1, 1983. You may find, however, that models from manufacturers in the USA are less expensive, and those from European manufacturers are more expensive. You should, however, be able to judge whether a model is likely to be from an expensive range or from one of the more inexpensive manufacturers. It always pays to shop around anyway to get the best price.

Price code A = under $3
Price code B = $3-5
Price code C = $5-8
Price code D = $8-15
Price code E = $15-23
Price code F = $23-30
Price code G = $30-38
Price code H = $38-46
Price code J = $46-61
Price code K = $61-76
Price code L = $76-114
Price code M = $114-152
Price code N = $152-228
Price code O = over $228
Price code Z = information not available

# Which Gauge?

If you are a newcomer to railway modeling, the various gauges (track and model sizes) can be confusing. To add to the problem, there is sometimes confusion between 'gauge' and 'scale', for the two are not the same.

All true models are reduced replicas of full-sized originals (what railway modelers call the prototype). A model is reduced by a specific proportion from its prototype – the exact reduction is expressed mathematically as 1:32 or 1/32 (for example). This is the *scale* of the model. *Gauge* is simply the distance between the running rails.

'Standard' gauge track in real life is 1435.5mm (4ft 8½in), and when reduced to a *scale* of 1:87, the model track becomes a 16.5mm – what we call HO gauge, the most common gauge used by modelers.

The only reason 4ft 8½in became the 'standard' gauge was because the first railways built in Great Britain had their wheels set at this distance. Tracks wider than this are called 'broad gauge' (in Spain and Ireland, for example, a broad gauge of 1600mm/5ft 3in is used). Tracks narrower than 4ft 8½in are known as 'narrow gauge'. Examples of narrow gauge can be found in countries such as the Isle of Man (914mm/3ft) and much of Africa (927mm/3ft 6in).

The various scales and gauges for modelers are described below.

## Gauge 1
Track width: 45mm
Scale: 1:32 (10mm to 1ft/305mm)
Historically this is the earliest of the miniature railway sizes, as well as the largest after LGB narrow-gauge models, which run on gauge 1 track. Models bigger than gauge 1 are normally considered to come under the heading of model engineering rather than model railways.

Gauge 1 dates back to about 1890, when Märklin in Germany was a major maker, using the lithographed tin-plate techniques of the time. Many other firms have produced models in this scale and gauge since then, but today Märklin remain the only manufacturer of ready-to-run gauge 1 models of any importance. Their gauge 1 models are all of German prototype.

Kits and accessories are produced by other manufacturers, however, and the gauge still has a surprisingly large following. A major drawback to gauge 1 is the large amount of space needed for even a modest layout.

## O gauge
Track width: 32mm
Scale: 1.43 (Great Britain and France), 1:45 (rest of Europe), 1:48 (USA); 7mm, 6.6mm, and 6.35mm to 1ft/305mm respectively.
O gauge was introduced in the early 1900s in an attempt to produce a more compact system. Although different countries interpreted the linear scale slightly differently, in practice the discrepancies are very small.

The famous Hornby tin-plate of yesteryear (still keenly collected) are O gauge models.

Today, only a few manufacturers produce ready-to-run models and the range is limited, but there are many kits and accessories for the gauge. The problems of modeling in O are the space required for a reasonable layout and the relatively high cost of models in comparison smaller sizes, but the gauge attracts many enthusiasts. The advantage of O gauge is the excellent detail that can be produced, allowing fine craftsmanship and running.

## S Gauge
Track width: .844in
Scale: 1:64 (4.8mm to 1ft/305mm)
S gauge models have not been included in this book because only a couple of ready-to-run locomotives are available (in the USA), and virtually everything has to be made by hand.

S gauge was originally called H1 (half gauge 1) when, earlier in the century, it was introduced as another attempt to evolve a more compact scale. In Great Britain a small band of enthusiasts keeps the gauge active; in the United States of America there is much more trade backing.

*The locomotive outlines show how the gauges compare.*

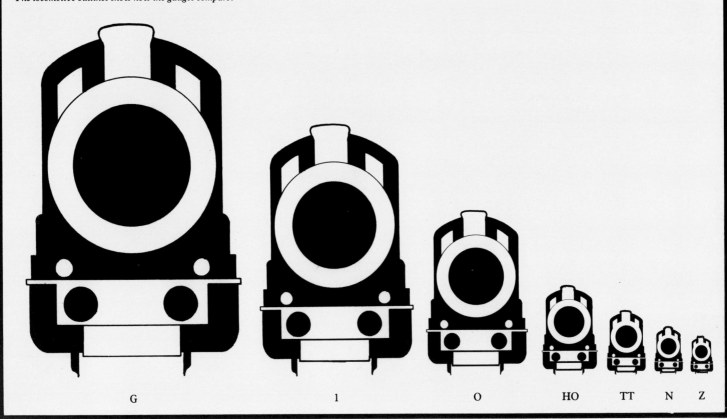

| G | 1 | O | HO | TT | N | Z |

### HO gauge
Track width: 16.5mm
Scale: 1:87 (3.5mm to 1ft/305mm)
This gauge is by far the most important commercially. It was evolved in the 1930s in yet another attempt to establish a compact miniature system. It is, as its name suggests, half of O scale and gauge. It has been estimated that about 80 per cent of the model railway industry is dedicated to producing HO models. All major manufacturers, except the British companies, produce some HO scale models.

### OO gauge
Track width: 16.5mm
Scale: 1:78 (4mm to 1ft/305mm)
In Great Britain, early kit and model makers found it difficult to fit British-outline superstructures over the motors and chassis used by the early German manufacturers for their HO models. To overcome this, the British designers enlarged the scale to 4mm to 1ft (305mm) – but they retained the HO gauge track of 16.5mm.

This discrepancy is substantial, as it is equivalent to running on prototype track about 8½in (216mm) narrower than standard gauge. Despite this, OO has become the most common in Britain, with many manufacturers supplying models of all kinds.

Some accessories are described as OO/HO gauge, and these should be suitable for either OO or HO, despite the discrepancy of almost 15 per cent in volume between models in the two scales.

### TT gauge
Track width: 12mm
Scale: 1:120 (2.5mm to 1ft/305mm)
TT stands for 'Table Top'. It was introduced in the USA in the 1950s, and for a time ready-to-run models were produced commercially in countries such as Britain (where a scale of 1:100 or 3mm to 1ft/305mm was used). Now trade support is minimal and only an East German manufacturer (TT Berliner Bahnen) remains.

### N gauge
Track width: 9mm
Scale: 1:160 (1.9mm to 1ft/305mm)
In Great Britain 1:148 (2.05mm to 1ft/305mm)
After HO and OO, this is the most popular size. There is a large selection of ready-to-run models, covering all the major countries for which model railways are produced. The British prototype models are fractionally larger in scale terms, again to accommodate foreign motors and chassis in British bodies.

The very small size of N gauge means that good layouts can be achieved in a very small area, making it attractive for anyone with limited space.

### Z gauge
Track width: 6.5mm
Scale: 1:220 (1.6mm to 1ft/305mm)
Z is the smallest commercially produced gauge. The minute models have a unique appeal. In this tiny size, a good layout could be built on a tea tray or in a desk drawer!

Because the main manufacturer is Märklin, most of the models are of German prototype. However, a few British and American Z gauge models are available.

### Narrow gauge
It became apparent to some of the more go-ahead railway enthusiasts in the late 1940s and 1950s that if a smaller gauge was adapted to a larger scale, it would be possible to duplicate in miniature the idea of narrow gauge modeling.

Narrow gauge trains have a fascination of their own and in real life they can be found on every continent. Narrow gauge largely came about for economic reasons. On hilly or rough terrain, the track was easier to lay in that less extensive land engineering was required. The locomotives and stock were smaller and less expensive, and also easier to lift and handle. Hence narrow gauge is often found in mountainous areas like Wales, Colorado, or the Austrian Tyrol. Also, industrial lines were often built in narrow gauge, again for economic reasons.

In miniature much narow gauge equipment is made from kits and parts, utilizing available chassis and track. To take an example, the popular smallest narrow gauge scale in Britain utilizes N-gauge track and loco chassis for a scale of 4mm to 1ft (305mm). This is the 1:76 scale of OO gauge. The 9mm track depicts a scale of 2ft 3in (686mm) in 1:76 – the gauge of most British narrow gauge railway lines. In practice the scale and gauge combinations can be chosen to suit the modeler's requirements. The main essential is that an existing model system be available to act as a source of track and chassis.

In recent years some firms have produced track in various gauges with sleepers that resemble the narrow gauge type more closely. Relatively few ready-to-run narrow gauge systems are available, but by using kits and adapting existing bodies the scope is enormous.

The main narrow gauge choices are given below, although there are others if you are prepared to build from scratch or from kits.

### G gauge
Track width: 45mm
Scale: 1:22.5 (13.55mm to 1ft/305mm)
This scale/gauge combination was started by LGB in West Germany. The 45mm track of gauge 1 is used but the models are scaled to 1:22.5 to depict mainly German and Austrian 750mm narrow gauge. The LGB range also includes some models scaled slightly smaller so that the 45mm track gauge can also serve for 1 metre (3ft 6in) narrow gauge.

### HOe, 009, HOm
Using 9mm (N) gauge track with 1:87 or 1:76 scale models enables 750mm gauge or 2ft 3in gauge models to be built for British and European models; HOm is the American equivalent. Several European HOe model ranges are available (Bemo, Liliput, Roco, for example), but for British prototype kits must be used for producing completed models (plenty are available).

Below: *The principal gauges (from left to right) G, 1, O, OO/HO, TT, N, Z.*

# Couplings

The scales for the models described have long been standardized, and an OO gauge model will be built to the same scale whatever the make . . . and will probably run on another manufacturer's OO track (you will have to use replacement wheels on Trix Express models). Unfortunately, it has not been possible to reach the same degree of agreement on wheels and couplers.

### Wheels
At one time popular makes such as Trix and Triang (now Hornby) produced wheels of very coarse profile and wide tread that would only run on their own tracks. However, most wheels are now much finer and made to a more acceptable standard so they will run on the standard Code 100 section track, and through the so-called 'universal' turnouts (what many of us used to call points), as well as the track of all the major manufacturers. Although some are much finer than others, you should not have a problem in using the rolling-stock of one manufacturer on the track of another (but as already mentioned, Trix Express in not compatible without exchange wheels; Trix International is).

In the United States of America virtually all manufacturers, and those outside the country supplying the American market, use wheels that conform to a profile known as RP25 – which was recommended some years ago by the National Model Railroad Association (NMRA). The RP25 standard has a 'fine scale' appearance, with a shallow flange; not only does this look good, but it will also run on 'fine scale' track, which is shallower than the Code 100 track standard in HO train sets.

### Couplers
It would be frustrating to buy a locomotive or a wagon only to find that it did not couple to the rest of your stock. This can be a particular problem if you try to mix the rolling stock of one country with that of another (although for the more recent scales such as N there is an internationally agreed standard). To ensure you buy stock that is suitable for your layout each model in this book has a symbol to identify which are compatible (see page 6).

The type of coupler is likely to vary with scale and country of origin. The main types of coupler are shown on these two pages.

### Z gauge
Because only one major manufacturer – Märklin – produces Z gauge, there are no problems. All stock is fitted with a simple claw-type coupling which engages when the models are pushed together. A ramp is required for remote uncoupling.

### N gauge
The wedge-shaped auto-coupler used for virtually all N gauge models is based on the design produced by Arnold, the pioneers of N gauge. A ramp, operated by hand or electrically, is required to uncouple remotely – though a cocktail stick is a good substitute if you do not

have any uncoupling ramps.

The Arnold Simplex and Kadee magnetic couplers are versions for easier or more realistic uncoupling.

### LBG and gauge 1
LBG rolling stock is also only produced by one manufacturer so there is no compatibility problem if you buy LBG models (which are 'narrow-gauge' using gauge 1 track). The models have a hook at one end and a bar at the other. Only one manufacturer produces gauge 1 ready-to-run models, so compatibility is not a problem.

### O gauge
All ready-to-run O gauge models have a claw-like coupler that is fitted as standard, but it is possible to buy an O gauge version of the Kadee magnetic coupler, which is similar to the Fleischmann HO coupler (see OO/HO gauge). However, most O gauge modelers refit ready-to-run models with scale hook and chain couplers.

### OO/HO gauge
It is among the OO/HO gauge models that most variation occurs, and you must take care when choosing your model unless you are prepared to change the coupling if it is not compatible. Some manufacturers, such as Roco, provide easily exchanged couplings on some of their models, but others are not easy to change.

In Great Britain the *tension-lock* (hook and bar) coupler has now become standard on ready-to-run models. This coupler was first introduced by Triang (now Hornby) about 1960. There is great

Below: *Z gauge coupling.*
Bottom left: *N gauge coupling.*
Bottom right: *HO Fleischmann coupling.*

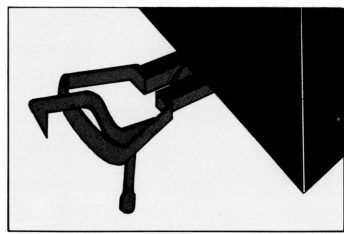

variety in the actual appearance of the tension-lock couplers – some are obtrusive, while others (such as the Mainline type) are commendably small and nicely sprung.

Unfortunately, there is no standardized method of fitting tension-lock couplers. Some makes, like Mainline, have a neat screw system allowing the coupler to be exchanged easily. A few have a plug-fit coupler, while others (Hornby, for example) sometimes have the coupler as part of the chassis moulding. However, if you standardize on tension-lock couplings for British-outline models, the problem of changing couplers should not arise.

The tension-lock coupler has a major advantage in that it can be worked from a sprung ramp without remote control. This can be positioned almost anywhere on the layout. The rolling stock to be uncoupled is stopped over the ramp, and the locomotive reversed slightly to ease the tension – the sprung ramp then lifts the hooks clear of the bars and uncouples. This convenience helps to offset the somewhat ugly appearance of this type of coupler, which is its major drawback.

Although tension-lock couplers will work one with the other, there is no standard way of fitting them and every model has to be dealt with in a different way.

In the rest of Europe, different couplers are used. There are three main types, but the principal one is the **NEM Class A**, sometimes called the Märklin coupler after its main user.

This is essentially a hook with a loop hinged above it. When two vehicles are pushed together, either one or both loops are pushed up over the hook on the adjacent vehicle, coupling them together. Märklin, Rivarossi, Roco, Liliput, Electrotren, Piko, and others, all use this common HO coupler. In a few cases the loops are magnetic (Rivarossi for instance) and magnets in the track uncouple the vehicles in a similar way to the American Kadee system. The loops lift when the coupling is stopped over the magnet. Most, however, require an uncoupling ramp, which must be lifted by hand or wired for remote operation.

Below: *HO Märklin-type coupling.*
Bottom left: *OO tension-lock coupling (Mainline).*
Bottom right: *HO tension-lock coupling (Hornby).*

The main alternative to the coupler just described is the Fleischmann type – named after the firm that uses it for all its HO models. It is like a smaller version of the British tension-lock in operation, but because the hook and bar is set at a different height it is not compatible with the British type. The Fleischmann coupler is very neat and inconspicuous, but it suffers from the disadvantage of requiring a hand or electrically-operated uncoupling ramp.

Roco, Piko, and Fleischmann (and to a lesser extent Märklin) all produce alternative couplers of the Fleischmann or Märklin type so that you can fit one or the other as required. These models have mounts that are easy to fit, and the catalogues list the exchange couplers to suit the various vehicles.

The third system available in Europe is the Roco close-coupler, a novel design with the hooks set in a vertical plane, being quite inconspicuous. It gives much closer spacing between vehicles on the straight (corridor connections actually touch), yet the coupling is cunningly shaped to space the vehicles apart on a curve. Roco produce this as an exchange coupling for all their models, and it can be fitted to some models made by other manufacturers.

Generally it is wise to decide at the outset when you model European railways other than British to standardize on either the Märkin, Fleischmann, or Roco coupler, and alter other stock to suit if you buy models with a different type. The greatest number of manufacturers, including those whose couplings are difficult to change (Liliput, for example), fit the Märklin (NEM Class A) coupler.

Models produced for the United States of America have a distinctive coupler called the 'horn-hook'. This is a type standardized in the early 1950s.

The horn-hook coupler works on the sideways-springing principle, having two 'hooks' that correspond roughly to the buck-eyes of a real auto-coupler. When pushed face-to-face these hooks are forced sideways, then spring together to join. For uncoupling there is a vertical pin hanging below the hook (known as the 'horn') and an uncoupling ramp for this type of coupler has two parallel strips between the rails to force the horns apart if the train stops over the ramps and tension is taken off the coupler. Tension of the ramps and good alignment are both essential for this uncoupling system to work: uncoupling is the least satisfactory of this otherwise easy and well-standardized coupler.

If you want to uncouple the horn-hook by hand, split an ice lolly stick in half diagonally, insert the pointed end of the stick gently between the two hooks and twist until the couplers are forced apart.

An alternative to the horn-hook – perhaps for the more advanced modeler – is the Kadee magnetic coupler, a very realistic miniature metal buck-eye that looks very much like the full-sized American auto-coupler. When vehicles are pushed together the buck-eyes join by spring action. For uncoupling the train is stopped with the couplers over a magnet in the track or beneath the baseboard. Working on the principle of 'like poles repel', the buck-eyes open by magnetic force. These Kadee couplers are made with fittings for many kinds of vehicle, but they must be purchased separately for HO or O gauge and fitted in place of the horn-hooks on ready-to-run stock.

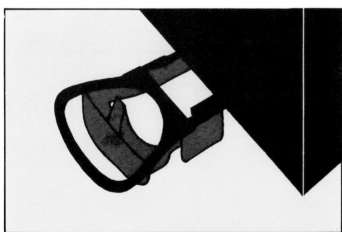

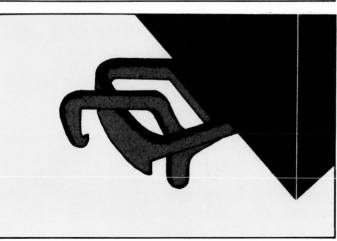

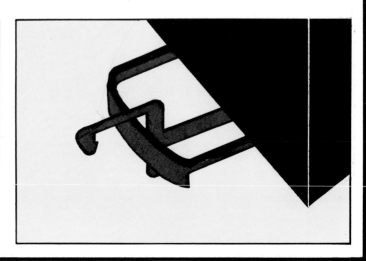

# Controlling the Trains

Most enthusiasts like to *run* trains. Building the layout, and perhaps some of the models, is fun but not an end in itself. A model railway layout is not something static, it is all about movement. All the models illustrated in this book *work* – they can be remotely controlled to perform most of the actions carried out by real trains. However, the *way* they operate depends on the system used by the manufacturer, so you can't mix all the different locomotives on the one layout.

The majority of models sold today are powered by electric motors and controlled through the tracks. The current supplied to the tracks is varied by a controller, and this affects the speed at which the motor revolves. Gears in the motor make sure the locomotive travels at a reasonably realistic speed.

In all cases the mains current is stepped down to a safe level through a transformer. Most motors operate at 12 volt DC (direct current), though there are important exceptions (explained later). When buying a transformer, it is important to remember that the mains voltage varies from country to country – 240V AC (alternating current) in Great Britain, 110-120V AC in the USA, for instance. In Germany it is 220V AC. The power point fittings also vary – so be particulary careful when buying electrical control equipment or accessories from another country. It could be dangerous. You should be able to buy something suitable from a reputable dealer or manufacturer, but be cautious about ordering anything from another country without checking first.

### Three-rail or two-rail?
In the early days of electric model railways, the trains ran on three-rail track, the centre rail carrying the pick-up. Some old three-rail track of this kind might still be seen in second-hand shops, but this is only suitable for trains designed for it.

One system, Ibertren of Spain, still has a centre-rail facility as an optional choice for their N gauge models, but these are not normally sold outside Spain. All other modern 12V systems use two-rail track, and the running rails act as pick-up and 'return'.

The two-rail 12V DC system is essentially simple provided you observe a few basic rules. Most trainsets come with a good control unit (you can also buy controllers separately), and all but the very simplest also have AC/DC outputs for operating equipment such as turnouts (points) if you motorize these.

On a simple layout – say an oval with a few sidings – you only need to plug in the two wires from the control unit, and you can operate your train. If you have a larger layout, and wish to run more than one train, or hold trains while others run, then the layout must be divided into sections so that some track areas are electrically 'dead' when trains are not to move. All the main trainset makers, and many

accessory manufacturers, sell all the necessary wires and levers or switches.

Most ready-made turnouts – those with insulated frogs – are of the isolating type, or can easily be converted to isolating turnouts. This means that if an engine is in a siding or loop and the turnout is set against it, then that section will be electrically isolated without the need for futher wiring.

One very important rule with two-rail systems is that reversing loops (that is where the train turns back on itself, also known as a turning triangle) or return loops (where the train changes direction on the same track), will not work unless special change-over or polarity reversing switches are put into the track circuit. This is because track turning on itself will set up opposite polarity in the two rails and cause a short-circuit.

All the main model railway companies, including Atlas, Hornby, Fleischmann, and Roco, produce excellent switch gear and button switches which can be used to do all the sectioning and isolating you might need. There is no shortage of equipment in the main ranges, nearly all with clear instructions.

The general principles apply whether you are modeling in any of the main gauges – O, OO/HO, TT, or N – if it operates at 12V DC.

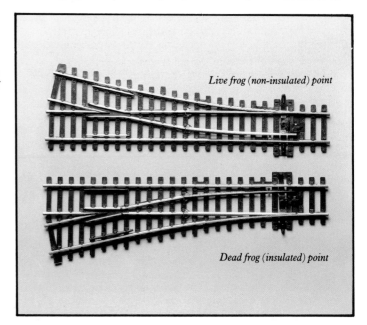

*Live frog (non-insulated) point*

*Dead frog (insulated) point*

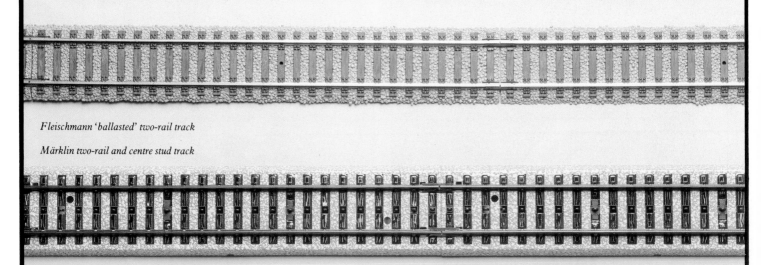

*Fleischmann 'ballasted' two-rail track*

*Märklin two-rail and centre stud track*

## AC systems

The one major manufacturer who uses a 16V AC system is Märklin. This system uses a centre-pick-up, but as a stud contact not a third rail. This is very unobtrusive in comparison with a third rail. A long, sprung pick-up skate beneath the locomotive collects the power from the studs.

The Märklin system is used for both HO and gauge 1 ranges. It has some advantages, one of which is that the reversing loop problem of 12V DC is not encountered. And there is little problem when it comes to isolating and sectionalizing. Märklin models will not run with DC equipment, so you must stay with Märklin track and equipment once you opt for this AC system. Gauge 1 locomotives are optionally available in DC form (the manufacturer will advise on availability). Incidentally, the Märklin gauge 1 system has two-rail track and no stud contact, so don't be tempted to use a DC control unit just because the track looks like DC track.

## Z gauge

Märklin are also producers of the world's smallest system, Z gauge, sometimes referred to as Miniclub. With trains so small that a shunting locomotive will fit into a matchbox, the motors have to be very tiny. Although a DC system, the small size of the motors means they are rated at 8V instead of 12V. Therefore it is essential to use a Märklin Miniclub controller, or if purchasing a controller from a special supplier to say that it is intended for use with Z gauge. They may be willing to alter a control unit to 8V.

If you try to use a 12V controller with Z gauge, you may burn out the motor.

## Command control

During the last few years new technology has given us 'command control'. Computer technology has enabled a chip to be wired into the locomotive so that the system can run several trains simultaneously on the same layout without all the wiring and sectionalizing complexity usually associated with big layouts. Several systems have been produced, of which Hornby's Zero-One is probably one of the best known.

The conventional 12V DC system depends on varying motor speed by use of the controller, the current acting directly through the track with one controller working on only one locomotive at a time (if you want to run two trains simultaneously on different parts of the layout you need a controller for each and the necessary sectionalizing). However, with command control a 20V AC current is fed into the rails continuously and signals are relayed down the track from the master controller covering stop, start, inertia, and other functions. Each locomotive is fitted with a differently coded 'memory' (or chip) module, which recognizes its own signal through the track and acts only on that. The 'instructions' for the different locomotives are tapped out on a keyboard that resembles that of a pocket calculator. Some manufacturers produce 'slave' units that can be plugged in around the layout in convenient positions.

On the Hornby system, up to 16 locomotives can be controlled

simultaneously, that being the number of coded 'memory modules' available for fitting to the locomotives. Other systems differ slightly, offering more or fewer 'memories'.

The module in each locomotive converts the current to 12V DC to suit its own requirements, depending on the commands keyed in.

As the voltage is different, it is obvious that the command control system in not compatible with the old systems (with a minor exception). But only locomotives fitted with the 'memory modules' will work on a command control system. These are sold separately and must be coded and fitted by the user. In the case of Hornby locomotives, fitting is easy, but some other makes require soldering or offer other difficulties. However, some firms offer a fitting service.

Command control is only suitable for HO/OO or larger. It is difficult to use with N gauge, partly because of the smaller motors and partly because the modules are too large for most locomotives.

A properly installed command control system greatly simplifies the running of a complex layout, but if you have a very small layout with room to run only one or two trains at a time, it may not be worth the extra time and expense. However, command control systems do offer a good way of controlling turnouts and other working features, again in a simple manner, and it is well worth watching command control demonstrations and reading manufacturer's leaflets before making a decision.

Further variations in command control include some smaller systems, notably the Trix EMS, which are simplified versions making provision for only two or three locomotives, instead of the 16 or more, and supplying the locomotives already fitted with the 'memory' modules.

## Overhead wiring

Many European models are replicas of electric locomotives and have the pantographs for overhead pick-up fitted accordingly. In some cases these are non-working dummies, but most models are actually wired so that the pantograph is 'live'. Several firms, among them Herpa, Märklin, and Piko, produce overhead wiring components which can be assembled over the track and clipped to it (in some cases) for further rigidity. Realistic poles, gantries, and wires can be erected for electric traction.

Locomotives designed for overhead pick-up usually have a change-over switch that can be set for either track or overhead. The advantage of having an overhead system is that two trains can be run simultaneously on the same electrical section – one locomotive picking up from the overhead wire, the other one from the track, each with its own controller.

If you want a realistic setting for running electric locomotives, but do not want the added work of making live overhead wiring then it is worth remembering that Arnold, and some other manufacturers, make dummy, elastic overhead wiring. This is set up from poles although it is not wired in and cannot carry current. It looks realistic and the pantographs run along it while the current is picked up from the tracks.

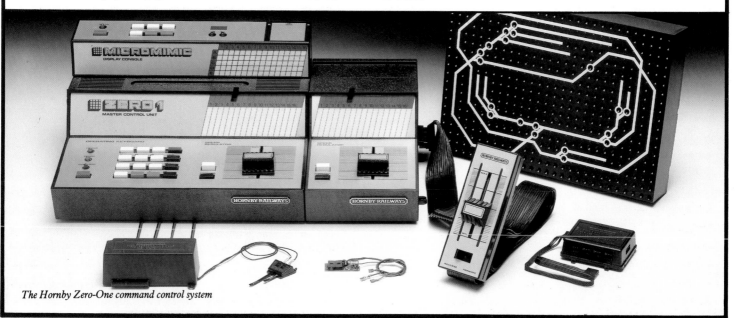

*The Hornby Zero-One command control system*

# Glossary

You may come across some words in this book that you don't understand. Terms that may be familiar in one country may be unfamiliar in another – the British 'brake van' is an American 'caboose', for instance. And there are railway terms such as 'compound' engines that may not be obvious to anyone who has not modeled the railways that used these locomotives. This glossary should put you on the right tracks if you come across an unfamiliar term or expression. It also contains a wealth of information about terms and abbreviations that are not mentioned in the book, but which will be invaluable to railway modelers.

**AC** Alternating current (power supply)

**AC1** Automatic Car Identification (USA)

**AIA-AIA** Diesel or electric locomotive wheel arrangement with non-driven centre axles on bogies.

**Alco** American Locomotive Co. A major steam and diesel locomotive builder.

**'American'** Nickname for 4-4-0 wheel arrangement.

**Amtrak** American National Railroad Passenger Company. Since 1972 responsible for passenger services in the USA.

**'Atlantic'** Nickname for 4-4-2 wheel arrangement.

**AT&SF** Atchinson, Topeka, & Santa Fe Railroad Co. Major American company.

**AWS** Automatic Warning System.

**Baldwin** American locomotive builder.

**Ballast** Bed of stones holding track.

**Belpaire** Type of firebox of squared-off shape, having increased efficiency over earlier fireboxes.

**Beyer-Garratt** See Garratt.

**Bi-level car** American double-deck passenger coach.

**'Bird cage'** Raised roof portion for guard's look-out on some old coaches or vans.

**BN** Burlington Northern. Major American company.

**Bo-Bo** Diesel or electric locomotive with two four-wheeled bogies, all wheels driven.

**Bogie** Swivelling wheel assembly (British term; truck in USA).

**B&O RR** Baltimore & Ohio (now part of Chessie Systems).

**BR** British Railways (British Rail). Formed by nationalization of separate private companies in 1948.

**Br** Baureike (class). Germany.

**Brake van** Vehicle in which train guard rides.

**Brakeman** Train crew member (USA) responsible for operating train brakes.

**BRMSB** British Railway Modelling Standards Bureau (now defunct)

**Brush** British diesel locomotive builder.

**Budd** American coach and railcar builder.

**Bulleid, O. V. S.,** Famous British locomotive designer, mainly with the Southern Railway.

**Bunker** Carrying bin for coal on a tank engine.

**Cab-forward** American steam locomotive type with cab at leading end.

**Caboose** Special van for train crew (USA). Equivalent to British brake van.

**Caledonian Railway** Famous Scottish company before 1923.

**Camelback** Type of locomotive in USA with wide firebox and cab astride boiler.

**Capitol Limited** Famous American express train.

**Churchward, G.J.** Famous locomotive designer of GWR.

**Clerestory** Raised portion of roof on some old coaches.

**Climax** Type of articulated steam locomotive.

**Co-Co (or C-C)** Diesel or electric locomotive with two six-wheeled bogies, all wheels driven.

**Compound** System by which exhaust steam is re-used in another cylinder on certain types of steam locomotives (the Midland 'Compounds' for example).

**Conductor** Train official either in charge of the train or passengers.

**Connecting rod** Rod on locomotive motion attached to cross-head at one end and main driving crank at the other.

**Conrail** Consolidated Rail Corporation. American railroad company.

**Consist** Train make-up/formation (American term).

**Coupling rod** Rod linking the driving wheels on a steam locomotive.

**'Cow-catcher'** Pilot (frame) on front of locomotive (American term).

**Crosshead** Sliding assembly that supports the piston rod on the cylinder on a steam locomotive.

**CSX** Very large operating merger (1983) between Chessie System and Seaboard System.

**CTC** Continuous Train Control (USA).

**DB** Deutsche Bundesbahn (post-war West German state railway company)

**DC** Direct current (power supply).

**Dean** Famous steam locomotive designer.

**Deltic** Type of diesel engine fitted to important British class of express locomotives.

**Diesel-electric** Diesel locomotive with electric drive (the most common type).

**Diesel hydraulic** Diesel locomotive with hydraulic transmission – common in Germany; once used in Great Britain.

**Diesel mechanical** Diesel locomotive with drive taken directly from the engine – mainly restricted to shunting locomotives.

**DMU** Diesel multiple unit.

**Dome** Steam chamber on top of boiler.

**Dome car** American passenger car with observation dome on top.

**Doodlebug** American slang for a petrol (gasoline) electric railcar.

**DR** Deutsche Reichsbahn (post-war East German state railway company).

**Drawbar** or **Drawgear** Couplers.

**DRG** Deutsche Reichsbahn Gesellschaft (pre-war state railway company of Germany).

**Driving wheels** Main wheels of a locomotive, the ones actually driven.

**Ducket** Look-out position inside of brake or guard's van.

**Dynamic brakes** Extra braking on large diesel locomotives utilising engine torque.

**Eilzug** Express train (Germany)

**EHT** Electric train heating.

**EMD** Electro-Motive Division (of General Motors). Major American diesel locomotive builder.

**EMU** Electric multiple unit.

**Engineer** Locomotive driver (American term).

**English Electric** Major builder of diesel and electric locomotives in UK.

**Espee** American slang for SP – Southern Pacific.

**Festiniog** Famous Welsh narrow gauge railway.

**Firebox** Part of locomotive (at cab end) where fire is built up.

**Fireman** Crew member who tends the fire.

**Fishplate** Rail joiner.

**Flagman** Train crew member or track gang member responsible for signalling warnings.

**Flange** Portion of railway wheel that is 'stepped' to keep the wheel running on the rail.

**Flexible track** Model track sold in lengths, to be shaped as required.

**Footplate** Horizontal plating forming working platform for crew and maintenance work on steam locomotive.

**Fowler, H.** Famous locomotive designer of the LMS.

**Frog** The actual junction piece between the two arms of a turnout (point). Can be 'dead frog' (insulated) or 'live frog' (carrying current). Applies to model track only.

**Gandy Dancer** American slang for railway ganger.

**Garratt** Locomotive of articulated type with twin chassis (UK).

**Gauge** Width between running rails. Can be standard gauge, narrow

gauge, or (rarely) broad gauge (see page 9).

**GE** General Electric Co. Major American builder of diesel and electric locomotives.

**GER** Great Eastern Railway. British railway company until 1923.

**GNR** Great Northern Railway. (1) in USA until 1970; (2) in Great Britain until 1923.

**Gondola** American term for open freight vehicle.

**Grate** Bars at bottom of firebox on which fire is built.

**Gresley, Sir N.** Famous locomotive designer of the LNER.

**Guard** Official in charge of train (Europe).

**Guard irons** Projecting plates at each end of chassis on locomotives and some coaches to clear track obstacles.

**Guard's van** Compartment for guard.

**GWR** Great Western Railway. (1) short line in USA; (2) famous British railway company until nationalization in 1948.

**Harriman** American railway baron of the 1900s, once owner of the Union Pacific and the Southern Pacific among others. Instituted several standard designs of locomotives and rolling stock.

**Head end** Front (American term).

**Heisler** Type of articulated steam locomotive (USA).

**HEP** Head-end power (USA).

**Herald** Company badge (American term).

**Hi-cube** High-capacity car (American term).

**'High iron'** American slang for main-line track.

**'Highball'** Signal clear – from early days when a ball was hoisted on a pole if the track was clear.

**'Highballing'** Running fast with a clear road ahead (American slang).

**Hopper** Wagon (car) with opening doors underneath for the transport of minerals.

**'Hudson'** Nickname for locomotive of 4-6-4 type, in USA.

**Hump yard** Large marshalling yard for freight trains, with raised ramp (hump) to enable rail wagons (cars) to be run under gravity.

**ICC** Interstate Commerce Commission. Regulating body for control of rail trade in USA.

**ICG** Illinois Central Gulf – leading USA railroad.

**Isolate** To make electrically dead (model term).

**Isolating rail** Track section specially wired to isolate part of the layout.

**Ivatt, H.A.** Locomotive designer of GNR. **Ivatt, H.G.** Locomotive designer of LMS.

**Jumper** Wire to carry common electrical feed.

**Kangarou** Flat cars carrying road trailers (Europe).

**Kleinlok** Small shunting locomotive (Germany).

**Live steam** In model terms, any locomotive using actual steam power.

**LMS** London Midland & Scottish Railway (1923-1948).

**LNER** London and North Eastern Railway (1923-1948).

**Lokalbahn** Local train (Germany).

**Mainframes** Longitudinal members of locomotive chassis.

**Mallet** Type of articulated steam locomotive (USA).

**META** Model Engineering Trade Association (UK).

**Metroliner** Famous modern American high-speed train.

**'Mikado'** Nickname for 2-8-2 wheel arrangement.

**'Mogul'** Nickname for 2-6-0 wheel arrangement.

**'Mountain'** Nickname for 4-8-2 wheel arrangement.

**MR** Midland Railway (until 1923).

**NMRA** National Model Railroad Association (of America).

**NS** Norfolk-Southern. Large American company (from 1982).

**N&W** Norfolk & Western Railroad Co. (USA until 1982).

**Observation car** Special coach with good viewing facilities for passengers.

**'Pacific'** Nickname for 4-6-2 wheel arrangement.

**Pacific Rail** Merger in 1983 of Union Pacific, Western Pacific, and Missouri Pacific, but with each company retaining its corporate name and style.

**Pantograph** Device for picking up current from overhead wires on electric locomotives.

**Pennsy** Pennsylvania Railroad, later Penn-Central (until 1975).

**Piggyback** Train of flat cars carrying trailers (USA).

**Pilot** Front end of locomotive (American term).

**Point** Old term for diverging track section (see **Turnout**)

**'Prairie'** Nickname for 2-6-2 wheel arrangement.

**Prototype** (1) First of a new design; (2) in model terms, the original full-size item.

**PSI** Pounds per square inch – old measure for locomotive boiler pressure.

**Pullman** (1) luxury coach; (2) company in USA building coaches and other rolling stock.

**Rangier lokomotive** Shunting locomotive (Germany)

**Reefer** Refrigerated car (American term).

**Regulator** Throttle controlling supply of steam to cylinders and hence controlling speed.

**Reporting marks** Abbreviated company name used on American rolling stock.

**Roster** (1) working pattern for locomotives or crew; (2) list of stock.

**Saddle tank** Tank locomotive with water tank over boiler.

**Safety valve** Spring-loaded valve on boiler to protect against high steam pressure.

**Seaboard System** New name (1983) for Family Lines.

**Sectional track**: Track in sections, as supplied with train sets. Also called **snap track**.

**Shunting** Moving rolling stock to form train, etc. American term for this is **switching**.

**Smoke box** Chamber at front end of boiler, carrying chimney.

**Smoke deflectors** Plates on side of locomotive at front to cause draught and so direct steam and smoke upwards so that it does not obstruct view.

**SP** Southern Pacific. Major American railroad.

**SR** Southern Railway. (1) USA until 1982; (2) Great Britain until 1948.

**Splashers** Covers over tops of wheels.

**Stock rail** Moving part of a turnout (point/switch).

**Super Chief** Famous American express passenger train.

**Switch** American term for turnout or point.

**Switcher** (1) shunting locomotive (USA); (2) one who controls shunting (USA).

**Thunderbox** Refurbished old 4-wheeled coach (Germany).

**Tractive effort** Pulling power of locomotive.

**Truck** Swivelling wheeled chassis. American; same as bogie in Britain.

**Turnout** Modern term for what used to be called a point in Great Britain.

**Twentieth Century Ltd** Famous American express train.

**USRA** United States Railroad Administration. Produced some standard designs from 1917.

**Valve gear** Regulates transmission of power to drive the wheels. Various types, including Baker, Stephenson, Walschearts, etc.

**Walschearts** The most common type of valve gear on steam locomotives; named after its inventor.

**Westinghouse** Main type of air brake, utilizing a pump to build up air pressure.

**Whyte system** Method of describing locomotive type by wheel arrangement (e.g. 4-6-2).

# Societies and Magazines

If your interest is model railways you will almost certainly be interested in reading about the hobby – and might consider the benefits of joining like-minded people in a model railway club. We cannot list them all here because most are local, but you may be able to find a club by asking in your model shop or reading suitable magazines. If this doesn't reveal a local club, try writing to the editor to see whether he can suggest one (enclose a stamped, self-addressed envelope).

The list below includes the major model railway magazines in the countries mentioned. You can obtain subscription details by writing to the addresses given.

**Australia**
Australian Model Railway Magazine,
PO Box 235,
Matraville,
NSW

**Great Britain**
Continental Modeller,
Peco Publications and Publicity Ltd.,
Beer,
Seaton,
Devon,
EX12 3NA

Model Railway Constructor,
Ian Allan Ltd.,
Terminal House,
Shepperton,
Middlesex

Model Railways,
Model & Allied Publications,
PO Box 35,
Wolsey House,
Wolsey Road,
Hemel Hempstead,
Herts,
HP2 4SS

Railway Modeller,
Peco Publications and Publicity Ltd.,
Beer,
Seaton,
Devon,
EX12 3NA

Scale Trains,
Blackfriars Press Ltd.,
PO Box 80,
Smith Dorrien Road,
Leicester,
LE5 4BS

**United States of America**
Mainline Modeler,
Hundman Publishing,
5115 Monticello Drive,
Edmonds,
Washington 98020

Model Railroad Craftsmen,
Carsten Publications Inc.,
Fredon-Springdale Road,
Fredon Township,
PO Box 700,
Newton,
New Jersey 07860

Model Railroader,
Kalmbach Publishing Co.,
1027 N. Seventh Street,
Milwaukee,
WI 53233

S Gaugian,
Heimburger House Publishing Co.,
310 Lathrop Avenue,
River Forest,
IL 60305

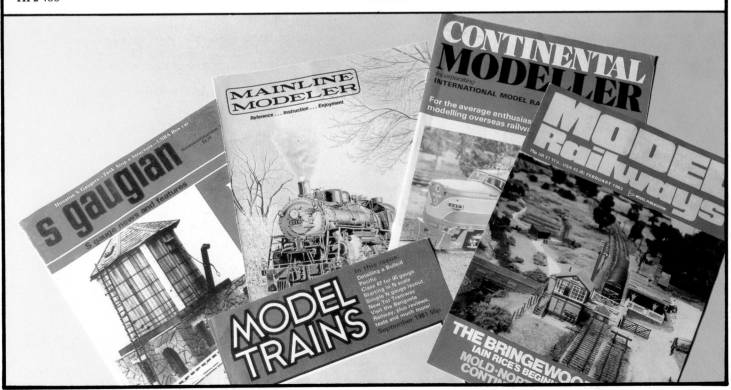

# Finishing Touches

Any model railway layout needs miniature figures to bring it to life. It is surprising how just one or two figures can add an extra dimension to a scene. Indeed, you sometimes quite literally need only one or two, as crowds of figures can very often make an otherwise realistic scene quite toy-like. A single well-placed figure, however, such as a railwayman coming out of a doorway, can have more impact than a whole box of figures!

All the major manufacturers offer figures of some sort. Typical are locomotive crews, passengers, and station personnel. There is certainly no shortage as a visit to any reasonably sized model shop will show.

LGB make their own large 1:22.5 scale figures to match their large narrow gauge trains. Märklin produce 1:32 scale figures for gauge 1, but in addition there are many model farm figures and accessories by firms like Britains, which all go with gauge 1 trains.

In the smaller scales there is a huge choice, with gauge 0 being the least well catered for (though small specialist suppliers offer good cast metal figures for this scale).

With OO/HO, N, and Z, the modeller is spoilt for choice. The major range for all these scales comes from the West German firm of Preiser, who offer many boxed sets of great realism and charm – the choice runs to well over 100 sets with royalty, military bands, a jazz band, weddings, hippies, train crews, track layers, luggage, police, nudists, artists, TV crews, cyclists, and a complete circus among the many delightful ready-painted sets.

There are also many plain plastic figures available that have to be painted but are much cheaper.

Several firms produce related accessories – platform slot machines, baggage, gas cylinders, crates, platform trolleys, and much more. Merit is a leading producer of these. Other firms with figure and accessory sets available include Airfix, Bachmann, and Hornby.

## Motor vehicles

Just as figures help build up a realistic scene, so do road vehicles. How many you'll need will naturally depend on the size of the layout. A very small, shelf-type layout might only have room for two or three models. However, normally you are likely to need taxis or buses in a station yard, trucks in a freight yard, cars parked outside model houses, and so on.

For HO and N scales the selection is superb, and firms like Brekina, Herpa, Praline, and Wiking, all from West Germany, have reached a high standard of perfection with their models covering both current and vintage vehicles. The models from these firms are so good that collecting HO model vehicles has become a hobby in its own right. The range is constantly changing with new releases always coming along to keep pace with new real vehicles.

There are numerous cast metal kits for all scales, covering all sorts of vehicles and in addition there are ready-made models by well-known firms like Corgi, Efsi, Majorette, Matchbox, and Solido. Most but not all of these models are to scales matching model railway equipment. If in doubt check the scale from the maker's catalogue for each type, or check the model or its carton as the scales are often marked.

## Model buildings

For the popular scales like OO/HO and N (and for TT), there is no shortage of plastic assembly kits. Faller, Heljan, Kibri, Pola, and Vollmer, are all well-known names and their imaginative kits are easy to make and are pre-coloured. In Britain, Ratio (who also make plastic kits of rolling stock and signals) produce some fine kits of buildings such as actual stations and signalboxes. Hornby and other model train manufacturers, such as Arnold and Lima, also make good, easily assembled kits for key buildings such as freight depots and stations. Other notable names are MKD (France), and Model Construction (UK), who make highly detailed structures of original types.

Besides plastic kits there are some good card cut-out models. Superquick and Builder Plus produce useful British outline models at modest prices.

Finally, there are some wood and card assembly kits requiring a fair skill, but giving you very fine models of character. Humbrol Euromodel in Britain, and Campbell in the USA are two of the big names.

For those who do not want to construct from kits, several major firms produce ready-made structures of key railway buildings – engine sheds, stations, freight sheds, and so on. Bachmann and Hornby are among the companies producing good ready-made buildings.

# LGB

The models shown on these pages are only a small part of the
LGB range. If you would like to know more about LGB model
trains, contact your nearest stockist for a catalogue. Only one
manufacturer – Lehmann – produces models in this gauge/
scale combination, though there are some ready-made live
steam locomotives produced from time to time in limited
batches.

There is considerable detail on many of these models,
including features like hinged toilet seats in the coaches, steam
or diesel sound from the locomotives, as well as working lights
and imitation 'steam' generators.

Lehmann, Waldenburg railway steam locomotive, 2073D, >340mm<, Price:N

Lehmann, US Western-type 0-4-0 steam locomotive, 2017, >480mm<, Price:N

Lehmann, ÖBB diesel, 2095 class, 2095, >460mm<, Price:O

Lehmann, DB 2nd class coach, 3070, >495mm<, Price:L

Lehmann, OEG ballast wagon, 4041, >300mm<, Price:G

# Gauge 1

The models illustrated on these pages are only a representative selection of the Märklin gauge 1 range. For a detailed list of models available, refer to a current Märklin catalogue.

Märklin, 55 class, ≃, 5714, >574mm<, ⚨, ⛭, Price:Z **Similar models:** with simulated locomotive sounds – 5713; DC version of 5714 – 5744; DC version of 5713 – 5743

Märklin, 212 class, ≃, 5772, >384mm<, ⚨, Price:Z **Similar models:** DC version – 5742

Märklin, 2nd class coach with brakeman's cab, 5805, ›391mm‹, Price:Z **Similar models:** without brakeman's cab - 5804

Märklin, hopper wagon, 5873, ›301mm‹, Price:Z

Märklin, low-sided wagon with cars, 5876, ›310mm‹, Price:Z **Similar models:** with load of timber – 5875; no load, stakes inserted – 5853

# Gauge O

A few other manufacturers produce a limited range of ready-to run O gauge models, but the Lionel trains, made by Fundimensions, are perhaps the best-known.

The models must be run on Lionel three-rail track, using AC or DC power between 5 and 15 volts.

The rolling stock illustrated here is only a selection. For information on the full range, and suppliers, consult American model railroad magazines, or write to the manufacturer (see page 255).

Lionel, 2-4-2 steam locomotive, Pennsylvania, 6-8214, Price:Z

Lionel, GP-7 diesel locomotive, Santa Fe, 6-8263, Price:Z

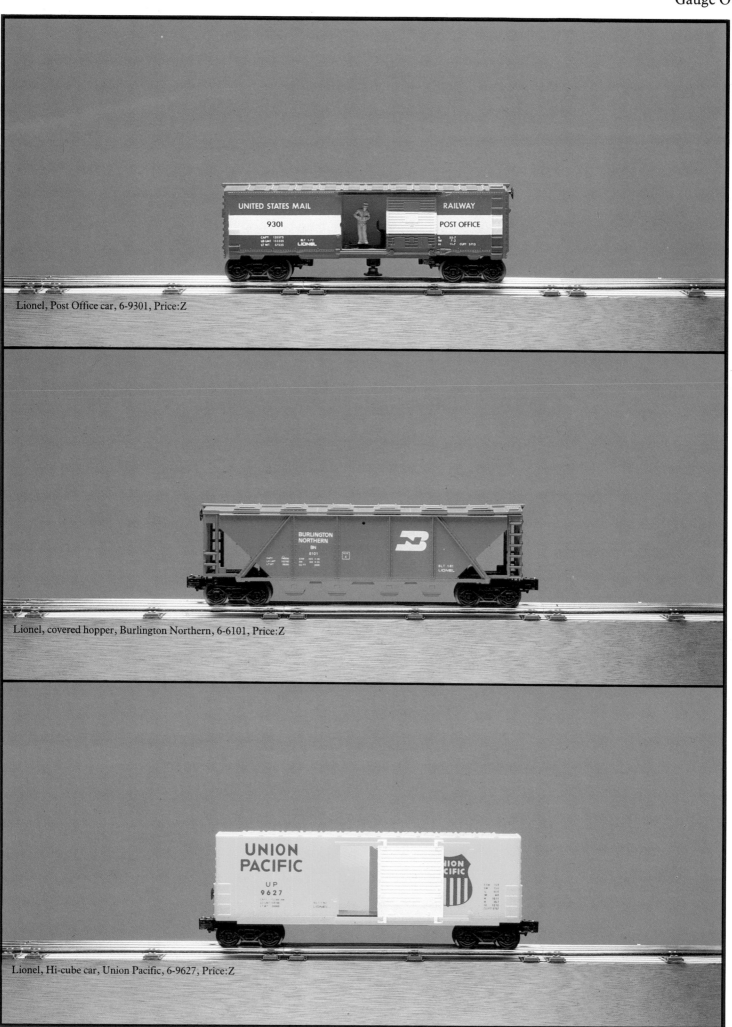

Lionel, Post Office car, 6-9301, Price:Z

Lionel, covered hopper, Burlington Northern, 6-6101, Price:Z

Lionel, Hi-cube car, Union Pacific, 6-9627, Price:Z

# Sweden

## Statens Järnvägar

The Statens Järnvägar (SJ), the Swedish state railway, was a nationalized company from the time it started in 1850. However, private rail development was allowed, and some used narrow gauge. There are over 11,000 route kilometres (7,000 miles) of track, most of it electrified. The current standard electric locomotive has been exported to several other countries, including Norway and the USA.

### N Gauge

⊕ Fleischmann, baggage car, 8170, >145mm<, Price:D

⊕ Fleischmann, 1st class coach, 8171, >145mm<, Price:D

⊕ Lima, old-time coach, 320351, >79mm<, Price:Z

⊖ Lima, Gullfiber covered wagon, 320409, >65mm<, Price:Z

**Also available**

**SJ electric locomotives**
⊕ Fleischmann, 2-6-2 locomotive, ⌂, 7368, >81mm<, ♀, Price:K

**SJ coaches**
⊖ Fleischmann, 2nd class coach, 8172, >145mm<, Price:D
⊖ Lima, old-time coach, 320350, >79mm<, Price:Z

### HO/OO Gauge

▣ Fleischmann, 0-8-0 locomotive, 4146, >223mm<, ♀, Price:L

▣ Fleischmann, ⌂, 4365, >179mm<, ♀, Price:L

◎ Märklin, Da class, ≲, ⌂, 3030, >147mm<, ♀, Price:Z

◎ Märklin, Rc class, ≲, ⌂, 3043, >175mm<, ♀, Price:Z

▣ Fleischmann, 2nd class coach, 5155, >240mm<, Price:E

◎ Liliput, 4-wheeled baggage van, 271 80, >138mm<, Price:C

◎ Märklin, 2nd class coach, 4072, >237mm<, Price:Z

◎ Märklin, dining car, 4073, >237mm<, Price:Z

◎ Roco, 1st and 2nd class coach, 4257B, >264mm<, Price:D

◎ Roco, 2nd class coach, 4289B, >236mm<, Price:D

◎ Liliput, covered van, 235 80, >117mm<, Price:C

◎ Liliput, ASG van, 235 81, >117mm<, Price:C **Similar models:** Felix – 235 82; Findus – 235 83; Milda – 235 84

## Also available

**SJ steam locomotives**
◎ Liliput, K24 shunting locomotive, 33 81, >100mm<, Price:L

**SJ electric locomotives**
◎ Lima, Rc2 class, ⟁, 208052LG, >176mm<, Price:Z

**SJ diesel locomotives**
◎ Lima, T43 class, 201627LG, >162mm<, Price:Z **Similar models:** red and grey livery – 201628LG
◎ Lima, diesel shunter, 205123MG, >115mm<, Price:Z **Similar models:** yellow livery – 205124MG

**SJ coaches**
◎ Liliput, 270 80, >138mm<, Price:D

**SJ coaches**
◎ Liliput, Red Cross coach, 270 81, >138mm<, Price:D
◎ Liliput, passenger coach, 844 80, >249mm<, Price:E
◎ Lima, 2nd class coach, 309158, >265mm<, Price:Z
◎ Lima, baggage car, 309335, >175mm<, Price:Z
◎ Lima, 1st class coach, 309141, >265mm<, Price:Z
◎ Lima, sleeping car, 309270, >270mm<, Price:Z

**SJ wagons**
◎ Liliput, milk tank, 251 80, >100mm<, Price:D
◎ Lima, sawdust wagon, 302832, >140mm<, Price:Z
◎ Lima, low-sided wagon with stakes, 302831, >140mm<, Price:Z

# Norway

## Norges Statsbaner

Norges Statsbaner (NSB) is the Norwegian state railway. Norway was one of the last countries to develop a proper rail network, party because of the mountainous terrain and partly due to its link with Sweden until 1905. As a result of the Swedish connection all lines led to Stockholm. After 1905 new routes were built linking the country north to south. Electric traction predominates, with relatively few diesel locomotives.

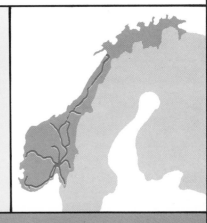

**N Gauge**

⊖ Fleischmann, 2-10-0 locomotive, 7178, >150mm<, ⚲ , Price:L

⊖ Roco, four-wheeled coach, 2200B, >74mm<, Price:C

**HO/OO Gauge**

◉ Fleischmann, 2-10-0 locomotive, 4178, >270mm<, ⚲ , Price:M

◎ Lima, ⚍, 208065LG, >167mm<, Price:Z

◎ Lima, ⚍, 208130LG, >200mm<, Price:Z

◎ Lima, 2nd class coach, 309150, >268mm<, Price:Z

◎ Lima, 1st class coach, 309222, >265mm<, Price:Z

◎ Lima, 2nd class coach with luggage compartment, 309308, >265mm<, Price:Z

◎ Roco, 3rd class coach, 4221A, >224mm<, Price:Z

◎ Roco, 1st, 2nd, 3rd class coach, 4221C, >224mm<, Price:Z

◎ Lima, timber wagon, 302834, >150mm<, Price:Z

◎ Lima, container wagon, 302851, >168mm<, Price:Z **Similar models:** with five small containers – 302853

◎ Lima, covered wagon, 303101, >126mm<, Price:Z

◎ Lima, covered wagon, 303568, >121mm<, Price:Z

**Also available**
**NSB steam locomotives**
◎ Liliput, 63a class (BR 52), 52 80, >268mm<, Price:N
**NSB coaches**
◎ Roco, 1st and 2nd class coach, 4221B, >224mm<, Price:Z
◎ Roco, 1st class coach, 4221D, >224mm<, Price:Z

# Denmark

## Danske Statsbaner

The Dankse Statsbaner (DSB) dates from 1885 when the main private lines in Denmark were taken over. Some private local lines still remain, however. Because of the many islands in Denmark, there are numerous bridges and several train ferries. DSB has all diesel traction except for a suburban electric service around Copenhagen. The DSB is a small system with only about 300 locomotives and 100 railcars.

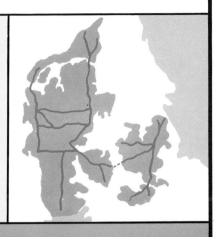

# DSB

### N Gauge

⊕ Fleischmann, 2-10-0 locomotive, 7178, >150mm<, ⚲, Price:L

⊕ Fleischmann, 2-6-0 tank locomotive, 7031, >68mm<, ⚲, Price:J

⊕ Minitrix, My1100 class, 2023, >118mm<, Price:J

⊕ Fleischmann, 2nd class coach, 8157, >165mm<, Price:D

⊕ Minitrix, express coach, 3140, >165mm<, Price:D

⊕ Lima, Carlsberg refrigerated wagon, 320467, >88mm<, Price:Z

**Also available**
**DSB coaches**
⊕, Roco, TEN sleeping car, 2278D, >165mm<, Price:D

### TT Gauge

Berliner Bahnen, My class, 2531, >158mm<, ⚲, Price:Z

Berliner Bahnen, refrigerated wagon, 4331, >76mm<, Price:Z

Berliner Bahnen, Carlsberg brewery wagon, 4333, >76mm<, Price:Z **Similar models:** Tuborg – 4332

### HO/OO Gauge

◎ Electrotren, ⬉, MZ 1400 class, 2051, >236mm<, Price:K **Similar models:** 12V DC, 2 rail – 2070 (Price:L)

◉ Fleischmann, 2-10-0 locomotive, 4178, >270mm<, ⚲ , Price:M

◉ Fleischmann, My 11 class, 4273, >223mm<, ⚲ , Price:L

◎ Märklin, My1100 class, ⊴, 3067, >205mm<, ⚲ , Price:Z

◉ Fleischmann, 2nd class coach, 5157, >245mm<, Price:E

◎ Roco, 2nd class coach, 4276S, >264mm<, Price:Z

### Also available

**DSB diesel locomotives**
◎ Lima, Mz class, 208109LG, >227mm<, Price:Z
◎ Lima, Mz class, 208153LG, >236mm<, Price:Z

**DSB diesel railcars**
◎ Lima, MR class, 201092LG, Price:Z **Similar models:** trailer (without motor) – 201090

**DSB coaches**
◎ Lima, 2nd class coach, 309164, >265mm<, Price:Z
◎ Lima, 2nd class coach with baggage compartment, 309346, >268mm<, Price:Z **Similar models:** red livery – 309339
◎ Lima, 2nd class coach, 309347, >268mm<, Price:Z

**DSB coaches**
◎ Märklin, 2nd class coach, 4045, >240mm<, Price:Z

**DSB wagons**
◎ Lima, open wagon, 303176, >121mm<, Price:Z
◎ Lima, covered wagon, 303567, >121mm<, Price:Z
◎ Roco, covered wagon, 4373B, >122mm<, Price:Z

**Private-owner wagons**
◎ Liliput, Albani refrigerated van, 214 62, >106mm<, Price:D
◎ Liliput, Star-Viking beer wagon, 221 64, >117mm>, Price:D
◎ Liliput, Carlsberg beer wagon, 235 64, >117mm<, Price:D **Similar models:** Faxe – 235 61; Tuborg - 235 65

# Great Britain

## British Railways

British Railways (which now uses the marketing name of British Rail for everyday use) was formed in 1948 when the 'Big Four' railway companies (the London, Midland and Scottish, London and North Eastern, Southern, and Great Western) were nationalized. A modernization programme was announced in 1955, and now over 9,000 kilometres (6,000 miles) of the total of about 42,000 kilometres (26,000 miles) are electrified.

⊕ Farish, 7P Castle class, 1445, >136mm<, Price:H **Similar models:** alternative name – 1447

⊕ Farish, 5MT Hall class, 1405, >132mm<, Price:H

⊖ Farish, 4F 94XX class pannier tank, 1105, >70mm<, Price:F

⊕ Farish, 4MT 61XX class prairie tank, 1605, >86mm<, Price:G **Similar models:** black livery – 1606

⊕ Farish, 8P Merchant Navy class, 1507, >143mm<, Price:H **Similar models:** Battle of Britain class (green) – 1505

⊖ Farish, 3F 0-6-0 tank locomotive, 1705, >71mm<, Price:F

⊕ Farish, 4P 'Compound', 1205, >122mm<, Price:H

⊕ Farish, 8P Duchess (Coronation) class, 1816, >150mm<, Price:J **Similar models:** blue livery – 1817

⊖ Minitrix, A4 class, N.211, >151mm<, ♀, Price:J

⊖ Minitrix, 7P6F Britannia class, N.203, >143mm<, ♀, Price:J

⊖ Minitrix, Ivatt 2MT 2-6-0, N.202, >110mm<, Price:J **Similar models:** green livery – N.213

⊖ Minitrix, 9F 2-10-0, N.207, >143mm<, Price:J **Similar models:** green livery – N.209

⊖ Minitrix, 0-6-0 dock tank, N.201, >56mm<, Price:F

⊖ Arnold, 0-4-0 shunter, 2059, >59mm<, Price:F

⊖ Farish, Class 08 shunter, 1007, >60mm<, Price:F **Similar models:** green livery – 1005

⊖ Farish, Class 37, 8015, >130mm<, Price:J, ☺, **Similar models:** green livery – 8014

⊖ Farish, Class 47, 8007, >130mm<, ☺, Price:J **Similar models:** earlier blue livery – 8005; green livery – 8004

⊖ Farish, Class 20, 8204, >95mm<, Price:G

⊖ Minitrix, Warship class, N.206, >115mm<, ☺, Price:H **Similar models:** green livery – N.208

⊖ Minitrix, Class 47 Co-Co, N.210, >129mm<, ☺, Price:H

⊖ Minitrix, Class 27 Bo-Bo, N.212, >103mm<, ☺, Price:H **Similar models:** green livery – N.204

⊖ Farish, Class 101 3-car set, 8145, >378mm<, Price:H **Similar models:** green livery – 8143; blue livery – 8146; white livery – 8147; 2-car set (252mm), blue and grey – 8135 (Price:H); 2-car set, blue – 8136 (Price:H); 2-car set, green – 8133 (Price:H); 2-car set, white – 8137 (Price:H)

⊖ Farish, High Speed Train, 8125, >405mm<, Price:K

⊖ Farish, 57ft suburban brake end coach, 0615, >125mm<, Price:C

⊖ Farish, 63ft coach, 0685, >136mm<, Price:C **Similar models:** maroon (MR) livery – 0681; green (SR) livery – 0683; brown and cream (WR) livery – 0684; crimson and cream livery – 0686

⊖ Farish, 63ft brake end coach, 0695, Price:C **Similar models:** maroon (MR) livery – 0691; green SR) livery – 0693; brown and cream (WR) livery – 0694; crimson and cream livery – 0696

⊖ Farish, 75ft buffet, 0745, >155mm<, Price:C

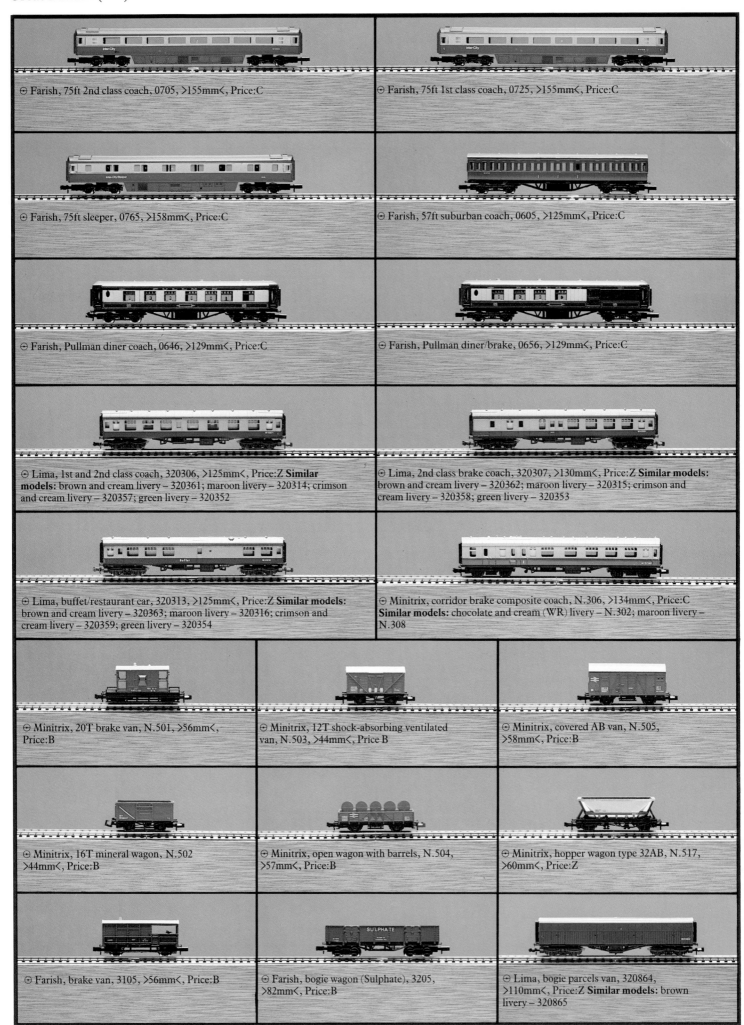

⊖ Farish, 75ft 2nd class coach, 0705, >155mm<, Price:C

⊖ Farish, 75ft 1st class coach, 0725, >155mm<, Price:C

⊖ Farish, 75ft sleeper, 0765, >158mm<, Price:C

⊖ Farish, 57ft suburban coach, 0605, >125mm<, Price:C

⊖ Farish, Pullman diner coach, 0646, >129mm<, Price:C

⊖ Farish, Pullman diner/brake, 0656, >129mm<, Price:C

⊖ Lima, 1st and 2nd class coach, 320306, >125mm<, Price:Z **Similar models:** brown and cream livery – 320361; maroon livery – 320314; crimson and cream livery – 320357; green livery – 320352

⊖ Lima, 2nd class brake coach, 320307, >130mm<, Price:Z **Similar models:** brown and cream livery – 320362; maroon livery – 320315; crimson and cream livery – 320358; green livery – 320353

⊖ Lima, buffet/restaurant car, 320313, >125mm<, Price:Z **Similar models:** brown and cream livery – 320363; maroon livery – 320316; crimson and cream livery – 320359; green livery – 320354

⊖ Minitrix, corridor brake composite coach, N.306, >134mm<, Price:C **Similar models:** chocolate and cream (WR) livery – N.302; maroon livery – N.308

⊖ Minitrix, 20T brake van, N.501, >56mm<, Price:B

⊖ Minitrix, 12T shock-absorbing ventilated van, N.503, >44mm<, Price B

⊖ Minitrix, covered AB van, N.505, >58mm<, Price:B

⊖ Minitrix, 16T mineral wagon, N.502 >44mm<, Price:B

⊖ Minitrix, open wagon with barrels, N.504, >57mm<, Price:B

⊖ Minitrix, hopper wagon type 32AB, N.517, >60mm<, Price:Z

⊖ Farish, brake van, 3105, >56mm<, Price:B

⊖ Farish, bogie wagon (Sulphate), 3205, >82mm<, Price:B

⊖ Lima, bogie parcels van, 320864, >110mm<, Price:Z **Similar models:** brown livery – 320865

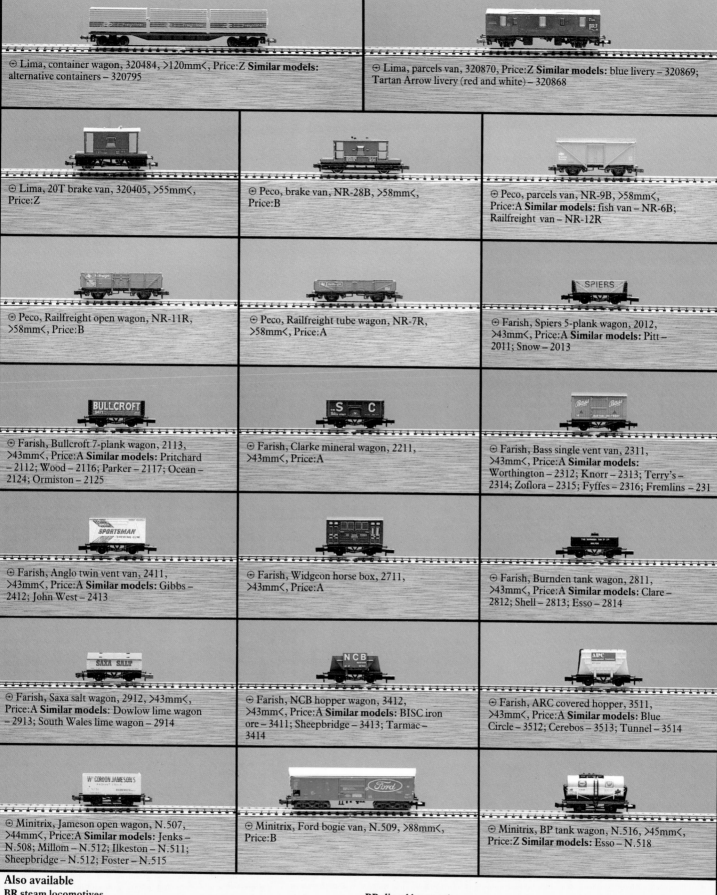

⊕ Lima, container wagon, 320484, >120mm<, Price:Z **Similar models:** alternative containers – 320795

⊕ Lima, parcels van, 320870, Price:Z **Similar models:** blue livery – 320869; Tartan Arrow livery (red and white) – 320868

⊕ Lima, 20T brake van, 320405, >55mm<, Price:Z

⊕ Peco, brake van, NR-28B, >58mm<, Price:B

⊕ Peco, parcels van, NR-9B, >58mm<, Price:A **Similar models:** fish van – NR-6B; Railfreight van – NR-12R

⊕ Peco, Railfreight open wagon, NR-11R, >58mm<, Price:B

⊕ Peco, Railfreight tube wagon, NR-7R, >58mm<, Price:A

⊕ Farish, Spiers 5-plank wagon, 2012, >43mm<, Price:A **Similar models:** Pitt – 2011; Snow – 2013

⊕ Farish, Bullcroft 7-plank wagon, 2113, >43mm<, Price:A **Similar models:** Pritchard – 2112; Wood – 2116; Parker – 2117; Ocean – 2124; Ormiston – 2125

⊕ Farish, Clarke mineral wagon, 2211, >43mm<, Price:A

⊕ Farish, Bass single vent van, 2311, >43mm<, Price:A **Similar models:** Worthington – 2312; Knorr – 2313; Terry's – 2314; Zoflora – 2315; Fyffes – 2316; Fremlins – 231

⊕ Farish, Anglo twin vent van, 2411, >43mm<, Price:A **Similar models:** Gibbs – 2412; John West – 2413

⊕ Farish, Widgeon horse box, 2711, >43mm<, Price:A

⊕ Farish, Burnden tank wagon, 2811, >43mm<, Price:A **Similar models:** Clare – 2812; Shell – 2813; Esso – 2814

⊕ Farish, Saxa salt wagon, 2912, >43mm<, Price:A **Similar models:** Dowlow lime wagon – 2913; South Wales lime wagon – 2914

⊕ Farish, NCB hopper wagon, 3412, >43mm<, Price:A **Similar models:** BISC iron ore – 3411; Sheepbridge – 3413; Tarmac – 3414

⊕ Farish, ARC covered hopper, 3511, >43mm<, Price:A **Similar models:** Blue Circle – 3512; Cerebos – 3513; Tunnel – 3514

⊕ Minitrix, Jameson open wagon, N.507, >44mm<, Price:A **Similar models:** Jenks – N.508; Millom – N.512; Ilkeston – N.511; Sheepbridge – N.512; Foster – N.515

⊕ Minitrix, Ford bogie van, N.509, >88mm<, Price:B

⊕ Minitrix, BP tank wagon, N.516, >45mm<, Price:Z **Similar models:** Esso – N.518

**Also available**

**BR steam locomotives**
⊕ Farish, 5MT 'Black 5' class, 1805, >133mm<, Price:J
⊕ Lima, King class, 220257G, Price:Z

**BR electric locomotives**
⊕ Lima, Class 81, 220205G, Price:Z
⊕ Lima, Class 86, 220249G, Price:Z

**BR diesel locomotives**
⊕ Lima, 0-4-0 shunter, 220211G, Price:Z

**BR diesel locomotives**
⊕ Lima, Class 31, 220209G, Price:Z **Similar models:** Railfreight blue livery – 220245G; green livery – 220214G
⊕ Lima, Class 55, 220217G, Price:Z **Similar models:** earlier green livery – 220253G

**BR coaches**
⊕ Minitrix, corridor composite coach, N.303, >134mm<, Price:C **Similar models:** chocolate and cream (WR) livery – N.301; maroon livery – N.305

# Great Britain (BR)

**HO/OO Gauge**

⊗ Hornby, 2-10-0 9F class, R.264, >270mm<, Price:J

⊗ Hornby, 4-6-0 B17/4 class, R.060, >255mm<, Price:J

⊗ Hornby, Coronation class, R.262, >297mm<, 💡, Price:J

⊗ Hornby, 2-6-4T 4P class, R.062, >185mm<, Price:G

⊗ Hornby, Britannia class, R.033, >280mm<, Price:J

⊗ Hornby, Patriot class, R.324, >255mm<, Price:J

⊗ Hornby, Schools class, R.257, Price:H

⊗ Lima, King class, 205104MG, >280mm<, Price:Z

⊗ Lima, 94XX class, 205118MG, >130mm<, Price:Z

⊗ Lima, J50 class, 205102MG, >140mm<, Price:Z

⊗ Mainline, Standard 4MT class, 937052, >235mm<, Price:G

⊗ Mainline, 66XX class, 937039, >149mm<, Price:H

⊗ Mainline, Manor class, 937043, >252mm<, Price:J

⊗ Mainline, 43XX class, 937045, >238mm<, Price:J

⊗ Mainline, 61XX class, 937086, >163mm<, Price:H

⊗ Mainline, 57XX class, 937085, >125mm<, Price:F

⊗ Mainline, Dean 0-6-0 class, 954157, >163mm<, Price:H

⊗ Mainline, Jubilee class, 937047, >253mm<, Price:J **Similar models:** black livery – 936153

⊗ Mainline, N2 class, 954155, >152mm<, Price:H

⊗ Mainline, 14XX class, 937097, >120mm<, Price:F

⊗ Mainline, Royal Scot class, 937088, >262mm<, Price:J

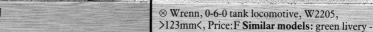

⊗ Mainline, parallel-boiler Royal Scot class, 937093, >262mm<, Price:J

⊗ Wrenn, 0-6-0 tank locomotive, W2205, >123mm<, Price:F **Similar models:** green livery - W2206

⊗ Wrenn, Castle class, W2223, >265mm<, Price:K **Similar models:** green livery, alternative names – W2221, W2221A, W2221B

⊗ Wrenn, A4 class, W2211, >287mm<, Price:K **Similar models:** alternative name – W2211A

⊗ Wrenn, West Country class, W2235, >277mm<, Price:K **Similar models:** alternative names – W2236, W2236A, W2239; Merchant Navy class, alternative name – W2238

⊗ Wrenn, Coronation class, W2229, >302mm<, Price:K **Similar models:** alternative name – W2229A; red livery – W2226; red livery, alternative name – W2226A; green livery – W2228; green livery, alternative name – W2228A

⊗ Wrenn, Battle of Britain class (before rebuilding), W2265, >275mm<, Price:K **Similar models:** alternative name (for Golden Arrow service W2265A, not for Golden Arrow service W2265A/X); blue livery, Merchant Navy group – W2267

⊗ Wrenn, Royal Scot class, W2262, >262mm<, Price:L **Similar models:** alternative name – W2262A

⊗ Hornby, Class 86, ⟐, R.360, >225mm<, ♀ , Price:G

⊗ Lima, Class 87, ⟐, 205125MG >231mm<, Price:Z **Similar models:** Railfreight blue livery – 205155MG

Hornby, Class 370 (Advanced Passenger Train), ⟐, R.794, >1360mm<, ♀ , Price:L

⊡ Fleischmann, Warship class, 4247, >210mm<, ♀ , Price:L **Similar models:** green livery – 4246

⊗ Hornby, Class 47, R.307, >255mm<, Price:G **Similar models:** earlier blue livery – R.319

⊗ Hornby, Class 35, R.335, >205mm<, Price:F

⊗ Hornby, Class 29, R.337, >205mm<, Price:F

⊗ Hornby, Class 25, R.326, >200mm<, 💡, Price:F **Similar models:** green livery – R.327

⊗ Hornby, Class 08 shunter, R.780, >120mm<, Price:E

⊗ Lima, Class 33, 205115MG, >199mm<, Price:Z

⊗ Lima, Class 55, 205105MG, >270mm<, Price:Z

⊗ Lima, Class 09, 205108MG, >115mm<, Price:Z **Similar models:** blue livery – 205107

⊗ Lima, Class 50, 205141MG, >272mm<, Price:Z **Similar models:** blue Railfreight livery – 205142MG

⊗ Lima, Class 52, 205121MG, Price:Z **Similar models:** blue livery – 205122

⊗ Lima, Class 42/43, 205135MG, >240mm<, Price:Z **Similar models:** blue livery – 205127MG

⊗ Mainline, Class 56, 937044, >252mm<, ♀, Price:H **Similar models:** earlier blue livery – 937035

⊗ Mainline, Class 03, 937036, >103mm<, Price:F **Similar models:** green livery – 937037

⊗ Mainline, Class 45, 937040, >273mm<, ♀, Price:G **Similar models:** Type 4, green livery – 937041

⊗ Wrenn, 0-6-0 diesel shunter, W2232, >113mm<, Price:L **Similar models:** green livery – W2231; blue livery, alternative number – W2232A

⊗ Hornby, Class 163 trailer 2nd, R.699, >240mm<, Price:H **Similar models:** green livery – R.688

⊗ Lima, 117/2 class, 205152MG (motor brake unit), 205153 (composite, not illustrated), 205154 (non-powered 2nd class driving car, not illustrated), Price:Z **Similar models:** 1981 blue and grey livery – 205147MG, 205148, 205149; 1974 blue livery – 205136MG, 205145, 205138; 1959 green livery – 205137MG, 205146, 205139

⊗ Lima, Inter-City 125 train, 149751G, >1077mm<, Price:Z Also available as separate items

◉ Fleischmann, 1st and 3rd class coach, 5146, >230mm<, Price:E

◉ Fleischmann, 3rd class coach, 5147, >230mm<, Price:E

◉ Fleischmann, 3rd class brake coach, 5148, >230mm<, Price:E

⊗ Hornby, composite coach, R.421, >240mm<, Price:D

⊗ Hornby, brake 3rd coach, R.424, >250mm<, Price:D

⊗ Hornby, 1st class open coach, R.425, >280mm<, Price:D

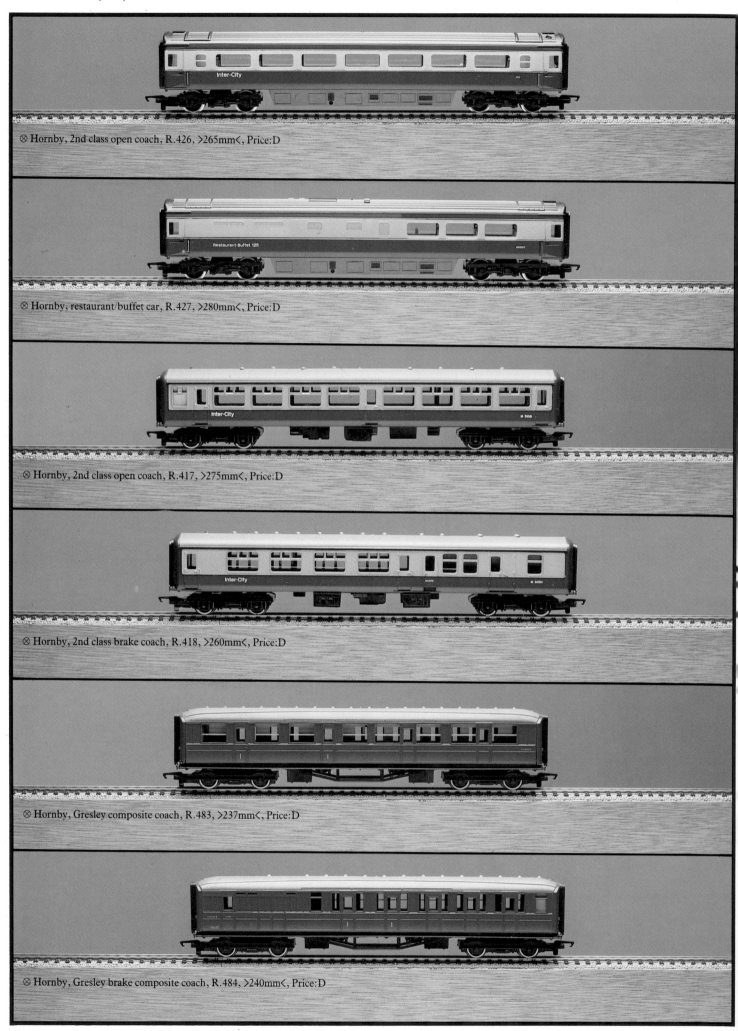

⊗ Hornby, 2nd class open coach, R.426, >265mm<, Price:D

⊗ Hornby, restaurant/buffet car, R.427, >280mm<, Price:D

⊗ Hornby, 2nd class open coach, R.417, >275mm<, Price:D

⊗ Hornby, 2nd class brake coach, R.418, >260mm<, Price:D

⊗ Hornby, Gresley composite coach, R.483, >237mm<, Price:D

⊗ Hornby, Gresley brake composite coach, R.484, >240mm<, Price:D

⊗ Hornby, 1st class sleeping car, R.485, >240mm<, Price:D

⊙ Liliput (UK), composite corridor coach, 1251, >250mm<, Price:D **Similar models:** maroon livery – 1201; brown and cream livery – 1211; green livery – 1221

⊙ Liliput (UK), brake end coach, 1252, >250mm<, Price:D **Similar models:** maroon livery – 1202; brown and cream livery – 1212; green livery – 1222

⊙ Liliput (UK), buffet, 1253, >250mm<, Price:D **Similar models:** maroon livery – 1203; brown and cream livery – 1213; green livery – 1223

⊗ Lima, gangwayed brake van (WR livery), 305345, >262mm<, Price:Z **Similar models:** green livery – 305348; crimson and cream livery – 305344; blue and grey livery – 305343

⊗ Lima, restaurant car (WR livery), 305322, >260mm<, Price:Z **Similar models:** green livery – 305324; crimson and cream – 305325; blue and grey livery – 305321

⊗ Lima, 2nd class brake coach (WR livery), 305333, >262mm<, Price:Z **Similar models:** green livery – 305334; crimson and cream livery – 305331; blue and grey livery – 305335

⊗ Lima, 3rd class coach (WR livery), 305362, >262mm<, Price:Z **Similar models:** green livery – 305365; crimson and cream livery – 305363; 2nd class blue and grey livery – 305361

⊗ Lima, mini buffet coach, 305308, >265mm<, Price:Z

⊗ Lima, 1st class coach, 305301, >265mm<, Price:Z

⊗ Lima, 2nd class coach, 305302, >265mm<, Price:Z

⊗ Lima, 1st class brake coach, 305303, >265mm<, Price:Z

⊗ Lima, gangwayed brake van, 305343, >261mm<, Price:Z

⊗ Lima, 2nd class brake coach, 205162, Price:Z

⊗ Mainline, 2nd class coach, 937107, >265mm<, Price:D

⊗ Mainline, 2nd class brake coach, 937108, >265mm<, Price:D

⊗ Mainline, buffet/restaurant car, 937114, >265mm<, Price:D

⊗ Mainline, 60ft 2nd class coach, 937309, >256mm<, Price:D

⊗ Mainline, 60ft 1st/2nd class brake coach, 937308, >256mm<, Price:D

⊗ Mainline, 60ft 1st and 2nd class coach, 937327, >254mm<, Price:D

⊗ Mainline, 2nd class brake coach, 937329, >242mm<, Price:D

⊗ Mainline, auto trailer (for push-pull trains), 937319, >266mm<, Price:D

⊗ Mainline, parcels van, 937307, >214mm<, Price:D **Similar models:** blue livery – 937117; blue and grey livery – 937304

⊗ Mainline, 60ft suburban brake coach, 937321, >250mm<, Price:D

⊗ Mainline, bogie milk van, 937325, >213mm<, Price:D

⊗ Mainline, gangwayed bogie milk van, 937323, >213mm<, Price:D

⊗ Mainline, 2nd class Inter-City coach, 937301, >273mm<, Price:D

⊗ Mainline, 2nd class brake Inter-City coach, 937303, >273mm<, Price:D

⊗ Mainline, buffet/restaurant car, 937113, >265mm<, Price:D

⊗ Hornby, 1st class parlour car, R.223, >260mm<, Price:D

⊗ Wrenn, Pullman 1st class coach with kitchen, W6002, >230mm<, Price:D **Similar models:** alternative name, for Brighton Belle – W6002A; alternative name, for Golden Arrow – W6012; blue and grey livery, for Golden Arrow – W6005; blue and grey livery, for Brighton Belle – W6005A; red livery – W6011; green livery – W6008

⊗ Wrenn, Pullman 2nd class coach, W6001, >230mm<, Price:D **Similar models:** alternative number, for Brighton Belle – W6001A; blue and grey livery – W6004; blue and grey livery, for Brighton Belle – W6004A; red livery – W6010; green livery – W6007

⊗ Wrenn, Pullman 2nd class brake coach, W6000, >230mm<, Price:D **Similar models:** blue and grey livery - W6003; red livery - W6009; green livery - W6006

⊗ Hornby, mineral wagon, R.239, >75mm<, Price:A

⊗ Hornby, 20T brake van, R.030, >107mm<, Price:C

⊗ Hornby, 45T steel carrier, R.246, >143mm<, Price:C

⊗ Hornby, 45T van, R.247, >145mm<, Price:C

⊗ Hornby, 45T wagon, R.248, >143mm<, Price:C

⊗ Hornby, hopper wagon, R.249, >120mm<, Price:C

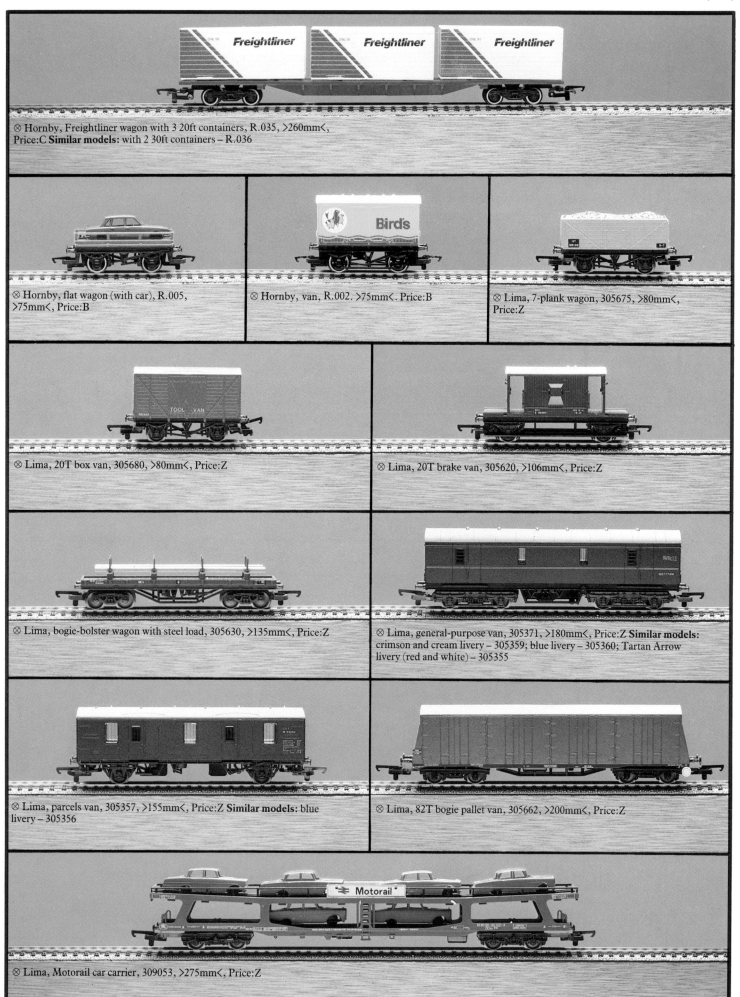

⊗ Hornby, Freightliner wagon with 3 20ft containers, R.035, >260mm<, Price:C **Similar models:** with 2 30ft containers – R.036

⊗ Hornby, flat wagon (with car), R.005, >75mm<, Price:B

⊗ Hornby, van, R.002. >75mm<. Price:B

⊗ Lima, 7-plank wagon, 305675, >80mm<, Price:Z

⊗ Lima, 20T box van, 305680, >80mm<, Price:Z

⊗ Lima, 20T brake van, 305620, >106mm<, Price:Z

⊗ Lima, bogie-bolster wagon with steel load, 305630, >135mm<, Price:Z

⊗ Lima, general-purpose van, 305371, >180mm<, Price:Z **Similar models:** crimson and cream livery – 305359; blue livery – 305360; Tartan Arrow livery (red and white) – 305355

⊗ Lima, parcels van, 305357, >155mm<, Price:Z **Similar models:** blue livery – 305356

⊗ Lima, 82T bogie pallet van, 305662, >200mm<, Price:Z

⊗ Lima, Motorail car carrier, 309053, >275mm<, Price:Z

# Great Britain (BR)

⊗ Lima, multiple wagon with transformer load, 309068, ›216mm‹, Price:Z **Similar models:** with British Steel load – 309067

⊗ Lima, 57ft general-purpose van, 305657, ›237mm‹, Price:Z **Similar models:** blue express parcels van – 305656

⊗ Lima, parcels van, 305350, ›210mm‹, Price:Z **Similar models:** blue livery – 305353

⊗ Mainline, hopper coal wagon, 937444, ›98mm‹, Price:B **Similar models:** grey livery – 937351

⊗ Mainline, bogie-bolster wagon, 937353, ›152mm‹, Price:C

⊗ Mainline, ventilated van, 937449, ›82mm‹, Price:C

⊗ Mainline, 3-plank wagon, 937420, ›82mm‹, Price:B

⊗ Mainline, Conflat wagon with container, 937352, ›82mm‹, Price:C

⊗ Mainline, brake van, 937366, ›107mm‹, Price:C

⊗ Wrenn, 16T steel mineral wagon, W4655, ›78mm‹, Price:B **Similar models:** with load of coal – W4655L; brown livery (no load) – W4655A

⊗ Wrenn, steel open wagon, W4640, ›78mm‹, Price:B

⊗ Wrenn, express parcels van, W5012, >94mm<, Price:B **Similar models:** BRT fish van – W5064

⊗ Wrenn, 20T brake van, W4310, >98mm<, Price:B

⊗ Wrenn, long-wheelbase fruit van (with Babycham poster), W4305, >120mm<, Price:C **Similar models:** blue livery (no poster) – W5055

⊗ Wrenn, 21T hopper wagon, W4644, >94mm<, Price:C

⊗ Wrenn, bulk grain hopper wagon, W4625, >86mm<, Price:C

⊗ Hornby, Scarwood 5-plank wagon, R.716, >76mm<, Price:A **Similar models:** Amos Benbow – R.116; Jif – R.222

⊗ Hornby, Barrow coke wagon, R.006, >75mm<, Price:B

⊗ Hornby, Perfection wagon with sheet rail, R.016, >75mm<, Price:B

⊗ Hornby, Hargreaves end tipping wagon, R.032, >75mm<, Price:B

⊗ Hornby, Black and Reoch mineral wagon, R.021, >100mm<, Price:B

⊗ Hornby, Esso tank wagon, R.014, >75mm<, Price:C **Similar models:** National Benzole – R.221

⊗ Hornby, Fisons twin silo wagon, R.011, >75mm<, Price:B

⊗ Hornby, Albright and Wilson tank wagon, R.026, >115mm<, Price:C **Similar models:** Fina – R.115; Pfizer (Traffic Services) – R.023

⊗ Hornby, Shell BP bogie tank wagon, R.669, >230mm<, Price:D

⊗ Hornby, Golden Shred van, R.009 >75mm<, Price:B **Similar models:** Wimpy – R.114

⦿ Liliput (UK), Charringtons mineral wagon, 1367, >77mm<, Price:C **Similar models:** ICI – 1365; Blue Circle Cement –1366; Wilkinson – 1368; Abbott – 1369; Stewarts and Lloyds – 1370

⊗ Lima, Pilkington Bros seven-plank wagon, 305670, >80mm<, Price:Z **Similar models:** Pontefract Collieries – 305671; Royal Arsenal Co-op – 305672; Black & Decker – 305673

⊗ Lima, Ford van, 305681, >80mm<, Price:Z **Similar models:** Pearl Fruit – 305682; Ever Ready – 305683

⊗ Lima, St Ivel milk tank wagon, 305641, >95mm<, Price:Z **Similar models:** I.M.S. – 305642; Express Dairy – 305643; CWS – 305644; Corn Products (oil tank) – 305640

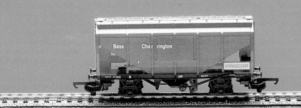

⊗ Lima, Bass Charrington hopper wagon, 305653, >112mm<, Price:Z

⊗ Lima, Haig 45T grain hopper wagon, 305651, >113mm<, Price:Z **Similar models:** Black and White – 305652; Vat 69 – 305650

⊗ Lima, British Leyland car carrier, 309057, >272mm<, Price:Z

⊗ Lima, NCB coal hopper wagon, 302892, >139mm<, Price:Z

⊗ Mainline, Coalite coke wagon, 937163, >82mm<, Price:B **Similar models:** Arthur H. Stabler – 937363

⊗ Mainline, E. Turner 3-plank wagon, 937362, >82mm<, Price:B **Similar models:** J. Carter – 937361

⊗ Mainline, B.A.C. 5-plank wagon, 937456, >82mm<, Price:B **Similar models:** Black Rock Quarries – 937455

⊗ Mainline, Stewarts and Lloyds 20T mineral wagon, 937439, >98mm<, Price:B **Similar models:** Blaenavon – 937437; Avon Tyres – 937459; Glenhafod – 937438

⊗ Mainline, Perfection Soap 7-plank wagon, 937457, >82mm<, Price:B **Similar models:** C.W.S. – 937129

⊗ Mainline, Charringtons hopper wagon, 937443, >98mm<, Price:B **Similar models:** Ministry of Transport – 937441

⊗ Mainline, Charringtons 20T mineral wagon, 937446, >98mm<, Price:B

⊗ Mainline, BP tank wagon, 937135, >82mm<, Price:C

⊗ Mainline, ICI tank wagon, 937453, >98mm<, Price:C

⊗ Mainline, ICI ventilated van, 937365, >82mm<, Price:C

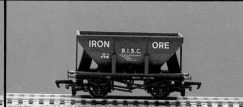

⊗ Mainline, B.I.S.C. iron ore hopper wagon, 937160, >82mm<, Price:B

⊗ Wrenn, Colman salt wagon, W5024, >78mm<, Price:C **Similar models:** Star Salt – W5018; Sifta – W4666; Saxa – W4665; DCL – W5070

⊗ Wrenn, Carter ore hopper wagon, W5025, >78mm<, Price:C **Similar models:** Pycroft – W5017; Southdown – W5006; Hinchley – W5015

⊗ Wrenn, Mobil tank wagon, W5041, >74mm<, Price:C **Similar models:** Esso – W5039; Shell – W5040; Esso – W5042

⊗ Wrenn, Auto Spares low-sided wagon, W5059, >78mm<, Price:B

⊗ Wrenn, North Sea Fish fish van, W5050, >92mm<, Price:C

⊗ Wrenn, Shell/BP tank wagon, W5061, >78mm<, Price:C **Similar models:** Royal Daylight – W5062; United Molasses – W5077; Power – W5076

⊗ Wrenn, British Anthracite Collieries steel wagon, W5073, >78mm<, Price:B

⊗ Hornby, track cleaning coach, R.296, >95mm<, Price:C

⊗ Hornby, 75T operating crane, R.749, >490mm<, Price:E

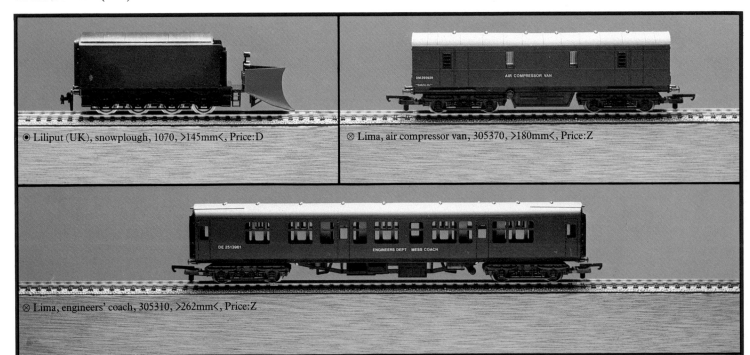

⊙ Liliput (UK), snowplough, 1070, >145mm<, Price:D

⊗ Lima, air compressor van, 305370, >180mm<, Price:Z

⊗ Lima, engineers' coach, 305310, >262mm<, Price:Z

## Also available

### BR steam locomotives
⊗ Hornby, A4 class, R.309, >288mm<, Price:J
⊗ Hornby, D49/1 class, R.259, Price:H
⊙ Liliput (UK), A3 class, 1037, >228mm<, 💡, Price:K **Similar models:** black livery, no working lights – 1039
⊙ Liliput (UK), A4 class, 1050, >290mm<, Price:K **Similar models:** alternative names – 1051, 1052, 1053, 1054, 1055
⊙ Liliput (UK), A2 class, 1061, >288mm<, Price:K **Similar models:** with tender drive – 1063; black livery, locomotive drive – 1064; black livery, tender drive – 1065
⊗ Lima, 2-6-0 'Crab' locomotive, 205120MG, Price:Z
⊗ Lima, 45XX class, 205110MG, Price:Z
⊗ Wrenn, 2-6-4 4MT tank locomotive, W2218, >178mm<, Price:J
⊗ Wrenn, 2-8-0 8F locomotive, W2224, >255mm<, Price:K
⊗ Wrenn, N2 class, W2216, >140mm<, Price:G

### BR electric locomotives
⊙ Liliput (UK), Class 81, 🚆, 1001, >222mm<, 💡, Price:J **Similar models:** with modern BR logo – 1005; fitted with two motors – 1002

### BR diesel locomotives
⊗ Hornby, Class 37, R.369, >247mm<, Price:F
⊗ Hornby, Class 58, R.250, >249mm<, Price:G
⊙ Liliput (UK), Western Class 52, 1010, >250mm<, 💡 Price:J **Similar models:** desert sand livery – 1009; maroon livery – 1012; green livery – 1011
⊗ Lima, Class 20, 205158MG, Price:Z **Similar models:** earlier blue livery – 205157MG, green livery – 205156MG
⊗ Wrenn, Class 20, W2230B, >185mm<, Price:H **Similar models:** green livery – W2230

### BR diesel railcars
⊗ Hornby, Class 110, R.698, >240mm<, Price:J **Similar models:** green livery – R.687
⊗ Hornby, Class 253 (Inter-City 125), R.332, >730mm<, 💡, Price:J
⊙ Liliput (UK), 'Trans-Pennine' 2-car set, 1020, >510mm<, 💡, Price:J **Similar models:** with interior lights – 1021; interior lights and two motors – 1022; green livery – 1025; green livery and interior lights – 1026; green livery, interior lights, and two motors – 1027
⊗ Lima, exGWR railcar, 205150MG, Price:Z **Similar models:** 1948 crimson and cream livery – 205133MG
⊗ Lima, exGWR parcels car, 205144MG, Price:Z

### BR coaches
⊗ Lima, 1st and 3rd class coach (WR livery), 305313, >262mm<, Price:Z **Similar models:** green livery – 305314; crimson and cream livery – 305311; 1st and 2nd class blue and grey livery – 305315
⊗ Lima, 2nd class coach, 305366, Price:Z
⊗ Lima, sleeping car, 305367, Price:Z

### Private-owner coaches
⊗ Hornby, 3rd class parlour brake, R.233, >262mm<, Price:D
⊙ Liliput (UK), Pullman coach, 1279, >250mm<, Price:D **Similar models:** brown and cream livery – 1278
⊗ Wrenn, Pullman electric Brighton Belle end driving coaches (one non-powered), W3006/7, >498mm<, Price:K **Similar models:** blue and grey livery - W3004/5

### BR wagons
⊗ Hornby, flat wagon with Freightliner container, R.017, >99mm<, Price:C
⊗ Hornby, ferry van, R.027, >181mm<, Price:C
⊗ Hornby, car transporter (with cars), R.124, >241mm<, Price:C
⊗ Hornby, Railfreight ventilated van, R.117, >77mm<, Price:B
⊗ Lima, 50T stone hopper wagon, 305637, Price:Z
⊗ Lima, iron ore tippler wagon, 305663, Price:Z **Similar models:** orange and grey livery – 305664
⊗ Lima, ballast wagon, 305666, Price:Z **Similar models:** green livery – 305665; grey and yellow livery – 305667
⊗ Wrenn, cattle wagon, W4630, >88mm<, Price:B
⊗ Wrenn, low-loader wagon, W4652, >129mm<, Price:A **Similar models:** grey livery – W4652A
⊗ Wrenn, gunpowder van, W5057, >78mm<, Price:B
⊗ Wrenn, utility van, W4324, >133mm<, Price:C **Similar models:** brown livery – W5053
⊗ Wrenn, low-sided wagon, W5060, >78mm<, Price:B

### Private-owner wagons
⊙ Liliput (UK), Esso, 1344, >85mm<, Price:C **Similar models:** Shell BP – 1340; BP – 1345
⊙ Liliput (UK), Johnnie Walker bulk grain van, 1380, >125mm<, Price:C **Similar models:** Haig – 1381; Vat 69 – 1383; King George IV – 1384; Dewars – 1385; Crawfords – 1386; White Horse Whisky – 1387; Jamie Stuart – 1388; Malsters Association – 1389; Abbot's Choice – 1390; plain grey – 1391
⊗ Lima, Tarmac 50T stone hopper wagon, 305639, Price:Z **Similar models:** Yeoman – 305635; Amey Roadstone Co – 305636; Tilcon – 305638; BP – 305668
⊗ Lima, Neill & Brown 82T pallet van, 305659, Price:Z **Similar models:** Fisons – 305660; UKF – 305661
⊗ Lima, Esso 102T bogie tank wagon, 305645, Price:Z **Similar models:** Fina – 305646; Philips Petroleum – 305647
⊗ Lima, Theakstons Beer 57ft bogie van, 305658, >240mm<, Price:Z
⊗ Wrenn, St. Ivel milk wagon, W5013, >93mm<, Price:C **Similar models:** Milk Marketing Board – W5023; United Dairies – W4657; Guinness beer tank wagon – W5003; Double Diamond beer tank wagon – W5044; Skol – W5066
⊗ Wrenn, Tunnel Cement hopper wagon, W5005, >78mm<, Price:C
⊗ Wrenn, Fisons fertiliser silo wagon, W4658, >78mm<, Price:C
⊗ Wrenn, Peak Frean's 12T ventilated van, W4318, >78mm<, Price:B
⊗ Wrenn, Royden Stables horse box, W4315, >120mm<, Price:C
⊗ Wrenn, BSA van, W5009, >78mm<, Price:C
⊗ Wrenn, Hoveringham ore hopper wagon, W5036, >96mm<, Price:C **Similar models:** Tarmac – W5056; W5068
⊗ Wrenn, NTG wagon with coal load, W5034, >78mm<, Price:C
⊗ Wrenn, National Coal Board 21T hopper wagon, W5035, >92mm<, Price:C
⊗ Wrenn, J. Bly & Co 5-plank wagon, W5000, >78mm<, Price:B **Similar models:** Higgs – W4635; Ayr Co-op – W5043; S. Harris – W5008; Cranston – W5048; Amos Benbow – W5067; British Soda – W5069; Twining – W5075; Bassetts – W5074
⊗ Wrenn, Park Ward steel mineral wagon, W5026, >78mm<, Price:B **Similar models:** Shell – W5051; Esso – W5051A
⊗ Wrenn, Kellogg's bulk grain wagon, W5020, >88mm<, Price:C **Similar models:** Quaker Oats – W5045; Bass Charington – W5071

# Great Britain

## Caledonian Railway

The Caledonian Railway, established in 1845, was one of the most famous and powerful of the early private companies in British railway history. It covered the western and central areas of Scotland, and had an intensive network of lines around Glasgow, serving industry and suburban passenger routes. Caledonian engines were pained a rich blue with red frames; the coaches were crimson and white.

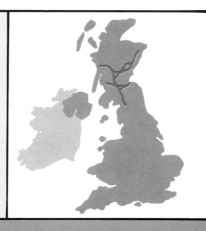

### N Gauge

⊕ Farish, 4P 4-4-0, 1217, >122mm<, Price:H

⊕ Farish, 57ft suburban coach, 0608, >125mm<, Price:C

⊕ Farish, 57ft brake end suburban coach, 1618, >125mm<, Price:C

⊕ Farish, 4-wheeled coach, 0668, >69mm<, Price:B

**Also available**
**Caledonian coaches**
⊕ Farish, 4-wheeled brake end coach, 0678, >69mm<, Price:B

# Great Britain

## Somerset & Dorset

The Somerset & Dorset Railway was jointly owned by the London and South Western Railway and the Midland Railway (after 1923, the SR and LMS). Its locomotives were supplied by the Midland Railway from its standard classes. There was also a 2-8-0 class specially built for the hilly, cross-country route over which the railway ran. It ran from Bristol and Bath to Bournemouth and Southampton.

### N Gauge

⊕ Farish, 4P 4-4-0, 1207, >122mm<, Price:H

**Also available**
**Somerset and Dorset coaches**
⊕ Farish, 4-wheeled, 0667, >69mm<, Price:B
⊕ Farish, 4-wheeled brake end coach, 0677, >69mm<, Price:B

# Great Britain

## Great Western Railway

The GWR was the only pre-1923 private company to retain its original name. It was already a big company and it merely absorbed some smaller lines, mostly in Wales. It was renowned for its style and public image. Its dark green locomotives and chocolate and cream coaches were probably the best-known of all the British railway colours. The company became the Western Region of British Railways in 1948.

**N Gauge**

⊖ Farish, Hall class, 1404, >132mm<, Price:H

⊖ Farish, pannier tank, 1104, >70mm<, Price:F

⊖ Farish, Castle class, 1444, >136mm<, Price:H **Similar models:** alternative name – 1446

⊖ Farish, 57ft suburban coach, 0604, >125mm<, Price:C

⊖ Farish, 57ft suburban brake end coach, 0614, >125mm<, Price:C

⊖ Farish, 57ft mainline coach, 0624, >125mm<, Price:C

⊖ Farish, 57ft mainline brake end coach, 0634, >125mm<, Price:C

⊖ Farish, 4-wheeled coach, 0664, >69mm<, Price:B

⊖ Farish, 4-wheeled brake end coach, 0674, >69mm<, Price:B

⊖ Farish, 5-plank wagon, 2004, >43mm<, Price:A

⊖ Farish, 7-plank wagon, 2104, >43mm<, Price:A

⊖ Farish, mineral wagon, 2204, >43mm<, Price:A

⊖ Farish, single vent van, 2304, >43mm<, Price:A

⊖ Farish, twin vent van, 2404, >43mm<, Price:A

⊖ Farish, cattle van, 2604, >43mm<, Price:A

⊕ Farish, brake van, 3104, >56mm<, Price:B

⊕ Farish, loco bogie wagon, 3211, >82mm<, Price:B

⊕ Lima, parcels van, 320862, >110mm<, Price:Z

⊕ Lima, brake van, 320410, >60mm<, Price:Z

⊕ Lima, box van, 320615, >50mm<, Price:Z

⊕ Lima, horse box, 320616, >50mm<, Price:Z

⊕ Peco, 5-plank mineral wagon, NR-40W, >41mm<, Price:A

⊕ Peco, 7-plank coal wagon, NR-41W, >41mm<, Price:A

⊕ Peco, steel coal wagon, NR-44W, >41mm<, Price:A

⊕ Peco, standard box van, NR-43W, >41mm<, Price:A

⊕ Peco, cattle truck, NR-45W, >41mm<, Price:A

⊕ Peco, plate wagon, NR-5W, >58mm<, Price:A

⊕ Peco, tube wagon, NR-7W, >58mm<, Price:A

⊕ Peco, Conflat container wagon, NR-20, >41mm<, Price:C

⊕ Lima, Palethorpes bogie van, 320863, Price:Z **Similar models:** Enparts – 320867

⊕ Lima, bogie milk tank wagon, 320625, >85mm<, Price:Z

⊕ Lima, London Brick brick wagon, 320720, Price:Z

⊕ Lima, Amoco bogie tank wagon, 320622, >85mm<, Price:Z

⊕ Lima, Typhoo box van, 320611, >45mm<, Price:Z **Similar models:** St Ivel – 320614; Lucas – 320618; Birds Custard Powder – 320619; Castrol – 320739

⊕ Lima, Black Park seven-plank wagon, 320602, >45mm<, Price:Z **Similar models:** Barrow Barnsley – 320604; J. K. Harrison – 320607; P. W. Spence – 320608

**Also available**
**GW steam locomotives**
⊕ Farish, prairie tank, 1604, >86mm<, Price:G
⊕ Lima, King class, 220256G, Price:Z

# Great Britain (GWR)

**HO/OO Gauge**

⊗ Hornby, King class, R.349, >275mm<, Price:H

⊗ Hornby, Hall class, R.313, >260mm<, Price:G

⊗ Hornby, County class, R.392, >235mm<, ⊷, Price:J

⊗ Hornby, Class 2721, R.059, >120mm<, Price:F

⊗ Lima, King class, 205103MG, Price:Z

⊗ Lima, 45XX class, 205111MG, Price:Z

⊗ Lima, 94XX class, 205117MG, >130mm<, Price:Z

⊗ Mainline, 66XX class, 937038, >149mm<, Price:H

⊗ Mainline, Manor class, 937100, >252mm<, Price:J

⊗ Mainline, 43XX class, 937090, >238mm<, Price:J

⊗ Mainline, 57XX class, 937084, >125mm<, Price:F

⊗ Mainline, Dean 0-6-0, 954156, >126mm<, Price:H

⊗ Mainline, 61XX class, 937083, >163mm<, Price:H

⊗ Mainline, 14XX class, 937096, >120mm<, Price:F

⊗ Hornby, clerestory composite, R.122, >230mm<, Price:D

⊗ Hornby, clerestory brake 3rd, R.123, >230mm<, Price:D

# Great Britain (GWR)

⊗ Hornby, composite coach, R.456, >230mm<, Price:C

⊗ Hornby, brake 3rd, R.457, >240mm<, Price:C

⊗ Hornby, restaurant car, R.458, >237mm<, Price:C

⊗ Hornby, 4-wheeled coach, R.213, >100mm<, Price:B

◉ Liliput (UK), composite corridor, 1235, >250mm<, Price:D

⊗ Mainline, 'Centenary' 1st and 3rd class coach, 937314, >254mm<, Price:D

⊗ Mainline, 'Centenary' 3rd class brake coach, 937316, >254mm<, Price:D

⊗ Mainline, bogie milk van, 937324, >213mm<, Price:D

⊗ Mainline, gangwayed bogie milk van, 937322, >213mm<, Price:D

⊗ Mainline, auto trailer (for push-pull trains), 937318, >266mm<, Price:D

⊗ Mainline, Collett 1st and 3rd class brake coach, 937123, >256mm<, Price:D

⊗ Mainline, Collett 3rd class coach, 937124, >256mm<, Price:D

⊗ Hornby, 20T brake van, R.714, >100mm<, Price:C          ⊗ Lima, horse box, 305625, >100mm<, Price:Z

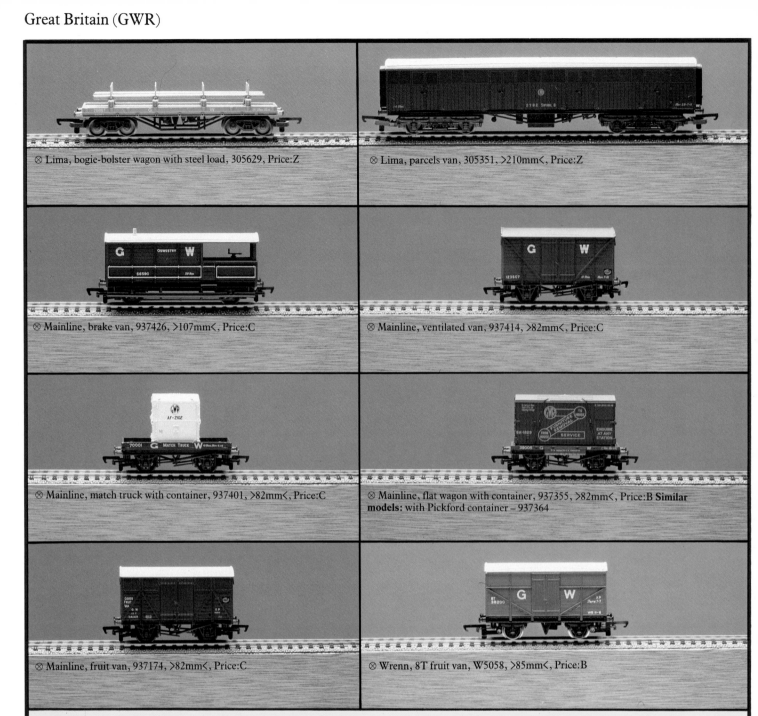

⊗ Lima, bogie-bolster wagon with steel load, 305629, Price:Z

⊗ Lima, parcels van, 305351, >210mm<, Price:Z

⊗ Mainline, brake van, 937426, >107mm<, Price:C

⊗ Mainline, ventilated van, 937414, >82mm<, Price:C

⊗ Mainline, match truck with container, 937401, >82mm<, Price:C

⊗ Mainline, flat wagon with container, 937355, >82mm<, Price:B **Similar models:** with Pickford container – 937364

⊗ Mainline, fruit van, 937174, >82mm<, Price:C

⊗ Wrenn, 8T fruit van, W5058, >85mm<, Price:B

**Also available**

**GWR steam locomotives**
⊗ Hornby, 0-4-0T No 101, R.333, >108mm<, Price:E
⊗ Wrenn, Castle class, W2222, >265mm<, Price:K **Similar models:** alternative name – W2247

**GWR diesel railcars**
⊗ Lima, diesel railcar, 205132MG, Price:Z
⊗ Lima, parcels car, 205143MG, Price:Z

**GWR wagons**
⊗ Wrenn, 12T steel mineral wagon, W5029, >78mm<, Price:B **Similar models:** with ore load – W5029L
⊗ Wrenn, refrigerated van, W5019, >78mm<, Price:C
⊗ Wrenn, brake van, W5037, >98mm<, Price:C
⊗ Wrenn, passenger fruit van, W5049, >120mm<, Price:C

# Great Britain

## London, Midland & Scottish Railway

The LMS (or LMSR) was formed in 1923 from the amalgamation of smaller private railway companies (such as the Midland Railway, London and North Western Railway, and Caledonian Railway). It was the largest of the four big British groups after amalgamation. With the exception of its Scottish area, it became the London Midland Region of British Railways after nationalization in 1948.

### N Gauge

⊖ Farish, Class 5 4-6-0 locomotive, 1801, >133mm<, Price:J **Similar models:** crimson lake livery – 1806

⊖ Farish, 0-6-0 tank locomotive, 1706, >71mm<, Price:F **Similar models:** maroon livery – 1701

⊖ Farish, 4P 'Compound', 1206, >122mm<, Price:H **Similar models:** maroon livery – 1201

⊖ Farish, Duchess (Coronation) class, 1811, >150mm<, Price:J

⊖ Peco, Jubilee class, NL-21, >134mm<, Price:J **Similar models:** maroon livery – NL-22

⊖ Farish, diesel shunter, 1001, >60mm<, Price:F

⊖ Farish, 57ft suburban coach, 0606, >125mm<, Price:C

⊖ Farish, 57ft suburban brake end coach, 0616, >125mm<, Price:C

⊖ Farish, 57ft mainline corridor coach, 0626, >125mm<, Price:C

⊖ Farish, 57ft brake end mainline corridor coach, 0636, >125mm<, Price:C

⊖ Farish, 4-wheeled coach, 0661, >69mm<, Price:B

⊖ Farish, 4-wheeled brake end coach, 0671, >69mm<, Price:B

⊖ Farish, 5-plank wagon, 2001, >43mm<, Price:A

⊖ Farish, 7-plank wagon, 2101, >43mm<, Price:A

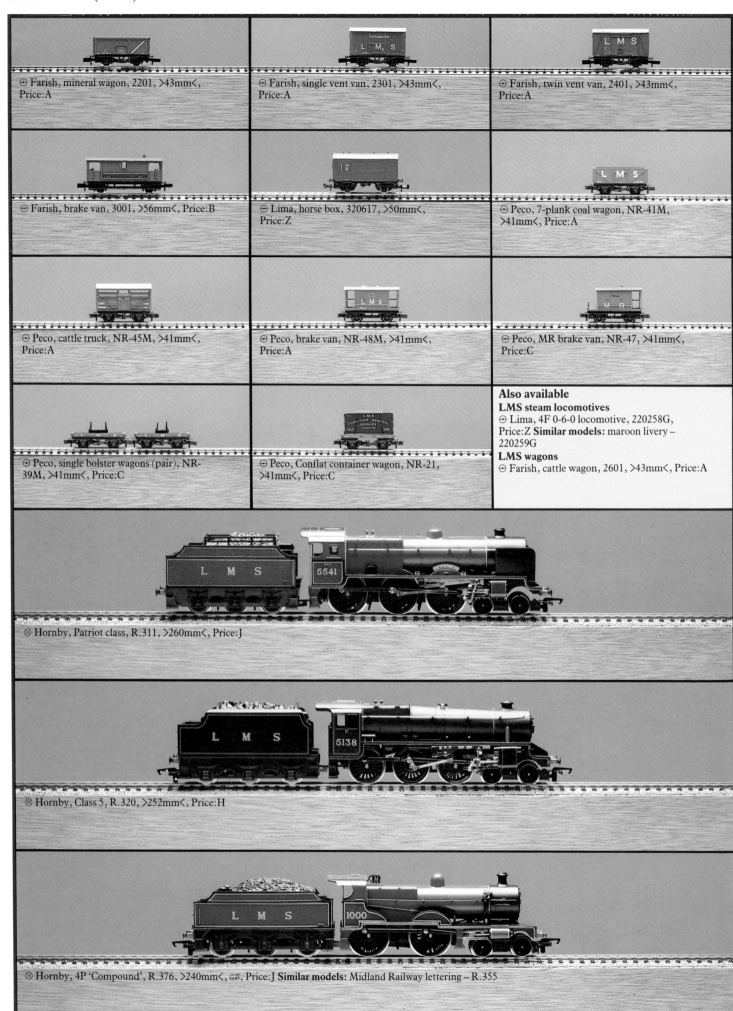

⊖ Farish, mineral wagon, 2201, >43mm<, Price:A

⊖ Farish, single vent van, 2301, >43mm<, Price:A

⊖ Farish, twin vent van, 2401, >43mm<, Price:A

⊖ Farish, brake van, 3001, >56mm<, Price:B

⊖ Lima, horse box, 320617, >50mm<, Price:Z

⊖ Peco, 7-plank coal wagon, NR-41M, >41mm<, Price:A

⊖ Peco, cattle truck, NR-45M, >41mm<, Price:A

⊖ Peco, brake van, NR-48M, >41mm<, Price:A

⊖ Peco, MR brake van, NR-47, >41mm<, Price:C

⊖ Peco, single bolster wagons (pair), NR-39M, >41mm<, Price:C

⊖ Peco, Conflat container wagon, NR-21, >41mm<, Price:C

**Also available**
**LMS steam locomotives**
⊖ Lima, 4F 0-6-0 locomotive, 220258G, Price:Z **Similar models:** maroon livery – 220259G
**LMS wagons**
⊖ Farish, cattle wagon, 2601, >43mm<, Price:A

⊗ Hornby, Patriot class, R.311, >260mm<, Price:J

⊗ Hornby, Class 5, R.320, >252mm<, Price:H

⊗ Hornby, 4P 'Compound', R.376, >240mm<, ⊛, Price:J **Similar models:** Midland Railway lettering – R.355

⊗ Hornby, 0-6-0T 3F 'Jinty', R.301, >140mm<, Price:F

⊗ Lima, 2-6-0 'Crab' locomotive, 205119MG, >250mm<, Price:Z

⊗ Mainline, Royal Scot class, 937092, >262mm<, Price:J

⊗ Mainline, Jubilee class, 937046, >253mm<, Price:J

⊗ Lima, 0-6-0 shunter, 205109MG, >115mm<, Price:Z

⊗ Hornby, composite coach, R.474, >237mm<, Price:D

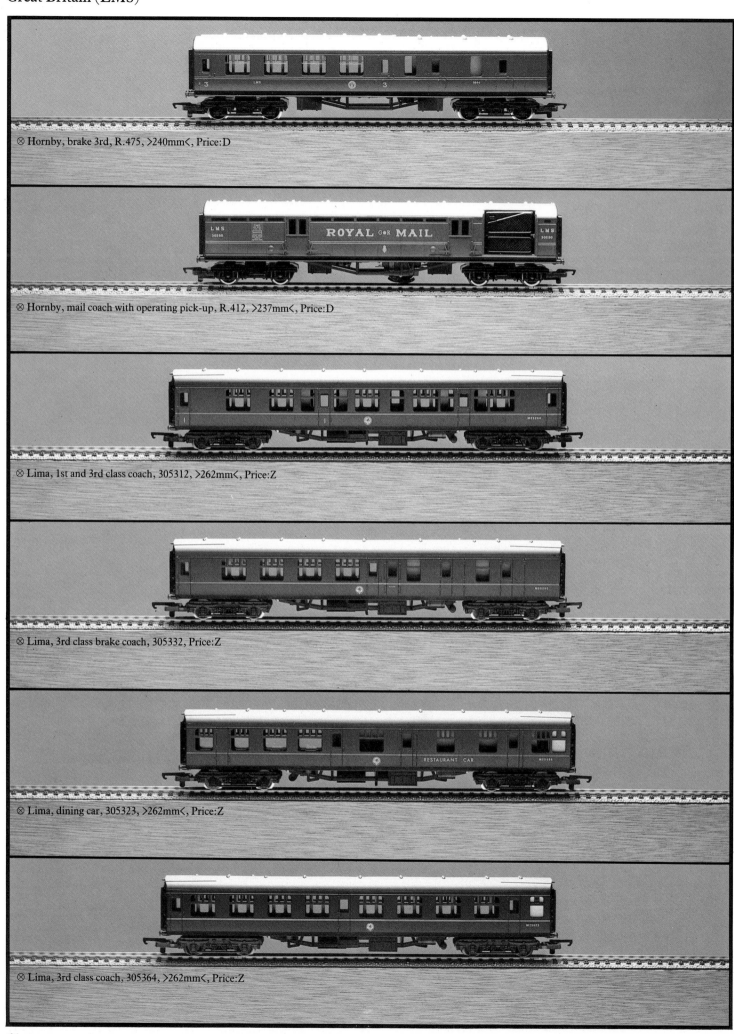

⊗ Hornby, brake 3rd, R.475, >240mm<, Price:D

⊗ Hornby, mail coach with operating pick-up, R.412, >237mm<, Price:D

⊗ Lima, 1st and 3rd class coach, 305312, >262mm<, Price:Z

⊗ Lima, 3rd class brake coach, 305332, Price:Z

⊗ Lima, dining car, 305323, >262mm<, Price:Z

⊗ Lima, 3rd class coach, 305364, >262mm<, Price:Z

⊗ Lima, gangwayed brake van, 305342, Price:Z

⊗ Mainline, parcels van, 937118, >214mm<, Price:D

⊗ Mainline, 3-plank wagon, 937419, >82mm<, Price:B

⊗ Mainline, 1-plank wagon with container, 937433, >82mm<, Price:B

⊗ Mainline, ventilated van, 937371, >82mm<, Price:C

⊗ Lima, van, 305658, >180mm<, Price:Z

## Also available

### LMS steam locomotives
⊗ Hornby, Coronation class, R.685, >297mm<, Price:J
⊗ Wrenn, 2-8-0 8F, W2225, >255mm<, Price:K
⊗ Wrenn, Coronation class, W2242, >300mm<, Price:K **Similar models:** black livery, without smoke deflectors – W2241; black, without smoke deflectors, alternative name – W2241A; black livery with smoke deflectors – W2227; black, smoke deflectors, alternative name – W2227A
⊗ Wrenn, Royal Scot class, W2260, >262mm<, Price:L **Similar models:** alternative name – W2260A; black livery, with smoke deflectors – W2261; black, alternative name – W2261A

### LMS diesel locomotives
⊗ Wrenn, 0-6-0 shunter, W2233, >113<, Price:G

### LMS coaches
⊗ Hornby, clerestory composite coach, R.452, >236mm<, Price:D
⊗ Hornby, 3rd class clerestory brake coach, R.453, >236mm<, Price:D
⊗ Hornby, composite coach (Coronation Scot livery), R.422, >266mm<, Price:D
⊗ Hornby, 3rd class brake coach (Coronation Scot livery), R.423, >266mm<, Price:D

### LMS wagons
⊗ Hornby, 20T brake van, R.718, >99mm<, Price:C
⊗ Lima, horse box, 305626, Price:Z
⊗ Wrenn, 5-plank open wagon with load, W5032, >78mm<, Price:B
⊗ Wrenn, 12T ventilated van, W5030, >93mm<, Price:B
⊗ Wrenn, 20T brake van, W4311, >98mm<, Price:B

# Great Britain

# London & North Eastern Railway

The LNER was formed in 1923 when several smaller railway companies radiating north-east and east from London, and those broadly in the east of Scotland, were amalgamated. The LNER was famous for its east-coast expresses, such as the Flying Scotsman, and for the sleek Pacific locomotives built by Sir Nigel Gresley. The LNER became the Eastern Region of British Railways in 1948.

**N Gauge**

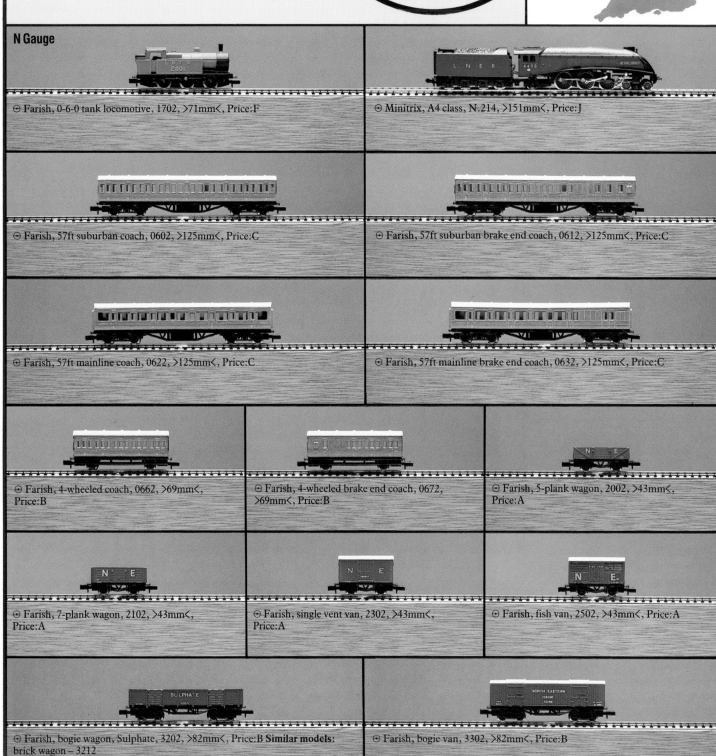

⊖ Farish, 0-6-0 tank locomotive, 1702, >71mm<, Price:F

⊖ Minitrix, A4 class, N.214, >151mm<, Price:J

⊖ Farish, 57ft suburban coach, 0602, >125mm<, Price:C

⊖ Farish, 57ft suburban brake end coach, 0612, >125mm<, Price:C

⊖ Farish, 57ft mainline coach, 0622, >125mm<, Price:C

⊖ Farish, 57ft mainline brake end coach, 0632, >125mm<, Price:C

⊖ Farish, 4-wheeled coach, 0662, >69mm<, Price:B

⊖ Farish, 4-wheeled brake end coach, 0672, >69mm<, Price:B

⊖ Farish, 5-plank wagon, 2002, >43mm<, Price:A

⊖ Farish, 7-plank wagon, 2102, >43mm<, Price:A

⊖ Farish, single vent van, 2302, >43mm<, Price:A

⊖ Farish, fish van, 2502, >43mm<, Price:A

⊖ Farish, bogie wagon, Sulphate, 3202, >82mm<, Price:B **Similar models:** brick wagon – 3212

⊖ Farish, bogie van, 3302, >82mm<, Price:B

⊖ Farish, loco sand wagon, 2911, >43mm<, Price:A

⊖ Peco, steel coal wagon, NR-44E, >41mm<, Price:A

⊖ Peco, refrigerator box van, NR-42E, >41mm<, Price:A

⊖ Peco, standard box van, NR-43E, >41mm<, Price:A

⊖ Peco, brake van, NR-49E, >41mm<, Price:A

⊖ Peco, bolster wagon, NR-4E, >41mm<, Price:A

⊖ Peco, brake van, NR-28E, >58mm<, Price:B

⊖ Peco, single bolster wagons (pair), NR-39E, >41mm<, Price:C

⊖ Peco, Mendip Mountain Quarries mineral wagon, NR-P81, >41mm<, Price:A **Similar models:** Charles Dunsdon – NR-P83; Garswood – NR-P80; A. Gresley & Co. – NR-P82

⊖ Peco, Ward & Son coal wagon, NR-P90, >41mm<, Price:A **Similar models:** Park End – NR-P91; Kingsbury – NR-P92; Hood & Son – NR-P93

⊖ Peco, Crawshay Brothers lime wagon, NR-P112, >41mm<, Price:A **Similar models:** Dowlow – NR-P111; S.L.B. – NR-P113

⊖ Peco, Charringtons steel coal wagon, NR-P100, >41mm<, Price:A **Similar models:** Denaby – NR-P101

⊖ Peco, Saxa salt wagon, NR-P120, >41mm<, Price:A **Similar models:** Shaka – NR-P121

⊖ Peco, Fyffes refrigerator box van, NR-P140, >41mm<, Price:A **Similar models:** Colman's – NR-P141

⊖ Peco, Worthington standard box van, NR-P130 >41mm<, Price:A **Similar models:** Bass – NR-P131

⊖ Peco, Shell/BP petrol wagon, NR-P160, >41mm<, Price:B **Similar models:** Esso – NR-P161

⊖ Peco, Express Dairy milk wagon, NR-P168, >41mm<, Price:B **Similar models:** United Dairies – NR-P167

⊖ Peco, container wagon with Raleigh Cycles container, NR-P30, >41mm<, Price:C **Similar models:** Lyons Tea – NR-P31

⊖ Peco, BP tank wagon (green), NR-P52, >41mm<, Price:B **Similar models:** black livery – NR-P53; white livery – NR-P50

⊖ Peco, Ford pallet van, NR-P55, >58mm<, Price:B **Similar models:** Izal – NR-P56; army – NR-P54

⊖ Peco, Haig grain whisky wagon, NR-P68, >58mm<, Price:B **Similar models:** Maltsters Association – NR-P70; White Horse – NR-P69; Abbot's Choice – NR-P67

**HO/OO Gauge**

⊗ Hornby, D49/1 class, R.378, ⟩240mm⟨, ⇔, Price:J

⊗ Hornby, A1 class, R.398, ⟩290mm⟨, Price:J

⊗ Lima, J50 class, 205101MG, ⟩130mm⟨, Price:Z

⊗ Mainline, N2 class, 954154, ⟩152mm⟨, Price:H **Similar models:** black livery – 954158

⊗ Hornby, composite coach, R.477, ⟩240mm⟨, Price:J

⊗ Hornby, brake composite, R.478, ⟩240mm⟨, Price:D

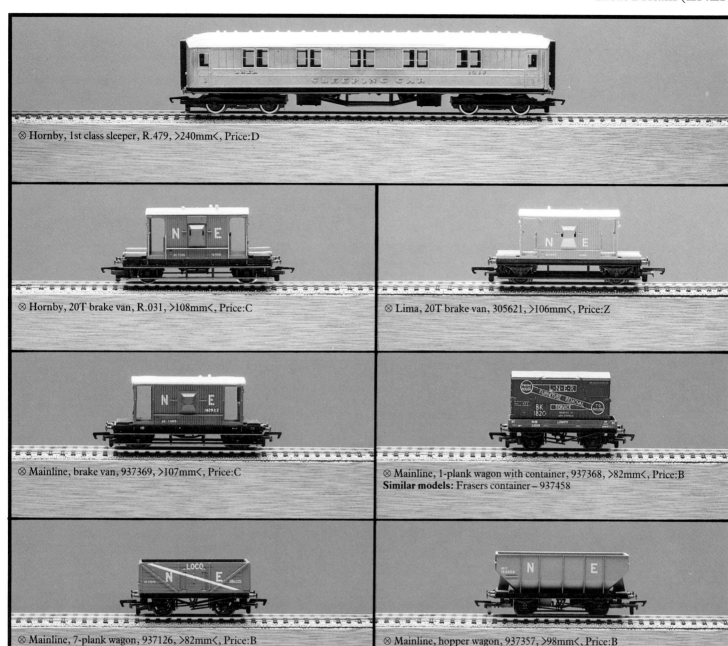

⊗ Hornby, 1st class sleeper, R.479, >240mm<, Price:D

⊗ Hornby, 20T brake van, R.031, >108mm<, Price:C

⊗ Lima, 20T brake van, 305621, >106mm<, Price:Z

⊗ Mainline, brake van, 937369, >107mm<, Price:C

⊗ Mainline, 1-plank wagon with container, 937368, >82mm<, Price:B
**Similar models:** Frasers container – 937458

⊗ Mainline, 7-plank wagon, 937126, >82mm<, Price:B

⊗ Mainline, hopper wagon, 937357, >98mm<, Price:B

## Also available
### LNER steam locomotives
◉ Liliput (UK), A3 class, 1030, >288mm<, 💡 , Price:K **Similar models:** with two tenders – 1035
◉ Liliput (UK), A4 class, 1040, >288mm<, 💡 , Price:K **Similar models:** alternative names – 1041, 1042, 1043; blue livery – 1045, 1046 (alternative names); blue without valances – 1048; black without valances – 1046
◉ Liliput (UK), A2 class, 1060, >288mm<, Price:K **Similar models:** with tender drive – 1062
⊗ Wrenn, A4 class, W2209, >287mm<, Price:K **Similar models:** alternative name – W2209A; blue livery, and alternative names – W2210, W2212, W2212A; black livery – 2213; black livery, alternative name – W2213A
⊗ Wrenn, N2 class, W2217, >140mm<, Price:G **Similar models:** black livery – W2217A
### LNER coaches
◉ Liliput (UK), composite corridor, 1271, >250mm<, Price:D **Similar models:** with interior lights – 1291; blue and white livery – 1252; blue and white livery with internal lights – 1295
◉ Liliput (UK), buffet, 1273, >250mm<, Price:D **Similar models:** with internal lights – 1293; blue and white livery – 1277; blue and white livery with internal lights – 1297
### LNER wagons
⊗ Wrenn, brake van, W5031, >95mm<, Price:C
⊗ Wrenn, 12T van, W5028, >78mm<, Price:B
### LNER miscellaneous
⊗ Lima, breakdown crane and flat car, 309059, Price:Z

# Great Britain

## Southern Railway

The SR was formed at the groupings of 1923, taking in the small companies operating south of London – the London, Brighton and South Coast, London, South Western, and South Eastern railways. It was the smallest of the 'Big Four' but was noted for its modern ideas, with extensive electrification of suburban routes even in the 1930s. The SR became the Southern Region of British Railways in 1948.

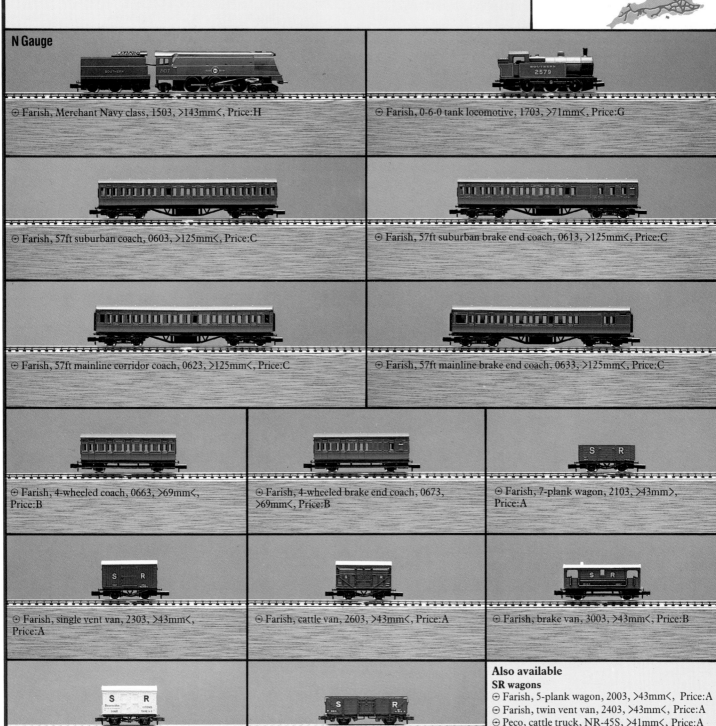

**N Gauge**

⊖ Farish, Merchant Navy class, 1503, >143mm<, Price:H

⊖ Farish, 0-6-0 tank locomotive, 1703, >71mm<, Price:G

⊖ Farish, 57ft suburban coach, 0603, >125mm<, Price:C

⊖ Farish, 57ft suburban brake end coach, 0613, >125mm<, Price:C

⊖ Farish, 57ft mainline corridor coach, 0623, >125mm<, Price:C

⊖ Farish, 57ft mainline brake end coach, 0633, >125mm<, Price:C

⊖ Farish, 4-wheeled coach, 0663, >69mm<, Price:B

⊖ Farish, 4-wheeled brake end coach, 0673, >69mm<, Price:B

⊖ Farish, 7-plank wagon, 2103, >43mm>, Price:A

⊖ Farish, single vent van, 2303, >43mm<, Price:A

⊖ Farish, cattle van, 2603, >43mm<, Price:A

⊖ Farish, brake van, 3003, >43mm<, Price:B

⊖ Peco, banana box van, NR-42S, >41mm<, Price:A

⊖ Peco, tarpaulin wagon, NR-10S, >58mm<, Price:A

**Also available**
**SR wagons**
⊖ Farish, 5-plank wagon, 2003, >43mm<, Price:A
⊖ Farish, twin vent van, 2403, >43mm<, Price:A
⊖ Peco, cattle truck, NR-45S, >41mm<, Price:A
⊖ Peco, 5-plank mineral wagon, NR-40S, >41mm<, Price:A
⊖ Peco, 7-plank coal wagon, NR-41S, >41mm<, Price:A

## HO/OO Gauge

⊗ Hornby, E2 class, R.261, >128mm<, Price:F

⊗ Hornby, Battle of Britain class, R.374, >270mm<, Price:H

⊗ Wrenn, West Country class, W2237, >277mm<, Price:K

⊗ Wrenn, West Country class (before rebuilding), W2266, >275mm<, Price:K **Similar models:** alternative name – (for Golden Arrow service W2266A, not Golden Arrow service W2266A/X)

⊗ Hornby, composite coach, R.486, >240mm<, Price:D

⊗ Hornby, 20T brake van, R.029, >105mm<, Price:C

⊗ Lima, horse box, 305628, >100mm<, Price:Z

**Also available**

**SR steam locomotives**
⊗ Hornby, Schools class, R.683, >238mm<, Price:H
⊗ Wrenn, R1 class, W2207, >123mm<, Price:F

**SR coaches**
⊗ Hornby, composite coach, R.441, >241mm<, Price:D
⊗ Hornby, 3rd class brake coach, R.445, >241mm<, Price:D
⊗ Hornby, brake coach, R.487, >240mm<, Price:D

**SR wagons**
⊗ Wrenn, brake van, W5038, >98mm<, Price:B
⊗ Wrenn, 12T ventilated van, W5033, >78mm<, Price:B
⊗ Wrenn, utility van, W4323, >133mm<, Price:C

# France

## Société Nationale des Chemins de Fer Français

The Société Nationale des Chemins de Fer Français (SNCF) was formed in January 1938 when the previous private French companies were nationalized. These included the Midi, Paris-Lyon Méditerranée (PLM), Paris-Orleans, Etat, Est, and Nord. The regions of the SNCF roughly match the old company areas. The SNCF is renowned for its very efficient equipment and operations – with such trains as the TGV.

### N Gauge

⊕ Arnold, 4-6-2 locomotive, 2535, >160mm<, ♀, Price:L *(shown in ETAT livery)*

⊖ Arnold, 0-8-0 locomotive, 2516, >118mm<, ♀, Price:K

⊖ Fleischmann, 2-10-0 locomotive, 7178, >150mm<, ♀, Price:L

⊖ Fleischmann, 4-6-0 locomotive, 7161, >122mm<, ♀, Price:K

⊖ Fleischmann, 0-10-0 tank locomotive, 7095, >79mm<, ♀, Price:K

⊖ Minitrix, 230-E class, 2089, >132mm<, ♀, Price:L

⊖ Minitrix, 150Y class, 2083, >148mm<, ♀, Price:L

⊖ Arnold, Bo-Bo type express locomotive, ♀, 2481, >100mm<, ♀, Price:K
**Similar models:** green livery – 2482; red livery – 2483

⊖ Fleischmann, 7200 class, ♀, 7362, >109mm<, ♀, Price:K **Similar models:** TEE livery – 7361; blue livery – 7360

⊖ Minitrix, CC6500 class, 2084, ♀, >125mm<, ♀, Price:K

⊖ Minitrix, BB20 000 class, 2934, ♀, >82mm<, ♀, Price:J

⊖ Roco, CC7100 class, ♀, 2157A, >108mm<, ♀, Price:J

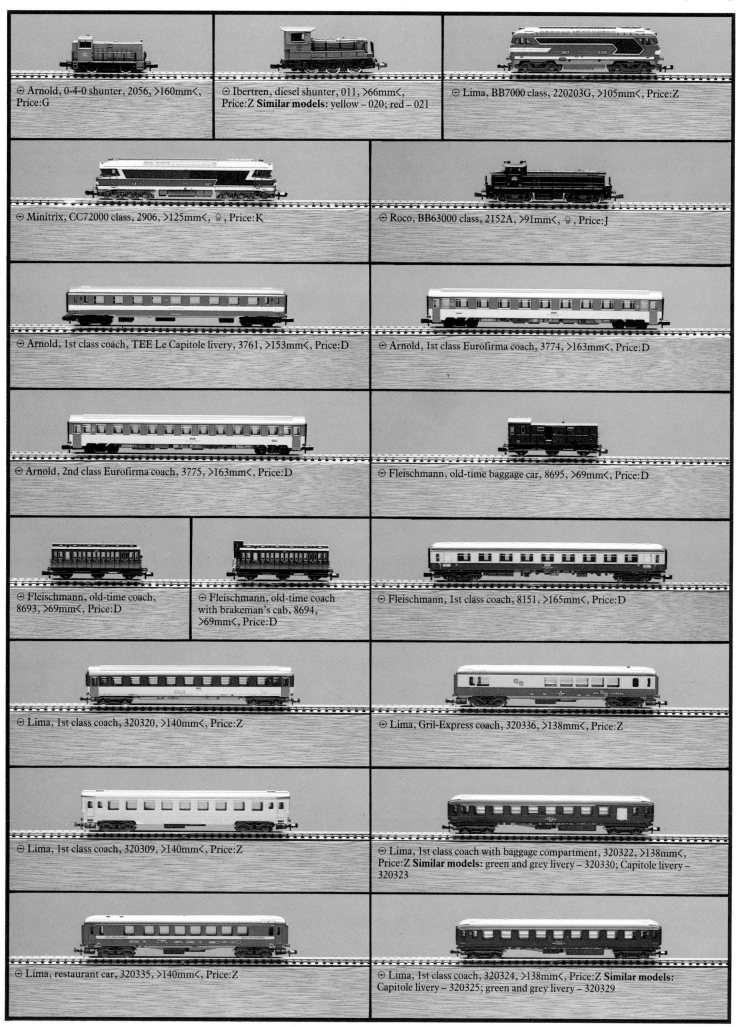

⊖ Arnold, 0-4-0 shunter, 2056, >160mm<, Price:G

⊖ Ibertren, diesel shunter, 011, >66mm<, Price:Z **Similar models:** yellow – 020; red – 021

⊖ Lima, BB7000 class, 220203G, >105mm<, Price:Z

⊖ Minitrix, CC72000 class, 2906, >125mm<, ♙, Price:K

⊖ Roco, BB63000 class, 2152A, >91mm<, ♙, Price:J

⊖ Arnold, 1st class coach, TEE Le Capitole livery, 3761, >153mm<, Price:D

⊖ Arnold, 1st class Eurofirma coach, 3774, >163mm<, Price:D

⊖ Arnold, 2nd class Eurofirma coach, 3775, >163mm<, Price:D

⊖ Fleischmann, old-time baggage car, 8695, >69mm<, Price:D

⊖ Fleischmann, old-time coach, 8693, >69mm<, Price:D

⊖ Fleischmann, old-time coach with brakeman's cab, 8694, >69mm<, Price:D

⊖ Fleischmann, 1st class coach, 8151, >165mm<, Price:D

⊖ Lima, 1st class coach, 320320, >140mm<, Price:Z

⊖ Lima, Gril-Express coach, 320336, >138mm<, Price:Z

⊖ Lima, 1st class coach, 320309, >140mm<, Price:Z

⊖ Lima, 1st class coach with baggage compartment, 320322, >138mm<, Price:Z **Similar models:** green and grey livery – 320330; Capitole livery – 320323

⊖ Lima, restaurant car, 320335, >140mm<, Price:Z

⊖ Lima, 1st class coach, 320324, >138mm<, Price:Z **Similar models:** Capitole livery – 320325; green and grey livery – 320329

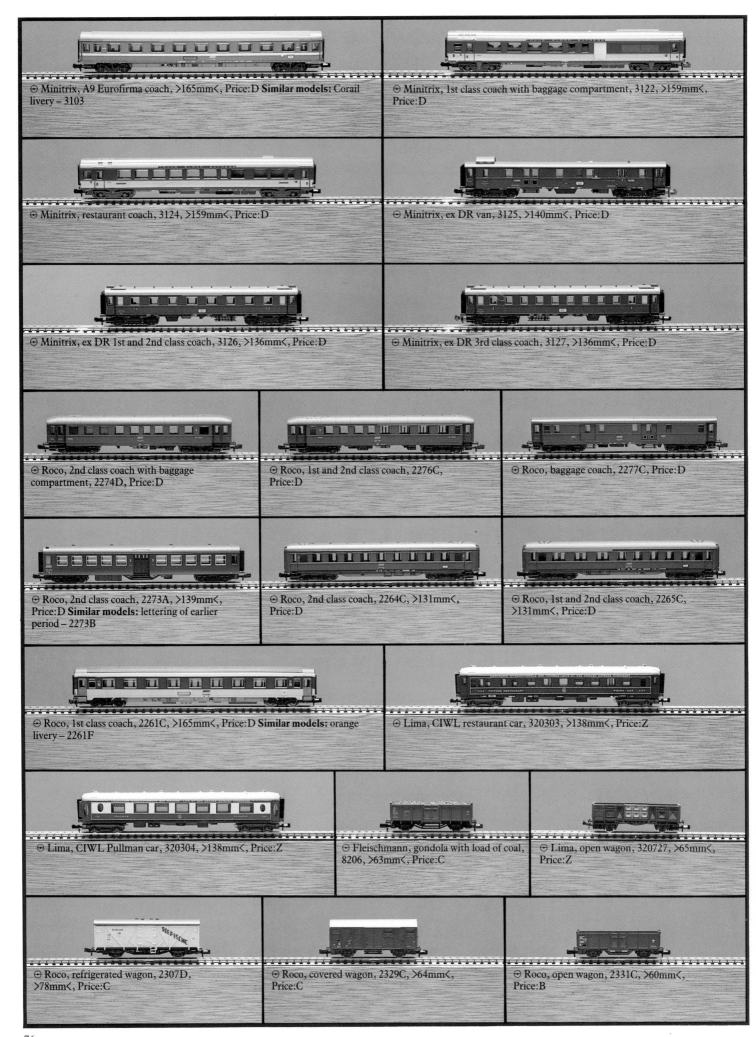

⊖ Minitrix, A9 Eurofirma coach, >165mm<, Price:D **Similar models:** Corail livery – 3103

⊖ Minitrix, 1st class coach with baggage compartment, 3122, >159mm<, Price:D

⊖ Minitrix, restaurant coach, 3124, >159mm<, Price:D

⊖ Minitrix, ex DR van, 3125, >140mm<, Price:D

⊖ Minitrix, ex DR 1st and 2nd class coach, 3126, >136mm<, Price:D

⊖ Minitrix, ex DR 3rd class coach, 3127, >136mm<, Price:D

⊖ Roco, 2nd class coach with baggage compartment, 2274D, Price:D

⊖ Roco, 1st and 2nd class coach, 2276C, Price:D

⊖ Roco, baggage coach, 2277C, Price:D

⊖ Roco, 2nd class coach, 2273A, >139mm<, Price:D **Similar models:** lettering of earlier period – 2273B

⊖ Roco, 2nd class coach, 2264C, >131mm<, Price:D

⊖ Roco, 1st and 2nd class coach, 2265C, >131mm<, Price:D

⊖ Roco, 1st class coach, 2261C, >165mm<, Price:D **Similar models:** orange livery – 2261F

⊖ Lima, CIWL restaurant car, 320303, >138mm<, Price:Z

⊖ Lima, CIWL Pullman car, 320304, >138mm<, Price:Z

⊖ Fleischmann, gondola with load of coal, 8206, >63mm<, Price:C

⊖ Lima, open wagon, 320727, >65mm<, Price:Z

⊖ Roco, refrigerated wagon, 2307D, >78mm<, Price:C

⊖ Roco, covered wagon, 2329C, >64mm<, Price:C

⊖ Roco, open wagon, 2331C, >60mm<, Price:B

⊖ Roco, telescopic cowl wagon, 2375C, >75mm<, Price:D

⊖ Arnold, Ermewa wine tank wagon, 4360, >60mm<, Price:D

⊖ Arnold, Stef refrigerated wagon, 4564, >74mm<, Price:C

⊖ Lima, Omya double-silo wagon, 320733, >56mm<, Price:Z **Similar models:** Européenne de Transport – 320731; Nouvelle de Cadres – 320732

⊖ Minitrix, Kronenbourg beer wagon, 3594, >68mm<, Price:C

⊖ Minitrix, Elf tank wagon, 3547, >55mm<, Price:C

## Also available

### SNCF steam locomotives
⊕ Arnold, 4-6-4 tank locomotive, 2271, >92mm<, ♀, Price:J
⊖ Fleischmann, 2-6-0 tank locomotive, 7031, ♀, >68mm<, Price:J
⊖ Roco, 150X class, 2106F, >141mm<, Price:L

### SNCF electric railcars
⊖ Lima, TGV, 123901, Price:Z. Also available as separate items

### SNCF diesel locomotives
⊖ Lima, MDT class, 220229G, >65mm<, Price:Z **Similar models:** blue livery – 220230G

### SNCF coaches
⊖ Fleischmann, 2nd class coach, 8152, >165mm<, Price:D
⊖ Lima, ambulance coach, 320328, Price:Z
⊖ Minitrix, 1st and 2nd class coach, 3023, >120mm<, Price:D **Similar models:** 2nd class – 3024; 2nd class with lights – 3025
⊖ Minitrix, 1st class coach, 3123, >159mm<, Price:D
⊖ Roco, 2nd class coach, 2274C, Price:D

### Private-owner coaches
⊖ Lima, CIWL wagon-lits coach, 320333, >138mm<, Price:Z
### SNCF wagons
⊖ Lima, high-sided wagon, 320643, Price:Z
⊖ Roco, open wagon with coal load, 2317C, >50mm<, Price:B
⊖ Roco, hopper wagon with coal load, 2318A, >60mm<, Price:B
⊖ Roco, flat wagon with stakes, 2308B, >86mm<, Price:B
⊖ Roco, open wagon with coal load, 2368C, >87mm<, Price:C
### Private-owner wagons
⊖ Roco, Sernam covered wagon, 2334A, >74mm<, Price:C
⊖ Roco, Dubonnet tank wagon. 2332D, >55mm<, Price:C

## TT Gauge

Berliner Bahnen, covered wagon, 4133, >76mm<, Price:Z

Berliner Bahnen, wine cask wagon, 4431, >76mm<, Price:Z

## HO/OO Gauge

▣ Fleischmann, 4-6-0 'P8' locomotive, 4161, >214mm<, ♀, Price:L  (supplied with transfers; shown here in NS livery)

▣ Fleischmann, 2-10-0 locomotive, 4178, >270mm<, ♀, Price:M

# France (SNCF)

▣ Fleischmann, 0-10-0 tank locomotive, 4095, >145mm<, ♀, Price:L

▣ Fleischmann, 0-8-0 locomotive, 4146, >223mm<, ♀, Price:L

◎ Liliput, 232TC class, 78 72, >170mm<, Price:L **Similar models:** black livery – 78 73

◎ Lima, 2-8-2 locomotive (oil-fired), 203002LG, Price:Z **Similar models:** coal-fired version – 203004LG

◎ Roco, 150C class, 4118S, >159mm<, ♀, Price:L

◎ Roco, 230G class, 4125A, >234mm<, ♀, Price:L

◎ Roco, BB15000 class, ☗, 4193S, >200mm<, ♀, Price:J **Similar models:** BB7200 class, Corail livery, two pantographs – 4199S

◎ Lima, CC7100 class, 🖧, 208029LG, ›217mm‹, Price:Z **Similar models:** 🖳 – 208029LGP

◎ Lima, BB15000 class, 🖧, 208045LG, ›200mm‹, Price:Z **Similar models:** 🖳 – 208045LGP; green livery, 🖧 – 208044LG

◎ Lima, BB7200 class, 🖧, 208107LG, ›200mm‹, Price:Z **Similar models:** 🖳 – 208107LGP; BB22000 class, 🖧 – 208111LG; BB22000 class, 🖳 – 208111LGP

◎ Lima, CC40100 class, 🖧, 208122LG, ›255mm‹, Price:Z **Similar models:** 🖳 – 208122LGP

◎ Lima, 67000 class, 208036, ›195mm‹, Price:Z

◎ Lima, 72000 class, 208058LG, ›225mm‹, Price:Z

# France (SNCF)

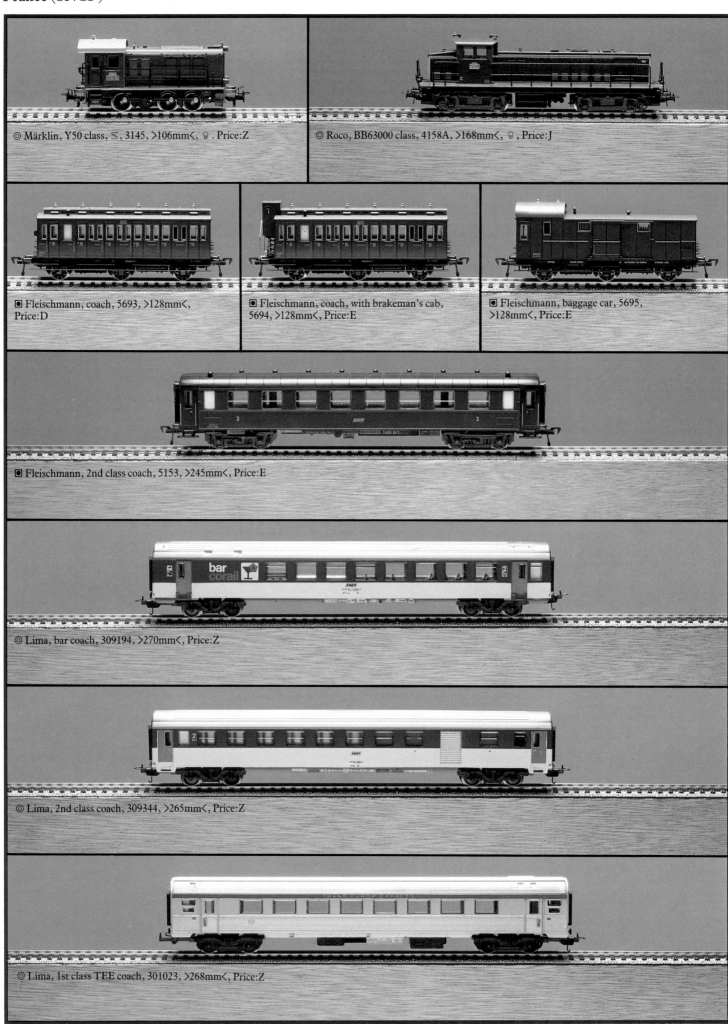

◎ Märklin, Y50 class, ≦, 3145, >106mm<, ♀, Price:Z

◎ Roco, BB63000 class, 4158A, >168mm<, ♀, Price:J

◉ Fleischmann, coach, 5693, >128mm<, Price:D

◉ Fleischmann, coach, with brakeman's cab, 5694, >128mm<, Price:E

◉ Fleischmann, baggage car, 5695, >128mm<, Price:E

◉ Fleischmann, 2nd class coach, 5153, >245mm<, Price:E

◎ Lima, bar coach, 309194, >270mm<, Price:Z

◎ Lima, 2nd class coach, 309344, >265mm<, Price:Z

◎ Lima, 1st class TEE coach, 301023, >268mm<, Price:Z

◎ Lima, 1st class TEE brake end coach, 301024, >240mm<, Price:Z

◎ Lima, 1st class coach, 309113, >265mm<, Price:Z

◎ Lima, 1st class coach, 309117, Price:Z **Similar models:** green and grey livery – 309128

◎ Lima, 1st class coach, 309124, Price:Z

◎ Lima, Grand Confort coach, 309129, >268mm<, Price:Z

◎ Lima, Wasteels 2nd class couchette coach, 309162, >270mm<, Price:Z **Similar models:** green and grey livery – 309191; 2nd class coach (not couchette), green – 309192

France (SNCF)

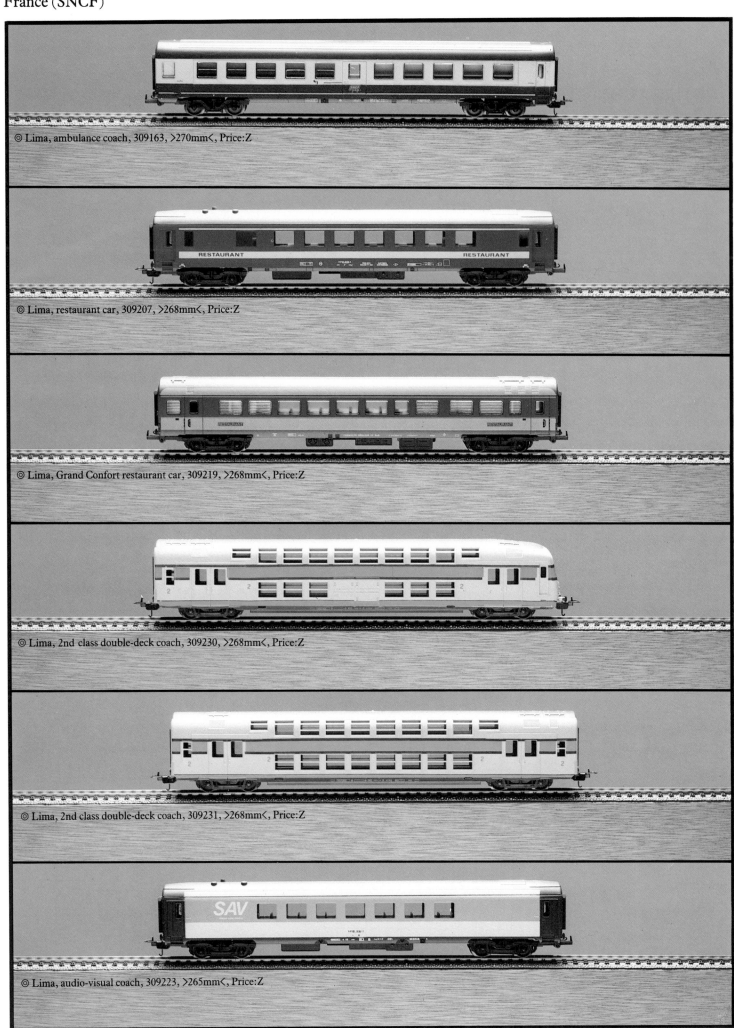

◎ Lima, ambulance coach, 309163, >270mm<, Price:Z

◎ Lima, restaurant car, 309207, >268mm<, Price:Z

◎ Lima, Grand Confort restaurant car, 309219, >268mm<, Price:Z

◎ Lima, 2nd class double-deck coach, 309230, >268mm<, Price:Z

◎ Lima, 2nd class double-deck coach, 309231, >268mm<, Price:Z

◎ Lima, audio-visual coach, 309223, >265mm<, Price:Z

◎ Lima, conference coach, 309224, >260mm<, Price:Z

◎ Lima, 1st and 2nd class coach, 309241, >268mm<, Price:Z

◎ Lima, 1st class coach with baggage compartment, 309306, >255mm<, Price:Z **Similar models:** red and cream livery – 309307; green and grey livery – 309312

◎ Lima, Grand Confort passenger and baggage coach, 309311, >268mm<, Price:Z

◎ Lima, mail coach, 309328, >270mm<, Price:Z

◎ Lima, 1st class coach with baggage compartment, 309318, >265mm<, Price:Z

# France (SNCF)

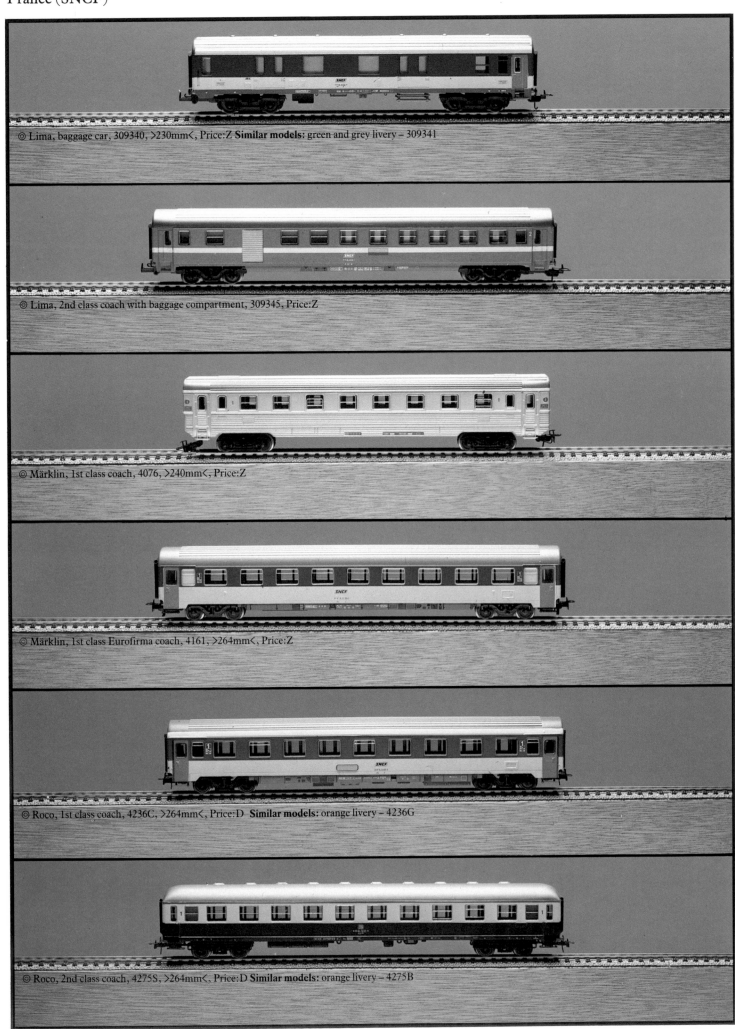

◎ Lima, baggage car, 309340, >230mm<, Price:Z **Similar models:** green and grey livery – 309341

◎ Lima, 2nd class coach with baggage compartment, 309345, Price:Z

◎ Märklin, 1st class coach, 4076, >240mm<, Price:Z

◎ Märklin, 1st class Eurofirma coach, 4161, >264mm<, Price:Z

◎ Roco, 1st class coach, 4236C, >264mm<, Price:D **Similar models:** orange livery – 4236G

◎ Roco, 2nd class coach, 4275S, >264mm<, Price:D **Similar models:** orange livery – 4275B

◎ Roco, 1st class coach, 4299S, >264mm<, Price: D

◎ Roco, 2nd class coach with baggage compartment, 4275S, >264mm<, Price: D **Similar models:** orange livery – 4223B

◎ Roco, 2nd class coach, 4222A, >256mm<, Price: K **Similar models:** lettering of earlier period – 4222B

◎ Roco, 2nd class coach, 44212A, >270mm<, Price: D

◎ Roco, 1st and 2nd class coach, 44214A, >270mm<, Price: D

◎ Roco, four-wheeled 2nd class coach, 4201F, >160mm<, Price: D

◎ Roco, four-wheeled 2nd class coach, 4202F, >160mm<, Price: D

# France (SNCF)

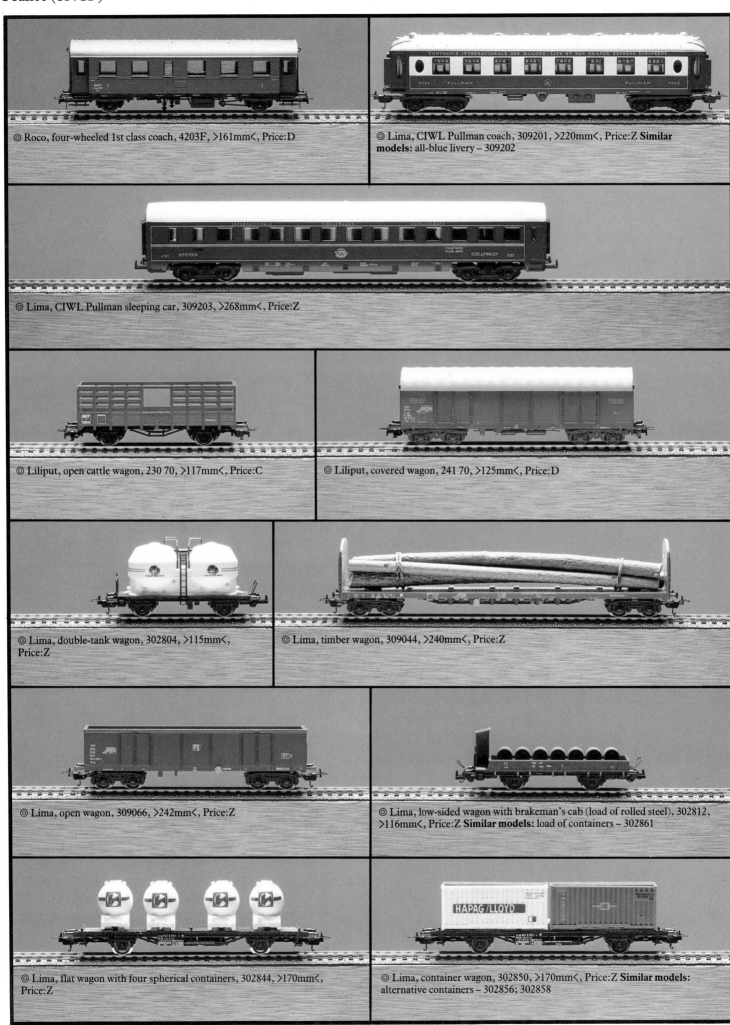

◎ Roco, four-wheeled 1st class coach, 4203F, >161mm<, Price:D

◎ Lima, CIWL Pullman coach, 309201, >220mm<, Price:Z **Similar models:** all-blue livery – 309202

◎ Lima, CIWL Pullman sleeping car, 309203, >268mm<, Price:Z

◎ Liliput, open cattle wagon, 230 70, >117mm<, Price:C

◎ Liliput, covered wagon, 241 70, >125mm<, Price:D

◎ Lima, double-tank wagon, 302804, >115mm<, Price:Z

◎ Lima, timber wagon, 309044, >240mm<, Price:Z

◎ Lima, open wagon, 309066, >242mm<, Price:Z

◎ Lima, low-sided wagon with brakeman's cab (load of rolled steel), 302812, >116mm<, Price:Z **Similar models:** load of containers – 302861

◎ Lima, flat wagon with four spherical containers, 302844, >170mm<, Price:Z

◎ Lima, container wagon, 302850, >170mm<, Price:Z **Similar models:** alternative containers – 302856; 302858

◎ Lima, covered wagon, 302863, >227mm<, Price:Z

◎ Lima, high-sided wagon, 303172, >121mm<, Price:Z

◎ Lima, bogie high-sided wagon, 309065, >242mm<, Price:Z

◎ Lima, covered wagon, 303205, Price:Z

◎ Lima, covered wagon with sliding roof, 303182, >161mm<, Price:Z

◎ Lima, telescopic covered wagon, 303184, >132mm<, Price:Z

◎ Lima, covered wagon with opening roof, 303187, >161mm<, Price:Z

◎ Roco, Sernam covered wagon, 44315A, >137mm<, Price:D

◎ Roco, open wagon, 4311D, >94mm<, Price:B

◎ Roco, refrigerated wagon, 4312D, >124mm<, Price:C

◎ Roco, covered wagon, 4375B, >122mm<, Price:D

◎ Roco, well wagon with tank load, 44313B, >124mm<, Price:C

◎ Roco, telescopic cowl wagon, 4395C, >138mm<, Price:D

◎ Electrotren, Transfesa car carrier with 10 cars, 6002, >305mm<, Price:D **Similar models:** without cars – 6000

◎ Electrotren, Transfesa articulated wagon with awnings, 6100, >305mm<, Price:D

◎ Lima, Pechine-Saint Gobain hopper wagon, 302893, >140mm<, Price:Z

◎ Lima, AGIP tank wagon, 302712, >126mm<, Price:Z

◎ Lima, Elf tank wagon, 302716, >116mm<, Price:Z

◎ Lima, Nouvelle des Cadres double tank wagon, 302803, >110mm<, Price:Z

◎ Lima, Beaujolais Village tank wagon, 302825, Price:Z

◎ Lima, Sernam covered wagon, 303106, >121mm<, Price:Z

◎ Lima, Chiquita covered wagon, 303167, >121mm<, Price:Z

◎ Lima, L'Air Liquide gas tank wagon, 302920, >190mm<, Price:Z

◎ Lima, Kronenbourg refrigerated wagon, 303551, >130mm<, Price:Z

◎ Lima, Martini refrigerated wagon, 303193, >242mm<, Price:Z

◎ Lima, Kronenbourg covered wagon, 303202, >240mm<, Price:Z

**Also available**

**SNCF steam locomotives**
◎ Liliput, 150Y class, 52 70, >268mm<, Price:N
◎ Liliput, 21D class, series 230F, 104 70, >214mm<, Price:L **Similar models:** ≲ – 104 75 (Price:K)
◎ Roco, 93 class, 4122B, >159mm<, ♀, Price:K

**SNCF electric locomotives**
◎ Lima, BB9200 class, ⛟, 208033LG, >185mm<, Price:Z **Similar models:** Corail livery – 208127LG
◎ Lima, CC6500 class, ⛟, 208050LG, >225mm<, Price:Z **Similar models:** ⛟ – 208050LGP; CC21000 class, ⛟ – 208047LG; CC21000, ⛟ – 208047LGP
◎ Lima, BB25170 class, ⛟, 208104LG, >???mm<, Price:Z
◎ Märklin, BB 9200 class, ≲, ⛟, 3165, >180mm<, ♀, Price:Z

**SNCF diesel locomotives**
◪ Fleischmann, 68 class, 4280, >208mm<, ♀,
◎ Lima, Y8000 class, 208141LG, >117mm<, Price:Z Price:L
◎ Mehanotehnika, CC 70000 locomotive, T151, >250mm<, Price:Z
◎ Roco, Y8000 class, 4126A, >115mm<, Price:L

**SNCF diesel railcars**
◎ Lima, TGV, 149711GP, Price:Z. Also available as separate items

**SNCF coaches**
◎ Liliput, 1st and 2nd class coach, 285 70, >240mm<, Price:D **Similar models:** 2nd class – 285 72; 3rd class – 285 73; 2nd class with interior – 286 70
◎ Liliput, passenger coach with baggage compartment, 285 74, >240mm<, Price:D
◎ Liliput, mail coach (old type), 291 70, >287mm<, Price:D
◎ Liliput, crew car, 295 70, >224mm<, Price:D
◎ Liliput, 'skirted' coach, 833 70, >240mm<, Price:E
◎ Liliput, 1st and 2nd class commuter coach, 287 70, >240mm<, Price:D
◎ Lima, gril-express dining car, 309267, >268mm<, Price:Z
◎ Lima, cinema coach, 309213, >268mm<, Price:Z
◎ Lima, Corail driving coach, 309266, >303mm<, Price:Z
◎ Roco, four-wheeled baggage coach, 4204F, >160mm<, Price:D

**SNCF wagons**
◪ Fleischmann, open wagon with coal load, 5206, >112mm<, Price:Z
◎ Liliput, high-sided open wagon, 244 70, >163mm<, Price:D
◎ Lima, covered wagon with brakeman's cab, 30315L, >142mm<, Price:Z
◎ Lima, bogie covered wagon, 309076, >190mm<, Price:Z
◎ Lima, six-wheeled covered wagon, 309073, >310mm<, Price:Z

**SNCF wagons**
◎ Roco, covered wagon, 4315A, >114mm<, Price:B
◎ Roco, low-sided wagon with load of tree trunks, 4397A, >124mm<, Price:C
◎ Roco, covered wagon, 4337S, >122mm<, Price:D

**Private-owner wagons**
◎ Roco, Interfrigo refrigerated wagon, 44310B, >167mm<, Price:D
◎ Roco, Dubonnet tank wagon, 4337F, >102mm<, Price:D

# Belgium

## Société Nationale des Chemins de Fer Belges

Belgian railways, Société Nationale des Chemins de Fer Belges (SNCB), were state owned from their beginning in the 1830s, though the French name (SNCB) was not used until 1926. It it also known in Flemish as the Nationale Maatschappij van Belgische Spoorwegen (NMBS). British companies were once major suppliers of steam locomotives, and the French Nord company managed one of the important routes.

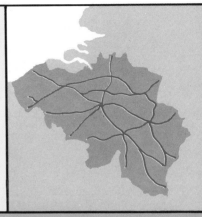

### Z Gauge

⊞ Märklin, 96 class, =, 8801, >55mm<, ⬙, Price:Z

### N Gauge

⊖ Arnold, 0-8-0 locomotive, 2516, >118mm<, ⬙, Price:K **Similar models:** green livery – 2517 (Price:L)

⊖ Fleischmann, 0-10-0 tank locomotive, 7095, >79mm<, ⬙, Price:K

⊖ Fleischmann, 4-6-0 locomotive, 7161, >122mm<, ⬙, Price:K

⊖ Fleischmann, 2-10-0 locomotive, 7178, >150mm<, ⬙, Price:L

⊖ Roco, 59 class, 2156B, >102mm<, ⬙, Price:H **Similar models:** alternative livery – 2156S

⊖ Arnold, 1st class Eurofirma coach, 3778, >163mm<, Price:D

⊖ Fleischmann, gondola with load of gravel, 8207, >63mm<, Price:C

⊖ Roco, open wagon, 2368D, >87mm<, Price:C

⊖ Roco, telescopic cowl wagon, 2375D, >75mm<, Price:D

### Also available

**SNCB steam locomotives**
⊖ Fleischmann, 2-6-0 tank locomotive, 7031, >68mm<, ⬙, Price:J

**SNCB coaches**
⊖ Arnold, 2nd class Eurofirma coach, 3775, >163mm<, Price:D

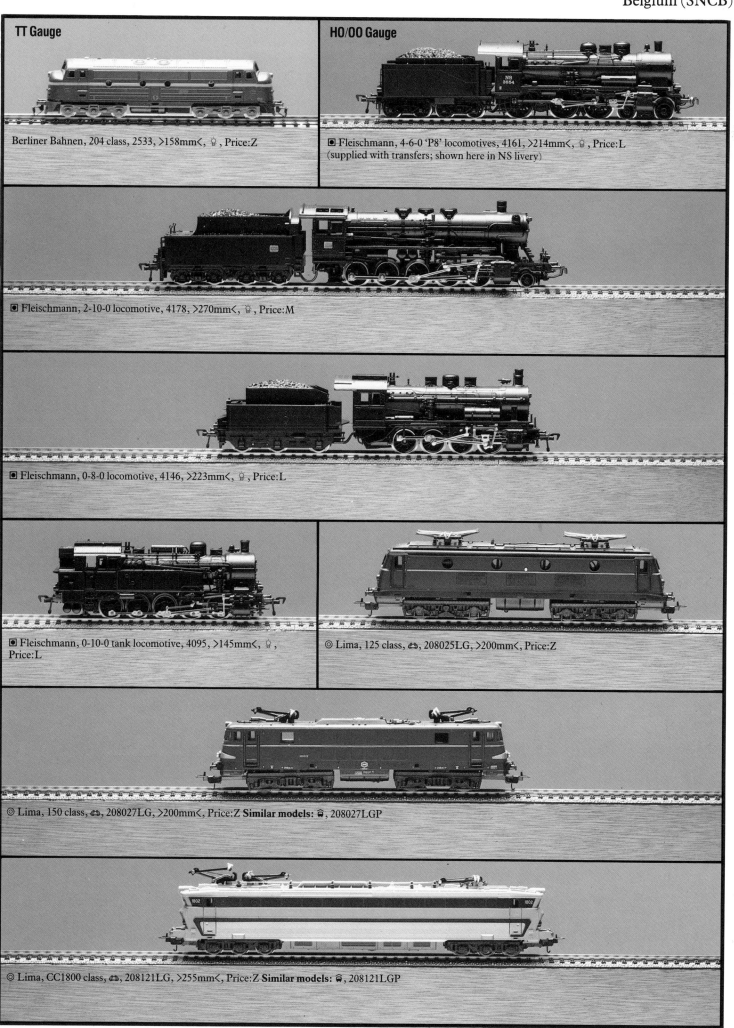

**TT Gauge**

Berliner Bahnen, 204 class, 2533, >158mm<, ♀ , Price:Z

**HO/OO Gauge**

◉ Fleischmann, 4-6-0 'P8' locomotives, 4161, >214mm<, ♀ , Price:L
(supplied with transfers; shown here in NS livery)

◉ Fleischmann, 2-10-0 locomotive, 4178, >270mm<, ♀ , Price:M

◉ Fleischmann, 0-8-0 locomotive, 4146, >223mm<, ♀ , Price:L

◉ Fleischmann, 0-10-0 tank locomotive, 4095, >145mm<, ♀ ,
Price:L

◎ Lima, 125 class, ⇌, 208025LG, >200mm<, Price:Z

◎ Lima, 150 class, ⇌, 208027LG, >200mm<, Price:Z **Similar models:** ♀, 208027LGP

◎ Lima, CC1800 class, ⇌, 208121LG, >255mm<, Price:Z **Similar models:** ♀, 208121LGP

91

# Belgium (SNCB)

◎ Märklin, 16 class, ⊑, 🔁, 3152, >194mm<, ♀, Price:Z

◎ Lima, 75 class, 149747GP, Price:Z Also available as separate items

◼ Fleischmann, BR 202 class, 4270, >223mm<, ♀, Price:L

◎ Märklin, 204 class, ⊑, 3066, >205mm<, ♀, Price:Z

◎ Märklin, 80 class, ⊑, 3149, >120mm<, ♀, Price:Z

◎ Roco, 59 class, 4152S, >188mm<, Price:H **Similar models:** new yellow and green livery – 4152B

◼ Fleischmann, 1st class express coach, 5151, >264mm<, Price:E

◎ Lima, 1st and 2nd class coach, 309108, >253mm<, Price:Z

◎ Märklin, 1st class Eurofirma coach, 4148, >264mm<, Price:Z

◎ Roco, four-wheeled 3rd class coach, 4201E, >160mm<, Price:D

◎ Roco, four-wheeled 2nd and 3rd class coach, 4202E, >160mm<, Price:D

◎ Roco, 2nd class coach, 4237D, >264mm<, Price:D

▣ Fleischmann, open wagon with gravel load, 5207, >112mm<, Price:C

◎ Roco, hopper wagon with coal load, 4335E, >111mm<, Price:D

◎ Roco, telescopic cowl wagon, 4395D, >138mm<, Price:D

## Also available
### SNCB steam locomotives
◎ Liliput, 26 class (BR52), 52 90, >268mm<, Price:N
◎ Liliput, 2-6-0 tank locomotive, 91 90, >120mm<, Price:L
### SNCB coaches
◎ Lima, 2nd class brake coach, 309303, >253mm<, Price:Z
◎ Roco, four-wheeled 1st class coach, 4203E, >160mm<, Price:D
◎ Roco, four-wheeled baggage car, 4204E, >160mm<, Price:D
◎ Roco, 1st class coach, 4236F, >264mm<, Price:D
### SNCB wagons
◎ Roco, steel coil transporter, 4396D, >138mm<, Price:D
◎ Roco, deep well flat wagon with load, 44311E, >189mm<, Price:E

# Netherlands

## Nederlandse Spoorwegen

The Dutch Nederlandse Spoorwegen (NS) was nationalized from the beginning of 1938, but the two major private companies were virtually merged in 1925 with the government having a majority shareholding. After much war damage, the system has been built into one of the most efficient and best-equipped in Europe. The passenger service in this quite densely populated country uses mainly electric multiple units.

⊖ Fleischmann, 0-10-0 tank locomotive, 7095, >79mm<, ⚲, Price:K

⊖ Arnold, 0-8-0 locomotive, 2516, >118mm<, ⚲, Price:K

⊖ Fleischmann, 4-6-0 locomotive, 7161, >122mm<, ⚲, Price:K

⊖ Fleischmann, 2-10-0 locomotive, 7178, >150mm<, ⚲, Price:L

⊖ Fleischmann, 1600 class, ⚡, 7363, >109mm<, ⚲, Price:K

⊖ Roco, 1310 class, ⚡, 2157C, >108mm<, ⚲, Price:J

⊖ Fleischmann, 2nd class Intercity coach, 8155, >165mm<, Price:D

⊖ Fleischmann, 2nd class suburban coach, 8156, >165mm<, Price:D

⊖ Minitrix, 2nd class coach, 3120, >143mm<, Price:D **Similar models:** with lighting – 3129

⊖ Minitrix, restaurant car with baggage compartment, 3121, >143mm<, Price:D

⊖ Roco, covered wagon, 2329B, >64mm<, Price:C

⊖ Roco, hopper wagon with coal load, 2318B, >60mm<, Price:B

⊖ Roco, mail wagon, 2333A, >98mm<, Price:C

⊖ Roco, VAMORA rubbish dump wagon, 2366A, >93mm<, Price:D **Similar models:** VAM Compost lettering – 2366B

**Also available**
**NS coaches**
⊖ Lima, TEN couchette coach, 320339, Price:Z
⊖ Roco, TEN sleeping car, 2278D, >165mm<, Price:D
**NS wagons**
⊖ Roco, open wagon with coal load, 2368F, >87mm<, Price:C
⊖ Roco, covered wagon, 2306S, >66mm<, Price:B

**HO/OO Gauge**

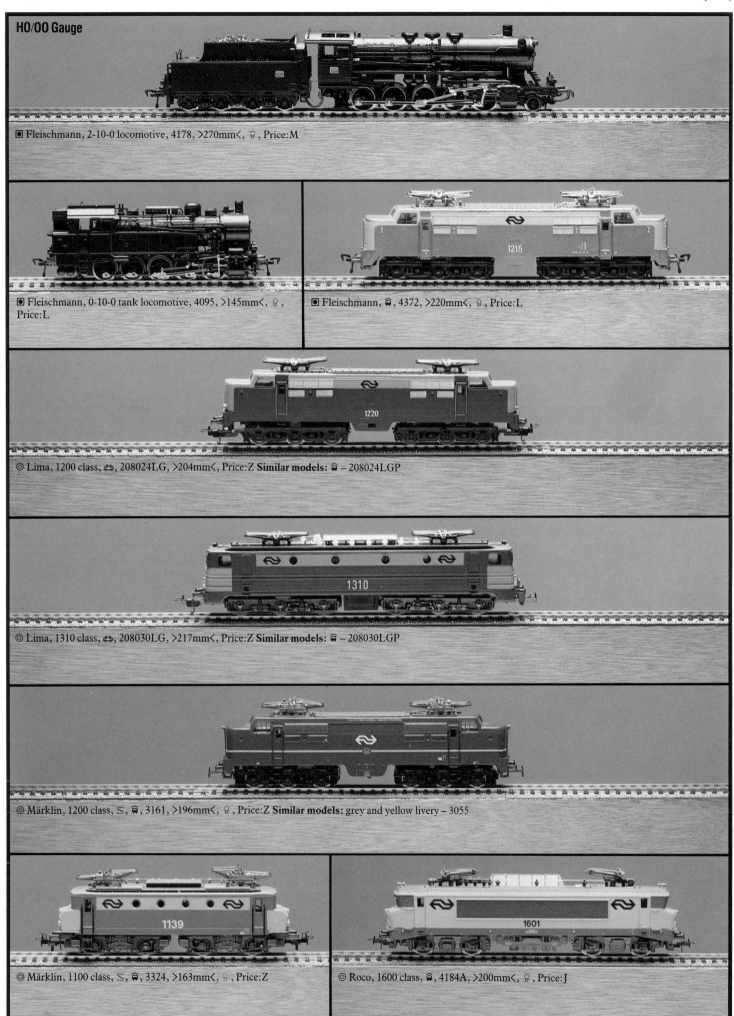

◉ Fleischmann, 2-10-0 locomotive, 4178, >270mm<, ⌂ , Price:M

◉ Fleischmann, 0-10-0 tank locomotive, 4095, >145mm<, ⌂ , Price:L

◉ Fleischmann, ⌂, 4372, >220mm<, ⌂ , Price:L

◎ Lima, 1200 class, ⌂, 208024LG, >204mm<, Price:Z **Similar models:** ⌂ – 208024LGP

◎ Lima, 1310 class, ⌂, 208030LG, >217mm<, Price:Z **Similar models:** ⌂ – 208030LGP

◎ Märklin, 1200 class, ≦, ⌂, 3161, >196mm<, ⌂ , Price:Z **Similar models:** grey and yellow livery – 3055

◎ Märklin, 1100 class, ≦, ⌂, 3324, >163mm<, ⌂ , Price:Z

◎ Roco, 1600 class, ⌂, 4184A, >200mm<, ⌂ , Price:J

◉ Fleischmann, 'Sprinter' Plan Y class, ⌂, 4470, >516mm<, ⚲, Price:M

◎ Lima, 500/600 class, 205129MG, Price:Z

◎ Roco, 600 class, 4160A, >106mm<, ⚲, Price:J **Similar models**: yellow and grey livery – 4160B

◉ Fleischmann, 2nd class coach , 5156, >245mm<, Price:E

◎ Lima, 1st class coach , 309109, >253mm<, Price:Z

◎ Märklin, 2nd class coach, 4049, >240mm<, Price:Z

◎ Märklin, TEN 1st and 2nd class sleeping coach, 4151, >270mm<, Price:Z

◎ Roco, 2nd class coach, 4218C, >258mm<, Price:D

◎ Roco, 2nd class coach, 4232A, >264mm<, Price:D **Similar models:** earlier markings – 4232B

◎ Roco, covered wagon, 4310B, >114mm<, Price:C **Similar models:** alternative lettering – 4310A

◎ Roco, open wagon, 4311B, >94mm<, Price:B **Similar model:** different lettering – 4311C

◎ Roco, open wagon with brakeman's cab, coal load, 4390B, >117mm<, Price:B

◎ Roco, mail wagon, 4387A, >181mm<, Price:D

◎ Roco, VAM Recycling rubbish dump wagon, 4368C, >173mm<, Price:D **Similar models:** VAM Potgrond lettering – 4368B; VAM Compost lettering – 4368S

## Also available

### NS steam locomotives
◎ Liliput, 'Tigerli' ex SBB E3/3, 33 40, >100mm<, Price:L
◎ Liliput, 2-6-0 tank locomotive, 91 40, >120mm<, Price:L

### NS electric railcars
◎ Lima, Intercity, ⏚, 149709, Price:Z. Also available as separate items
◎ Roco, mB4D class, 🚃, 4184A, >200mm<, 💡, Price:L

### NS diesel locomotives
◎ Roco, 2200/2300 class, 4155A, >161mm<, 💡, Price:J **Similar models:** brown livery – 4155B
◎ Roco, 200/300 class, 4153A, >83mm<, Price:F **Similar models:** green and yellow livery – 4153B

### NS coaches
◙ Fleischmann, 1st and 2nd class coach, 5154, >245mm<, Price:E
◎ Lima, 2nd class coach (with advertising), 309110, >253mm<, Price:Z
◎ Lima, restaurant car (with advertising), 309305, >253mm<, Price:Z
◎ Lima, TEN couchette coach, 309235, >268mm<, Price:Z
◎ Märklin, 1st class Intercity coach, 4164, >264mm<, Price:Z
◎ Roco, 1st class coach, 4218A, >258mm<, Price:D

### NS wagons
◎ Märklin, open wagon, 4639, >115mm<, Price:Z
◎ Roco, open wagon, 4314B, >94mm<, Price:C
◎ Roco, covered wagon, 4315B, >114mm<, Price:C
◎ Roco, covered wagon, 4373D, >122mm<, Price:D

### NS wagons
◎ Roco, covered wagon, 4301F, >104mm<, Price:C
◎ Roco, low-sided wagon, 4303B, >104mm<, Price:B
◎ Roco, hopper wagon with coal load, 4335C, >111mm<, Price:D

# German Federal Republic

## Deutsche Bundesbahn

The Deutsche Bundesbahn (DB) came into being with its headquarters in Frankfurt in the late 1940s. It was an amalgamation of all the existing West German railways. Diesel-hydraulic locomotives were introduced and electrification of the main line was undertaken. Now, over 8,000 kilometres (approx. 5,000 miles) of the total of almost 30,000 kilometres (approx. 18,750 miles) are electrified.

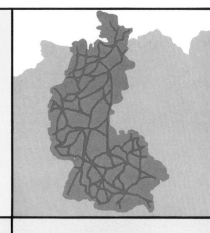

**Z Gauge**

⊞ Märklin, 038 class, =, 8899, >89mm<, ⚲, Price:Z

⊞ Märklin, 18 class, =, 8893, >106mm<, ⚲, Price:Z

⊞ Märklin, 89 class, =, 8800, >45mm<, Price:Z

⊞ Märklin, 24 class, =, 8803, >82mm<, ⚲, Price:Z

⊞ Märklin, 41 class, =, 8827, >112mm<, ⚲, Price:Z

⊞ Märklin, 74 class, =, 8895, >55mm<, ⚲, Price:Z

⊞ Märklin, 86 class, =, 8896, >63mm<, ⚲, Price:Z

⊞ Märklin, 003 class, =, 8885, >112mm<, ⚲, Price:Z

⊞ Märklin, 103 class, =, 🔌, 8854, >88mm<, ⚲, Price:Z

⊞ Märklin, 111 class, =, 🔌, 8842, >76mm<, ⚲, Price:Z **Similar models:** orange and beige livery – 8855

⊞ Märklin, 120 class, =, 🔌, 8853, >87mm<, ⚲, Price:Z

⊞ Märklin, 144 class, =, 🔌, 8811, >68mm<, ⚲, Price:Z

⊞ Märklin, 151 class, =, 🔌, 8858, >88mm<, ⚲, Price:Z **Similar models:** green livery – 8857

⊞ Märklin, 260 class, =, 8804, >49mm<, Price:Z **Similar models:** red livery – 8864

⊞ Märklin, 221 class, =, 8821, >84mm<, ⚲, Price:Z

⊞ Märklin, 216 class, =, 8875, >75mm<, ⚲, Price:Z **Similar models:** alternative livery – 8874

⊞ Märklin, 798 railbus, =, 8816, >62mm<, ⚲, Price:Z

⊞ Märklin, 1st and 2nd class coach, 8750, >63mm<, Price:Z

⊞ Märklin, 2nd class coach, 8751, >63mm<, Price:Z

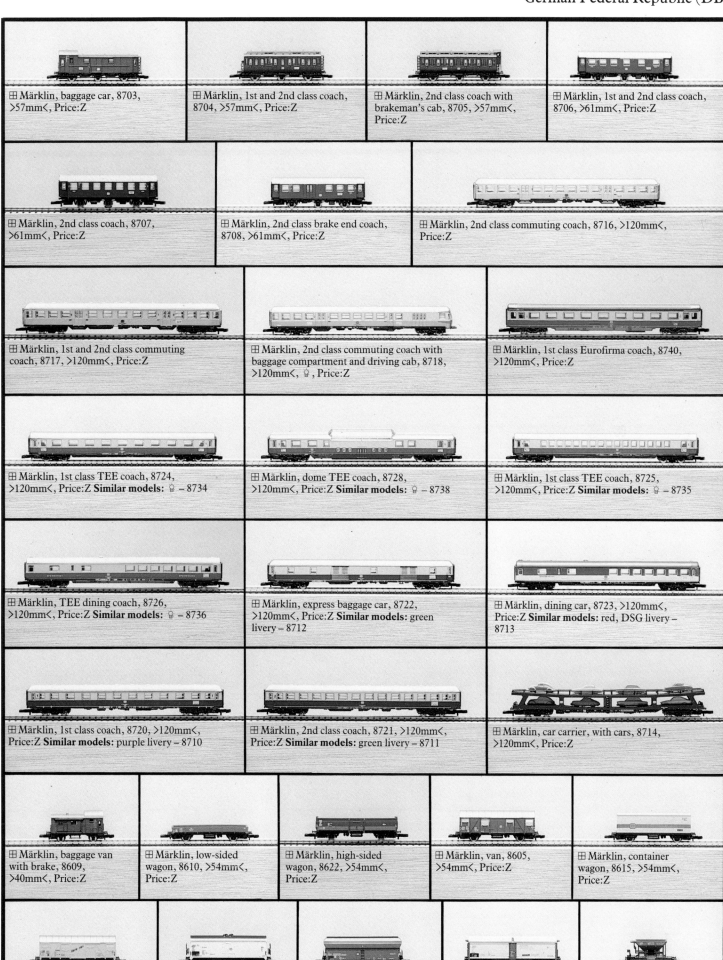

⊞ Märklin, baggage car, 8703, >57mm<, Price:Z

⊞ Märklin, 1st and 2nd class coach, 8704, >57mm<, Price:Z

⊞ Märklin, 2nd class coach with brakeman's cab, 8705, >57mm<, Price:Z

⊞ Märklin, 1st and 2nd class coach, 8706, >61mm<, Price:Z

⊞ Märklin, 2nd class coach, 8707, >61mm<, Price:Z

⊞ Märklin, 2nd class brake end coach, 8708, >61mm<, Price:Z

⊞ Märklin, 2nd class commuting coach, 8716, >120mm<, Price:Z

⊞ Märklin, 1st and 2nd class commuting coach, 8717, >120mm<, Price:Z

⊞ Märklin, 2nd class commuting coach with baggage compartment and driving cab, 8718, >120mm<, ⌕, Price:Z

⊞ Märklin, 1st class Eurofirma coach, 8740, >120mm<, Price:Z

⊞ Märklin, 1st class TEE coach, 8724, >120mm<, Price:Z **Similar models:** ⌕ – 8734

⊞ Märklin, dome TEE coach, 8728, >120mm<, Price:Z **Similar models:** ⌕ – 8738

⊞ Märklin, 1st class TEE coach, 8725, >120mm<, Price:Z **Similar models:** ⌕ – 8735

⊞ Märklin, TEE dining coach, 8726, >120mm<, Price:Z **Similar models:** ⌕ – 8736

⊞ Märklin, express baggage car, 8722, >120mm<, Price:Z **Similar models:** green livery – 8712

⊞ Märklin, dining car, 8723, >120mm<, Price:Z **Similar models:** red, DSG livery – 8713

⊞ Märklin, 1st class coach, 8720, >120mm<, Price:Z **Similar models:** purple livery – 8710

⊞ Märklin, 2nd class coach, 8721, >120mm<, Price:Z **Similar models:** green livery – 8711

⊞ Märklin, car carrier, with cars, 8714, >120mm<, Price:Z

⊞ Märklin, baggage van with brake, 8609, >40mm<, Price:Z

⊞ Märklin, low-sided wagon, 8610, >54mm<, Price:Z

⊞ Märklin, high-sided wagon, 8622, >54mm<, Price:Z

⊞ Märklin, van, 8605, >54mm<, Price:Z

⊞ Märklin, container wagon, 8615, >54mm<, Price:Z

⊞ Märklin, banana wagon, 8606, >54mm<, Price:Z

⊞ Märklin, refrigerated wagon, 8600, >54mm<, Price:Z

⊞ Märklin, self-unloading hopper wagon, 8630, >53mm<, Price:Z

⊞ Märklin, bulk freight van, 8623, >64mm<, Price:Z

⊞ Märklin, ballast wagon, 8624, >33mm<, Price:Z

# German Federal Republic (DB)

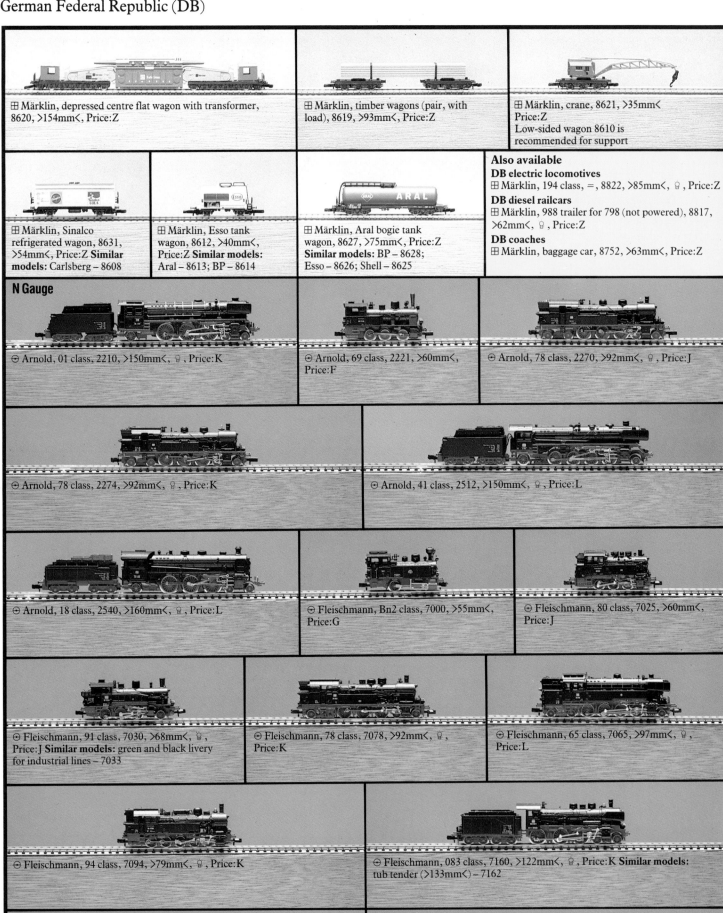

⊞ Märklin, depressed centre flat wagon with transformer, 8620, >154mm<, Price:Z

⊞ Märklin, timber wagons (pair, with load), 8619, >93mm<, Price:Z

⊞ Märklin, crane, 8621, >35mm<
Price:Z
Low-sided wagon 8610 is recommended for support

⊞ Märklin, Sinalco refrigerated wagon, 8631, >54mm<, Price:Z **Similar models:** Carlsberg – 8608

⊞ Märklin, Esso tank wagon, 8612, >40mm<, Price:Z **Similar models:** Aral – 8613; BP – 8614

⊞ Märklin, Aral bogie tank wagon, 8627, >75mm<, Price:Z **Similar models:** BP – 8628; Esso – 8626; Shell – 8625

**Also available**
**DB electric locomotives**
⊞ Märklin, 194 class, =, 8822, >85mm<, ⚲, Price:Z
**DB diesel railcars**
⊞ Märklin, 988 trailer for 798 (not powered), 8817, >62mm<, ⚲, Price:Z
**DB coaches**
⊞ Märklin, baggage car, 8752, >63mm<, Price:Z

## N Gauge

⊖ Arnold, 01 class, 2210, >150mm<, ⚲, Price:K

⊖ Arnold, 69 class, 2221, >60mm<, Price:F

⊖ Arnold, 78 class, 2270, >92mm<, ⚲, Price:J

⊖ Arnold, 78 class, 2274, >92mm<, ⚲, Price:K

⊖ Arnold, 41 class, 2512, >150mm<, ⚲, Price:L

⊖ Arnold, 18 class, 2540, >160mm<, ⚲, Price:L

⊖ Fleischmann, Bn2 class, 7000, >55mm<, Price:G

⊖ Fleischmann, 80 class, 7025, >60mm<, Price:J

⊖ Fleischmann, 91 class, 7030, >68mm<, ⚲, Price:J **Similar models:** green and black livery for industrial lines – 7033

⊖ Fleischmann, 78 class, 7078, >92mm<, ⚲, Price:K

⊖ Fleischmann, 65 class, 7065, >97mm<, ⚲, Price:L

⊖ Fleischmann, 94 class, 7094, >79mm<, ⚲, Price:K

⊖ Fleischmann, 083 class, 7160, >122mm<, ⚲, Price:K **Similar models:** tub tender (>133mm<) – 7162

⊖ Fleischmann, 011 class, 7170, >158mm<, ⚲, Price:L **Similar models:** 012 class (oil-firing tender) – 7171

⊖ Fleischmann, 050 Kab class, 7175, >150mm<, ⚲, Price:L **Similar models:** 051 class (alternative tender) – 7177

⊖ Ibertren, S.66 class, 017, >96mm<, Price:Z

⊖ Minitrix, 01 class, 2076, >153mm<, ♀, Price:K **Similar models:** ems-fitted – 2176 (Price:L)

⊖ Minitrix, 52 class, 2051, >148m<, ♀, Price:L **Similar models:** ems-fitted – 2151

⊖ Minitrix, 85 class, 2053, >102mm<, ♀, Price:K

⊖ Minitrix, 64 class, 2030, >79mm<, ♀, Price:J

⊖ Fleischmann, 0-10-0 tank locomotive, 7095, >79mm<, ♀, Price:K

⊖ Roco, 80 class, 2100A, >60mm<, Price:H

⊖ Roco, 44 class, 2106B, >141mm<, Price:L

⊖ Arnold, 141 class, ⚏, 2321, >98mm<, ♀, ⊞, Price:K **Similar models:** blue and beige livery, without Simplex coupling – 2322

⊖ Arnold, 103 class, ⚏, 2350, >123mm<, ♀, Price:K

⊖ Arnold, 150 class, ⚏, 2355, >122mm<, ♀, Price:K

⊖ Arnold, 169 class, ⚏, 2402, >54mm<, ♀, Price:G

⊖ Arnold, E16 class, ⚏, 2450, >102mm<, ♀, Price:K

⊖ Arnold, 117 class, ⚏, 2456, >100mm<, ♀, Price:L

⊖ Arnold, ES88 driving trailer, 2936, >120mm<, ♀, Price:E

⊖ Arnold, ET88 motor coach, ⚏, 2935, >106mm<, ♀, Price:K

⊖ Arnold, ET420 class, ⚏, 2940, >420mm<, ♀, Price:L **Similar models:** orange and white livery – 2950

⊖ Ibertren, Alsthom electric, 018, >124mm<, Price:Z **Similar models:** ≠ – 955

⊖ Lima, 184 class, ⊂⊃, 220215G, >108mm<, Price:Z

⊖ Lima, E410 class, ⊂⊃, 220226G, >108mm<, Price:Z

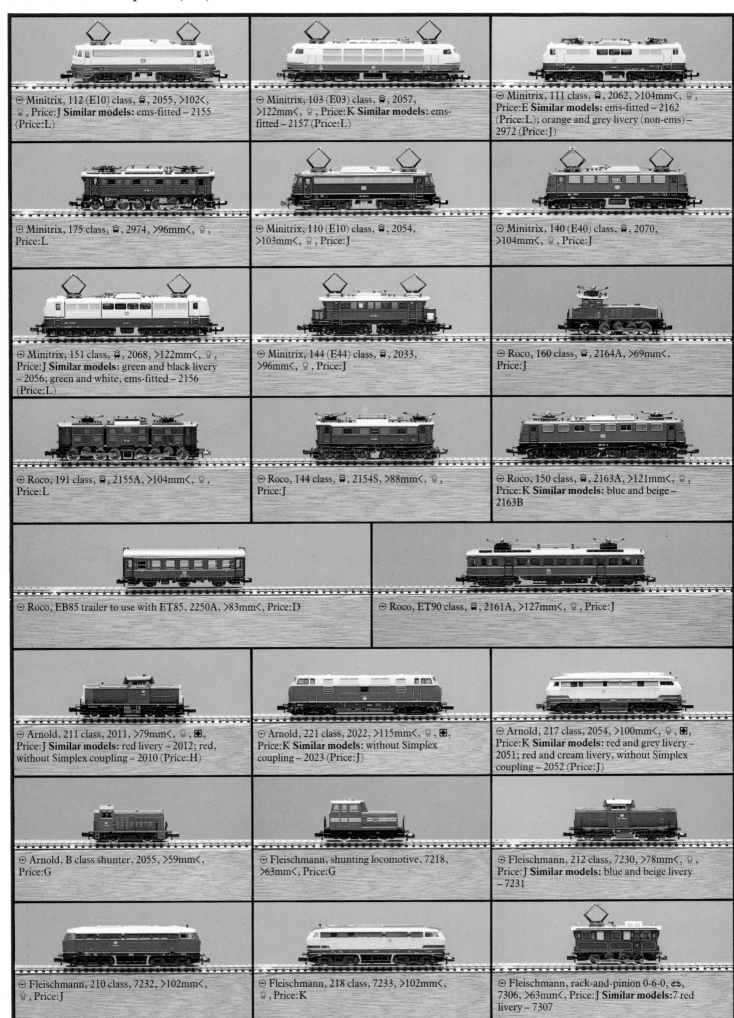

⊖ Minitrix, 112 (E10) class, ⌂, 2055, >102<, ⌂, Price:J **Similar models:** ems-fitted – 2155 (Price:L)

⊖ Minitrix, 103 (E03) class, ⌂, 2057, >122mm<, ⌂, Price:K **Similar models:** ems-fitted – 2157 (Price:L)

⊖ Minitrix, 111 class, ⌂, 2062, >104mm<, ⌂, Price:E **Similar models:** ems-fitted – 2162 (Price:L); orange and grey livery (non-ems) – 2972 (Price:J)

⊖ Minitrix, 175 class, ⌂, 2974, >96mm<, ⌂, Price:L

⊖ Minitrix, 110 (E10) class, ⌂, 2054, >103mm<, ⌂, Price:J

⊖ Minitrix, 140 (E40) class, ⌂, 2070, >104mm<, ⌂, Price:J

⊖ Minitrix, 151 class, ⌂, 2068, >122mm<, ⌂, Price:J **Similar models:** green and black livery – 2056; green and white, ems-fitted – 2156 (Price:L)

⊖ Minitrix, 144 (E44) class, ⌂, 2033, >96mm<, ⌂, Price:J

⊖ Roco, 160 class, ⌂, 2164A, >69mm<, Price:J

⊖ Roco, 191 class, ⌂, 2155A, >104mm<, ⌂, Price:L

⊖ Roco, 144 class, ⌂, 2154S, >88mm<, ⌂, Price:J

⊖ Roco, 150 class, ⌂, 2163A, >121mm<, ⌂, Price:K **Similar models:** blue and beige – 2163B

⊖ Roco, EB85 trailer to use with ET85, 2250A, >83mm<, Price:D

⊖ Roco, ET90 class, ⌂, 2161A, >127mm<, ⌂, Price:J

⊖ Arnold, 211 class, 2011, >79mm<, ⌂, ▣, Price:J **Similar models:** red livery – 2012; red, without Simplex coupling – 2010 (Price:H)

⊖ Arnold, 221 class, 2022, >115mm<, ⌂, ▣, Price:K **Similar models:** without Simplex coupling – 2023 (Price:J)

⊖ Arnold, 217 class, 2054, >100mm<, ⌂, ▣, Price:K **Similar models:** red and grey livery – 2051; red and cream livery, without Simplex coupling – 2052 (Price:J)

⊖ Arnold, B class shunter, 2055, >59mm<, Price:G

⊖ Fleischmann, shunting locomotive, 7218, >63mm<, Price:G

⊖ Fleischmann, 212 class, 7230, >78mm<, ⌂, Price:J **Similar models:** blue and beige livery – 7231

⊖ Fleischmann, 210 class, 7232, >102mm<, ⌂, Price:J

⊖ Fleischmann, 218 class, 7233, >102mm<, ⌂, Price:K

⊖ Fleischmann, rack-and-pinion 0-6-0, ⛓, 7306, >63mm<, Price:J **Similar models:** 7 red livery – 7307

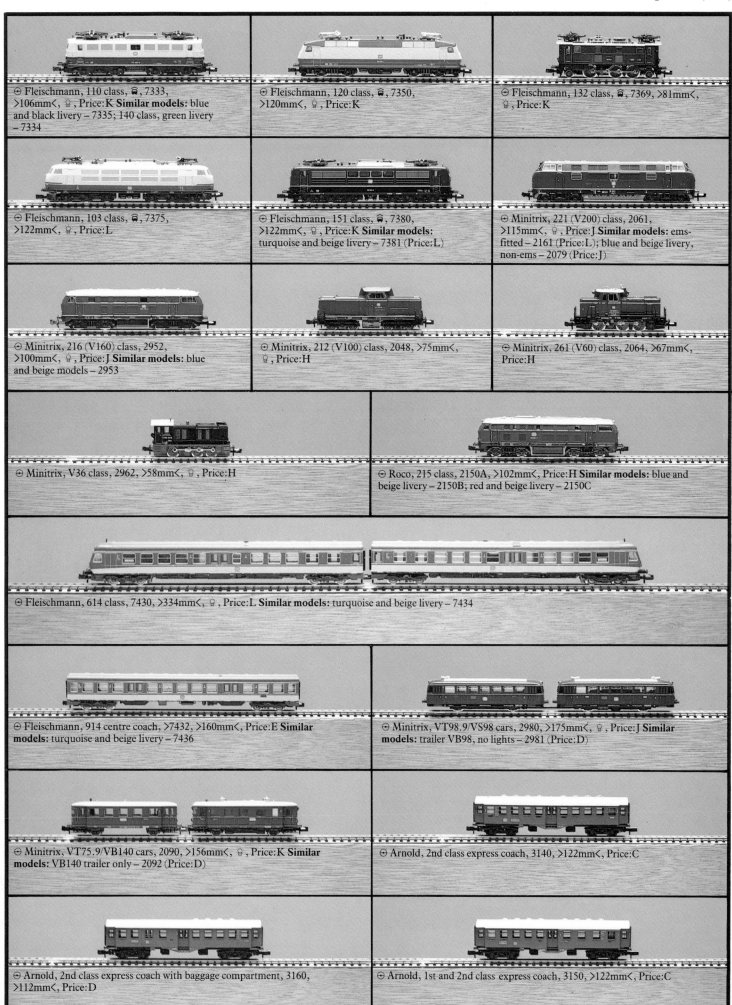

⊕ Fleischmann, 110 class, 🚈, 7333, >106mm<, ⚲, Price:K **Similar models:** blue and black livery – 7335; 140 class, green livery – 7334

⊖ Fleischmann, 120 class, 🚈, 7350, >120mm<, ⚲, Price:K

⊖ Fleischmann, 132 class, 🚈, 7369, >81mm<, ⚲, Price:K

⊕ Fleischmann, 103 class, 🚈, 7375, >122mm<, ⚲, Price:L

⊖ Fleischmann, 151 class, 🚈, 7380, >122mm<, ⚲, Price:K **Similar models:** turquoise and beige livery – 7381 (Price:L)

⊖ Minitrix, 221 (V200) class, 2061, >115mm<, ⚲, Price:J **Similar models:** ems-fitted – 2161 (Price:L); blue and beige livery, non-ems – 2079 (Price:J)

⊕ Minitrix, 216 (V160) class, 2952, >100mm<, ⚲, Price:J **Similar models:** blue and beige models – 2953

⊖ Minitrix, 212 (V100) class, 2048, >75mm<, ⚲, Price:H

⊖ Minitrix, 261 (V60) class, 2064, >67mm<, Price:H

⊖ Minitrix, V36 class, 2962, >58mm<, ⚲, Price:H

⊖ Roco, 215 class, 2150A, >102mm<, Price:H **Similar models:** blue and beige livery – 2150B; red and beige livery – 2150C

⊖ Fleischmann, 614 class, 7430, >334mm<, ⚲, Price:L **Similar models:** turquoise and beige livery – 7434

⊕ Fleischmann, 914 centre coach, >7432, >160mm<, Price:E **Similar models:** turquoise and beige livery – 7436

⊖ Minitrix, VT98.9/VS98 cars, 2980, >175mm<, ⚲, Price:J **Similar models:** trailer VB98, no lights – 2981 (Price:D)

⊕ Minitrix, VT75.9/VB140 cars, 2090, >156mm<, ⚲, Price:K **Similar models:** VB140 trailer only – 2092 (Price:D)

⊖ Arnold, 2nd class express coach, 3140, >122mm<, Price:C

⊖ Arnold, 2nd class express coach with baggage compartment, 3160, >112mm<, Price:D

⊖ Arnold, 1st and 2nd class express coach, 3150, >122mm<, Price:C

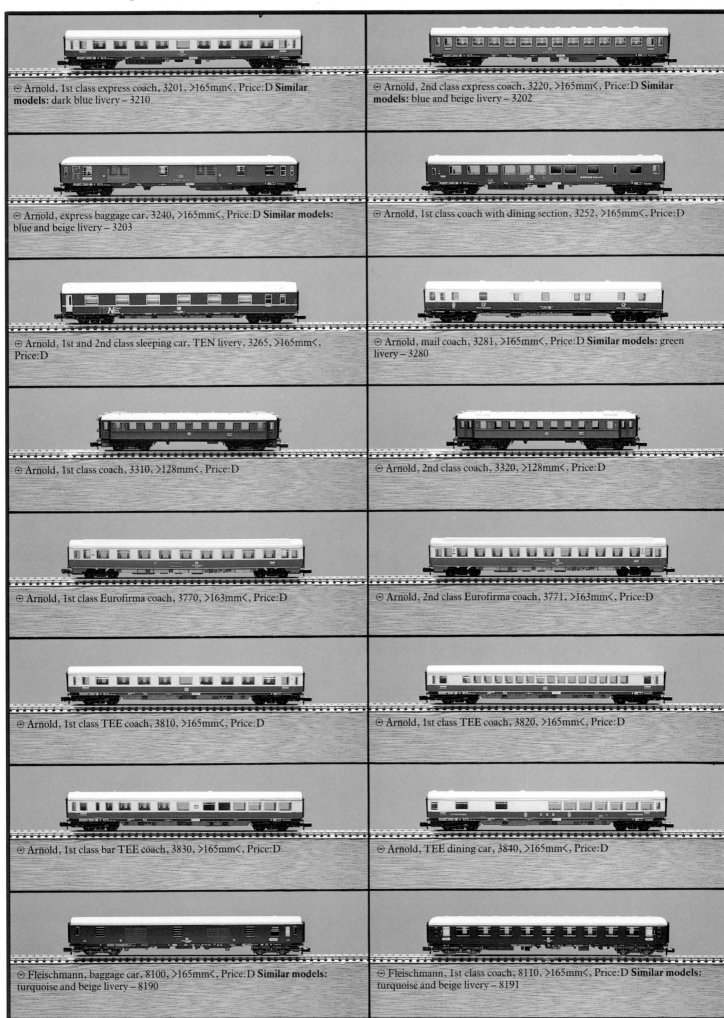

⊖ Arnold, 1st class express coach, 3201, >165mm<, Price:D **Similar models:** dark blue livery – 3210

⊖ Arnold, 2nd class express coach, 3220, >165mm<, Price:D **Similar models:** blue and beige livery – 3202

⊖ Arnold, express baggage car, 3240, >165mm<, Price:D **Similar models:** blue and beige livery – 3203

⊖ Arnold, 1st class coach with dining section, 3252, >165mm<, Price:D

⊖ Arnold, 1st and 2nd class sleeping car, TEN livery, 3265, >165mm<, Price:D

⊖ Arnold, mail coach, 3281, >165mm<, Price:D **Similar models:** green livery – 3280

⊖ Arnold, 1st class coach, 3310, >128mm<, Price:D

⊖ Arnold, 2nd class coach, 3320, >128mm<, Price:D

⊖ Arnold, 1st class Eurofirma coach, 3770, >163mm<, Price:D

⊖ Arnold, 2nd class Eurofirma coach, 3771, >163mm<, Price:D

⊖ Arnold, 1st class TEE coach, 3810, >165mm<, Price:D

⊖ Arnold, 1st class TEE coach, 3820, >165mm<, Price:D

⊖ Arnold, 1st class bar TEE coach, 3830, >165mm<, Price:D

⊖ Arnold, TEE dining car, 3840, >165mm<, Price:D

⊖ Fleischmann, baggage car, 8100, >165mm<, Price:D **Similar models:** turquoise and beige livery – 8190

⊖ Fleischmann, 1st class coach, 8110, >165mm<, Price:D **Similar models:** turquoise and beige livery – 8191

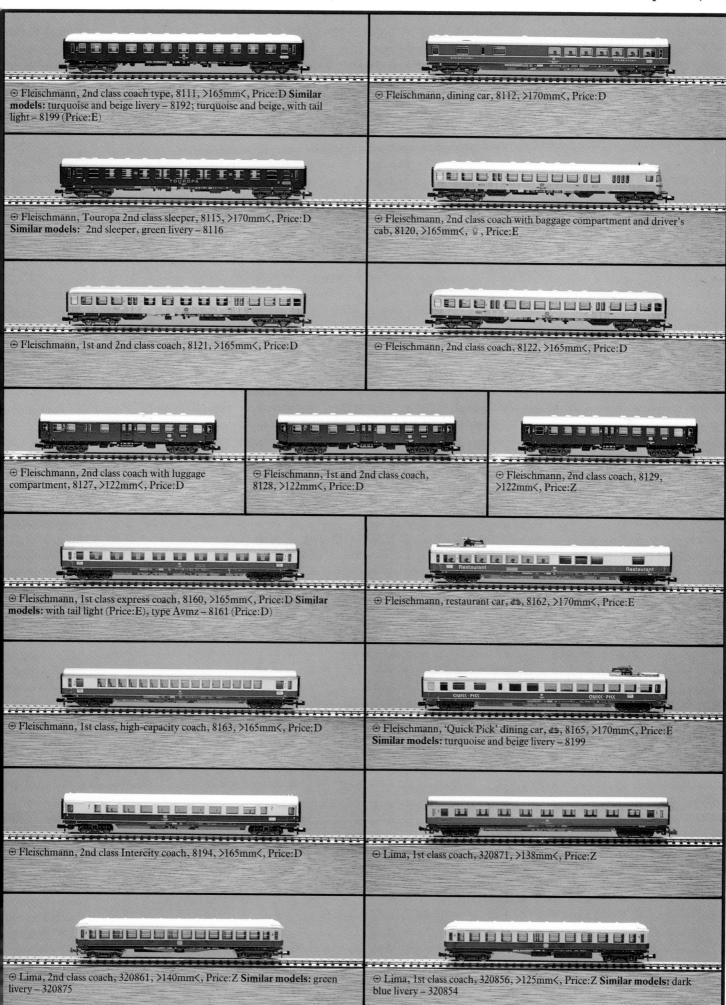

⊖ Fleischmann, 2nd class coach type, 8111, >165mm<, Price:D **Similar models:** turquoise and beige livery – 8192; turquoise and beige, with tail light = 8199 (Price:E)

⊖ Fleischmann, dining car, 8112, >170mm<, Price:D

⊖ Fleischmann, Touropa 2nd class sleeper, 8115, >170mm<, Price:D **Similar models:** 2nd sleeper, green livery – 8116

⊖ Fleischmann, 2nd class coach with baggage compartment and driver's cab, 8120, >165mm<, Price:E

⊖ Fleischmann, 1st and 2nd class coach, 8121, >165mm<, Price:D

⊖ Fleischmann, 2nd class coach, 8122, >165mm<, Price:D

⊖ Fleischmann, 2nd class coach with luggage compartment, 8127, >122mm<, Price:D

⊖ Fleischmann, 1st and 2nd class coach, 8128, >122mm<, Price:D

⊖ Fleischmann, 2nd class coach, 8129, >122mm<, Price:Z

⊖ Fleischmann, 1st class express coach, 8160, >165mm<, Price:D **Similar models:** with tail light (Price:E), type Avmz – 8161 (Price:D)

⊖ Fleischmann, restaurant car, 8162, >170mm<, Price:E

⊖ Fleischmann, 1st class, high-capacity coach, 8163, >165mm<, Price:D

⊖ Fleischmann, 'Quick Pick' dining car, 8165, >170mm<, Price:E **Similar models:** turquoise and beige livery – 8199

⊖ Fleischmann, 2nd class Intercity coach, 8194, >165mm<, Price:D

⊖ Lima, 1st class coach, 320871, >138mm<, Price:Z

⊖ Lima, 2nd class coach, 320861, >140mm<, Price:Z **Similar models:** green livery – 320875

⊖ Lima, 1st class coach, 320856, >125mm<, Price:Z **Similar models:** dark blue livery – 320854

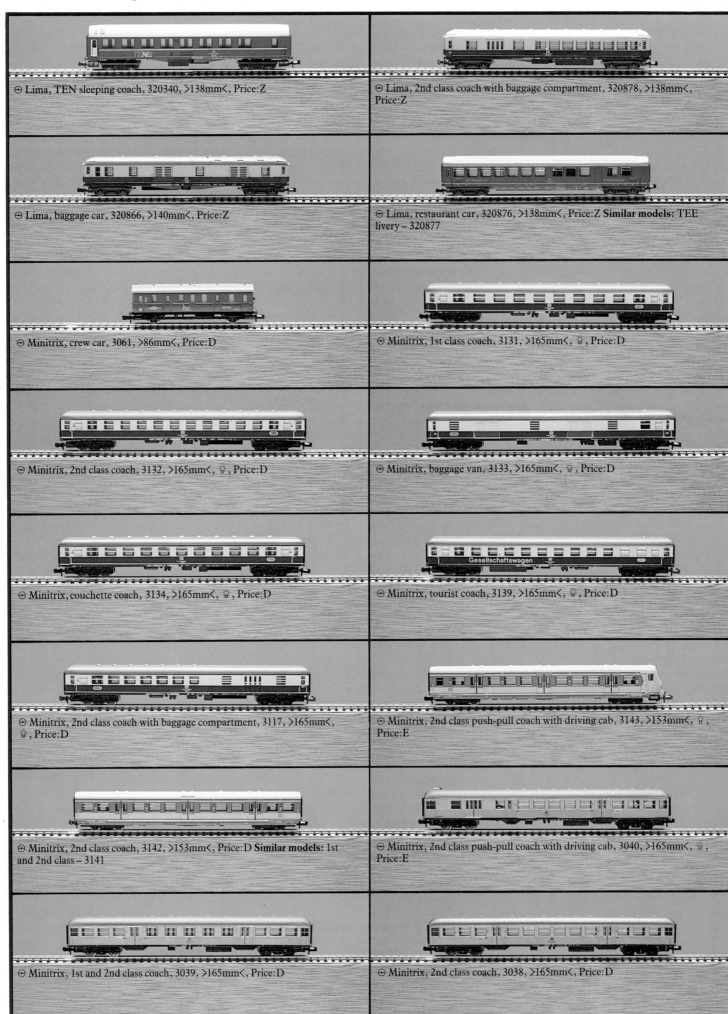

⊖ Lima, TEN sleeping coach, 320340, >138mm<, Price:Z

⊖ Lima, 2nd class coach with baggage compartment, 320878, >138mm<, Price:Z

⊖ Lima, baggage car, 320866, >140mm<, Price:Z

⊖ Lima, restaurant car, 320876, >138mm<, Price:Z **Similar models:** TEE livery – 320877

⊖ Minitrix, crew car, 3061, >86mm<, Price:D

⊕ Minitrix, 1st class coach, 3131, >165mm<, ♀, Price:D

⊖ Minitrix, 2nd class coach, 3132, >165mm<, ♀, Price:D

⊖ Minitrix, baggage van, 3133, >165mm<, ♀, Price:D

⊖ Minitrix, couchette coach, 3134, >165mm<, ♀, Price:D

⊖ Minitrix, tourist coach, 3139, >165mm<, ♀, Price:D

⊖ Minitrix, 2nd class coach with baggage compartment, 3117, >165mm<, ♀, Price:D

⊖ Minitrix, 2nd class push-pull coach with driving cab, 3143, >153mm<, ♀, Price:E

⊖ Minitrix, 2nd class coach, 3142, >153mm<, Price:D **Similar models:** 1st and 2nd class – 3141

⊖ Minitrix, 2nd class push-pull coach with driving cab, 3040, >165mm<, ♀, Price:E

⊖ Minitrix, 1st and 2nd class coach, 3039, >165mm<, Price:D

⊖ Minitrix, 2nd class coach, 3038, >165mm<, Price:D

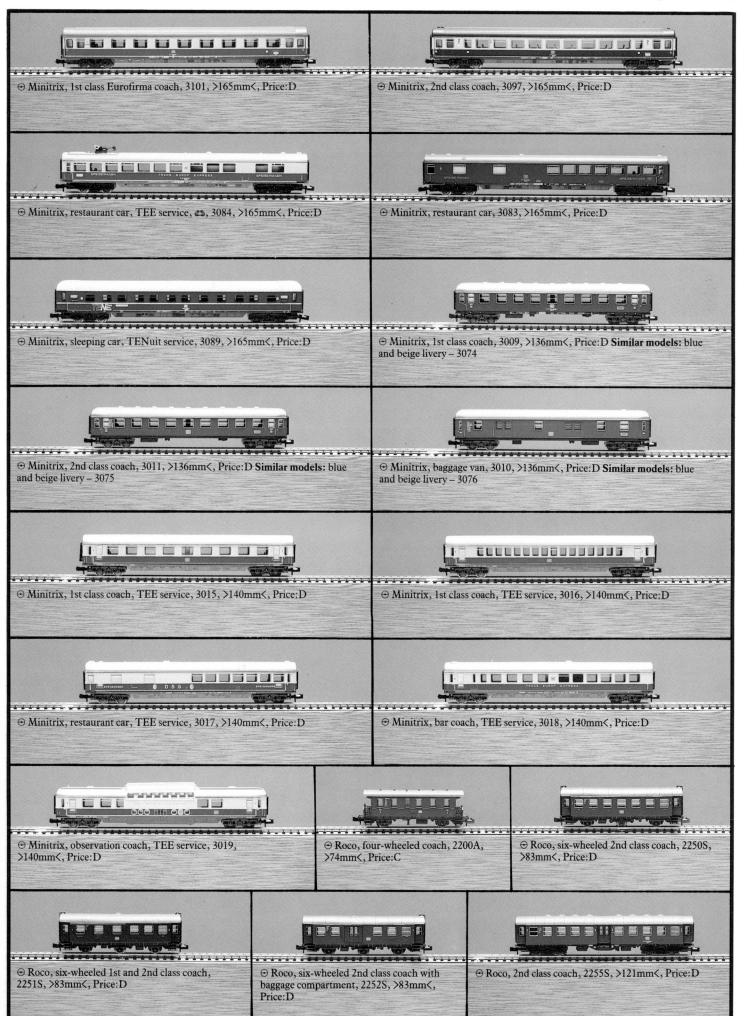

⊕ Minitrix, 1st class Eurofirma coach, 3101, >165mm<, Price:D

⊕ Minitrix, 2nd class coach, 3097, >165mm<, Price:D

⊕ Minitrix, restaurant car, TEE service, ⏣, 3084, >165mm<, Price:D

⊕ Minitrix, restaurant car, 3083, >165mm<, Price:D

⊕ Minitrix, sleeping car, TENuit service, 3089, >165mm<, Price:D

⊕ Minitrix, 1st class coach, 3009, >136mm<, Price:D **Similar models:** blue and beige livery – 3074

⊕ Minitrix, 2nd class coach, 3011, >136mm<, Price:D **Similar models:** blue and beige livery – 3075

⊕ Minitrix, baggage van, 3010, >136mm<, Price:D **Similar models:** blue and beige livery – 3076

⊕ Minitrix, 1st class coach, TEE service, 3015, >140mm<, Price:D

⊕ Minitrix, 1st class coach, TEE service, 3016, >140mm<, Price:D

⊕ Minitrix, restaurant car, TEE service, 3017, >140mm<, Price:D

⊕ Minitrix, bar coach, TEE service, 3018, >140mm<, Price:D

⊕ Minitrix, observation coach, TEE service, 3019, >140mm<, Price:D

⊕ Roco, four-wheeled coach, 2200A, >74mm<, Price:C

⊕ Roco, six-wheeled 2nd class coach, 2250S, >83mm<, Price:D

⊕ Roco, six-wheeled 1st and 2nd class coach, 2251S, >83mm<, Price:D

⊕ Roco, six-wheeled 2nd class coach with baggage compartment, 2252S, >83mm<, Price:D

⊕ Roco, 2nd class coach, 2255S, >121mm<, Price:D

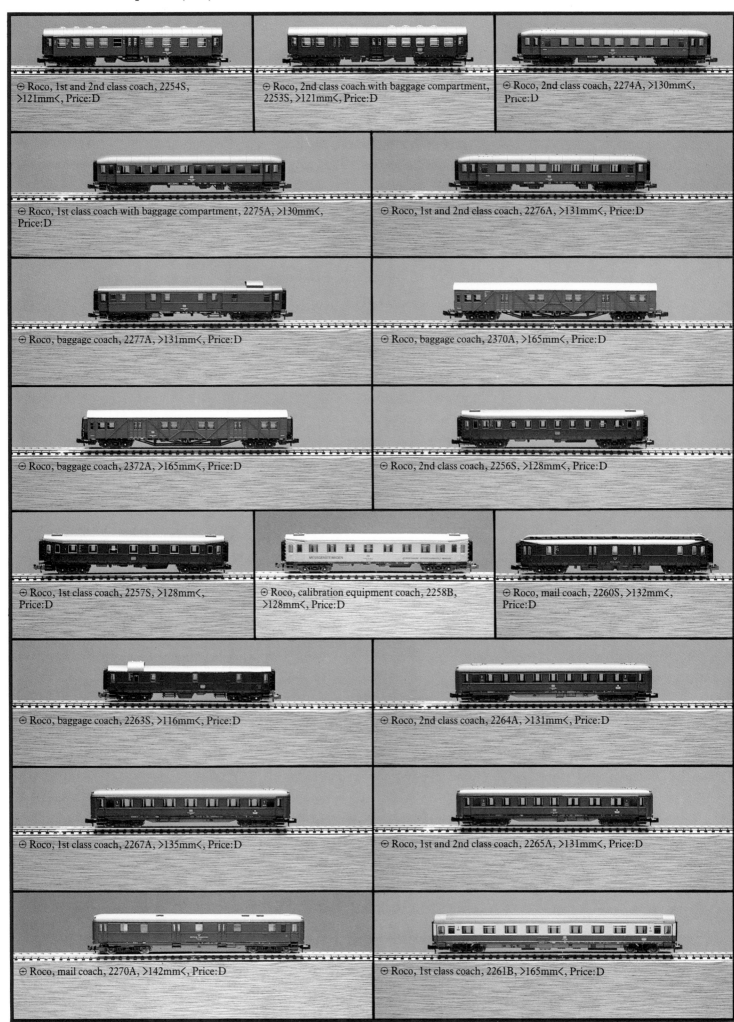

⊖ Roco, 1st and 2nd class coach, 2254S, >121mm<, Price:D

⊖ Roco, 2nd class coach with baggage compartment, 2253S, >121mm<, Price:D

⊖ Roco, 2nd class coach, 2274A, >130mm<, Price:D

⊖ Roco, 1st class coach with baggage compartment, 2275A, >130mm<, Price:D

⊖ Roco, 1st and 2nd class coach, 2276A, >131mm<, Price:D

⊖ Roco, baggage coach, 2277A, >131mm<, Price:D

⊖ Roco, baggage coach, 2370A, >165mm<, Price:D

⊖ Roco, baggage coach, 2372A, >165mm<, Price:D

⊖ Roco, 2nd class coach, 2256S, >128mm<, Price:D

⊖ Roco, 1st class coach, 2257S, >128mm<, Price:D

⊖ Roco, calibration equipment coach, 2258B, >128mm<, Price:D

⊖ Roco, mail coach, 2260S, >132mm<, Price:D

⊖ Roco, baggage coach, 2263S, >116mm<, Price:D

⊖ Roco, 2nd class coach, 2264A, >131mm<, Price:D

⊖ Roco, 1st class coach, 2267A, >135mm<, Price:D

⊖ Roco, 1st and 2nd class coach, 2265A, >131mm<, Price:D

⊖ Roco, mail coach, 2270A, >142mm<, Price:D

⊖ Roco, 1st class coach, 2261B, >165mm<, Price:D

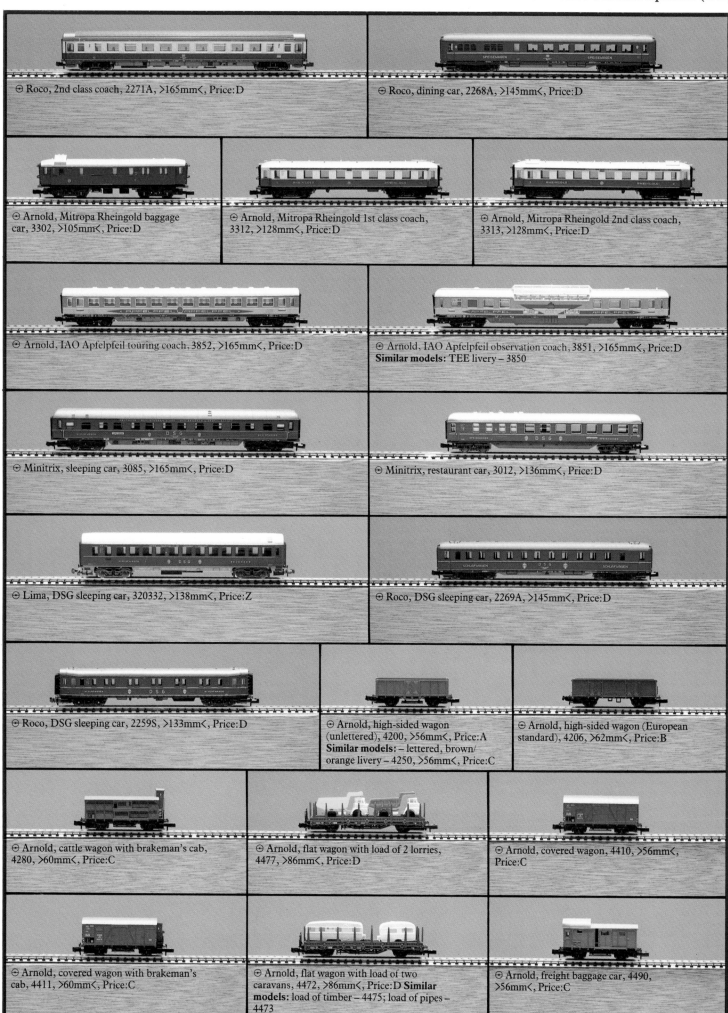

⊕ Roco, 2nd class coach, 2271A, >165mm<, Price:D

⊕ Roco, dining car, 2268A, >145mm<, Price:D

⊕ Arnold, Mitropa Rheingold baggage car, 3302, >105mm<, Price:D

⊕ Arnold, Mitropa Rheingold 1st class coach, 3312, >128mm<, Price:D

⊕ Arnold, Mitropa Rheingold 2nd class coach, 3313, >128mm<, Price:D

⊕ Arnold, IAO Apfelpfeil touring coach, 3852, >165mm<, Price:D

⊕ Arnold, IAO Apfelpfeil observation coach, 3851, >165mm<, Price:D
**Similar models:** TEE livery – 3850

⊕ Minitrix, sleeping car, 3085, >165mm<, Price:D

⊕ Minitrix, restaurant car, 3012, >136mm<, Price:D

⊕ Lima, DSG sleeping car, 320332, >138mm<, Price:Z

⊕ Roco, DSG sleeping car, 2269A, >145mm<, Price:D

⊕ Roco, DSG sleeping car, 2259S, >133mm<, Price:D

⊕ Arnold, high-sided wagon (unlettered), 4200, >56mm<, Price:A
**Similar models:** – lettered, brown/orange livery – 4250, >56mm<, Price:C

⊕ Arnold, high-sided wagon (European standard), 4206, >62mm<, Price:B

⊕ Arnold, cattle wagon with brakeman's cab, 4280, >60mm<, Price:C

⊕ Arnold, flat wagon with load of 2 lorries, 4477, >86mm<, Price:D

⊕ Arnold, covered wagon, 4410, >56mm<, Price:C

⊕ Arnold, covered wagon with brakeman's cab, 4411, >60mm<, Price:C

⊕ Arnold, flat wagon with load of two caravans, 4472, >86mm<, Price:D **Similar models:** load of timber – 4475; load of pipes – 4473

⊕ Arnold, freight baggage car, 4490, >56mm<, Price:C

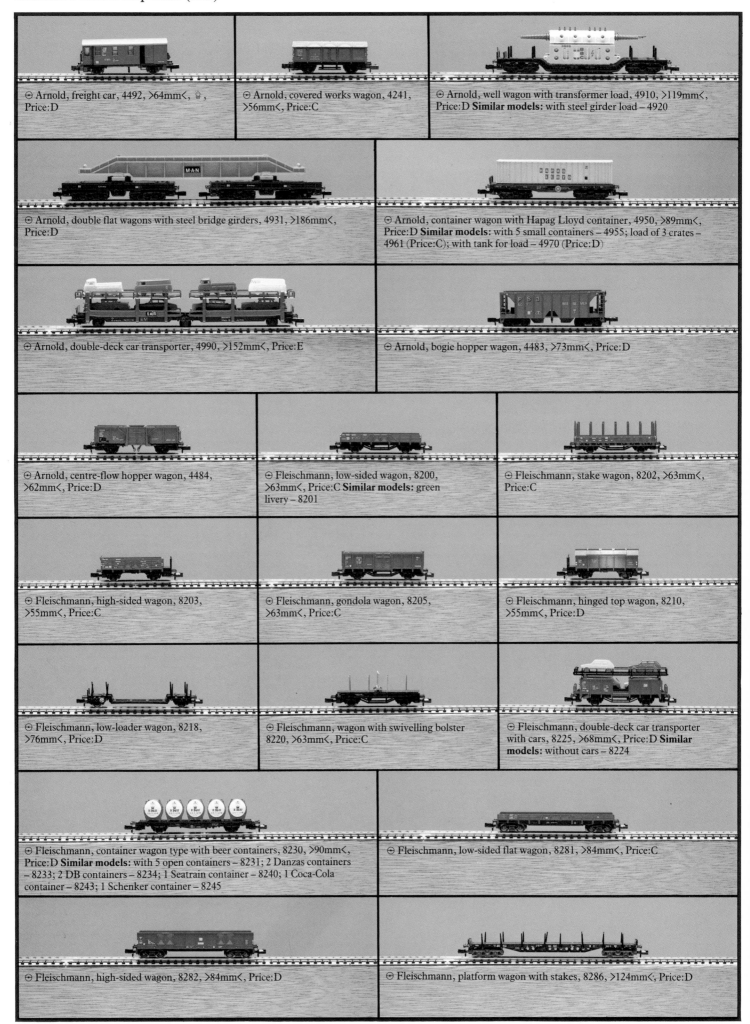

⊖ Arnold, freight car, 4492, >64mm<, 💡, Price:D

⊖ Arnold, covered works wagon, 4241, >56mm<, Price:C

⊕ Arnold, well wagon with transformer load, 4910, >119mm<, Price:D **Similar models:** with steel girder load – 4920

⊖ Arnold, double flat wagons with steel bridge girders, 4931, >186mm<, Price:D

⊖ Arnold, container wagon with Hapag Lloyd container, 4950, >89mm<, Price:D **Similar models:** with 5 small containers – 4955; load of 3 crates – 4961 (Price:C); with tank for load – 4970 (Price:D)

⊖ Arnold, double-deck car transporter, 4990, >152mm<, Price:E

⊖ Arnold, bogie hopper wagon, 4483, >73mm<, Price:D

⊖ Arnold, centre-flow hopper wagon, 4484, >62mm<, Price:D

⊖ Fleischmann, low-sided wagon, 8200, >63mm<, Price:C **Similar models:** green livery – 8201

⊖ Fleischmann, stake wagon, 8202, >63mm<, Price:C

⊖ Fleischmann, high-sided wagon, 8203, >55mm<, Price:C

⊖ Fleischmann, gondola wagon, 8205, >63mm<, Price:C

⊖ Fleischmann, hinged top wagon, 8210, >55mm<, Price:D

⊖ Fleischmann, low-loader wagon, 8218, >76mm<, Price:D

⊖ Fleischmann, wagon with swivelling bolster 8220, >63mm<, Price:C

⊖ Fleischmann, double-deck car transporter with cars, 8225, >68mm<, Price:D **Similar models:** without cars – 8224

⊖ Fleischmann, container wagon type with beer containers, 8230, >90mm<, Price:D **Similar models:** with 5 open containers – 8231; 2 Danzas containers – 8233; 2 DB containers – 8234; 1 Seatrain container – 8240; 1 Coca-Cola container – 8243; 1 Schenker container – 8245

⊖ Fleischmann, low-sided flat wagon, 8281, >84mm<, Price:C

⊖ Fleischmann, high-sided wagon, 8282, >84mm<, Price:D

⊖ Fleischmann, platform wagon with stakes, 8286, >124mm<, Price:D

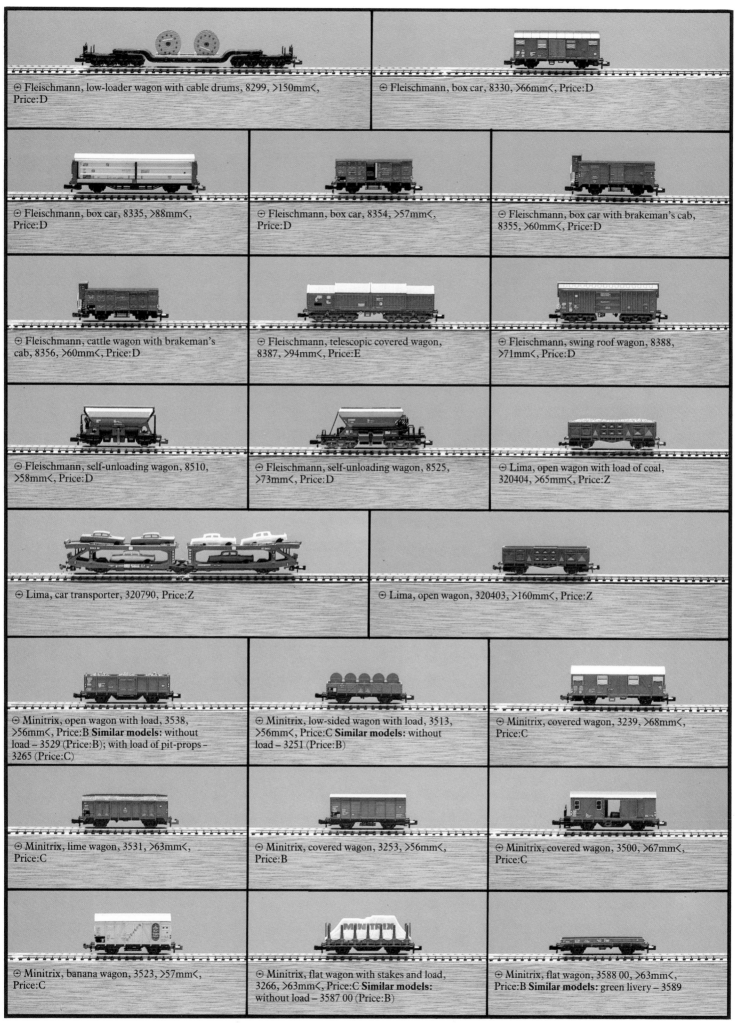

⊖ Fleischmann, low-loader wagon with cable drums, 8299, >150mm<, Price:D

⊖ Fleischmann, box car, 8330, >66mm<, Price:D

⊖ Fleischmann, box car, 8335, >88mm<, Price:D

⊖ Fleischmann, box car, 8354, >57mm<, Price:D

⊖ Fleischmann, box car with brakeman's cab, 8355, >60mm<, Price:D

⊖ Fleischmann, cattle wagon with brakeman's cab, 8356, >60mm<, Price:D

⊖ Fleischmann, telescopic covered wagon, 8387, >94mm<, Price:E

⊖ Fleischmann, swing roof wagon, 8388, >71mm<, Price:D

⊖ Fleischmann, self-unloading wagon, 8510, >58mm<, Price:D

⊖ Fleischmann, self-unloading wagon, 8525, >73mm<, Price:D

⊖ Lima, open wagon with load of coal, 320404, >65mm<, Price:Z

⊖ Lima, car transporter, 320790, Price:Z

⊖ Lima, open wagon, 320403, >160mm<, Price:Z

⊖ Minitrix, open wagon with load, 3538, >56mm<, Price:B **Similar models:** without load – 3529 (Price:B); with load of pit-props – 3265 (Price:C)

⊖ Minitrix, low-sided wagon with load, 3513, >56mm<, Price:C **Similar models:** without load – 3251 (Price:B)

⊖ Minitrix, covered wagon, 3239, >68mm<, Price:C

⊖ Minitrix, lime wagon, 3531, >63mm<, Price:C

⊖ Minitrix, covered wagon, 3253, >56mm<, Price:B

⊖ Minitrix, covered wagon, 3500, >67mm<, Price:C

⊖ Minitrix, banana wagon, 3523, >57mm<, Price:C

⊖ Minitrix, flat wagon with stakes and load, 3266, >63mm<, Price:C **Similar models:** without load – 3587 00 (Price:B)

⊖ Minitrix, flat wagon, 3588 00, >63mm<, Price:B **Similar models:** green livery – 3589

111

# German Federal Republic (DB)

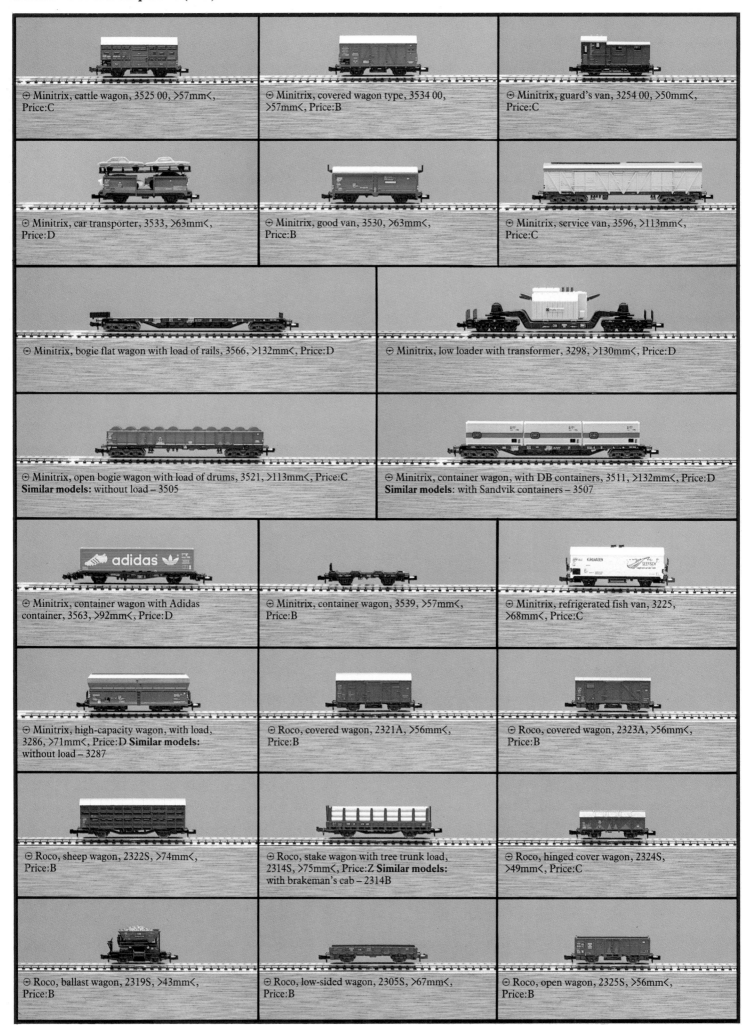

⊕ Minitrix, cattle wagon, 3525 00, >57mm<, Price:C

⊕ Minitrix, covered wagon type, 3534 00, >57mm<, Price:B

⊕ Minitrix, guard's van, 3254 00, >50mm<, Price:C

⊕ Minitrix, car transporter, 3533, >63mm<, Price:D

⊕ Minitrix, good van, 3530, >63mm<, Price:B

⊕ Minitrix, service van, 3596, >113mm<, Price:C

⊕ Minitrix, bogie flat wagon with load of rails, 3566, >132mm<, Price:D

⊕ Minitrix, low loader with transformer, 3298, >130mm<, Price:D

⊕ Minitrix, open bogie wagon with load of drums, 3521, >113mm<, Price:C
**Similar models**: without load – 3505

⊕ Minitrix, container wagon, with DB containers, 3511, >132mm<, Price:D
**Similar models**: with Sandvik containers – 3507

⊕ Minitrix, container wagon with Adidas container, 3563, >92mm<, Price:D

⊕ Minitrix, container wagon, 3539, >57mm<, Price:B

⊕ Minitrix, refrigerated fish van, 3225, >68mm<, Price:C

⊕ Minitrix, high-capacity wagon, with load, 3286, >71mm<, Price:D **Similar models:** without load – 3287

⊕ Roco, covered wagon, 2321A, >56mm<, Price:B

⊕ Roco, covered wagon, 2323A, >56mm<, Price:B

⊕ Roco, sheep wagon, 2322S, >74mm<, Price:B

⊕ Roco, stake wagon with tree trunk load, 2314S, >75mm<, Price:Z **Similar models:** with brakeman's cab – 2314B

⊕ Roco, hinged cover wagon, 2324S, >49mm<, Price:C

⊕ Roco, ballast wagon, 2319S, >43mm<, Price:B

⊕ Roco, low-sided wagon, 2305S, >67mm<, Price:B

⊕ Roco, open wagon, 2325S, >56mm<, Price:B

⊖ Roco, open wagon with coal load, 2317A, >50mm<, Price:B

⊖ Roco, open wagon with pit-props load, 2313S, >50mm<, Price:B

⊖ Roco, refrigerated fish van, 2307A, >78m<, Price:B

⊖ Roco, covered wagon, 2328A, >64mm<, Price:C

⊖ Roco, covered wagon, 2329A, >64mm<, Price:C

⊖ Roco, covered wagon, 2330A, >64mm<, Price:C

⊖ Roco, open wagon, 2331A, >60mm<, Price:B

⊖ Roco, open wagon with coal load, 2315S, >63mm<, Price:B

⊖ Roco, hopper wagon with coal load, 2318A, >60mm<, Price:B

⊖ Roco, flat wagon with stakes, 2308S, >86mm<, Price:B

⊖ Roco, covered wagon, 2304S, >87mm<, Price:B

⊖ Roco, bogie open wagon with coal load, 2368A, >87mm<, Price:C

⊖ Roco, bogie flat wagon, 2352S, >89mm<, Price:B

⊖ Roco, container wagon, 2361S, >132mm<, Price:C
Set of five containers - 2050S

⊖ Roco, 12-wheeled hopper wagon, 2365B, >93mm<, Price:D

⊖ Roco, 12-wheeled telescopic cowl wagon, 2373A, >94mm<, Price:D

⊖ Roco, telescopic cowl wagon, 2374A, >75mm<, Price:D

⊖ Arnold, Dortmunder Union covered wagon with brakeman's cab, 4271, >60mm<, Price:C **Similar models:** Badische Staatsbrauerei Rothaus – 4272; Kaiser Friedrich Quelle – 4273

⊖ Arnold, Aral tank wagon, 4310, >55mm<, Price:C **Similar models:** Shell – 4350; Esso – 4331; Mobil – 4320 (this item has transfers for Aral, Gulf, Seca, Elan, and Texaco)

⊖ Arnold, Kühne & Nagel flat wagon with plastic cover, 4474, >86mm<, Price:D

⊖ Arnold, Wacker-Chemie tank wagon, 4523, >56mm<, Price:C **Similar models:** BP – 4522

⊖ Arnold, Shell Butan pressurised gas tank, 4510, >60mm<, Price:D

⊖ Arnold, BASF hopper wagon, 4482, >60mn.<, Price:D

⊖ Fleischmann, refrigerated van, 8320, >73mm<, Price:C **Similar models:** Interfrigo – 8321; Gullfiber – 8323; Grolsch-Bier – 8325; Reichelbräu – 8326

113

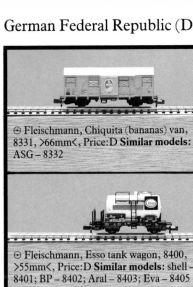

⊖ Fleischmann, Chiquita (bananas) van, 8331, >66mm<, Price:D **Similar models:** ASG – 8332

⊖ Fleischmann, Pilsener Urquell beer wagon with brakeman's cab, 8357, >60mm<, Price:D

⊕ Fleischmann, Bauknecht high-capacity refrigerated wagon, 8389, >124mm<, Price:D

⊕ Fleischmann, Esso tank wagon, 8400, >55mm<, Price:D **Similar models:** shell – 8401; BP – 8402; Aral – 8403; Eva – 8405

⊖ Fleischmann, Shell bogie tank wagon, 8481, >88mm<, Price:D **Similar models:** Esso – 8480; BP – 8482; Aral – 8483; Eva – 8485

⊕ Lima, Mobiloil bogie tank wagon, 320620, >85mm<, Price:Z

⊕ Lima, Henniez covered wagon, 320459, >65mm<, Price:Z

⊖ Minitrix, Patrizier beer wagon, 3227, >55mm<, Price:C **Similar models:** Mela refrigerated fruit van – 3226

⊖ Minitrix, Minitrix tilting roof van, 3280, >88mm<, Price:C **Similar models:** Kabafit – 3568

⊕ Minitrix, BASF chemical carrier, 3586, >88mm<, Price:D **Similar models:** Südzucker – 3518

⊖ Minitrix, AEG wagon with sliding roof, 3567, >113mm<, Price:D

⊕ Minitrix, Shell tank wagon, 3541, >55mm<, Price:C **Similar models:** Aral – 3543; Esso – 3542; BP – 3544; Texaco – 3546

⊖ Minitrix, Esso bogie tank wagon, 3552, >78mm<, Price:D **Similar models:** Shell – 3551; Aral – 3553; BP – 3554

⊖ Minitrix, Rhein-Kies ballast wagon, 3569, >76mm<, Price:D

⊕ Roco, VTG tank wagon, 2320A, >55mm<, Price:C **Similar models:** Shell – 2320B

⊖ Roco, VTG tank wagon, 2332A, >55mm<, Price:C **Similar models:** Shell – 2332B; Aral – 2332C

⊖ Roco, Shell bogie tank wagon, 2364A, >89mm<, Price:D **Similar models:** Aral – 2364B

⊕ Roco, Stuttgarter Hofbräu covered wagon, 2323B, >56mm<, Price:C **Similar models:** Königsbacher – 2323C

⊕ Roco, Dortmunder Union covered wagon, 2321E, >56mm<, Price:C **Similar models:** Dinkelacker – 2321C

⊖ Roco, Pschorr-Bräu covered wagon, 2307B, >78mm<, Price:C

⊕ Roco, Peine Salzgitter 12-wheeled hopper wagon, 2365A, >93mm<, Price:D

⊕ Roco, VTG high-capacity covered wagon, 2367A, >125mm<, Price:D

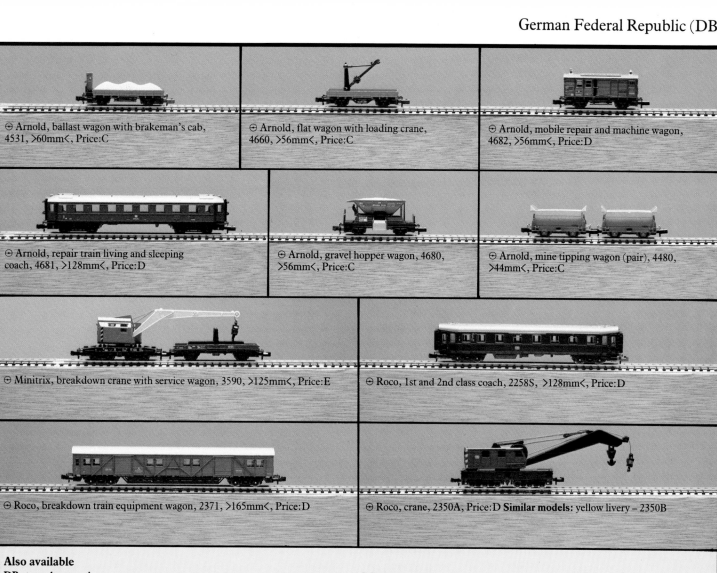

⊖ Arnold, ballast wagon with brakeman's cab, 4531, >60mm<, Price:C

⊖ Arnold, flat wagon with loading crane, 4660, >56mm<, Price:C

⊖ Arnold, mobile repair and machine wagon, 4682, >56mm<, Price:D

⊖ Arnold, repair train living and sleeping coach, 4681, >128mm<, Price:D

⊖ Arnold, gravel hopper wagon, 4680, >56mm<, Price:C

⊖ Arnold, mine tipping wagon (pair), 4480, >44mm<, Price:C

⊖ Minitrix, breakdown crane with service wagon, 3590, >125mm<, Price:E

⊖ Roco, 1st and 2nd class coach, 2258S, >128mm<, Price:D

⊖ Roco, breakdown train equipment wagon, 2371, >165mm<, Price:D

⊖ Roco, crane, 2350A, Price:D **Similar models:** yellow livery – 2350B

## Also available

### DB steam locomotives
⊕ Arnold, 23 class, 2231, >140mm<, ♀, Price:K

### DB electric locomotives
⊕ Arnold, 194 class, ⌂, 2310, >118mm<, ♀, Price:K **Similar models:** blue livery – 2311
⊕ Arnold, E 111 class, ⌂, 2325, >105mm<, ♀, Price:J **Similar models:** BR 111 class, orange and grey livery – 2327
⊕ Arnold, 118 class, ⌂, 2455, >116mm<, ♀, Price:L
⊕ Lima, 184 class, ⌂, 220207G, >108mm<, Price:Z
⊕ Lima, 151 class, ⌂, 220225G, Price:Z **Similar models:** green livery – 220224G

### DB electric railcars
⊕ Lima, ET403/404 class, ⌂, 123903G, >???mm<, Price:Z **Similar models:** Lufthansa Airport Express livery – 123902G. Also available as separate items
⊕ Roco, ET85 class, ⌂, 2160A, >255mm<, ♀, Price:K

### DB diesel locomotives
⊖ Ibertren, BB diesel, 019, >117mm<, Price:Z **Similar models:** ≠ – 956
⊕ Lima, V100 class, 220208G, Price:Z
⊕ Lima, 212 class, 220220G, >81mm<, Price:Z
⊕ Lima, shunting locomotive, 220222G, >65mm<, Price:Z **Similar models:** red livery – 220221G

### DB diesel railcars
⊕ Arnold, DB 798 class (motor unit), 2910, >87mm<, ♀, Price:H
⊕ Arnold, 998 class (intermediate unit), 2911, >87mm<, Price:D **Similar models:** driving trailer – 2912 (Price:E)

### DB coaches
⊕ Arnold, express baggage car, 3301, >105mm<, Price:D
⊕ Lima, 1st and 2nd class coach, 320874, >138mm<, Price:Z
⊕ Lima, observation coach, 320874, >138mm<, Price:Z
⊕ Roco, 1st and 2nd class coach, 2280A, >165mm<, Price:D
⊕ Roco, TEN sleeping car, 2278A, >165mm<, Price:D

### DB wagons
⊕ Arnold, high-sided wagon with sliding roof, 4401, >63mm<, Price:D
⊕ Arnold, high-sided wagon with load of wood, 4471, >56mm<, Price:C
⊕ Fleischmann, brake van, 8301, >52mm<, ♀, Price:D
⊕ Fleischmann, high-capacity self-unloading hopper wagon, 8520, >72mm<, Price:D

### DB wagons
⊕ Lima, covered wagon, 320402, Price:Z
⊕ Lima, high-sided wagon, 320640, Price:Z
⊕ Lima, car transporter, 320645, Price:Z

### Private-owner wagons
⊕ Lima, Shell bogie tank wagon, 320621, Price:Z
⊕ Lima, Spatenbräu refrigerated wagon, 320469, Price:Z **Similar models:** Patrizier – 320480

### Miscellaneous
⊕ Arnold, breakdown crane with support wagon, 4650, >143m<, Price:E
⊕ Fleischmann, dump truck, 8500, >47mm<, Price:B
⊕ Roco, jib wagon to work with crane, 2305S, >67mm<, Price:B

# German Federal Republic (DB)

**TT Gauge**

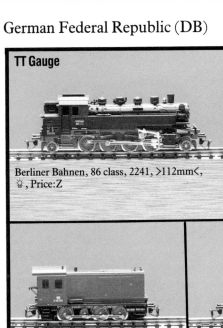

Berliner Bahnen, 86 class, 2241, >112mm<, ☼, Price:Z

Berliner Bahnen, 81 class, 2211, >93mm<, Price:Z

Berliner Bahnen, 221 class, 2510, >152mm<, Price:Z

Berliner Bahnen, 103 class, 2632, >82mm<, Price:Z

Berliner Bahnen, 194 class, ☗, 2411, >154mm<, ☼, Price:Z

Berliner Bahnen, four-wheeled coach, 3212, >116mm<, Price:Z

Berliner Bahnen, four-wheeled baggage van, 3412, >116mm<, Price:Z

Berliner Bahnen, 2nd class coach, 3614, >195mm<, Price:Z

Berliner Bahnen, refrigerated wagon, 4342, >98mm<, Price:Z

Berliner Bahnen, silo wagon, 4421, >76mm<, Price:Z

Berliner Bahnen, ASG covered wagon, 4152, >116mm<, Price:Z **Similar models:** Interfrigo – 4153

Berliner Bahnen, Transfesa refrigerated wagon, 4341, >98mm<, Price:Z **Similar models:** Interfrigo - 4340; Margon-water – 4343; Transthermos – 4344

Berliner Bahnen, Minol tank wagon, 4410, >76mm<, Price:Z **Similar models:** Buna – 4418; Lacke und Farben – 4401; Schwedt – 4402, Esso – 4415; Aral – 4417

Berliner Bahnen, EKS bogie tank wagon, 5410, >104mm<, Price:Z **Similar models:** Shell – 4414; Esso – 4415; BP – 4416; Aral – 4417; Schwedt – 5416; Texaco – 5417; Primagaz – 5413; Fina – 5411; Gasolin – 5414

Berliner Bahnen, Radeberger Pilsner refrigerated wagon, 5313, >137mm<, Price:Z **Similar models:** Staropramen – 5315

**HO/OO Gauge**

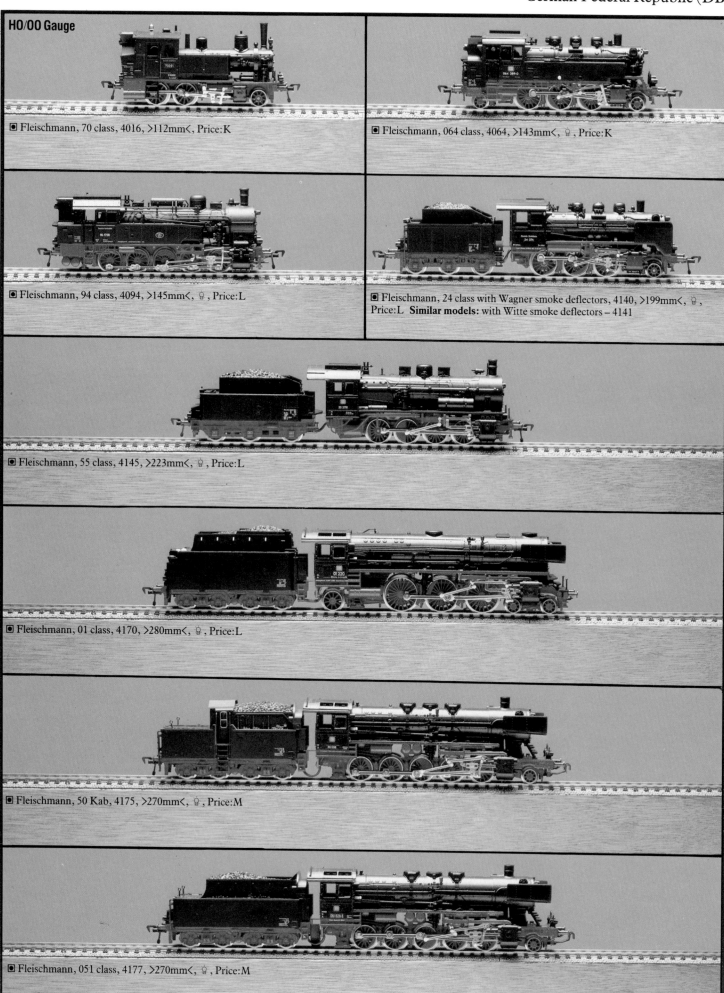

◉ Fleischmann, 70 class, 4016, >112mm<, Price:K

◉ Fleischmann, 064 class, 4064, >143mm<, ⚲ , Price:K

◉ Fleischmann, 94 class, 4094, >145mm<, ⚲ , Price:L

◉ Fleischmann, 24 class with Wagner smoke deflectors, 4140, >199mm<, ⚲ , Price:L  **Similar models:** with Witte smoke deflectors – 4141

◉ Fleischmann, 55 class, 4145, >223mm<, ⚲ , Price:L

◉ Fleischmann, 01 class, 4170, >280mm<, ⚲ , Price:L

◉ Fleischmann, 50 Kab, 4175, >270mm<, ⚲ , Price:M

◉ Fleischmann, 051 class, 4177, >270mm<, ⚲ , Price:M

# German Federal Republic (DB)

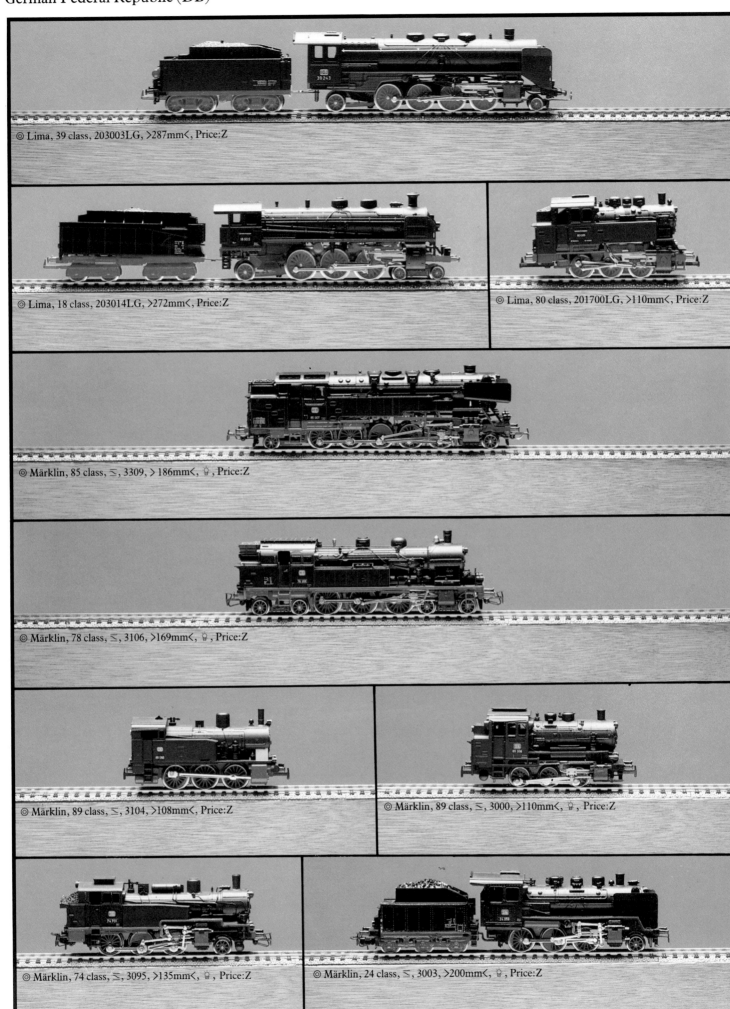

◎ Lima, 39 class, 203003LG, >287mm<, Price:Z

◎ Lima, 18 class, 203014LG, >272mm<, Price:Z

◎ Lima, 80 class, 201700LG, >110mm<, Price:Z

◎ Märklin, 85 class, ≦, 3309, >186mm<, ⚲, Price:Z

◎ Märklin, 78 class, ≦, 3106, >169mm<, ⚲, Price:Z

◎ Märklin, 89 class, ≦, 3104, >108mm<, Price:Z

◎ Märklin, 89 class, ≦, 3000, >110mm<, ⚲, Price:Z

◎ Märklin, 74 class, ≦, 3095, >135mm<, ⚲, Price:Z

◎ Märklin, 24 class, ≦, 3003, >200mm<, ⚲, Price:Z

◎ Märklin, 18 class, ≲, 3093, ⟩249mm⟨, ♙, Price:Z

◎ Märklin, 86 class, ≲, 3096, ⟩158mm⟨, ♙, Price:Z

◎ Märklin, 050 class, ≲, 3084, ⟩261mm⟨, ♙, Price:Z

◎ Märklin, 41 class, ≲, 3082, ⟩275mm⟨, ♙, Price:Z

◎ Märklin, 003 class, ≲, 3085, ⟩277mm⟨, ♙, Price:Z

◎ Roco, 043 class, 4126A, ⟩260mm⟨, ♙, Price:L **Similar models:** ≲ – 14126A

◎ Roco, 23 class, 4120A, >245mm<, ♀, Price:L **Similar models:** ⋚ – 14120A

◎ Roco, 01 class, 4119A, >275mm<, ♀, Price:L **Similar models:** later smoke deflectors – 4119B

✪ Trix, BR 54 class, ≡, 2225, >208mm<, ♀, Price:L **Similar models:** ◎ coupling, 12V DC – 2425

✪ Trix, 01 class, ≡, 2204, >280mm<, ♀, Price:L

✪ Trix, 64 class, ≡, 2203, >145mm<, ♀, Price:K

✪ Trix, 24 class, ≡, 2202, >200mm<, Price:K

✪ Trix, 80 class, ≡, 2217, >110mm<, Price:H

▣ Fleischmann, E69 class, 🚋, 4300, >97mm<, Price:G **Similar models:** red livery – 4303

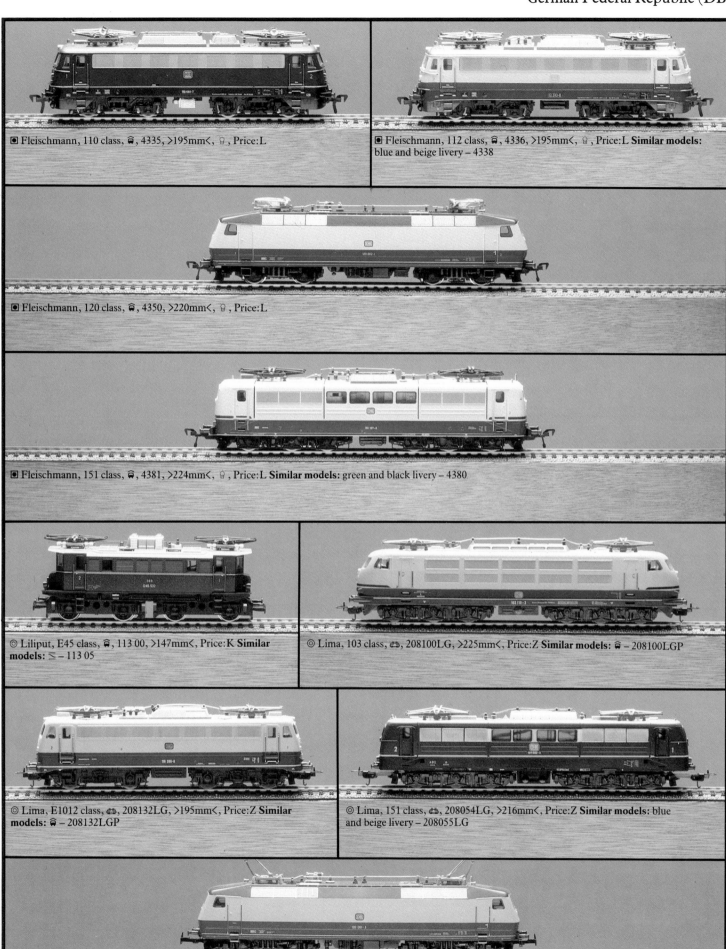

◉ Fleischmann, 110 class, 🔲, 4335, >195mm<, 🔲, Price: L

◉ Fleischmann, 112 class, 🔲, 4336, >195mm<, 🔲, Price: L **Similar models:** blue and beige livery – 4338

◉ Fleischmann, 120 class, 🔲, 4350, >220mm<, 🔲, Price: L

◉ Fleischmann, 151 class, 🔲, 4381, >224mm<, 🔲, Price: L **Similar models:** green and black livery – 4380

◎ Liliput, E45 class, 🔲, 113 00, >147mm<, Price: K **Similar models:** ≲ – 113 05

◎ Lima, 103 class, 🖘, 208100LG, >225mm<, Price: Z **Similar models:** 🔲 – 208100LGP

◎ Lima, E1012 class, 🖘, 208132LG, >195mm<, Price: Z **Similar models:** 🔲 – 208132LGP

◎ Lima, 151 class, 🖘, 208054LG, >216mm<, Price: Z **Similar models:** blue and beige livery – 208055LG

◎ Märklin, 120 class, ≲, 🔲, 3153, >221mm<, 🔲, Price: Z

# German Federal Republic (DB)

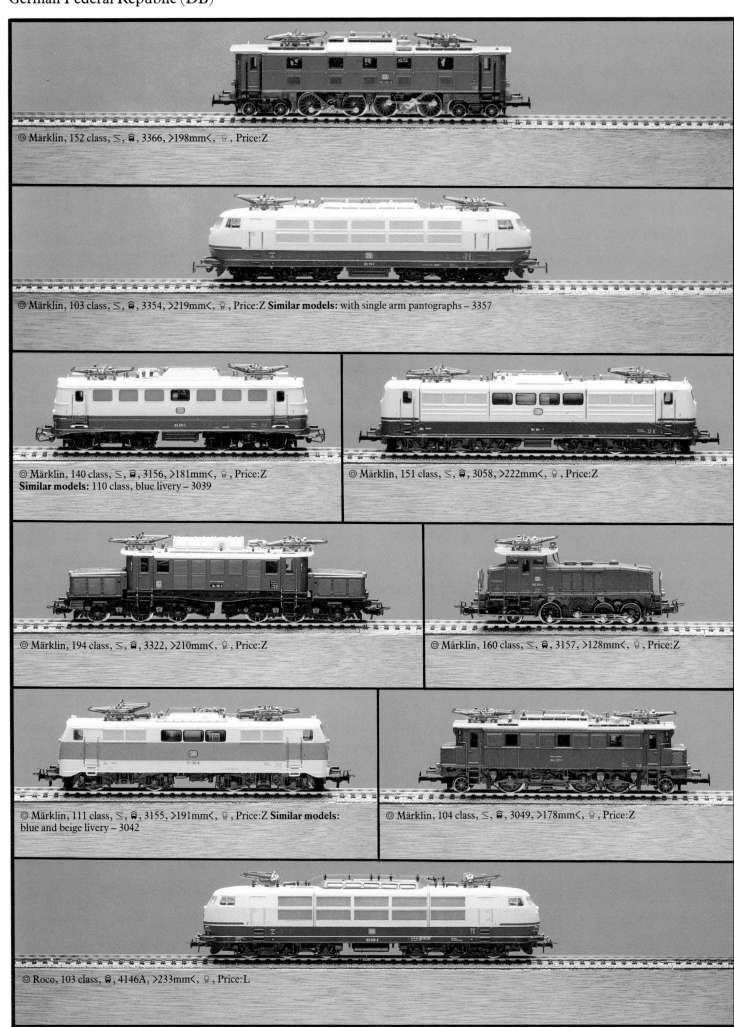

◎ Märklin, 152 class, ⊆, ⌂, 3366, >198mm<, ⚲, Price:Z

◎ Märklin, 103 class, ⊆, ⌂, 3354, >219mm<, ⚲, Price:Z **Similar models:** with single arm pantographs – 3357

◎ Märklin, 140 class, ⊆, ⌂, 3156, >181mm<, ⚲, Price:Z
**Similar models:** 110 class, blue livery – 3039

◎ Märklin, 151 class, ⊆, ⌂, 3058, >222mm<, ⚲, Price:Z

◎ Märklin, 194 class, ⊆, ⌂, 3322, >210mm<, ⚲, Price:Z

◎ Märklin, 160 class, ⊆, ⌂, 3157, >128mm<, ⚲, Price:Z

◎ Märklin, 111 class, ⊆, ⌂, 3155, >191mm<, ⚲, Price:Z **Similar models:**
blue and beige livery – 3042

◎ Märklin, 104 class, ⊆, ⌂, 3049, >178mm<, ⚲, Price:Z

◎ Roco, 103 class, ⌂, 4146A, >233mm<, ⚲, Price:L

122

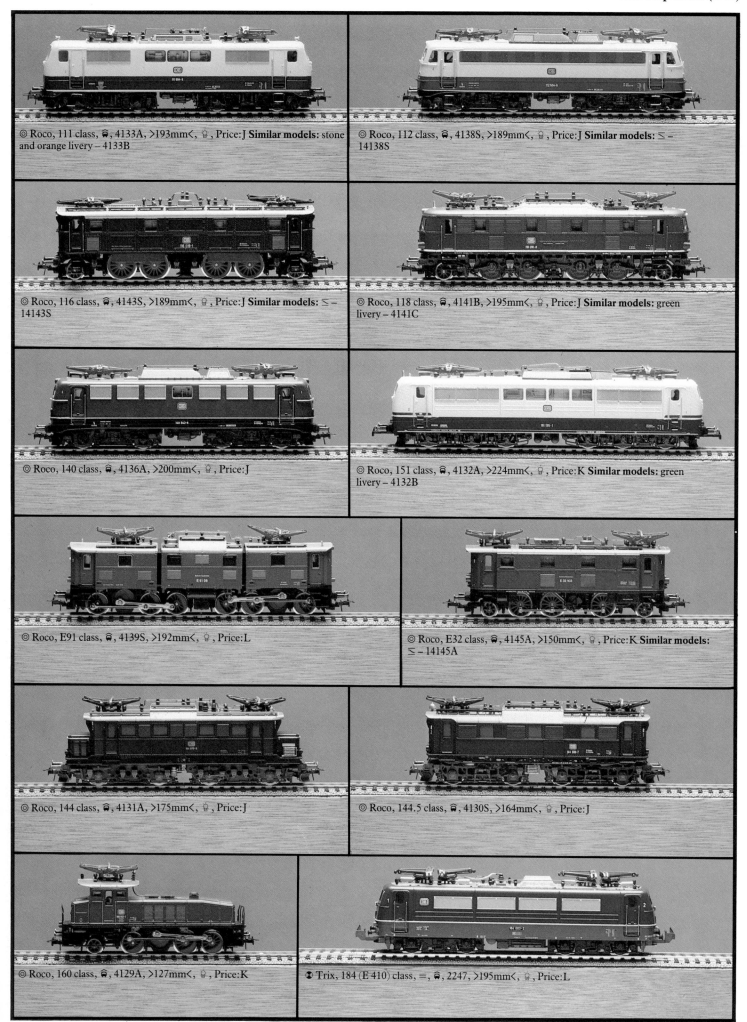

◎ Roco, 111 class, 🔝, 4133A, >193mm<, ♀, Price: J **Similar models:** stone and orange livery – 4133B

◎ Roco, 112 class, 🔝, 4138S, >189mm<, ♀, Price: J **Similar models:** ≲ – 14138S

◎ Roco, 116 class, 🔝, 4143S, >189mm<, ♀, Price: J **Similar models:** ≲ – 14143S

◎ Roco, 118 class, 🔝, 4141B, >195mm<, ♀, Price: J **Similar models:** green livery – 4141C

◎ Roco, 140 class, 🔝, 4136A, >200mm<, ♀, Price: J

◎ Roco, 151 class, 🔝, 4132A, >224mm<, ♀, Price: K **Similar models:** green livery – 4132B

◎ Roco, E91 class, 🔝, 4139S, >192mm<, ♀, Price: L

◎ Roco, E32 class, 🔝, 4145A, >150mm<, ♀, Price: K **Similar models:** ≲ – 14145A

◎ Roco, 144 class, 🔝, 4131A, >175mm<, ♀, Price: J

◎ Roco, 144.5 class, 🔝, 4130S, >164mm<, ♀, Price: J

◎ Roco, 160 class, 🔝, 4129A, >127mm<, ♀, Price: K

☒ Trix, 184 (E 410) class, ≡, 🔝, 2247, >195mm<, ♀, Price: L

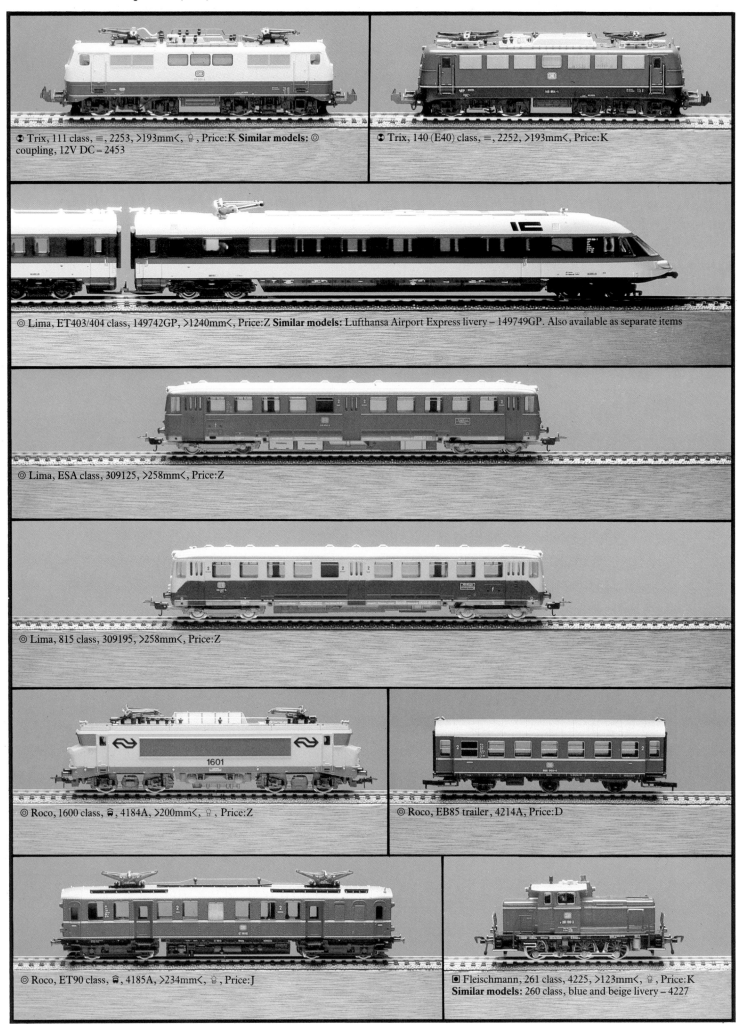

☫ Trix, 111 class, ≡, 2253, >193mm<, ⌂, Price:K **Similar models:** ◎ coupling, 12V DC – 2453

☫ Trix, 140 (E40) class, ≡, 2252, >193mm<, Price:K

◎ Lima, ET403/404 class, 149742GP, >1240mm<, Price:Z **Similar models:** Lufthansa Airport Express livery – 149749GP. Also available as separate items

◎ Lima, ESA class, 309125, >258mm<, Price:Z

◎ Lima, 815 class, 309195, >258mm<, Price:Z

◎ Roco, 1600 class, ⌂, 4184A, >200mm<, ⌂, Price:Z

◎ Roco, EB85 trailer, 4214A, Price:D

◎ Roco, ET90 class, ⌂, 4185A, >234mm<, ⌂, Price:J

◉ Fleischmann, 261 class, 4225, >123mm<, ⌂, Price:K **Similar models:** 260 class, blue and beige livery – 4227

◉ Fleischmann, 212 class, 4231, >145mm<, ⚲, Price:K **Similar models:** red livery – 4230

◉ Fleischmann, 218 class, 4232, >188mm<, ⚲, Price:L

◉ Fleischmann, 221 class, 4235, >213mm<, ⚲, Price:L **Similar models:** blue and beige livery – 4236

◎ Lima, 288 class, 208114LG, >258mm<, Price:Z **Similar models:** 208115LG

◎ Lima, 280 class, 201626LG, >147mm<, Price:Z

◎ Lima, 221 class, 201640LG, >212mm<, Price:Z **Similar models:** blue and beige livery – 201641LG

◎ Märklin, 260 class, ≲, 3064, >120mm<, ⚲, Price:Z **Similar models:** with Telex coupler – 3065; blue and cream livery – 3141

◎ Märklin, 236 class, ≲, 3146, >106mm<, ⚲, Price:Z

◎ Märklin, 212 class, ≲, 3147, >141mm<, ⚲, Price:Z **Similar models:** red livery – 3072

◎ Märklin, 220 class, ≲, 3021, >210mm<, ⚲, Price:Z

◎ Märklin, 216 class, ≲, 3074, >182mm<, ⚲, Price:Z **Similar models:** red and grey livery – 3075

◎ Mehanotehnika, V-160 class, T041, >183mm<, Price:Z

◎ Roco, 215 class, 4151A, >189mm<, ♀, Price:H **Similar models:** blue and beige livery – 4151B; red and beige livery – 4151C

◎ Roco, 290 class, 4154A, >165mm<, ♀, Price:J **Similar models:** blue and beige livery – 4145B

☮ Trix, 221 (V200) class, ≡, 2256, >212mm<, ♀, Price:K **Similar models:** ◎ coupling, 12V DC – 2456

☮ Trix, 217 (V160) class, ≡, 2251, >188mm<, ♀, Price:K **Similar models:** ◎ coupling, 12V DC – 2451

☮ Trix, 236 (V36) class, ≡, 2263, >110mm<, ♀, Price:H **Similar models:** ◎ coupler, 12V DC, black – 2464

▣ Fleischmann, VT98 and VS98, 4400, >305mm<, ♀, Price:K

▣ Fleischmann, 614 class, 4434, >537mm<, ♀, Price:L **Similar models:** red and grey livery – 4430

▣ Fleischmann, 914 centre coach for 614 units (no motor), 4436, >257mm<, Price:E **Similar models:** red and grey livery – 4432

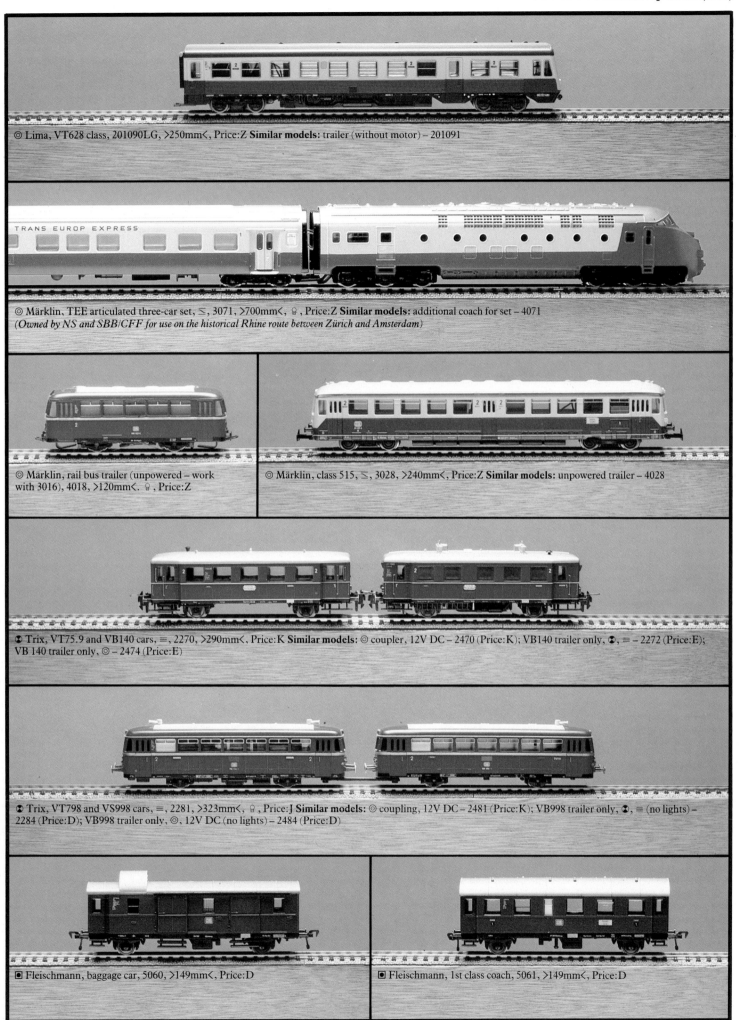

⊚ Lima, VT628 class, 201090LG, >250mm<, Price:Z **Similar models:** trailer (without motor) – 201091

⊚ Märklin, TEE articulated three-car set, ≦, 3071, >700mm<, ☺, Price:Z **Similar models:** additional coach for set – 4071
(*Owned by NS and SBB/CFF for use on the historical Rhine route between Zürich and Amsterdam*)

⊚ Märklin, rail bus trailer (unpowered – work with 3016), 4018, >120mm<. ☺, Price:Z

⊚ Märklin, class 515, ≦, 3028, >240mm<, Price:Z **Similar models:** unpowered trailer – 4028

☼ Trix, VT75.9 and VB140 cars, ≡, 2270, >290mm<, Price:K **Similar models:** ⊚ coupler, 12V DC – 2470 (Price:K); VB140 trailer only, ☺, ≡ – 2272 (Price:E); VB 140 trailer only, ⊚ – 2474 (Price:E)

☼ Trix, VT798 and VS998 cars, ≡, 2281, >323mm<, ☺, Price:J **Similar models:** ⊚ coupling, 12V DC – 2481 (Price:K); VB998 trailer only, ☺, ≡ (no lights) – 2284 (Price:D); VB998 trailer only, ⊚, 12V DC (no lights) – 2484 (Price:D)

◉ Fleischmann, baggage car, 5060, >149mm<, Price:D

◉ Fleischmann, 1st class coach, 5061, >149mm<, Price:D

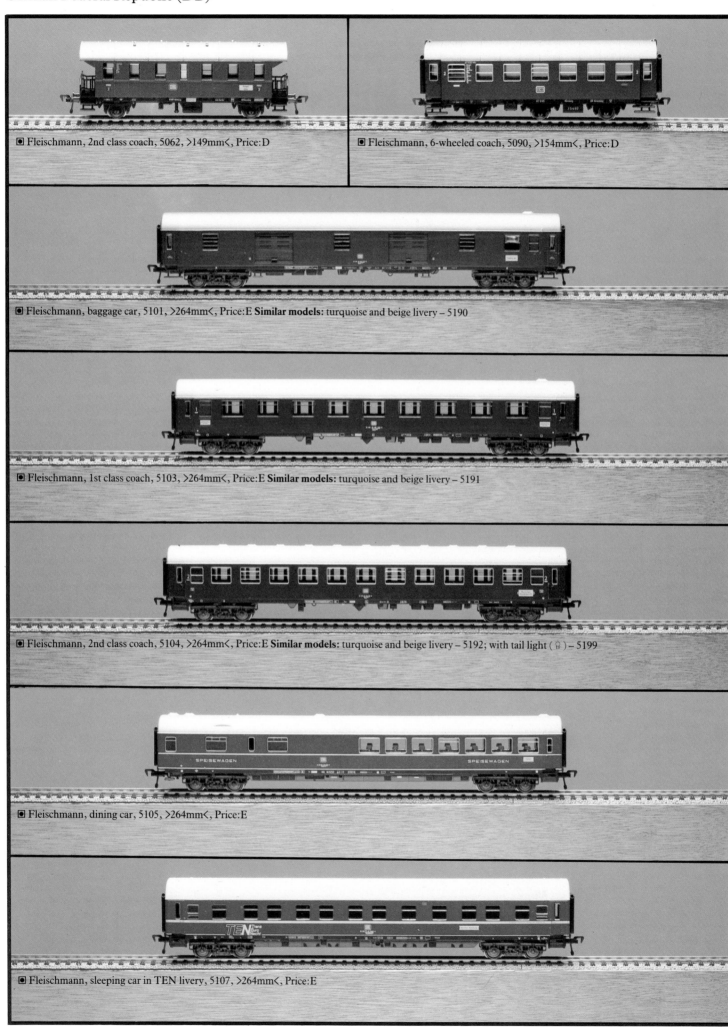

◉ Fleischmann, 2nd class coach, 5062, >149mm<, Price:D

◉ Fleischmann, 6-wheeled coach, 5090, >154mm<, Price:D

◉ Fleischmann, baggage car, 5101, >264mm<, Price:E **Similar models:** turquoise and beige livery – 5190

◉ Fleischmann, 1st class coach, 5103, >264mm<, Price:E **Similar models:** turquoise and beige livery – 5191

◉ Fleischmann, 2nd class coach, 5104, >264mm<, Price:E **Similar models:** turquoise and beige livery – 5192; with tail light ( ) – 5199

◉ Fleischmann, dining car, 5105, >264mm<, Price:E

◉ Fleischmann, sleeping car in TEN livery, 5107, >264mm<, Price:E

◉ Fleischmann, 2nd class coach with driver's cab (push-pull trains), 5120, ›245mm‹, ⚲, Price:F

◉ Fleischmann, 2nd class coach, 5122, ›245mm‹, Price:E

◉ Fleischmann, 1st class coach, 5160, ›264mm‹, Price:E **Similar models:** with tail light (⚲) – 5169

◉ Fleischmann, 1st class coach, 5161, ›264mm‹, Price:E

◉ Fleischmann, restaurant car, ⛴, 5162, ›264mm‹, Price:E

◉ Fleischmann, 1st class coach, 5163, ›264mm‹, Price:E

◉ Fleischmann, 'Quick Pick' dining coach, 🍴, 5165, >264mm<, Price:E

◉ Fleischmann, 2nd class Intercity coach, 5194, >264mm<, Price:E

◎ Liliput, 2nd class, converted E30, coach, 286 00, >240mm<, Price:D

◎ Liliput, 1st and 2nd class coach, 287 00, >240mm<, Price:D

◎ Liliput, baggage car for Rheingold, 289 03, >250mm<, Price:D

◎ Liliput, 'party' coach, 829 00, >270mm<, 💡, Price:E

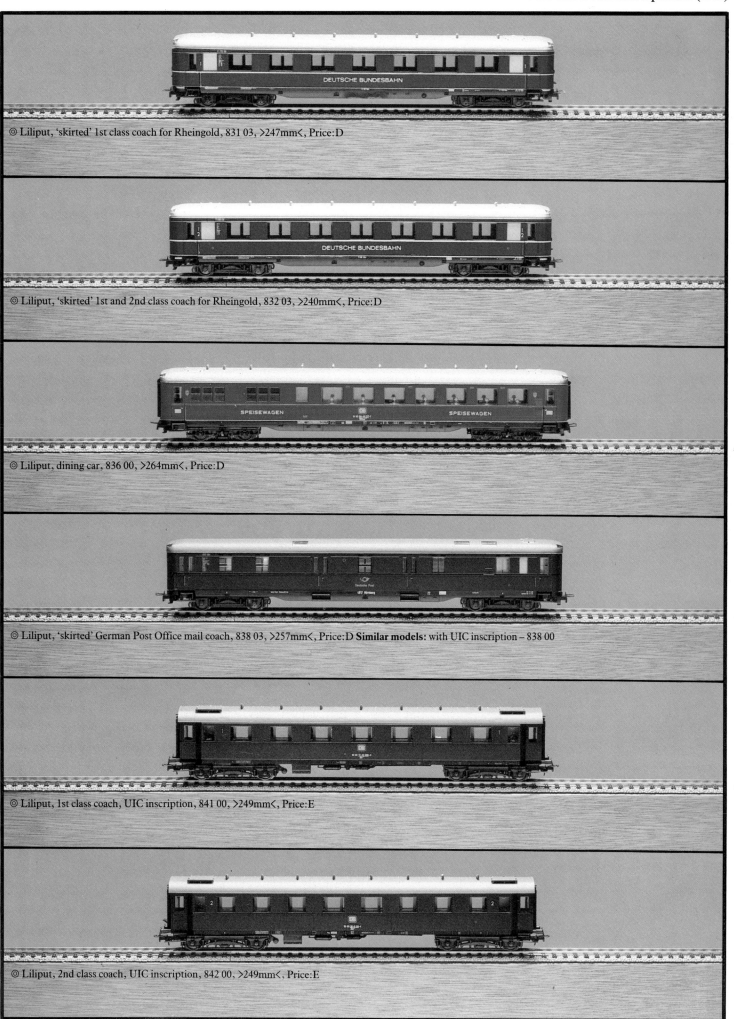

◎ Liliput, 'skirted' 1st class coach for Rheingold, 831 03, >247mm<, Price:D

◎ Liliput, 'skirted' 1st and 2nd class coach for Rheingold, 832 03, >240mm<, Price:D

◎ Liliput, dining car, 836 00, >264mm<, Price:D

◎ Liliput, 'skirted' German Post Office mail coach, 838 03, >257mm<, Price:D **Similar models:** with UIC inscription – 838 00

◎ Liliput, 1st class coach, UIC inscription, 841 00, >249mm<, Price:E

◎ Liliput, 2nd class coach, UIC inscription, 842 00, >249mm<, Price:E

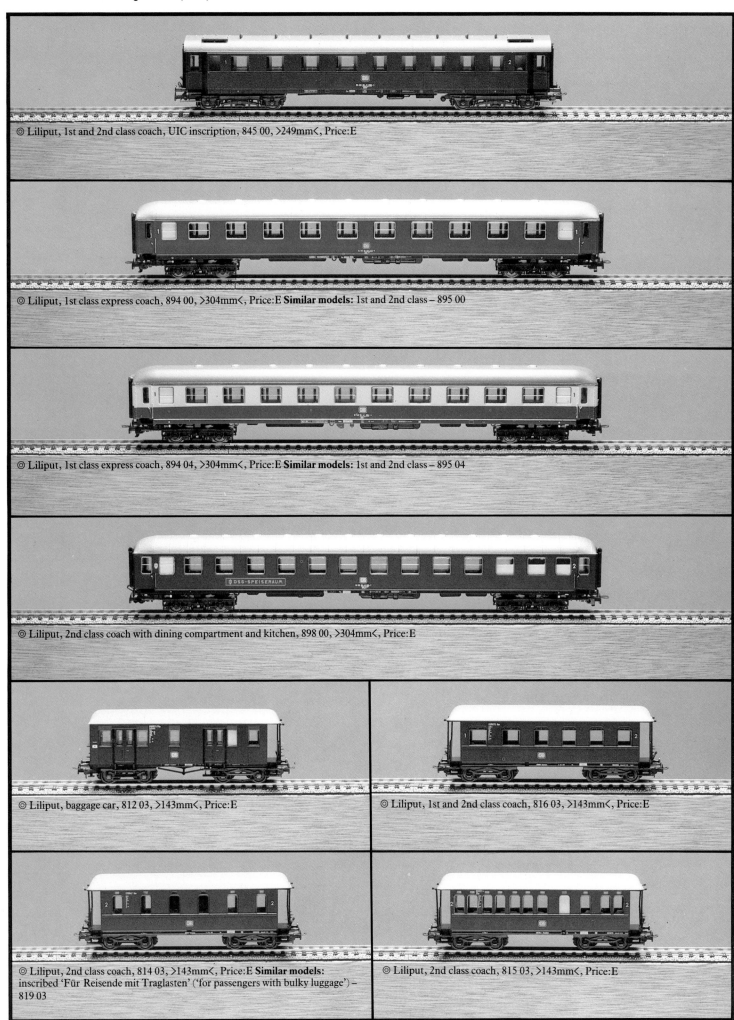

◎ Liliput, 1st and 2nd class coach, UIC inscription, 845 00, >249mm<, Price:E

◎ Liliput, 1st class express coach, 894 00, >304mm<, Price:E **Similar models:** 1st and 2nd class – 895 00

◎ Liliput, 1st class express coach, 894 04, >304mm<, Price:E **Similar models:** 1st and 2nd class – 895 04

◎ Liliput, 2nd class coach with dining compartment and kitchen, 898 00, >304mm<, Price:E

◎ Liliput, baggage car, 812 03, >143mm<, Price:E

◎ Liliput, 1st and 2nd class coach, 816 03, >143mm<, Price:E

◎ Liliput, 2nd class coach, 814 03, >143mm<, Price:E **Similar models:** inscribed 'Für Reisende mit Traglasten' ('for passengers with bulky luggage') – 819 03

◎ Liliput, 2nd class coach, 815 03, >143mm<, Price:E

◎ Liliput, 2nd class coach, 813 03, >143mm<, Price:E **Similar models:** inscribed 'Für Reisende Traglasten' ('for passengers with bulky luggage') – 818 03 alternative type – 817 03

◎ Lima, baggage car, 309309, >149mm<, Price:Z

◎ Lima, 1st class coach, 309153, >149mm<, Price:Z

◎ Lima, 1st and 2nd class coach, 309156, >257mm<, Price:Z

◎ Lima, Rheingold coach, 309167, >270mm<, Price:Z

◎ Lima, 2nd class driving coach, 309157, >255mm<, Price:Z

◎ Lima, 2nd class coach, 309155, >257mm<, Price:Z

◎ Lima, 1st class coach, 309167, >268mm<, Price:Z **Similar models:** Rheingold livery – 309180

◎ Lima, 1st class coach, 309172, >268mm<, Price:Z **Similar models:** blue and beige livery – 309174

◎ Lima, 2nd class coach, 309179, >268mm<, Price:Z **Similar models:** green livery – 309178

◎ Lima, dining car, 309214, >268mm<, Price:Z **Similar models:** TEE livery – 309217

◎ Lima, TEE dining car, 309169, >268mm<, Price:Z **Similar models:** DSG Rheingold livery – 309182; Rheingold Salonwagen livery – 309226

◎ Lima, observation car, 309170, >268mm<, Price:Z

◎ Lima, sleeping car, 309238, >268mm<, Price:Z

◎ Lima, baggage car, 309337, >255mm<, Price:Z **Similar models:** green livery – 309314

◎ Lima, 1st class coach, 309330, >268mm<, Price:Z

◎ Lima, 2nd class brake coach, 309336, >268mm<, Price:Z

◎ Märklin, 1st and 2nd class commuter coach, 4158, >264mm<, Price:Z

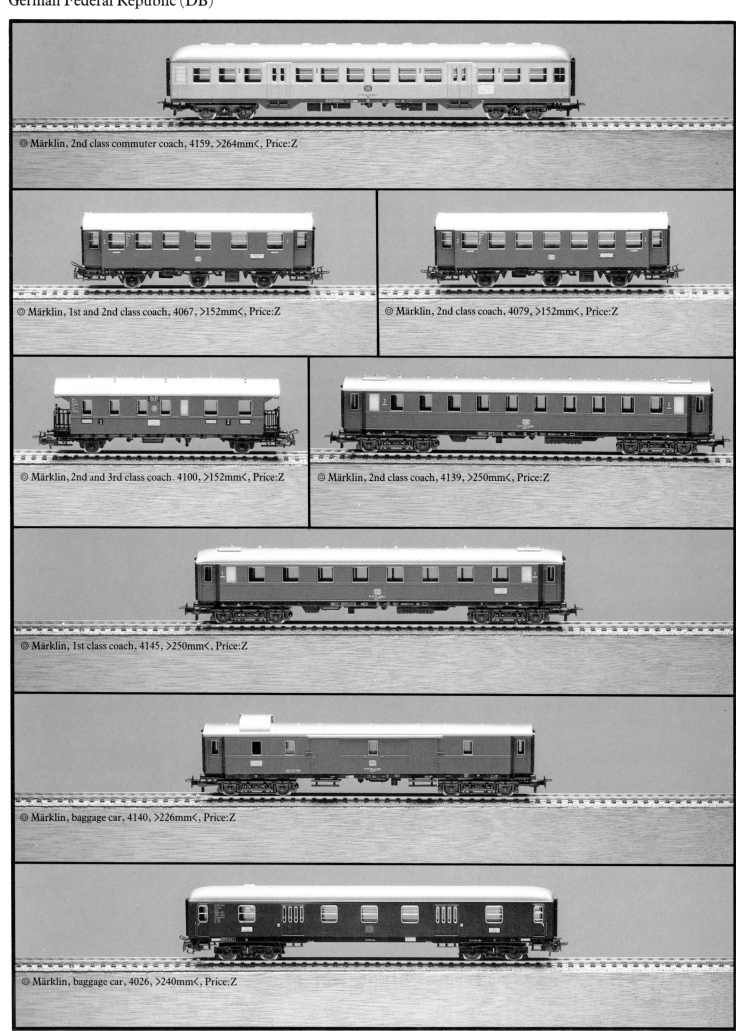

◎ Märklin, 2nd class commuter coach, 4159, >264mm<, Price:Z

◎ Märklin, 1st and 2nd class coach, 4067, >152mm<, Price:Z

◎ Märklin, 2nd class coach, 4079, >152mm<, Price:Z

◎ Märklin, 2nd and 3rd class coach, 4100, >152mm<, Price:Z

◎ Märklin, 2nd class coach, 4139, >250mm<, Price:Z

◎ Märklin, 1st class coach, 4145, >250mm<, Price:Z

◎ Märklin, baggage car, 4140, >226mm<, Price:Z

◎ Märklin, baggage car, 4026, >240mm<, Price:Z

◎ Märklin, 1st class coach, 4051, >240mm<, Price:Z **Similar models:** ♀ – 4053; blue and cream livery, no lights – 4111

◎ Märklin, 2nd class coach, 4052, >240mm<, Price:Z **Similar models:** blue and cream livery – 4112

◎ Märklin, dining car, 4054, >240mm<, Price:Z **Similar models:** TEE, DSG livery – 4087

◎ Märklin, 1st class coach with side corridor, 4085, >240mm<, Price:Z **Similar models:** ♀ – 4089

◎ Märklin, vista dome car, 4090, >240mm<, Price:Z

◎ Märklin, 1st class coach, 4095, >270mm<, Price:Z **Similar models:** ♀ – 4098

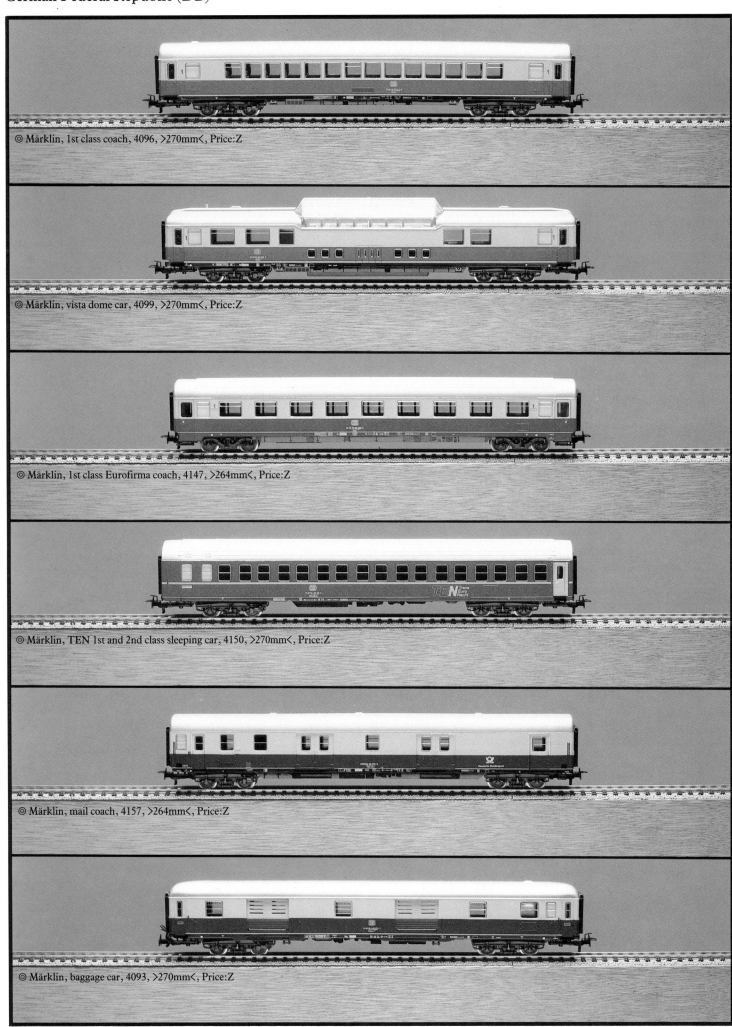

◎ Märklin, 1st class coach, 4096, >270mm<, Price:Z

◎ Märklin, vista dome car, 4099, >270mm<, Price:Z

◎ Märklin, 1st class Eurofirma coach, 4147, >264mm<, Price:Z

◎ Märklin, TEN 1st and 2nd class sleeping car, 4150, >270mm<, Price:Z

◎ Märklin, mail coach, 4157, >264mm<, Price:Z

◎ Märklin, baggage car, 4093, >270mm<, Price:Z

◎ Märklin, dining car, 4094 >270mm<, Price:Z

◎ Märklin, 1st class coach, 4091, >270mm<, Price:Z

◎ Märklin, 2nd class coach, 4092, >270mm<, Price:Z **Similar models:** ⬙ – 4154

◎ Roco, four-wheeled mail coach, 4217S, >139mm<, Price:D

◎ Roco, four-wheeled 2nd class coach, 4201A, >160mm<, Price:D

◎ Roco, four-wheeled 1st and 2nd class coach, 4202S, >160mm<, Price:D

◎ Roco, four-wheeled 1st class coach, 4203A, >161mm<, Price:D

◎ Roco, four-wheeled baggage coach, 4204S, >160mm<, Price:D

◎ Roco, six-wheeled 2nd class coach with brakeman's cab, 44205A, >140mm<, Price:D

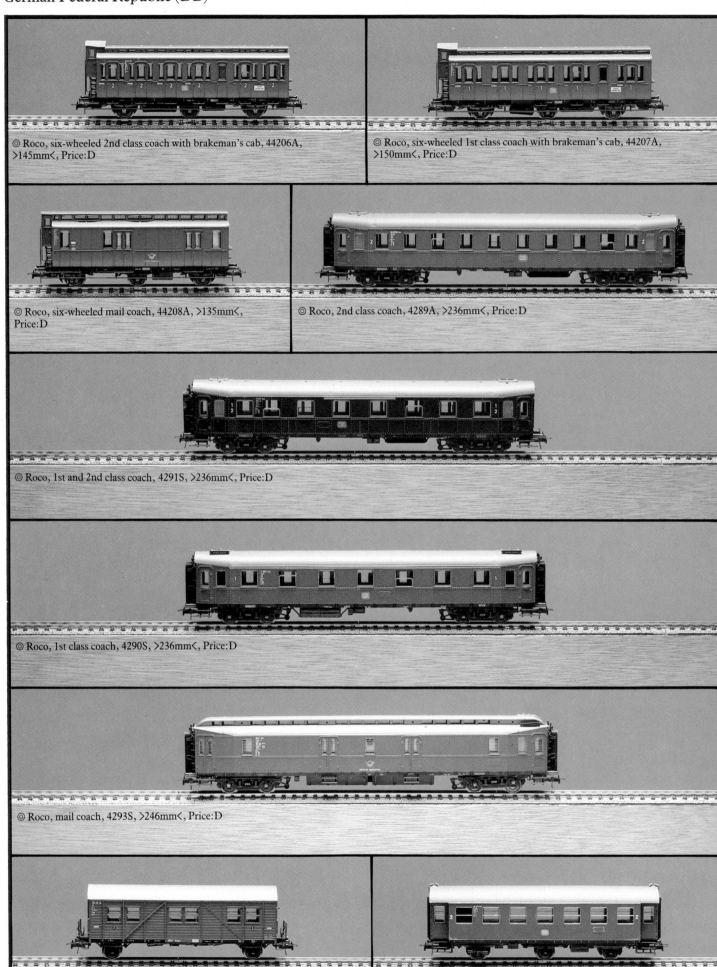

◎ Roco, six-wheeled 2nd class coach with brakeman's cab, 44206A, >145mm<, Price:D

◎ Roco, six-wheeled 1st class coach with brakeman's cab, 44207A, >150mm<, Price:D

◎ Roco, six-wheeled mail coach, 44208A, >135mm<, Price:D

◎ Roco, 2nd class coach, 4289A, >236mm<, Price:D

◎ Roco, 1st and 2nd class coach, 4291S, >236mm<, Price:D

◎ Roco, 1st class coach, 4290S, >236mm<, Price:D

◎ Roco, mail coach, 4293S, >246mm<, Price:D

◎ Roco, baggage car, 4220S, >226mm<, Price:D **Similar models:** earlier livery – 4220B

◎ Roco, six-wheeled 2nd class coach, 4214S, >153mm<, Price:D

◎ Roco, six-wheeled 1st and 2nd class coach, 4215S, >153mm<, Price:D

◎ Roco, six-wheeled 2nd class coach with baggage compartment, 4216S, >153mm<, Price:D

◎ Roco, 2nd class coach, 4250S, >224mm<, Price:D

◎ Roco, 1st and 2nd class coach, 4252S, >224mm<, Price:D

◎ Roco, 2nd class coach with baggage compartment, 4254S, >224mm<, Price:D

◎ Roco, 2nd class coach with baggage compartment and driver's cab, 4264S, >264mm<, ☼, Price:E

◎ Roco, 2nd class coach, 4265S, >264mm<, Price:D

◎ Roco, 1st and 2nd class coach, 4266S, >264mm<, Price:D

◎ Roco, 2nd class coach, 4279S, >264mm<, Price:D

◎ Roco, 1st and 2nd class coach, 4280S, >264mm<, Price:D

◎ Roco, 2nd class coach with baggage compartment and driver's cab, 4281S, >264mm<, ⚲, Price:E

◎ Roco, mail coach, 4262S, >264mm<, Price:D

◎ Roco, 2nd class coach, 4256S, >264mm<, Price:D **Similar models:** green livery – 4294S

◎ Roco, 1st and 2nd class coach, 4288S, >264mm<, Price:D **Similar models:** green livery – 4295S

◎ Roco, 2nd class coach with baggage compartment, 4258S, >264mm<, Price:D **Similar models:** green livery – 4298S

◎ Roco, baggage coach, 4259S, >264mm<, Price:D

◎ Roco, baggage coach, 4297S, >264mm<, Price:D

◎ Roco, 1st class coach, 4267S, >264mm<, Price:D

◎ Roco, 1st class open coach, 4268S, >264mm<, Price:D

# German Federal Republic (DB)

◎ Roco, 2nd class coach, 4235A, >264mm<, Price:D

◎ Roco, 1st class coach, 4236B, >264mm<, Price:D

◎ Roco, 1st class bar coach, 4270S, >275mm<, Price:D

◎ Roco, dining car, 4269S, >275mm<, Price:D

◎ Roco, dining car, 🍴, 4272A, >275mm<, Price:E

◎ Roco, observation car, 4271S, >264mm<, Price:E

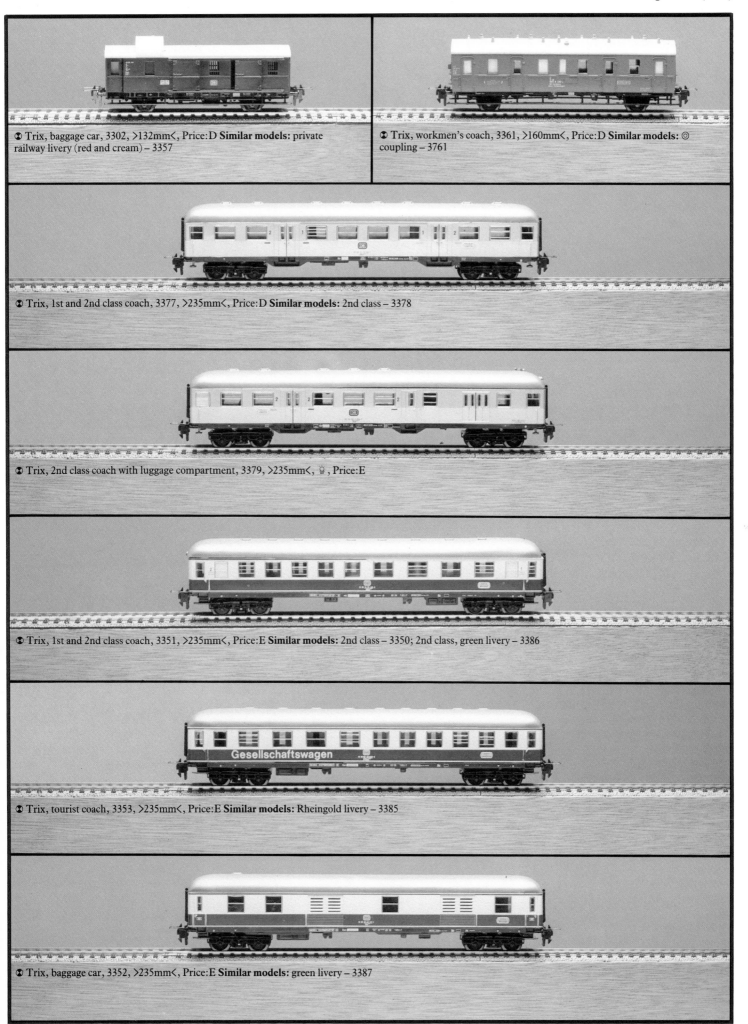

✪ Trix, baggage car, 3302, >132mm<, Price:D **Similar models:** private railway livery (red and cream) – 3357

✪ Trix, workmen's coach, 3361, >160mm<, Price:D **Similar models:** ◎ coupling – 3761

✪ Trix, 1st and 2nd class coach, 3377, >235mm<, Price:D **Similar models:** 2nd class – 3378

✪ Trix, 2nd class coach with luggage compartment, 3379, >235mm<, 🔌, Price:E

✪ Trix, 1st and 2nd class coach, 3351, >235mm<, Price:E **Similar models:** 2nd class – 3350; 2nd class, green livery – 3386

✪ Trix, tourist coach, 3353, >235mm<, Price:E **Similar models:** Rheingold livery – 3385

✪ Trix, baggage car, 3352, >235mm<, Price:E **Similar models:** green livery – 3387

✪ Trix, 1st and 2nd class coach, 3374, >194mm<, Price:D

✪ Trix, 2nd class coach, 3375, >194mm<, Price:D

✪ Trix, 2nd class coach with luggage compartment, 3376, >194mm<, Price:D

◎ Liliput, Mitropa dining car, 827 02, >270mm<, Price: E

◎ Liliput, DSG sleeping car, 837 03, >264mm<, ♀ , Price:Z

◎ Lima, DSG sleeping car, 309204, >268mm<, Price:Z

◎ Lima, DSG sleeping car, 309206, >268mm<, Price:Z

◎ Märklin, DSG 1st and 2nd class sleeper, 4064, Price:Z

◎ Märklin, sleeping car, 4029, >240mm<, Price:Z

◎ Roco, TUI treff (meeting) holiday coach, 4226A, >264mm<, Price:E

◎ Roco, TUI holiday coach, 4227A, >264mm<, Price:E

◎ Roco, DSG dining car, 4261B, >264mm<, Price:D

◎ Roco, DSG sleeping car, 4292S, >246mm<, Price:D

# German Federal Republic (DB)

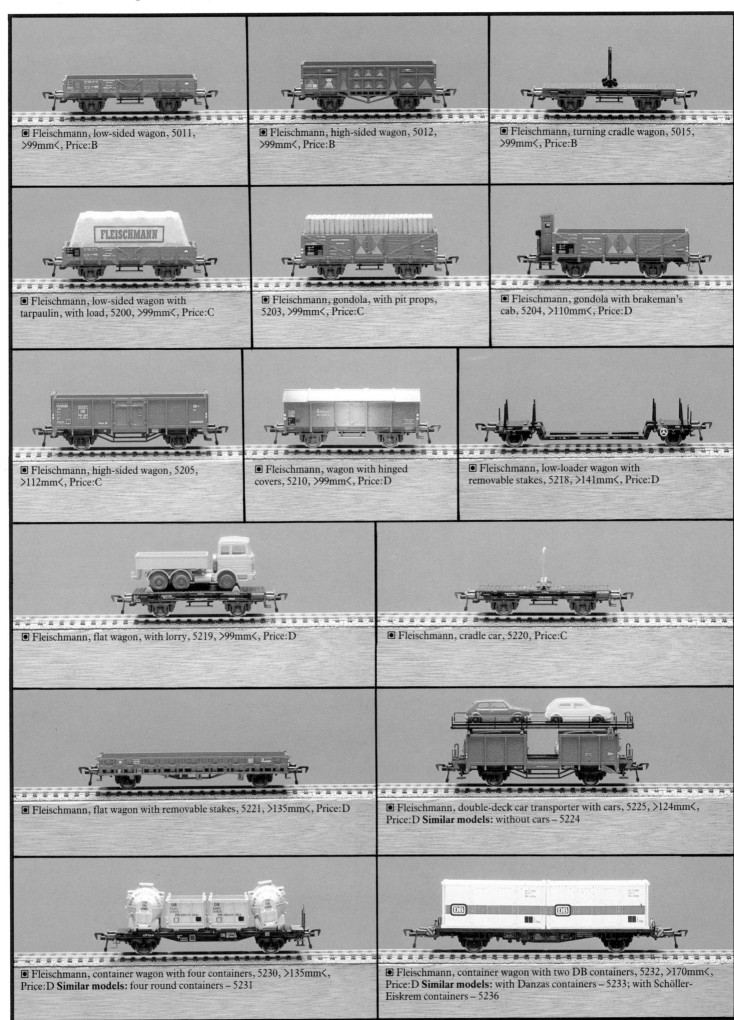

◉ Fleischmann, low-sided wagon, 5011, >99mm<, Price:B

◉ Fleischmann, high-sided wagon, 5012, >99mm<, Price:B

◉ Fleischmann, turning cradle wagon, 5015, >99mm<, Price:B

◉ Fleischmann, low-sided wagon with tarpaulin, with load, 5200, >99mm<, Price:C

◉ Fleischmann, gondola, with pit props, 5203, >99mm<, Price:C

◉ Fleischmann, gondola with brakeman's cab, 5204, >110mm<, Price:D

◉ Fleischmann, high-sided wagon, 5205, >112mm<, Price:C

◉ Fleischmann, wagon with hinged covers, 5210, >99mm<, Price:D

◉ Fleischmann, low-loader wagon with removable stakes, 5218, >141mm<, Price:D

◉ Fleischmann, flat wagon, with lorry, 5219, >99mm<, Price:D

◉ Fleischmann, cradle car, 5220, Price:C

◉ Fleischmann, flat wagon with removable stakes, 5221, >135mm<, Price:D

◉ Fleischmann, double-deck car transporter with cars, 5225, >124mm<, Price:D **Similar models:** without cars – 5224

◉ Fleischmann, container wagon with four containers, 5230, >135mm<, Price:D **Similar models:** four round containers – 5231

◉ Fleischmann, container wagon with two DB containers, 5232, >170mm<, Price:D **Similar models:** with Danzas containers – 5233; with Schöller-Eiskrem containers – 5236

◉ Fleischmann, low-sided wagon, 5281, Price: D

◉ Fleischmann, high-sided wagon, 5282, ＞155mm＜, Price: D

◉ Fleischmann, double-deck car carrier with cars, 5285, ＞264mm＜, Price: E **Similar models:** without cars – 5284

◉ Fleischmann, bogie-bolster wagon, 5286, ＞228mm＜, Price: D

◉ Fleischmann, low-bed flat wagon with generator, 5299, ＞290mm＜, Price: F

◉ Fleischmann, parcels and freight crew wagon, 5300, ＞98mm＜, Price: D
**Similar models:** with tail lights (⚲) – 5301 (Price: E)

◉ Fleischmann, covered wagon, 5330, ＞125mm＜, Price: D

◉ Fleischmann, covered wagon, 5335, ＞169mm＜, Price: D

◉ Fleischmann, box van, 5350, ＞105mm＜, Price: D

◉ Fleischmann, box van with brakeman's cab, 5355, ＞110mm＜, Price: Z

# German Federal Republic (DB)

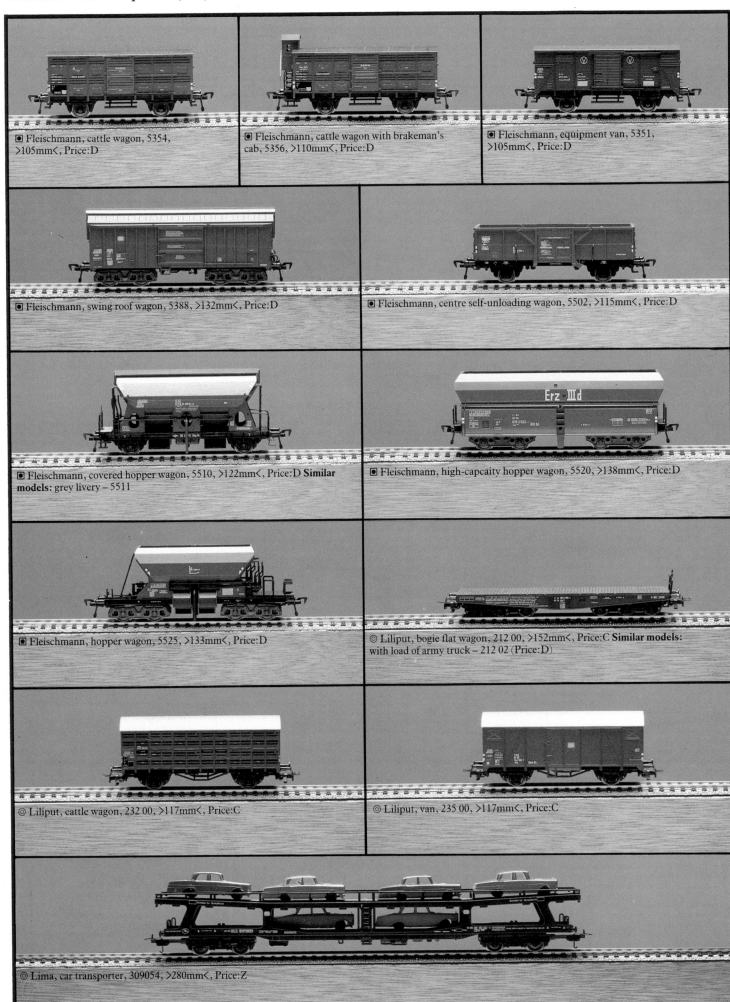

◉ Fleischmann, cattle wagon, 5354, >105mm<, Price:D

◉ Fleischmann, cattle wagon with brakeman's cab, 5356, >110mm<, Price:D

◉ Fleischmann, equipment van, 5351, >105mm<, Price:D

◉ Fleischmann, swing roof wagon, 5388, >132mm<, Price:D

◉ Fleischmann, centre self-unloading wagon, 5502, >115mm<, Price:D

◉ Fleischmann, covered hopper wagon, 5510, >122mm<, Price:D **Similar models:** grey livery – 5511

◉ Fleischmann, high-capcaity hopper wagon, 5520, >138mm<, Price:D

◉ Fleischmann, hopper wagon, 5525, >133mm<, Price:D

◎ Liliput, bogie flat wagon, 212 00, >152mm<, Price:C **Similar models:** with load of army truck – 212 02 (Price:D)

◎ Liliput, cattle wagon, 232 00, >117mm<, Price:C

◎ Liliput, van, 235 00, >117mm<, Price:C

◎ Lima, car transporter, 309054, >280mm<, Price:Z

◎ Lima, car transporter, 309062, >280mm<, Price:Z

◎ Lima, hopper wagon, 302891, >139mm<, Price:Z

◎ Lima, bogie low-sided wagon with stakes, 309042, >160mm<, Price:Z

◎ Lima, covered wagon, 303566, Price:Z

◎ Lima, high-sided wagon, 309064, >160mm<, Price:Z

◎ Lima, flat wagon with four spherical containers, 302841, >168mm<, Price:Z **Similar models:** 'Slottenap' containers – 302842

◎ Lima, container wagon, 302845, >170mm<, Price:Z **Similar model:** with one DB container – 302859

◎ Lima, covered wagon with sliding roof, 303181, >161mm<, Price:Z

◎ Lima, high-sided wagon, 309043, >205mm<, Price:Z

◎ Lima, special wagon with load, 309052, >220mm<, Price:Z **Similar models:** with transformer – 309056 (Price:Z)

◎ Lima, open wagon with cover, 303178, >121mm<, Price:Z

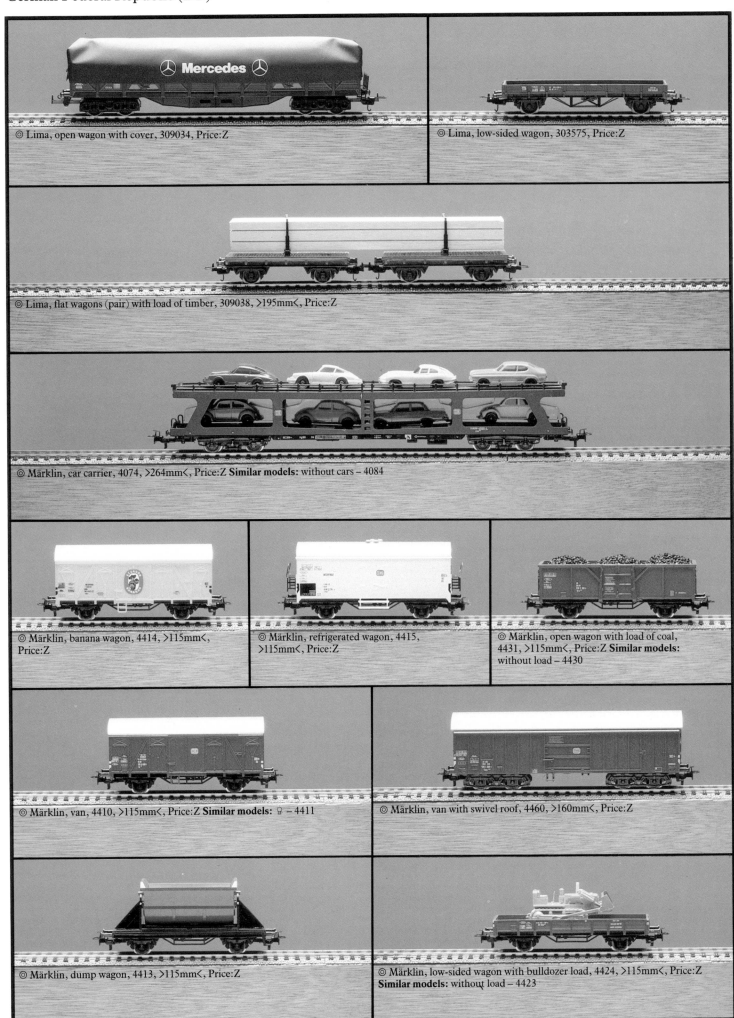

◎ Lima, open wagon with cover, 309034, Price:Z

◎ Lima, low-sided wagon, 303575, Price:Z

◎ Lima, flat wagons (pair) with load of timber, 309038, >195mm<, Price:Z

◎ Märklin, car carrier, 4074, >264mm<, Price:Z **Similar models:** without cars – 4084

◎ Märklin, banana wagon, 4414, >115mm<, Price:Z

◎ Märklin, refrigerated wagon, 4415, >115mm<, Price:Z

◎ Märklin, open wagon with load of coal, 4431, >115mm<, Price:Z **Similar models:** without load – 4430

◎ Märklin, van, 4410, >115mm<, Price:Z **Similar models:** ⚲ – 4411

◎ Märklin, van with swivel roof, 4460, >160mm<, Price:Z

◎ Märklin, dump wagon, 4413, >115mm<, Price:Z

◎ Märklin, low-sided wagon with bulldozer load, 4424, >115mm<, Price:Z **Similar models:** without load – 4423

◎ Märklin, bogie low-sided wagon with load of bulldozer and shovel loader, 4474, >160mm<, Price:Z **Similar models:** without load – 4473; with tarpaulin cover – 4475

◎ Märklin, telescoping wagon, 4693, >138mm<, Price:Z

◎ Märklin, crane, 4671, >90mm<, Price:Z (low-sided wagon 4423 recommended as support wagon)

◎ Märklin, car carrier, 4613, >115mm<, Price:Z **Similar models:** without load of cars – 4612

◎ Märklin, ore wagon, 4610, >95mm<, Price:Z

◎ Märklin, depressed centre flat wagon loaded with crate, 4618, >250mm<, Price:Z **Similar models:** loaded with transformer – 4617

◎ Märklin, van, 4627, >133mm<, Price:Z

◎ Märklin, wagon with sliding roof and sides, 4633, >157mm<, Price:Z

◎ Märklin, wagon with sliding roof, 4619, >115mm<, Price:Z

◎ Märklin, timber wagon, 4665, >195mm<, Price:Z

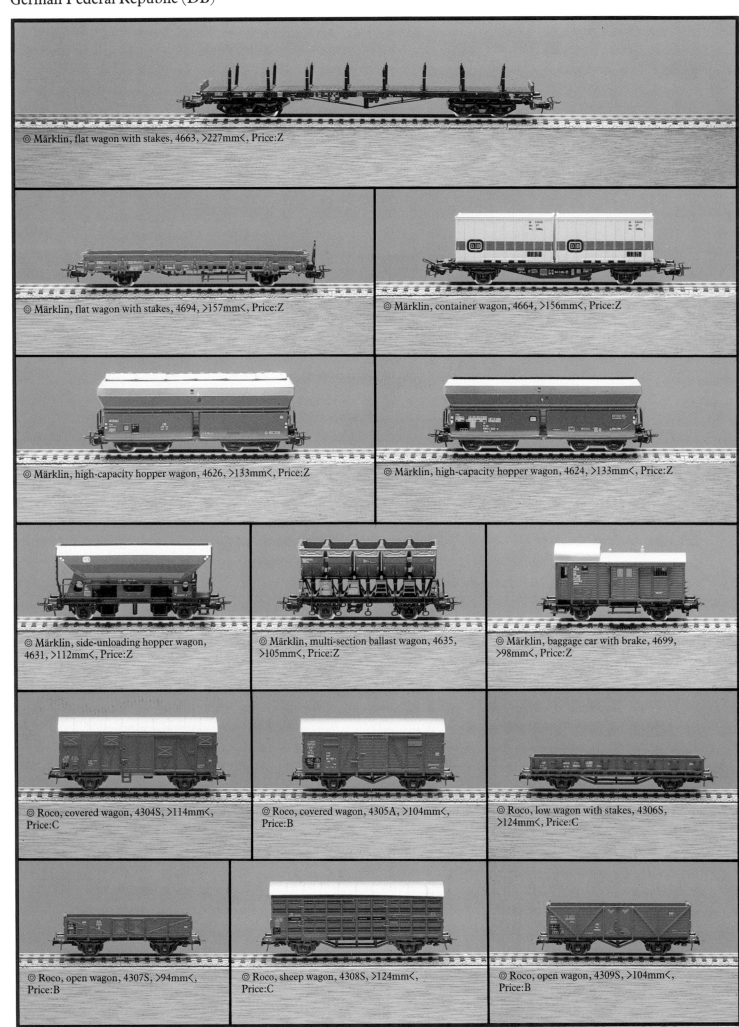

◎ Märklin, flat wagon with stakes, 4663, >227mm<, Price:Z

◎ Märklin, flat wagon with stakes, 4694, >157mm<, Price:Z

◎ Märklin, container wagon, 4664, >156mm<, Price:Z

◎ Märklin, high-capacity hopper wagon, 4626, >133mm<, Price:Z

◎ Märklin, high-capacity hopper wagon, 4624, >133mm<, Price:Z

◎ Märklin, side-unloading hopper wagon, 4631, >112mm<, Price:Z

◎ Märklin, multi-section ballast wagon, 4635, >105mm<, Price:Z

◎ Märklin, baggage car with brake, 4699, >98mm<, Price:Z

◎ Roco, covered wagon, 4304S, >114mm<, Price:C

◎ Roco, covered wagon, 4305A, >104mm<, Price:B

◎ Roco, low wagon with stakes, 4306S, >124mm<, Price:C

◎ Roco, open wagon, 4307S, >94mm<, Price:B

◎ Roco, sheep wagon, 4308S, >124mm<, Price:C

◎ Roco, open wagon, 4309S, >104mm<, Price:B

◎ Roco, covered wagon, 4310S, >114mm<, Price:C

◎ Roco, open wagon, 4302S, >114mm<, Price:B

◎ Roco, low-sided wagon, 4303A, >94mm<, Price:B

◎ Roco, refrigerated fish wagon, 4312A, >124mm<, Price:C

◎ Roco, lime wagon, 4313S, >94mm<, Price:C

◎ Roco, open wagon, 4314S, >94mm<, Price:C

◎ Roco, hinged top wagon with brakeman's cab, 4389A, >107mm<, Price:D

◎ Roco, bogie covered wagon, 4369A, >206mm<, Price:D

◎ Roco, brake van, 4372S, >122mm<, Price:D

◎ Roco, ballast wagon, 4334A, >79mm<, Price:D

◎ Roco, covered wagon with brake platform, 4374S, >127mm<, Price:D

◎ Roco, covered wagon, 4375S, >122mm<, Price:D

◎ Roco, hopper wagon with coal load, 4335A, >111mm<, Price:D

◎ Roco, centre well wagon, 44313A, >124mm<, Price:C

◎ Roco, refrigerated wagon, 4339S, >167mm<, Price:D **Similar models:** without outside compressor – 44310A

# German Federal Republic (DB)

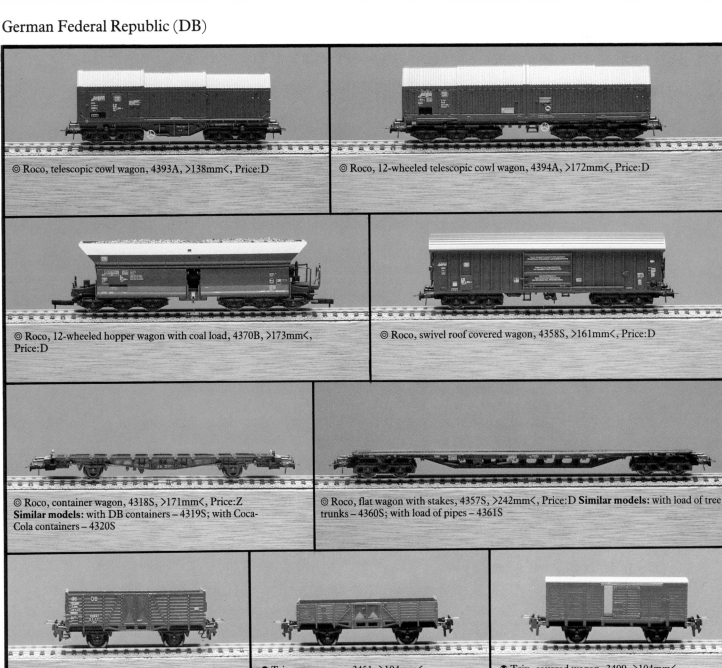

◎ Roco, telescopic cowl wagon, 4393A, >138mm<, Price:D

◎ Roco, 12-wheeled telescopic cowl wagon, 4394A, >172mm<, Price:D

◎ Roco, 12-wheeled hopper wagon with coal load, 4370B, >173mm<, Price:D

◎ Roco, swivel roof covered wagon, 4358S, >161mm<, Price:D

◎ Roco, container wagon, 4318S, >171mm<, Price:Z **Similar models:** with DB containers – 4319S; with Coca-Cola containers – 4320S

◎ Roco, flat wagon with stakes, 4357S, >242mm<, Price:D **Similar models:** with load of tree trunks – 4360S; with load of pipes – 4361S

☻ Trix, open wagon, 3414, >104mm<, Price:D

☻ Trix, open wagon, 3451, >104mm<, Price:C **Similar models:** with load – 3452; green, without load – 3413

☻ Trix, covered wagon, 3409, >104mm<, Price:C **Similar model:** brown livery – 3453; banana wagon (yellow) – 3408

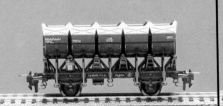

☻ Trix, hopper wagon, 3455, >102mm<, Price:D

☻ Trix, low wagon with stakes and brakeman's cab, 3436, >141mm<, Price:D

☻ Trix, open wagon, 3450, >74mm<, Price:B

☻ Trix, guard's van, 3454, >95mm<, Price:C

☻ Trix, car transporter, 3463, >255mm<, Price:E **Similar models:** ◎ coupling – 3663

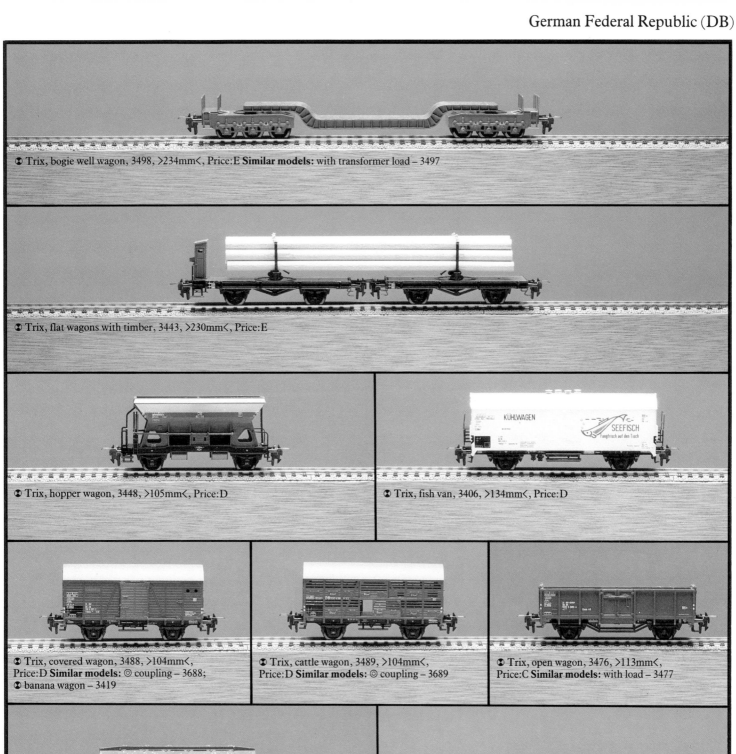

⚙ Trix, bogie well wagon, 3498, >234mm<, Price:E **Similar models:** with transformer load – 3497

⚙ Trix, flat wagons with timber, 3443, >230mm<, Price:E

⚙ Trix, hopper wagon, 3448, >105mm<, Price:D

⚙ Trix, fish van, 3406, >134mm<, Price:D

⚙ Trix, covered wagon, 3488, >104mm<, Price:D **Similar models:** ◎ coupling – 3688; ⚙ banana wagon – 3419

⚙ Trix, cattle wagon, 3489, >104mm<, Price:D **Similar models:** ◎ coupling – 3689

⚙ Trix, open wagon, 3476, >113mm<, Price:C **Similar models:** with load – 3477

⚙ Trix, lime wagon, 3433, >113mm<, Price:D **Similar models:** ◎ coupling – 3633

⚙ Trix, container wagon, 3466, >110mm<, Price:C **Similar models:** ◎ coupling – 3666

⚙ Trix, high-capacity wagon, 3487, >130mm<, Price:D

◎ Electrotren, Transfesa van, 1403, >145mm<, Price:D

157

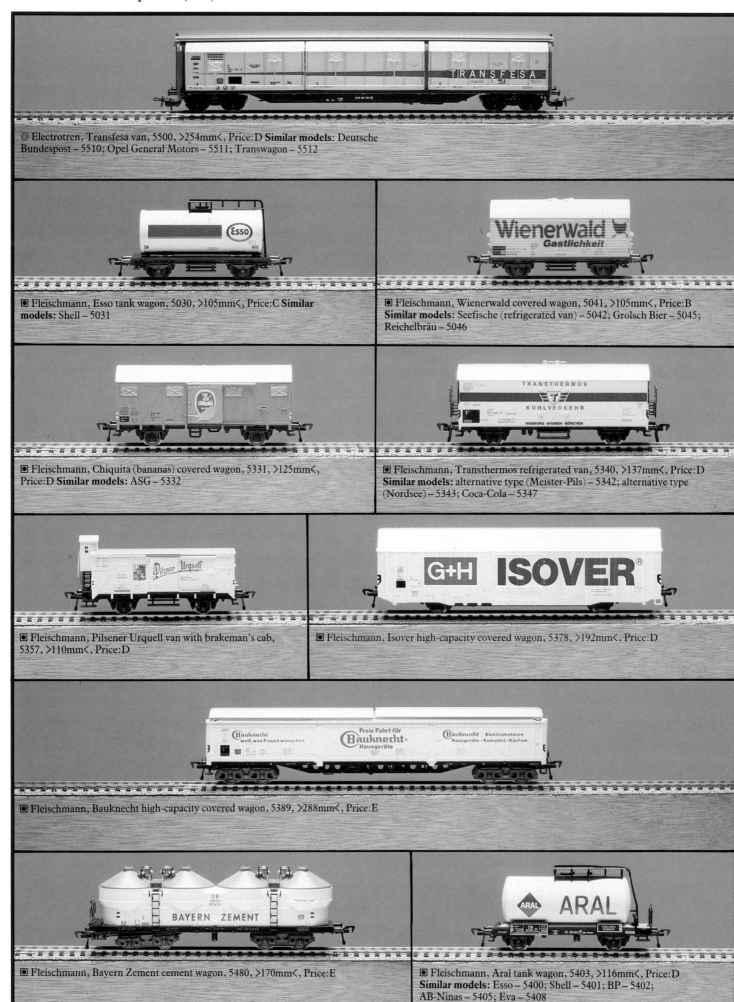

◎ Electrotren, Transfesa van, 5500, >254mm<, Price:D **Similar models**: Deutsche Bundespost – 5510; Opel General Motors – 5511; Transwagon – 5512

◙ Fleischmann, Esso tank wagon, 5030, >105mm<, Price:C **Similar models**: Shell – 5031

◙ Fleischmann, Wienerwald covered wagon, 5041, >105mm<, Price:B **Similar models**: Seefische (refrigerated van) – 5042; Grolsch Bier – 5045; Reichelbräu – 5046

◙ Fleischmann, Chiquita (bananas) covered wagon, 5331, >125mm<, Price:D **Similar models**: ASG – 5332

◙ Fleischmann, Transthermos refrigerated van, 5340, >137mm<, Price:D **Similar models**: alternative type (Meister-Pils) – 5342; alternative type (Nordsee) – 5343; Coca-Cola – 5347

◙ Fleischmann, Pilsener Urquell van with brakeman's cab, 5357, >110mm<, Price:D

◙ Fleischmann, Isover high-capacity covered wagon, 5378, >192mm<, Price:D

◙ Fleischmann, Bauknecht high-capacity covered wagon, 5389, >288mm<, Price:E

◙ Fleischmann, Bayern Zement cement wagon, 5480, >170mm<, Price:E

◙ Fleischmann, Aral tank wagon, 5403, >116mm<, Price:D **Similar models**: Esso – 5400; Shell – 5401; BP – 5402; AB-Ninas – 5405; Eva – 5408

◉ Fleischmann, BP bogie tank wagon, 5472, >165mm<, Price:D
**Similar models:** Esso – 5470; Shell – 5471; Aral – 5473; Eva – 5475

◎ Liliput, Löwenbräu beer wagon, with brakeman's cab, 215 00, >106mm<, Price:D

◎ Liliput, Interfrigo refrigerated wagon, 221 00, >117mm<, Price:C **Similar models:** Coco-Cola – 221 01

◎ Liliput, Thyssen waterproof wagon, 222 00, >152mm<, Price:D

◎ Liliput, Texaco tank wagon, 250 11, >100mm<, Price:C **Similar models:** BP – 250 03; Aral – 250 04; Gulf – 250 15; Shell – 250 00

◎ Lima, Esso tank wagon, 302711, >116mm<, Price:Z **Similar models:** Shell – 302713; Aral – 302714

◎ Lima, Uces cement wagon, 302806, >113mm<, Price:Z **Similar models:** Phoenix – 302807

◎ Lima, Shell bogie gas tank wagon, 302904, >190mm<, Price:Z

◎ Lima, ÖMV bogie tank wagon, 302915, >190mm<, Price:Z

◎ Lima, Interfrigo refrigerated wagon, 303103, >126mm<, Price:Z **Similar models:** Spatenbräu – 303111

◎ Lima, Gullfiber covered wagon, 303112, >126mm<, Price:Z

◎ Lima, ASG covered wagon, 303164, >121mm<, Price:Z

◎ Lima, VAW telescopic covered wagon, 303186, >132mm<, Price:Z

# German Federal Republic (DB)

◎ Lima, Staufen-Bräu refrigerated wagon, 303192, >242mm<, Price:Z

◎ Märklin, König-Brauerei refrigerated wagon, 4418, >115mm<, Price:Z **Similar models:** Apollinaris – 4426; Bitburger – 4421; Capri-Sonne – 4425; Pepsi – 4419; Wicküler-Küpper – 4422

◎ Märklin, Aral tank wagon, 4440, >115mm<, Price:Z **Similar models:** Esso – 4441; Shell – 4442

◎ Märklin, wine wagon (Upper Rhine Wine Producers), 4432, >115mm<, Price:Z

◎ Märklin, BP tank wagon, 4644, >100mm<, Price:Z **Similar models:** Aral – 4646

◎ Märklin, Esso bogie tank wagon, 4650, >164mm<, Price:Z **Similar models:** BP – 4653; Shell – 4651; Texaco – 4652

◎ Roco, VTG high-capacity covered wagon, 4380A, >230mm<, Price:D

◎ Roco, Peine-Salzgitter 12-wheeled hopper wagon with coal load, 4370A, >173mm<, Price:D

◎ Roco, Königsbacher covered wagon, 4301C, >104mm<, Price:C

◎ Roco, Dinckelacker covered wagon, 4305C, >104mm<, Price:B

◎ Roco, Stuttgarter Hofbräu refrigerated wagon, 4339B, >167mm<, Price:D

◎ Roco, VTG tank wagon, 4336A, >102mm<, Price:D **Similar models:** Esso – 4336B; Calpam – 4336C; Texaco – 4336E

◎ Roco, VTG tank wagon, 4337A, >102mm<, Price:D **Similar models:** Shell – 4337B; ÖMV – 4337D; Aral – 4337E

◎ Roco, VTG bogie tank wagon, 4356A, >166mm<, Price:Z

◎ Roco, VTG bogie tank wagon, 4365A, >179mm<, Price: D **Similar models:** AGIP – 4365C; Esso – 4365D

◉ Fleischmann, dump truck, 5500, >83mm<, Price: A

◉ Fleischmann, brakedown train, 5597, >485mm<, Price: K (also available as separate items)

◉ Fleischmann, crane, 5019, >99mm<, Price: D

◎ Liliput, steam crane, 210 00, >122mm<, Price: E **Similar models:** red – 210 01; yellow – 210 02; blue – 210 03

◎ Lima, crane with support wagon, 309058, Price: Z

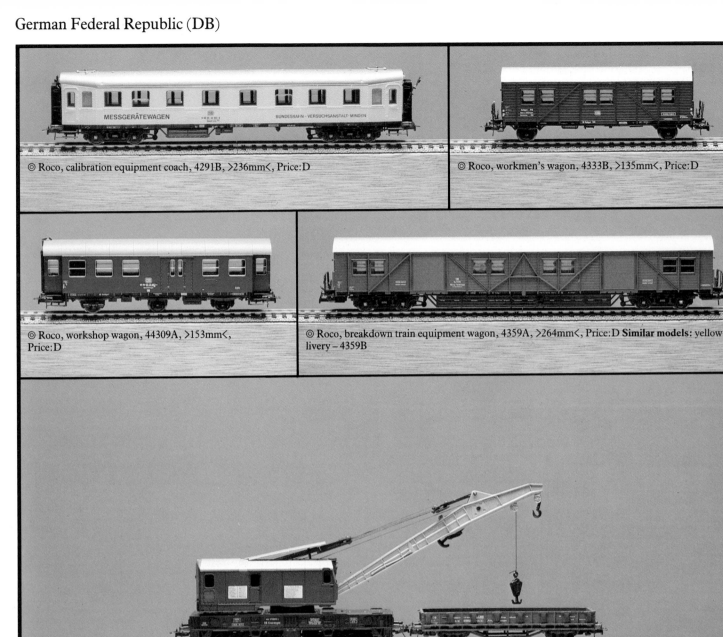

◎ Roco, calibration equipment coach, 4291B, >236mm<, Price:D

◎ Roco, workmen's wagon, 4333B, >135mm<, Price:D

◎ Roco, workshop wagon, 44309A, >153mm<, Price:D

◎ Roco, breakdown train equipment wagon, 4359A, >264mm<, Price:D **Similar models:** yellow livery – 4359B

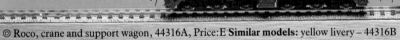

◎ Roco, crane and support wagon, 44316A, Price:E **Similar models:** yellow livery – 44316B

## HOe Narrow Gauge

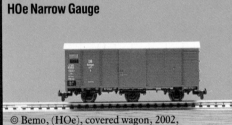

◎ Bemo, (HOe), covered wagon, 2002, >97mm<, Price:D **Similar models:** HOm – 2202

◎ Bemo, (HOe), low-sided wagon, 2001, >97mm<, Price:D **Similar models:** HOm – 2201

◎ Bemo, (HOe), covered wagon, 2004, >97mm<, Price:D **Similar models:** HOm – 2204; white livery, HOe – 2005; white livery, HOm – 2205

◎ Bemo, (HOe), timber or log carrier, 2006, >97mm<, Price:D **Similar models:** HOm – 2206

◎ Bemo, (HOe), Buffer wagon, 2003, >101mm<, Price:D **Similar models:** HOm – 2203

◎ Bemo, wagon for carrying 9mm and 12mm rolling stock, 2401, >145mm<, Price:D

## Also available

### DB steam locomotives

◎ Liliput, 42 class, 42 03, >268mm<, Price:M **Similar models:** ≲ – 42 08
◎ Liliput, 45 class, 45 03, >310mm<, Price:N **Similar models:** with Witte smoke deflectors – 45 04 (Price:N); Witte smoke deflectors, ≲ – 45 09 (Price:M)
◎ Liliput, 52 class, 52 03, >268mm<, Price:M **Similar models:** ≲ – 52 08 (Price:M)
◎ Liliput, 078 class (ex Prussian T18), UIC inscription, 78 01, >170mm<, ♀, Price:L **Similar models:** with straight cab roof – 78 03; with standard cab – 78 04
◎ Liliput, 62 class, 103 00, >190mm<, Price:K **Similar models:** with large smoke deflectors – 103 01
◎ Liliput, 050 class, 105 03, >307mm<, Price:N **Similar models:** ≲ – 105 08 (Price:M)
◎ Liliput, 38 class, 109 00, >236mm<, Price:L **Similar models:** ≲ – 109 05; O38 class with box-type tender, UIC inscription, DC – 109 01 (Price:L); 038 class with box tender, ≲ – 109 06 (Price:K)
◎ Liliput, 40 03, Price:N **Similar models:** with Witte smoke deflectors – 40 04
◎ Lima, 10 class, 203016LG, Price:Z
◎ Roco, 80 class, 4114A, >111mm<, Price:J

### DB electric locomotives

▣ Fleischmann, E44 class, ⊟, 4330, >182mm<, ♀, Price:L
▣ Fleischmann, 132 class, ⊟, 4369, >160mm<, ♀, Price:L
◎ Liliput, E94 class, ⊟, 119 00, >212mm<, ♀, Price:L **Similar models:** ≲ – 119 05
◎ Lima, 120 class, ⊕, 208143LG, Price:Z **Similar models:** ⊟, 208143LGP
◎ Roco, 181 class, ⊟, 4142A, >205mm<, ♀, Price:K **Similar models:** dark blue livery – 4142B
◎ Roco, 169 class, ⊟, 4128A, >89mm<, Price:F **Similar models:** red livery – 4128B
☮ Trix, 112 (E10) class, ≡, ⊟, 2245, >189mm<, ♀, Price:K **Similar models:** ◎, 12V DC, ems fitted – 2648 (Price:L)

### DB electric railcars

◎ Lima, ET30 class, 149800GP, Price:Z **Similar models:** 430 class (green and grey livery) – 149801GP. Also available as separate items

### DB diesel locomotives

◎ Lima, V300 class, 201644LG, Price:Z **Similar models:** red and black livery – 201643LG
☮ Trix, 211 (V100) class, ≡, 2267, >142mm<, ♀, Price:J

### DB diesel railcars

◎ Lima, VT137 class, 208141LG, Price:Z
◎ Lima, VS145 class trailer (no motor), 309123, Price:Z
◎ Lima, 515 class, 208037LG, >258mm<, Price:Z **Similar models:** blue and beige – 208039LG
◎ Märklin, rail bus, ≲, 3016, >147mm<, ♀, Price:Z

### DB coaches

▣ Fleischmann, track cleaning wagon, 5569, >99mm<, Price:E
▣ Fleischmann, 1st and 2nd class coach, 5121, >245mm<, Price:E
☮ Fleischmann, 6-wheeled 2nd class coach, 5091, >154mm<, Price:D
◎ Liliput, baggage car, 289 00, >250mm<, Price:D
◎ Liliput, baggage car with mail compartment, 292 03, >254mm<, Price:E **Similar models:** without look-out – 293 03
◎ Liliput, 'skirted' 1st class coach with UIC inscription, 831 00, >247mm<, Price:D
◎ Liliput, 'skirted' 3rd class coach for Rheingold, 833 03, >240mm<, Price:D
◎ Liliput, 'skirted' 1st, 2nd, and 3rd class coach for Rheingold, 835 03, >240mm<, Price:D
◎ Liliput, 'skirted' composite coach with UIC inscription, 832 00, >240mm<, Price:D
◎ Liliput, 'skirted' 2nd class coach with UIC inscription, 833 00, >240mm<, Price:D
◎ Liliput, luggage van with UIC inscription, 839 00 **Similar models:** 1960s (epoch III) lettering – 841 03
◎ Liliput, 3rd class coach, UIC inscription, 843 00, >249mm<, Price:E
◎ Liliput, 1st class express coach, 842 03, >249mm<, Price:E **Similar models:** green livery – 841 03
◎ Liliput, 2nd class express coach, 843 03, >249mm<, Price:E **Similar models:** – 844 03
◎ Liliput, 1st and 2nd class express, 845 03, >240mm<, Price:E ◎ Liliput, 2nd class express coach, 896 00, >304mm<, Price:E **Similar models:** beige and blue livery – 896 04
◎ Liliput, couchette coach, 897 04, >304mm<, Price:E **Similar models:** blue livery – 897 00
◎ Liliput, 2nd class coach hired from SBB, 878 03, >261mm<, Price:D
◎ Lima, 1st and 2nd class double-deck coach, 309264L, Price:Z
◎ Märklin, dining car, 4097, >270mm<, Price:Z
◎ Märklin, 2nd class driving end commuter coach, 4160, >264mm<, ♀, Price:Z
◎ Märklin, TEE dining car, ⊕, 4153, >264mm<, Price:Z

### DB coaches

◎ Mehanotehnika, Pullman restaurant car, T201, >254mm<, Price:Z
◎ Roco, 1st class coach, 4257A, >264mm<, Price:D **Similar models:** blue livery – 4296S
☮ Trix, 2nd class coach, 3303, >132mm<, Price:D **Similar models:** red livery – 3310; private railway livery (red and cream) – 3312

### Private-owner coaches

◎ Liliput, Mitropa dining car, 262 00, >228mm<, Price:Z
◎ Liliput, Mitropa sleeping car, 267 00, >228mm<, Price:Z
◎ Liliput, Mitropa 'skirted' dining car, 836 02, >264mm<, ♀, Price:Z
◎ Liliput, DSG dining car, 836 03, >264mm<, Price:D
◎ Roco, DSG sleeping car, 4260S, >264mm<, Price:E
☮ Trix, DSG dining car, 3384, >235mm<, Price:Z
☮ Trix, DSG sleeping car, 3383, >235mm<, Price:Z
☮ Trix, Mitropa dining car, 3373, >233mm<, Price:Z **Similar models:** ◎ coupling – 3773

### DB wagons

◎ Liliput, low-loader for trucks or lorries, 200 00, >158mm<, Price:E
◎ Liliput, 14-axle carrier, with transformer, 209 00, >380mm<, Price:F
◎ Liliput, centre tipper wagon, 211 00, Price:D
◎ Liliput, acid carrier with brakeman's cab, 207 00, >127mm<, Price:C
◎ Liliput, covered wagon with brakeman's cab, 214 00, >106mm<, Price:C
◎ Liliput, bogie hopper wagon, 220 00, >114mm<, Price:D
◎ Liliput, high-sided open wagon, 244 00, >163mm<, Price:D
◎ Liliput, van, 253 00, >103mm<, Price:C
◎ Lima, bogie flat wagon, 309075, >168mm<, Price:Z
◎ Lima, hopper wagon, 303570, Price:Z
◎ Lima, car transporter, 303573, Price:Z
◎ Roco, open wagon, 4311A, >94mm<, Price:B
◎ Roco, covered wagon, 4301, >104mm<, Price:B
☮ Trix, open wagon with brakeman's cab, 3416, >113mm<, Price:D

### Private-owner wagons

◎ Electrotren, Transfesa phosphorus tank wagon, 5420, >160mm<, Price:D
◎ Liliput, VAW bulk carrier, 240 00, >158mm<, Price:D
◎ Liliput, Hoechst-Frigen high-pressure gas tank wagon, 251 00, >100mm<, Price:D
◎ Liliput, Texaco bogie tank wagon, 258 09, >172mm<, Price:D
◎ Lima, Isover covered wagon, 303576, Price:Z
◎ Roco, VTG bogie tank wagon, 4335A, >166mm<, Price:D **Similar models:** Shell – 4335B; Aral – 4335C
☮ Trix, Donau-Kies hopper wagon type Ed 084, 3421, >105mm<, Price:Z
☮ Trix, Mela fruit and vegetable wagon, 3445, >134mm<, Price:Z **Similar models:** ◎ coupling – 3645; Patrizier-Bräu beer wagon, ☮ – 3467; Patrizier-Bräu beer wagon, ◎ – 3667
☮ Trix, Shell tank wagon, 3427, >103mm<, Price:Z **Similar models:** Aral – 3428; Esso – 3429; BP – 3432
☮ Trix, BP bogie tank wagon, 3491, >140mm<, Price:Z **Similar models:** Esso – 3492; Aral – 3494; Shell – 3496

### Miscellaneous

◎ Liliput, Snowplough on tender, 309 09, >130mm<, Price:D
◎ Roco, workmen's dormitory wagon, 44308A, >153mm<, Price:D

## Also available

### DB diesel locomotives

◎ Bemo, (HOe) V51 class, 1001, >113mm<, Price:K **Similar models:** HOe 251 class – 1003; HOm V52 class – 1201; HOm 252 class – 1203

# German Federal Republic

## Königlich Bayrische Staatsbahn

What are now the states of West and East Germany result from a turbulent history. The small states that made up Germany were unified into Imperial Germany in 1871 but the largest states all retained a degree of autonomy and all were responsible for their own railway systems. The Royal Bavarian State Railway (Königlich Bayrische Staatsbahn, the K.Bay.Sts.B) was the most important. It became part of Deutsche Reichsbahn in the 1920s.

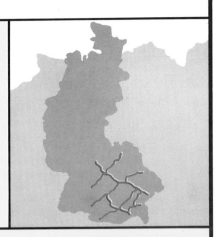

### Z Gauge

⊞ Märklin, 3rd class coach, 8730, >87mm<, Price:Z

**K.BAY.STS.B steam locomotives**
⊞ Märklin, S3/6 class, =, 8892, >106mm<, ☼, Price:Z

### N Gauge

⊖ Arnold, Gt2 x 4/4 class, 2276, >110mm<, ☼, Price:L

⊖ Minitrix, G3/4H class, 2903, >114mm<, ☼, Price:L

⊖ Minitrix, baggage/mail van, 3001, >60mm<, Price:C **Similar models:** maroon livery – 3068

⊖ Minitrix, passenger coach, 3002, >64mm<, Price:C **Similar models:** brown livery – 3069

⊖ Minitrix, 1st and 2nd class coach, 3160, >85mm<, Price:D

⊖ Minitrix, 3rd class coach, 3161, >85mm<, Price:D

⊖ Minitrix, luggage van, 3162, >85mm<, Price:D

⊖ Minitrix, 3rd class coach (old type), 3064, >53mm<, Price:D

⊖ Minitrix, brake van, 3200, >53mm<, ☼, Price:D

⊖ Minitrix, covered goods wagon, 3202, >58mm<, Price:C

⊖ Minitrix, open goods wagon, 3203, >60mm<, Price:C

**Also available**
**K.BAY.STS.B steam locomotives**
⊖ Arnold, S3/6 class, 2530, >160mm<, ☼, Price:L

**K.BAY.STS.B. wagons**
⊖ Minitrix, special 'overseas' wagon, 3212, >58mm<, Price:C

**Private-owner wagons**
⊖ Minitrix, Hacker-Bräu beer wagon, 3218, >55mm<, Price:D

**HO/OO Gauge**

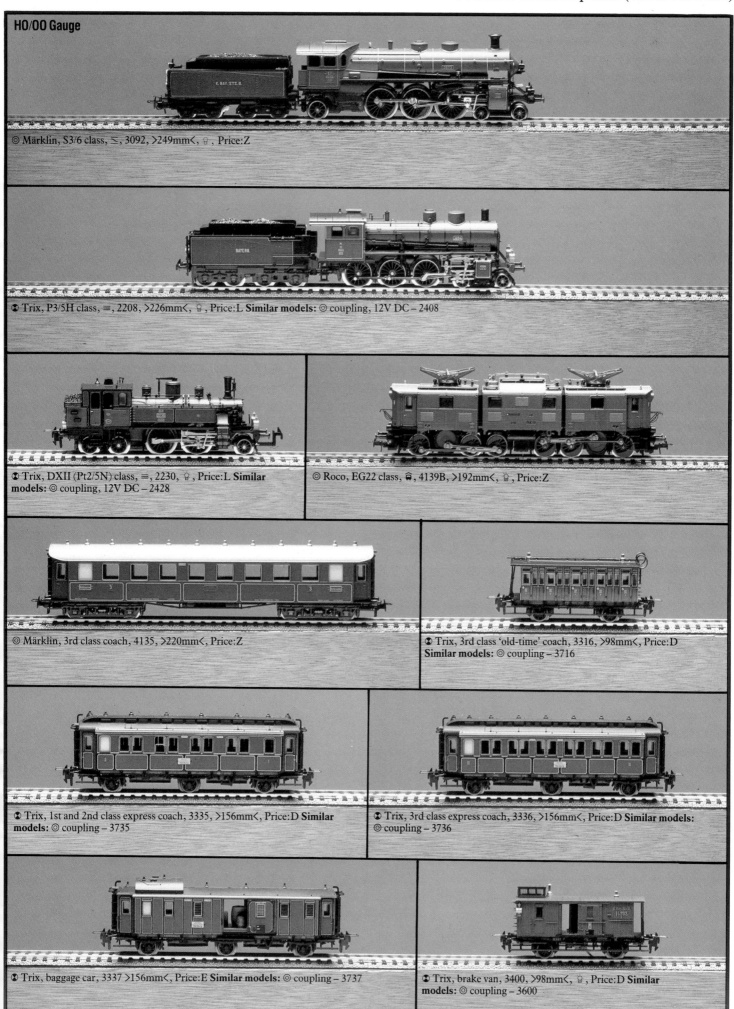

◎ Märklin, S3/6 class, ⌣, 3092, >249mm<, ♀, Price:Z

☻ Trix, P3/5H class, ≡, 2208, >226mm<, ♀, Price:L **Similar models:** ◎ coupling, 12V DC – 2408

☻ Trix, DXII (Pt2/5N) class, ≡, 2230, ♀, Price:L **Similar models:** ◎ coupling, 12V DC – 2428

◎ Roco, EG22 class, ☗, 4139B, >192mm<, ♀, Price:Z

◎ Märklin, 3rd class coach, 4135, >220mm<, Price:Z

☻ Trix, 3rd class 'old-time' coach, 3316, >98mm<, Price:D **Similar models:** ◎ coupling – 3716

☻ Trix, 1st and 2nd class express coach, 3335, >156mm<, Price:D **Similar models:** ◎ coupling – 3735

☻ Trix, 3rd class express coach, 3336, >156mm<, Price:D **Similar models:** ◎ coupling – 3736

☻ Trix, baggage car, 3337 >156mm<, Price:E **Similar models:** ◎ coupling – 3737

☻ Trix, brake van, 3400, >98mm<, ♀, Price:D **Similar models:** ◎ coupling – 3600

# German Federal Republic (K.BAY.STS.B)

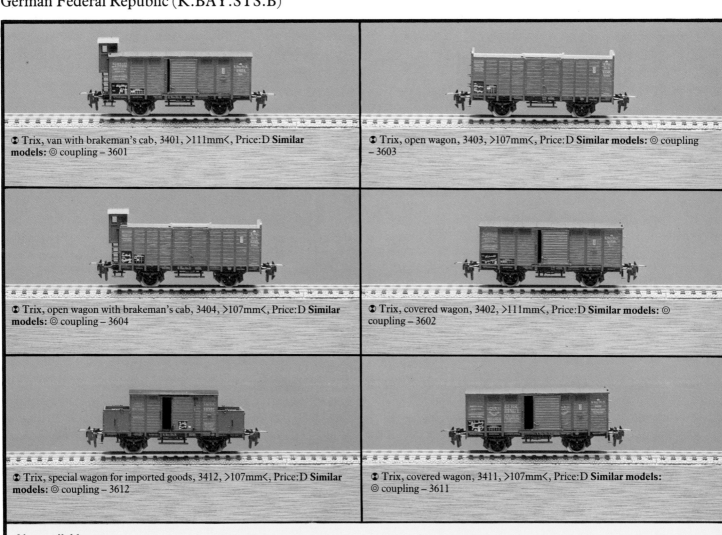

⚙ Trix, van with brakeman's cab, 3401, >111mm<, Price:D **Similar models:** ◎ coupling – 3601

⚙ Trix, open wagon, 3403, >107mm<, Price:D **Similar models:** ◎ coupling – 3603

⚙ Trix, open wagon with brakeman's cab, 3404, >107mm<, Price:D **Similar models:** ◎ coupling – 3604

⚙ Trix, covered wagon, 3402, >111mm<, Price:D **Similar models:** ◎ coupling – 3602

⚙ Trix, special wagon for imported goods, 3412, >107mm<, Price:D **Similar models:** ◎ coupling – 3612

⚙ Trix, covered wagon, 3411, >107mm<, Price:D **Similar models:** ◎ coupling – 3611

**Also available**

**K.BAY.STS.B steam locomotives**

◎ Liliput, S3/6 class, 18 00, >262mm<, Price:N **Similar models:** ⊆ – 18 05

⚙ Trix, G3/4H class, ≡, 2226, >208mm<, 💡, Price:L **Similar models:** ◎ coupling, 12V DC – 2426

**K.BAY.STS.B coaches**

⚙ Trix, 3rd class 'old-time' coach with mail compartment, 3317, >98mm<, Price:D **Similar models:** ◎ coupling – 3717

**Private-owner wagons**

⚙ Trix, Hacker-Bräu beer wagon with brakeman's cab, 3418, >104mm<, Price:D **Similar models:** ◎ coupling –3618

⚙ Trix, old-time tank wagon with brakeman's cab, 3417, >104mm<, Price:D **Similar models:** ◎ coupling – 3618

⚙ Trix, covered wagon, 3411, >107mm<, Price:D **Similar models:** ◎ coupling – 3611

# German Federal Republic

## Königlich Preussische Eisenbahn-Verwaltung

The Königlich Preussische Eisenbahn-Verwaltung (KPEV) was the Royal Prussian state railway system. Its locomotives were well designed and several Prussian standard types like the P8 (over 4,000 built) and G5 (later classes 38 and 55) were adopted as standard types for the newly formed Deutsche Reichsbahn when all the German systems were nationalized in the 1920s. Many of these locomotives lasted until the 1970s.

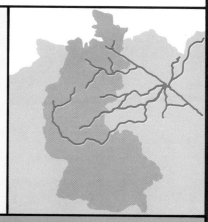

**N Gauge**

⊖ Arnold, prT18 class, 2273, >92mm<, ♀, Price:J

⊖ Arnold, prG8 class, 2518, >118mm<, ♀, Price:K

⊖ Arnold, 36 class, 2545, >110mm<, ♀, Price:L

⊖ Minitrix, T3 class, 2047, >52mm<, Price:F

⊖ Arnold, ET88 class, motor unit, ♀, 2930, >106mm<, ♀, Price:K

⊖ Arnold, EB88 class, intermediate coach, 3394, >121mm<, Price:D

⊖ Arnold, ES88 class, driving trailer, 2931, >120mm<, Price:E

⊖ Arnold, 3rd class coach, 3041, >76mm<, Price: D

⊖ Arnold, 4th class coach, 3042, >76mm<, Price:D

⊖ Arnold, 2nd and 3rd class coach, 3043, >76mm<, Price:D

⊖ Arnold, old-time 3rd class coach, 3030, >55mm<, Price:C

⊖ Arnold, old-time baggage car, 3050, >62mm<, Price:C

⊖ Arnold, baggage car, 3044, >76mm<, Price:D

⊖ Arnold, 1st class coach, 3051, >78mm<, Price:D **Similar models:** green livery – 3055

⊖ Arnold, 2nd and 3rd class coach, 3052, >78mm<, Price:D **Similar models:** 1st and 2nd class coach (green livery) – 3056

⊖ Arnold, baggage car, 3053, >78mm<, Price:D **Similar models:** green livery – 3057

⊖ Arnold, 3rd class coach with brakeman's cab, 3391, >115mm<, Price:D

**Also available**
**KPEV steam locomotives**
⊖ Minitrix, S10 class, 2088, >132mm<, ♀, Price:L
**KPEV coaches**
⊖ Arnold, old-time 2nd and 3rd class coach, 3040, >69mm<, Price:C

## HO/OO Gauge

◙ Fleischmann, G.8 class, 4147, >223mm<, ⚲, Price:L

◎ Liliput, 91 (pr.T9) class, 91 01, >120mm<, Price:L
**Similar models:** DRG black livery – 91 02; DB black-red livery – 91 03

◎ Roco, baggage coach, 4209S, >118mm<, Price:D **Similar models:** green livery – 4205S

◎ Roco, 3rd class coach, 4210S, >125mm<, Price:D **Similar models:** green livery – 4206S

◎ Roco, 2nd and 3rd class coach, 4211S, >135mm<, Price:D **Similar models:** green livery – 4207S

◎ Roco, 4th class coach, 4229S, >125mm<, Price:D

◎ Roco, 3rd class coach, 4208S, >128mm<, Price:D

# German Democratic Republic

# Deutsche Reichsbahn

Deutsche Reichsbahn Gesellschaft (DRG) was the government railway system set up in the 1920s to take over the individual state railway companies. DRG disappeared in 1945 but the pre-war name of Deutsche Reichsbahn (DR) was retained for the East German railways. Lines in West Germany were called Deutsche Bundesbahn (DB). Modern DR has nearly 14,500 kilometres (9000 miles) of track, and branch lines are still very much in use.

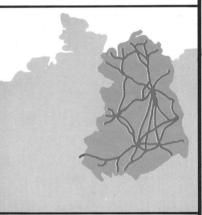

## Z Gauge

⊞ Märklin, 3rd class coach, 8731, >87mm<, Price:Z

⊞ Märklin, express baggage car, 8732, >78mm<, Price:Z

**Also available**
**DR steam locomotives**
⊞ Märklin, 18 class, =, 8891, >106mm<, ⚲, Price:Z

## N Gauge

⊖ Arnold, 89 class, 2222, >60mm<, Price:G

⊖ Arnold, 89 class (with tender), 2223, >105mm<, Price:H

⊖ Arnold, 41 class, 2511, >150mm<, ⚲, ▱, Price:L

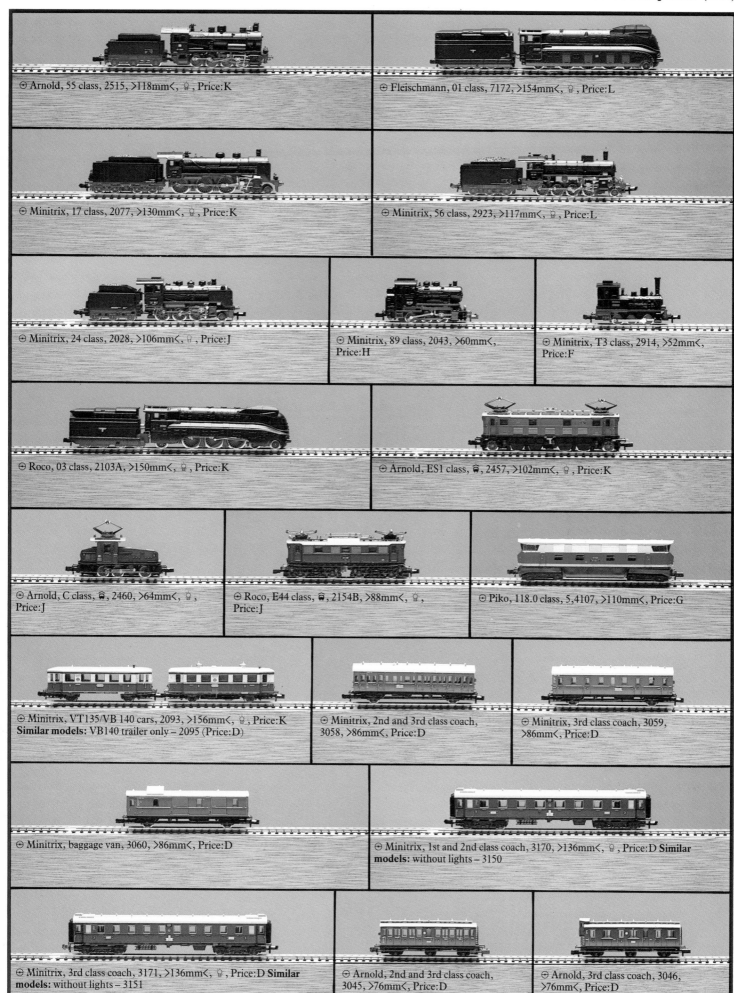

⊖ Arnold, 55 class, 2515, >118mm<, ♀, Price:K

⊖ Fleischmann, 01 class, 7172, >154mm<, ♀, Price:L

⊖ Minitrix, 17 class, 2077, >130mm<, ♀, Price:K

⊖ Minitrix, 56 class, 2923, >117mm<, ♀, Price:L

⊖ Minitrix, 24 class, 2028, >106mm<, ♀, Price:J

⊖ Minitrix, 89 class, 2043, >60mm<, Price:H

⊖ Minitrix, T3 class, 2914, >52mm<, Price:F

⊖ Roco, 03 class, 2103A, >150mm<, ♀, Price:K

⊖ Arnold, ES1 class, ☝, 2457, >102mm<, ♀, Price:K

⊖ Arnold, C class, ☝, 2460, >64mm<, ♀, Price:J

⊖ Roco, E44 class, ☝, 2154B, >88mm<, ♀, Price:J

⊖ Piko, 118.0 class, 5,4107, >110mm<, Price:G

⊖ Minitrix, VT135/VB 140 cars, 2093, >156mm<, ♀, Price:K **Similar models:** VB140 trailer only – 2095 (Price:D)

⊖ Minitrix, 2nd and 3rd class coach, 3058, >86mm<, Price:D

⊖ Minitrix, 3rd class coach, 3059, >86mm<, Price:D

⊖ Minitrix, baggage van, 3060, >86mm<, Price:D

⊖ Minitrix, 1st and 2nd class coach, 3170, >136mm<, ♀, Price:D **Similar models:** without lights – 3150

⊖ Minitrix, 3rd class coach, 3171, >136mm<, ♀, Price:D **Similar models:** without lights – 3151

⊖ Arnold, 2nd and 3rd class coach, 3045, >76mm<, Price:D

⊖ Arnold, 3rd class coach, 3046, >76mm<, Price:D

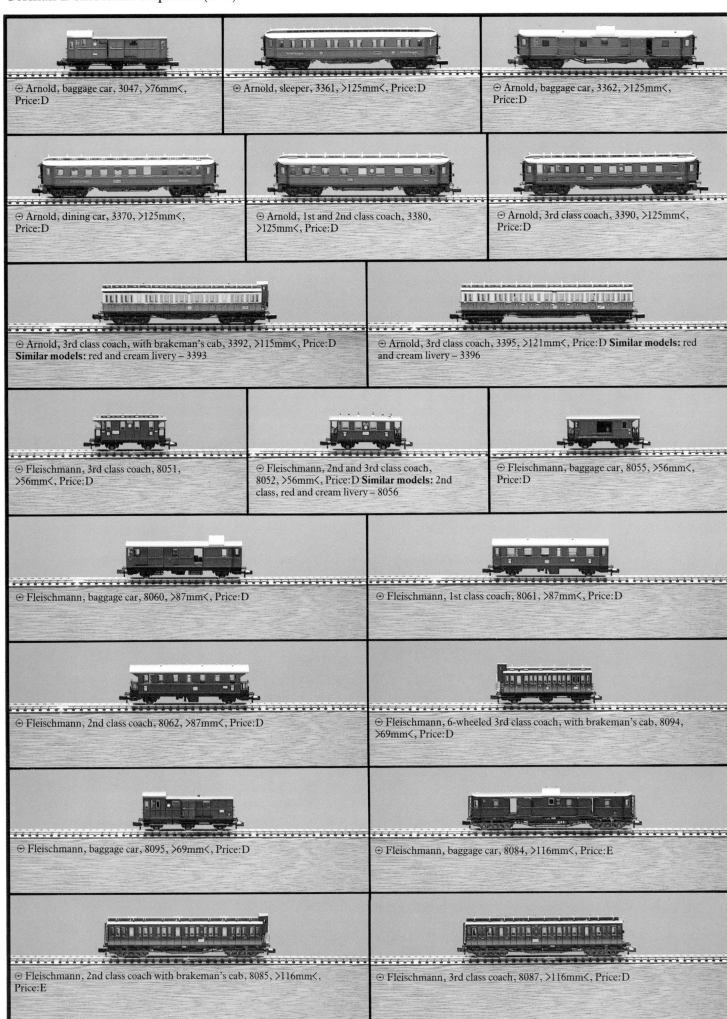

⊖ Arnold, baggage car, 3047, >76mm<, Price:D

⊖ Arnold, sleeper, 3361, >125mm<, Price:D

⊖ Arnold, baggage car, 3362, >125mm<, Price:D

⊖ Arnold, dining car, 3370, >125mm<, Price:D

⊖ Arnold, 1st and 2nd class coach, 3380, >125mm<, Price:D

⊖ Arnold, 3rd class coach, 3390, >125mm<, Price:D

⊖ Arnold, 3rd class coach, with brakeman's cab, 3392, >115mm<, Price:D **Similar models:** red and cream livery – 3393

⊖ Arnold, 3rd class coach, 3395, >121mm<, Price:D **Similar models:** red and cream livery – 3396

⊖ Fleischmann, 3rd class coach, 8051, >56mm<, Price:D

⊖ Fleischmann, 2nd and 3rd class coach, 8052, >56mm<, Price:D **Similar models:** 2nd class, red and cream livery – 8056

⊖ Fleischmann, baggage car, 8055, >56mm<, Price:D

⊖ Fleischmann, baggage car, 8060, >87mm<, Price:D

⊖ Fleischmann, 1st class coach, 8061, >87mm<, Price:D

⊖ Fleischmann, 2nd class coach, 8062, >87mm<, Price:D

⊖ Fleischmann, 6-wheeled 3rd class coach, with brakeman's cab, 8094, >69mm<, Price:D

⊖ Fleischmann, baggage car, 8095, >69mm<, Price:D

⊖ Fleischmann, baggage car, 8084, >116mm<, Price:E

⊖ Fleischmann, 2nd class coach with brakeman's cab, 8085, >116mm<, Price:E

⊖ Fleischmann, 3rd class coach, 8087, >116mm<, Price:D

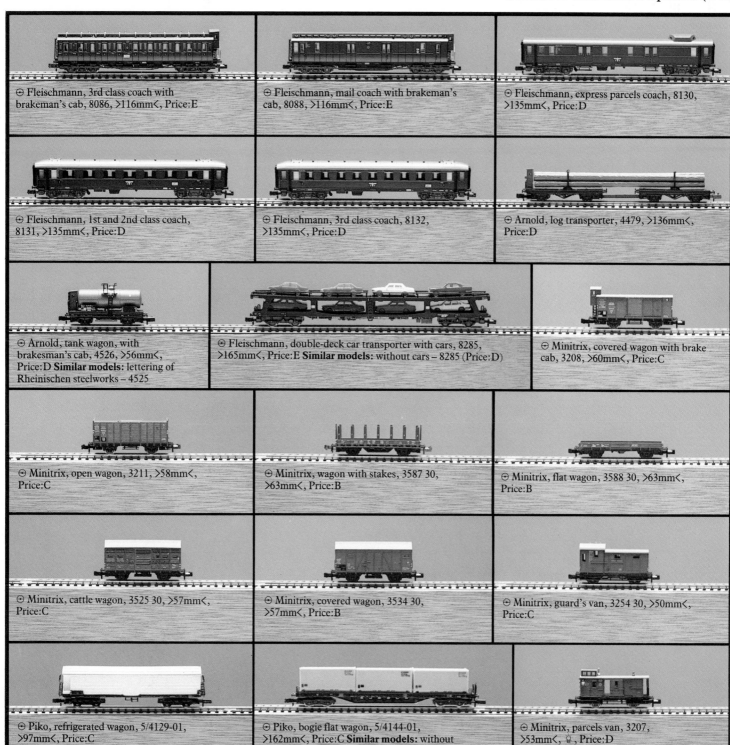

⊖ Fleischmann, 3rd class coach with brakeman's cab, 8086, >116mm<, Price:E

⊖ Fleischmann, mail coach with brakeman's cab, 8088, >116mm<, Price:E

⊖ Fleischmann, express parcels coach, 8130, >135mm<, Price:D

⊖ Fleischmann, 1st and 2nd class coach, 8131, >135mm<, Price:D

⊖ Fleischmann, 3rd class coach, 8132, >135mm<, Price:D

⊖ Arnold, log transporter, 4479, >136mm<, Price:D

⊖ Arnold, tank wagon, with brakesman's cab, 4526, >56mm<, Price:D **Similar models:** lettering of Rheinischen steelworks – 4525

⊖ Fleischmann, double-deck car transporter with cars, 8285, >165mm<, Price:E **Similar models:** without cars – 8285 (Price:D)

⊖ Minitrix, covered wagon with brake cab, 3208, >60mm<, Price:C

⊖ Minitrix, open wagon, 3211, >58mm<, Price:C

⊖ Minitrix, wagon with stakes, 3587 30, >63mm<, Price:B

⊖ Minitrix, flat wagon, 3588 30, >63mm<, Price:B

⊖ Minitrix, cattle wagon, 3525 30, >57mm<, Price:C

⊖ Minitrix, covered wagon, 3534 30, >57mm<, Price:B

⊖ Minitrix, guard's van, 3254 30, >50mm<, Price:C

⊖ Piko, refrigerated wagon, 5/4129-01, >97mm<, Price:C

⊖ Piko, bogie flat wagon, 5/4144-01, >162mm<, Price:C **Similar models:** without containers – 5/4146-01

⊖ Minitrix, parcels van, 3207, >53mm<, ⚲, Price:D

## Also available

**DR steam locomotives**
⊖ Minitrix, 54 class, 2902, >114mm<, ⚲, Price:L
⊖ Piko, 65 class, 5/4130, >110mm<, Price:H

**DR diesel locomotives**
⊖ Piko, 118.1 class, 5/4124, >110mm<, Price:G

**DR diesel railcars**
⊖ Minitrix, VT62.904 class, 2096, >132mm<, ⚲, Price:L
⊖ Minitrix, baggage car, 3172, >140mm<, ⚲, Price:D **Similar models:** without lights – 3152
⊖ Piko, VT4.12 class, 5/4105, >137mm<, ⚲, Price:F **Similar models:** trailer (unpowered) – 5/4141 (Price:D)

**DR coaches**
⊖ Piko, double-deck coaches, 5/4136-01, >450mm<, Price:F
⊖ Piko, 4-wheeled coach, 5/4135, Price:C
⊖ Piko, 4-wheeled coach, 5/4401, >86mm<, Price:C
⊖ Piko, 4-wheeled coach, 5/4403, >86mm<, Price:C
⊖ Piko, 4-wheeled coach with mail compartment, 5/4402, >86mm<, Price:C
⊖ Piko, 4-wheeled coach, 5/4405, Price:C

**DR coaches**
⊖ Piko, 4-wheeled coach with brakeman's cab, 5/4406, Price:C
⊖ Piko, 4-wheeled coach, 5/4404, >86mm<, Price:C
⊖ Piko, 4-wheeled coach, 5/4407, Price:Z

**Private-owner coaches**
⊖ Minitrix, sleeping car, 3153, >147mm<, Price:D
⊖ Minitrix, dining car, 3154, >147mm<, Price:D

**DR wagons**
⊖ Piko, open wagon, 5/4125-01, >55mm<, Price:B **Similar models:** green livery – 5/4125-015
⊖ Piko, bogie open wagon, 5/4142-01, >87mm<, Price:B
⊖ Piko, bogie open wagon, 5/4143-01, >87mm<, Price:C
⊖ Piko, covered wagon, 5/4126-01, >55mm<, Price:C **Similar models:** white livery – 5/4126-015
⊖ Piko, stool wagon, 5/4134-01, >55mm<, Price:A
⊖ Piko, cement wagon, 5/4407, Price:B
⊖ Piko, van with brakeman's compartment, 5/4133-01, >52mm<, Price:C
**Similar models:** brown livery – 5/4133-015

# German Democratic Republic (DR)

**TT Gauge**

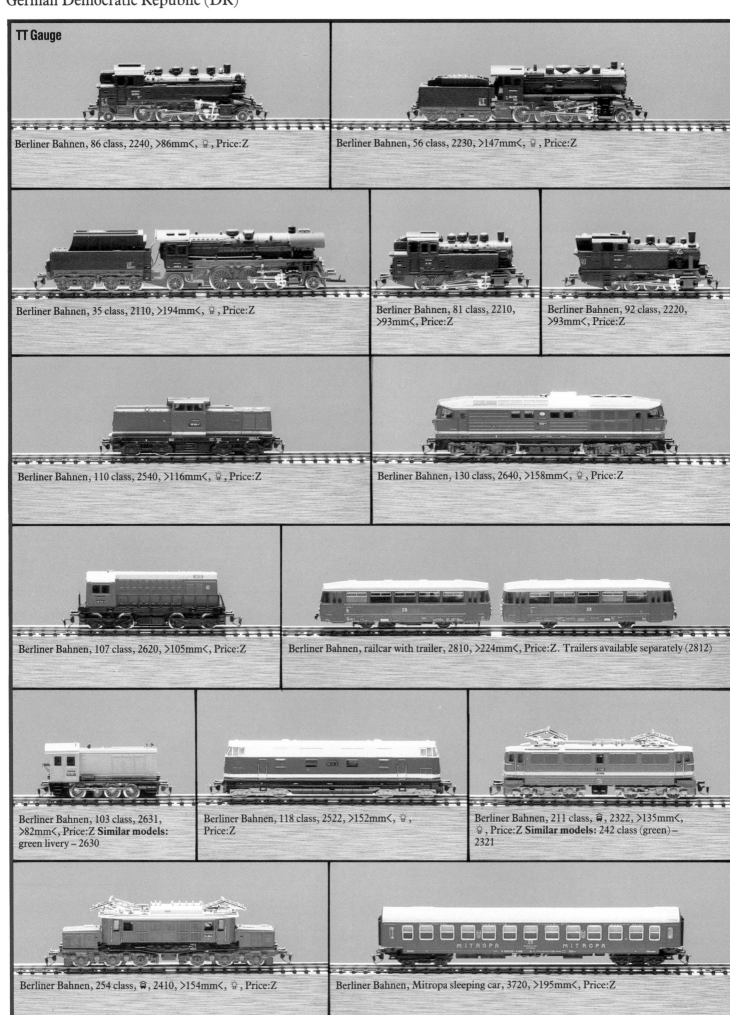

Berliner Bahnen, 86 class, 2240, >86mm<, ⚱, Price:Z

Berliner Bahnen, 56 class, 2230, >147mm<, ⚱, Price:Z

Berliner Bahnen, 35 class, 2110, >194mm<, ⚱, Price:Z

Berliner Bahnen, 81 class, 2210, >93mm<, Price:Z

Berliner Bahnen, 92 class, 2220, >93mm<, Price:Z

Berliner Bahnen, 110 class, 2540, >116mm<, ⚱, Price:Z

Berliner Bahnen, 130 class, 2640, >158mm<, ⚱, Price:Z

Berliner Bahnen, 107 class, 2620, >105mm<, Price:Z

Berliner Bahnen, railcar with trailer, 2810, >224mm<, Price:Z. Trailers available separately (2812)

Berliner Bahnen, 103 class, 2631, >82mm<, Price:Z **Similar models:** green livery – 2630

Berliner Bahnen, 118 class, 2522, >152mm<, ⚱, Price:Z

Berliner Bahnen, 211 class, ⌂, 2322, >135mm<, ⚱, Price:Z **Similar models:** 242 class (green) – 2321

Berliner Bahnen, 254 class, ⌂, 2410, >154mm<, ⚱, Price:Z

Berliner Bahnen, Mitropa sleeping car, 3720, >195mm<, Price:Z

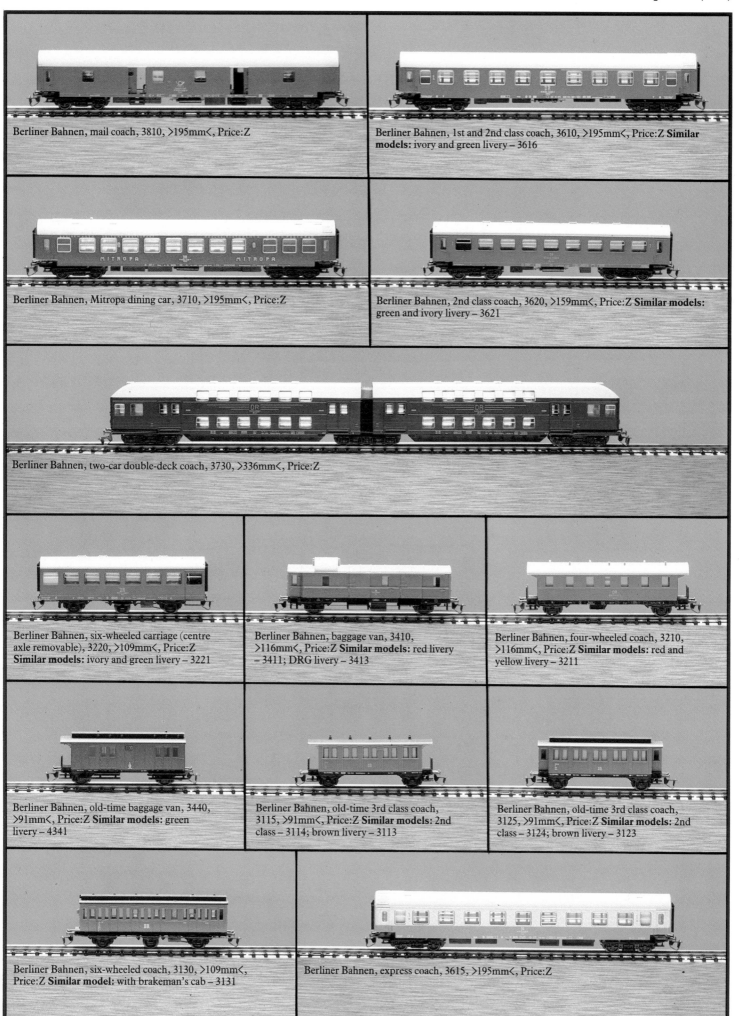

Berliner Bahnen, mail coach, 3810, >195mm<, Price:Z

Berliner Bahnen, 1st and 2nd class coach, 3610, >195mm<, Price:Z **Similar models:** ivory and green livery – 3616

Berliner Bahnen, Mitropa dining car, 3710, >195mm<, Price:Z

Berliner Bahnen, 2nd class coach, 3620, >159mm<, Price:Z **Similar models:** green and ivory livery – 3621

Berliner Bahnen, two-car double-deck coach, 3730, >336mm<, Price:Z

Berliner Bahnen, six-wheeled carriage (centre axle removable), 3220, >109mm<, Price:Z **Similar models:** ivory and green livery – 3221

Berliner Bahnen, baggage van, 3410, >116mm<, Price:Z **Similar models:** red livery – 3411; DRG livery – 3413

Berliner Bahnen, four-wheeled coach, 3210, >116mm<, Price:Z **Similar models:** red and yellow livery – 3211

Berliner Bahnen, old-time baggage van, 3440, >91mm<, Price:Z **Similar models:** green livery – 4341

Berliner Bahnen, old-time 3rd class coach, 3115, >91mm<, Price:Z **Similar models:** 2nd class – 3114; brown livery – 3113

Berliner Bahnen, old-time 3rd class coach, 3125, >91mm<, Price:Z **Similar models:** 2nd class – 3124; brown livery – 3123

Berliner Bahnen, six-wheeled coach, 3130, >109mm<, Price:Z **Similar model:** with brakeman's cab – 3131

Berliner Bahnen, express coach, 3615, >195mm<, Price:Z

# German Democratic Republic (DR)

Berliner Bahnen, covered wagon with brakeman's cab, 4120, >81mm<, Price:Z

Berliner Bahnen, bogie covered wagon, 5110, >132mm<, Price:Z

Berliner Bahnen, open wagon, 4240, >83mm<, Price:Z **Similar models:** with load of timber – 4244; with load of coal – 4245

Berliner Bahnen, covered wagon, 4150, >116mm<, Price:Z **Similar models:** alternative inscription - 4154; banana wagon – 4151

Berliner Bahnen, refrigerated wagon, 5310, >137mm<, Price:Z

Berliner Bahnen, brake and luggage van, 3420, >76mm<, Price:Z

Berliner Bahnen, hinged lid wagon, 4710, >76mm<, Price:Z

Berliner Bahnen, silo wagon, 4420, >76mm<, Price:Z

Berliner Bahnen, container wagon, 4910, >91mm<, Price:Z **Similar models:** With different containers – 4520; 4521; 4522; 4523

Berliner Bahnen, low-sided wagon with stakes, 4620, >96mm<, Price:Z

Berliner Bahnen, coal hopper wagon, 5210, >108mm<, Price:Z

Berliner Bahnen, tank wagon, 4412, >76mm<, Price:Z **Similar models:** silver – 4413

Berliner Bahnen, covered wagon with barrel roof, 4160, >91mm<, Price:Z

## Also available
**DR diesel locomotives**
Berliner Bahnen, 118 class, 2520, >152mm<, ⚲, Price:Z
**DR coaches**
Berliner Bahnen, double-deck centre unit, 3740, >336mm<, Price:Z
Berliner Bahnen, DRG coach, 3213, Price:Z
**DR wagons**
Berliner Bahnen, acid carrier, 4440, >81mm<, Price:Z

## HO/OO Gauge

◉ Fleischmann, 89 class, 4019, >111mm<, ⚲, Price:J **Similar models:** with working Heusinger valve gear – 4020 (Price:K)

◉ Fleischmann, 53 class, 4124, >184mm<, ⚲, Price:K

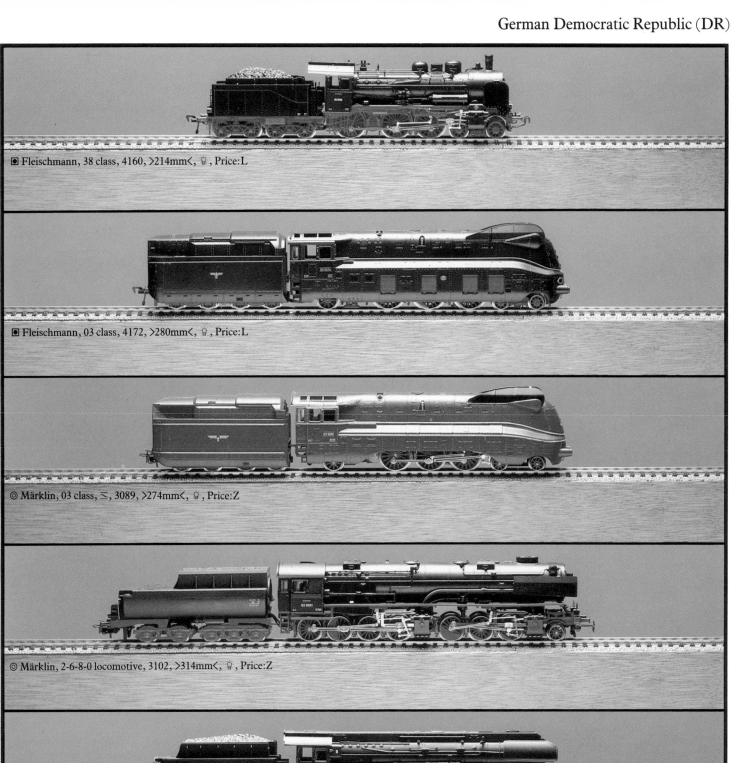

◉ Fleischmann, 38 class, 4160, ⟩214mm⟨, ⚲ , Price:L

◉ Fleischmann, 03 class, 4172, ⟩280mm⟨, ⚲ , Price:L

◎ Märklin, 03 class, ≦, 3089, ⟩274mm⟨, ⚲ , Price:Z

◎ Märklin, 2-6-8-0 locomotive, 3102, ⟩314mm⟨, ⚲ , Price:Z

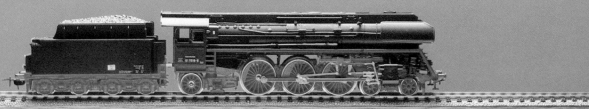

◎ Piko, 01 class, 5/6325, ⟩281mm⟨, Price:L **Similar models:** with box spoke wheels – 5/6329; oil-fired, spoked wheels – 5/6320; oil-fired, box spoke wheels – 5/6327

◎ Piko, 41 class, 5/6326, ⟩278mm⟨, Price:L

◎ Piko, 55 class, 5/6302, >210mm<, Price:H

◎ Piko, 75 class, 190/16/1, >145mm<, Price:H

◎ Piko, 86 class, 190/27, >160mm<, Price:H

◎ Roco, 58 class, 4112A, >159mm<, ♀, Price:L

◎ Roco, 93 class, 4122A, >159mm<, ♀, Price:K

◎ Roco, E71 class, 4196A, >133mm<, ♀, Price:Z

☻ Trix, T13 class, ≡, 2228, >128mm<, ♀, Price:L **Similar models:** ◎ coupling, 12V DC – 2428

☻ Trix, 01 class, ≡, 2222, >280mm<, ♀, Price:L

◎ Piko, 211 class, ☻, 5/6213, >187mm<, Price:J

☻ Trix, E 05 class, ≡, ☻, 2240, >177mm<, ♀, Price:L **Similar models:** ◎ coupling, 12V DC – 2240

◎ Piko, 110 class, 190/EM/18, >160mm<, Price:G **Similar models:** V100 class (blue livery) – 190/17

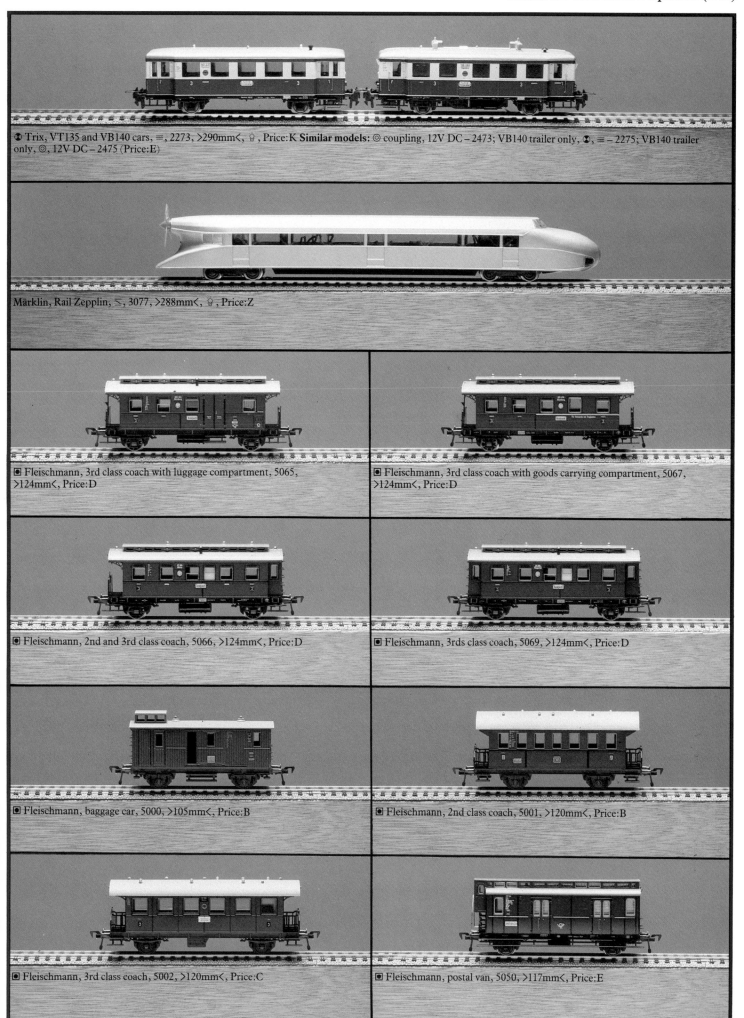

Trix, VT135 and VB140 cars, =, 2273, >290mm<, Price:K **Similar models:** coupling, 12V DC – 2473; VB140 trailer only, ≡ – 2275; VB140 trailer only, , 12V DC – 2475 (Price:E)

Märklin, Rail Zepplin, ≲, 3077, >288mm<, Price:Z

Fleischmann, 3rd class coach with luggage compartment, 5065, >124mm<, Price:D

Fleischmann, 3rd class coach with goods carrying compartment, 5067, >124mm<, Price:D

Fleischmann, 2nd and 3rd class coach, 5066, >124mm<, Price:D

Fleischmann, 3rds class coach, 5069, >124mm<, Price:D

Fleischmann, baggage car, 5000, >105mm<, Price:B

Fleischmann, 2nd class coach, 5001, >120mm<, Price:B

Fleischmann, 3rd class coach, 5002, >120mm<, Price:C

Fleischmann, postal van, 5050, >117mm<, Price:E

# German Democratic Republic (DR)

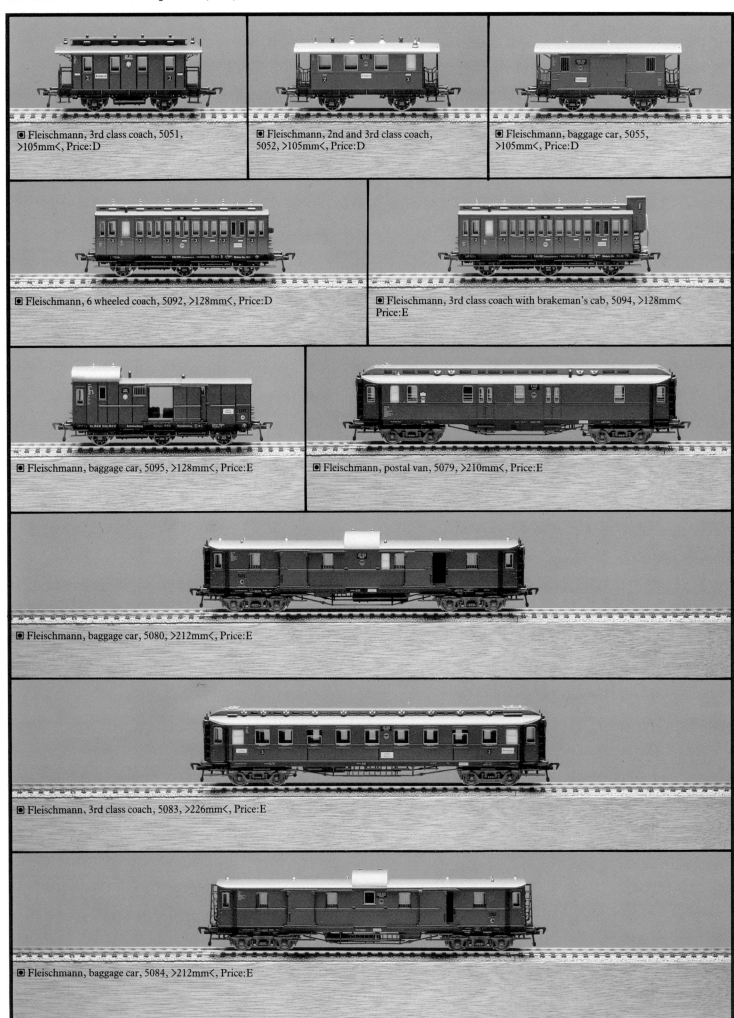

◉ Fleischmann, 3rd class coach, 5051, >105mm<, Price:D

◉ Fleischmann, 2nd and 3rd class coach, 5052, >105mm<, Price:D

◉ Fleischmann, baggage car, 5055, >105mm<, Price:D

◉ Fleischmann, 6 wheeled coach, 5092, >128mm<, Price:D

◉ Fleischmann, 3rd class coach with brakeman's cab, 5094, >128mm< Price:E

◉ Fleischmann, baggage car, 5095, >128mm<, Price:E

◉ Fleischmann, postal van, 5079, >210mm<, Price:E

◉ Fleischmann, baggage car, 5080, >212mm<, Price:E

◉ Fleischmann, 3rd class coach, 5083, >226mm<, Price:E

◉ Fleischmann, baggage car, 5084, >212mm<, Price:E

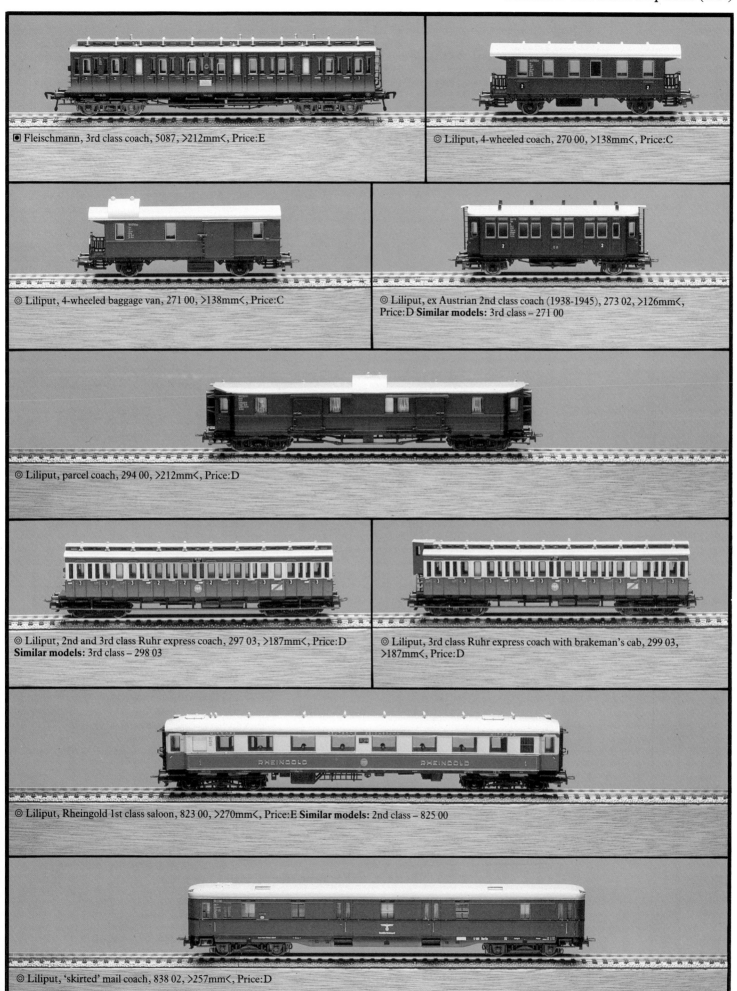

◨ Fleischmann, 3rd class coach, 5087, >212mm<, Price:E

◎ Liliput, 4-wheeled coach, 270 00, >138mm<, Price:C

◎ Liliput, 4-wheeled baggage van, 271 00, >138mm<, Price:C

◎ Liliput, ex Austrian 2nd class coach (1938-1945), 273 02, >126mm<, Price:D **Similar models:** 3rd class – 271 00

◎ Liliput, parcel coach, 294 00, >212mm<, Price:D

◎ Liliput, 2nd and 3rd class Ruhr express coach, 297 03, >187mm<, Price:D **Similar models:** 3rd class – 298 03

◎ Liliput, 3rd class Ruhr express coach with brakeman's cab, 299 03, >187mm<, Price:D

◎ Liliput, Rheingold 1st class saloon, 823 00, >270mm<, Price:E **Similar models:** 2nd class – 825 00

◎ Liliput, 'skirted' mail coach, 838 02, >257mm<, Price:D

◎ Liliput, 2nd class coach, 842 02, >249mm<, Price: E **Similar models:** – 844 02

◎ Liliput, 2nd class coach, 843 02, >249mm<, Price: E

◎ Liliput, 2nd class coach, 286 02, >240mm<, Price: D

◎ Liliput, ex Austrian mail coach with DR inscription (1938-1945), 272 00, >127mm<, Price: C

◎ Liliput, baggage car, 812 02, >143mm<, Price: E

◎ Liliput, 3rd class coach, 814 02, >143mm<, Price: E **Similar models:** inscribed 'Für Reisende mit Traglasten' ('for passengers with bulky luggage') – 819 02

◎ Liliput, 2nd and 3rd class coach, 815 02, >143mm<, Price: E

◎ Liliput, 2nd and 3rd class coach, 816 02, >143mm<, Price: E

◎ Märklin, baggage car, 4102, >160mm<, Price: Z **Similar models:** with illuminated end markers – 4103

◎ Märklin, 3rd class coach, 4101, >160mm<, Price:Z

◎ Märklin, coach with platforms, 4040, >115mm<, Price:Z

◎ Märklin, 2nd class coach, 4004, >130mm<, Price:Z

◎ Märklin, 2nd class coach with brakeman's cab, 4005, >130mm<, Price:Z

◎ Märklin, 3rd class coach, 4136, >220mm<, Price:Z

◎ Märklin, baggage car, 4137, >200mm<, Price:Z

◎ Märklin, 1st, 2nd and 3rd class coach, 4143, >232mm<, Price:Z

◎ Märklin, 3rd class coach, 4141, >250mm<, Price:Z

◎ Märklin, 2nd class coach, 4144, >250mm<, Price:Z

◎ Märklin, baggage car, 4142, >226mm<, Price:Z

◎ Piko, 1st class coach, 5/6507, >244mm<, Price:C

◎ Piko, 1st and 2nd class coach, 5/6508, >244mm<, ☼, Price:C

◎ Piko, 2nd class coach, 5/6509, >244mm<, ☼,Price:C

◎ Piko, buffet coach, 5/6510, >244mm<, ☼, Price:C

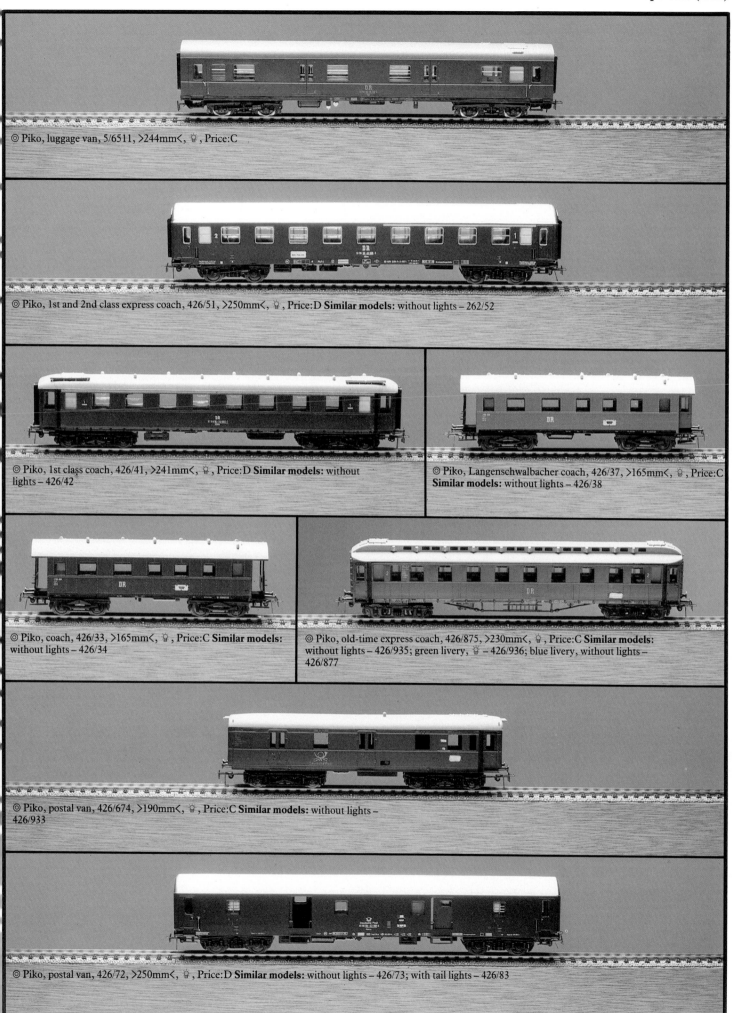

◎ Piko, luggage van, 5/6511, >244mm<, 💡, Price:C

◎ Piko, 1st and 2nd class express coach, 426/51, >250mm<, 💡, Price:D **Similar models:** without lights – 262/52

◎ Piko, 1st class coach, 426/41, >241mm<, 💡, Price:D **Similar models:** without lights – 426/42

◎ Piko, Langenschwalbacher coach, 426/37, >165mm<, 💡, Price:C **Similar models:** without lights – 426/38

◎ Piko, coach, 426/33, >165mm<, 💡, Price:C **Similar models:** without lights – 426/34

◎ Piko, old-time express coach, 426/875, >230mm<, 💡, Price:C **Similar models:** without lights – 426/935; green livery, 💡 – 426/936; blue livery, without lights – 426/877

◎ Piko, postal van, 426/674, >190mm<, 💡, Price:C **Similar models:** without lights – 426/933

◎ Piko, postal van, 426/72, >250mm<, 💡, Price:D **Similar models:** without lights – 426/73; with tail lights – 426/83

# German Democratic Republic (DR)

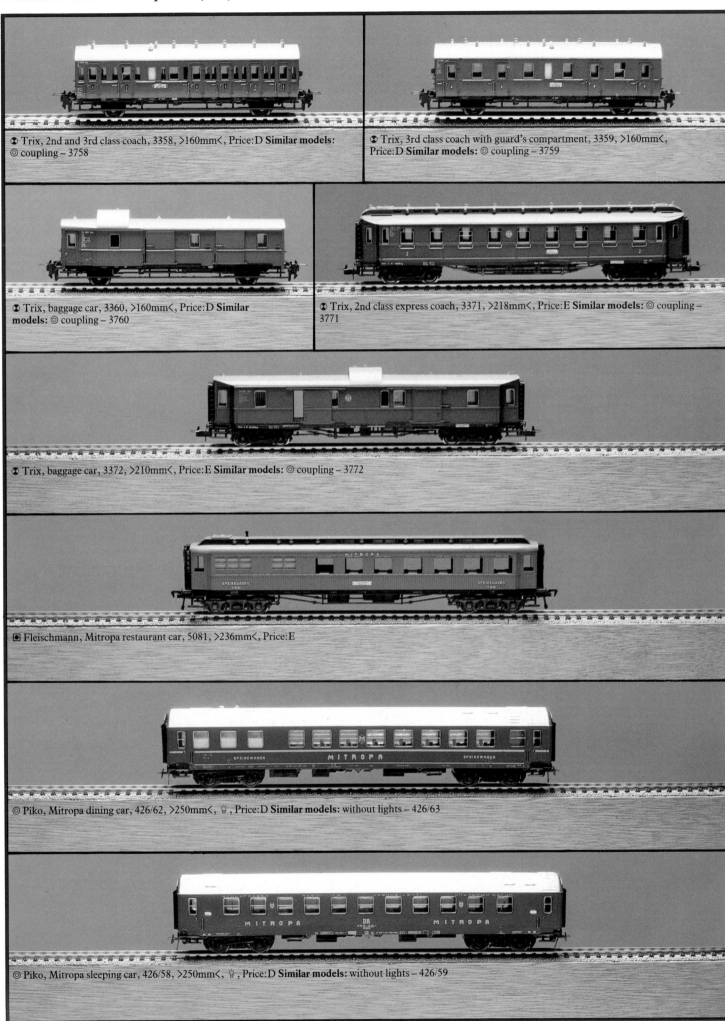

➐ Trix, 2nd and 3rd class coach, 3358, >160mm<, Price:D **Similar models:** ◎ coupling – 3758

➐ Trix, 3rd class coach with guard's compartment, 3359, >160mm<, Price:D **Similar models:** ◎ coupling – 3759

➐ Trix, baggage car, 3360, >160mm<, Price:D **Similar models:** ◎ coupling – 3760

➐ Trix, 2nd class express coach, 3371, >218mm<, Price:E **Similar models:** ◎ coupling – 3771

➐ Trix, baggage car, 3372, >210mm<, Price:E **Similar models:** ◎ coupling – 3772

▣ Fleischmann, Mitropa restaurant car, 5081, >236mm<, Price:E

◎ Piko, Mitropa dining car, 426/62, >250mm<, ♙, Price:D **Similar models:** without lights – 426/63

◎ Piko, Mitropa sleeping car, 426/58, >250mm<, ♙, Price:D **Similar models:** without lights – 426/59

◎ Piko, old-time Mitropa dining car, 426/874, >230mm<, Price:D **Similar models:** ⬛ – 426/875

◨ Fleischmann, open wagon, 5208, >99mm<, Price:C

◨ Fleischmann, open wagon with brakeman's cab, 5209, >110mm<, Price:D

◎ Märklin, covered wagon, 4692, >105mm<, Price:Z

◎ Märklin, open wagon with brakeman's cab, 4696, >101mm<, Price:Z

◎ Märklin, flat wagon with brakeman's cab, 4697, >115mm<, Price:Z

◎ Märklin, van with brakeman's cab, 4695, >110mm<, Price:Z

◎ Piko, wooden open bogie wagon, 5/6423/010, >157mm<, Price:C

◎ Piko, steel open bogie wagon, 5/6422/010, >157mm<, Price:C

◎ Piko, open wagon, 5/6412/010, >114mm<, Price:C

◎ Piko, open wagon, 5/6413/010, >114mm<, Price:C

◎ Piko, open wagon, 5/6410/011, >114mm<, Price:C

◎ Piko, covered wagon, 5/6446/010, >105mm<, Price:C **Similar models:** white livery – 5/6446/015; marked 'Seefische' – 5/6446/016

◎ Piko, covered wagon with brakeman's cab, 5/6452/010, >110mm<, Price:C

◎ Piko, covered wagon, 5/6445/010, >105mm<, Price:C **Similar models:** Feuerlöschwagen – 5/6445/012; Wasserstott – 5/6445/018; Seefische – 5/6445/015

◎ Piko, covered wagon with brakeman's cab, 5/6450/010, >109mm<, Price:C

◎ Piko, Bahndienstwagen covered wagon, 5/6449/012, >105mm<, Price:C

◎ Piko, covered wagon, 5/6448/010, >105mm<, Price:C

◎ Piko, refrigerated van, 5/6407/010, >5/6407/011, Price:C

◎ Piko, bogie refrigerated van, 426/101, >207mm<, Price:C

◎ Piko, brake van, 5/6605/015, >100mm<, Price:C **Similar models:** green livery – 5/6605/010

◎ Piko, wagon with hinged top, 5/6432/010, >122mm<, Price:C

◎ Piko, low-sided wagon with containers, 5/6416/018, >131mm<, Price:C **Similar models:** green livery – 5/6416/017; with stakes – 5/6416/015

◎ Piko, hopper wagon, 5/6426/010, >147mm<, Price:Z

◎ Piko, bogie tank wagon, 5/6424/019, >142mm<, Price:C

◎ Piko, acid wagon, 426/103, >100mm<, Price:C

✪ Trix, brake van, 3422, >98mm<, Price:E **Similar models:** ◎ coupling – 3622

✪ Trix, covered wagon with brakeman's cab, 3423, >111mm<, Price:D **Similar models:** ◎ coupling – 3623

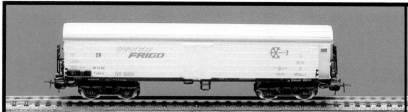

◎ Piko, Interfrigo bogie refrigerated van, 5/6425/011, >185mm<, Price:C

◎ Piko, Schwedt bogie tank wagon, 5/6424/017, >142mm<, Price:C
**Similar models:** Minol – 5/6424; Buna – 5/6242/017; Leuna – 5/6424/018

## HOe Narrow Gauge

◎ Bemo, (HOe), post and baggage car, 3401, >97mm<, Price:D **Similar models:** HOm – 3601

◎ Bemo, (HOe), 3rd class coach, 3402, >97mm<, Price:D **Similar models:** HOm – 3602

◎ Bemo, (HOe), 3rd class coach, 3403, >97mm<, Price:D **Similar models:** HOm – 3603

◎ Bemo, (HOe), 3rd class coach, 3408, >126mm<, Price:D **Similar models:** HOm – 3608

◎ Bemo, (HOe), 3rd class coach, 3411, >126mm<, Price:D **Similar models:** HOm – 3611

## Also available

### DR steam locomotives
◎ Liliput, ex S3/6 2'Cl', 18 02, >262mm<, Price:N
◎ Liliput, 42 class in war livery, 42 01, >268mm<, Price:M **Similar models:** superdetailed, tender drive, black livery – 42 02 (Price:M)
◎ Liliput, 45 class, 45 01, >310mm<, Price:N **Similar models:** ≲ – 45 06; ex works livery, DC – 45 02 (Price:N)
◎ Liliput, 52 class in war livery, 52 01, >268mm<, Price:M **Similar models:** black livery – 52 02
◎ Liliput, 1E1 class, type 95, 95 00, >174mm<, Price:M **Similar models:** type GT 57.18 – 95 01; type 95, grey livery – 95 02; type 95 black and red 1950s livery – 95 03; type pr.T20 – 95 04
◎ Liliput, 05 class, 105 01, >316mm<, Price:M **Similar models:** ≲ – 105 06 (Price:L)
◎ Liliput, BR 050 03 class, 105 02, >307mm<, Price:N **Similar models:** ≲ – 105 07
◎ Liliput, 2'C2' express locomotive, 105 04, >307mm<, Price:N **Similar models:** ≲ – 105 09 (Price:M); war livery, DC – 105 22 (Price:N); war livery, ≲ – 105 27 (Price:N)
◎ Liliput, 214 class, 106 01, Price:M **Similar models:** ≲ – 106 06
◎ Liliput, 4-6-2 locomotive, 40 00, Price:N **Similar models:** black and red – 40 01; black and red, with smoke deflectors – 40 02
◎ Märklin, 38 class, ≲, 3099, >218mm<, ☼ Price:Z
◎ Piko, 52 class, 190/23/1, >305mm<, Price:K
◎ Piko, 89 class, 5/6300, >109mm<, Price:F
◎ Roco, 17 class, 4115S, >243mm<, ☼, Price:L **Similar models:** with standard boiler – 3125B
◎ Roco, E60 class, 4129B, >127mm<, ☼, Price:Z
❂ Trix, 38 class, ≡, 2209, >226mm<, ☼, Price:L **Similar models:** ◎ coupling, 12V DC – 2409
❂ Trix, 92 class, ≡, 2212, >128mm<, ☼, Price:K **Similar models:** ◎ coupling, 12V DC – 2412

### DR electric locomotives
◎ Piko, E11 class, ⬓, 5/6205, >187mm<, Price:J
◎ Piko, E42 class, ⬓, 5/6212, >187mm<, Price:J
◎ Piko, 244 class, ⬓, 5/6201, >142mm<, Price:H
◎ Piko, E69 class, ⬓, 5/6200, >106mm<, Price:E

### DR diesel locomotives
◎ Piko, 120 class, 190/21/1, >201mm<, Price:G
◎ Piko, 130 class, 5/6010, >236mm<, Price:G

### DR diesel locomotives
◎ Piko, 118.1 class, 190/19/1, >223mm<, Price:G
◎ Piko, 118.0 class, 190/20/1, >223mm<, Price:G **Similar models:** blue and cream livery – 190/20/2

### DR diesel railcars
◎ Lima, VT137 class, 208140LG, Price:Z
◎ Lima, VS145 class trailer (no motor), 309122, Price:Z
◎ Piko, VT137 class, 190/14/1, >700mm<, Price:J **Similar models:** red and ivory livery – 190/14/5/1

### DR coaches
◙ Fleischmann, 1st, 2nd, and 3rd class coach, 5082, >226mm<, Price:E
◙ Fleischmann, 2nd class coach with brakeman's cab, 5085, >212mm<, Price:E
◙ Fleischmann, 3rd class coach with brakeman's cab, 5086, >212mm<, Price:E
◎ Liliput, baggage car with guard's compartment, 289 02, >250mm<, Price:D
◎ Liliput, Prussian-type compartment coach, 290 00, >187mm<, Price:D
◎ Liliput, Prussian-type compartment coach with brakeman's cab, 290 03, >187mm<, Price:D
◎ Liliput, Prussian-type mail coach with brakeman's cab, 291 00, >187mm<, Price:D
◎ Liliput, mail/baggage coach, 292 02, >254mm<, Price:E
◎ Liliput, Prussian-type, 295 00, >224mm<, Price:D **Similar models:** Epoch II livery – 295 02
◎ Liliput, Rheingold baggage coach, 821 00, >226mm<, Price:E
◎ Liliput, Rheingold 1st class saloon with kitchen, 822 00, >270mm<, Price:E **Similar models:** 2nd class – 824 00
◎ Liliput, 1st and 2nd class 'skirted' coach, 832 02, >240mm< Price:D **Similar models:** 3rd class – 833 02; 2nd and 3rd class – 834 02; 1st, 2nd, and 3rd class – 835 02
◎ Liliput, luggage van with conductor's cabin, 839 02, >250mm<, Price:D
◎ Liliput, 1st class coach, 841 02, >249mm<, Price:E
◎ Liliput, 1st, 2nd, and 3rd class coach, 845 02, >249mm<, Price:E
◎ Liliput, 1st and 2nd class, 287 02, >240mm<, Price:D
◎ Märklin, 2nd and 3rd class coach, 4100, >160mm<, Price:Z

## Also available
### DR steam locomotives
◎ Bemo, (HOe) 99 class, 1007, >99mm<, Price:L

# Switzerland

# Bern-Lötschberg-Simplon

The Bern-Lötschberg-Simplon (BLS) railway is an important privately owned line on a major trunk route through Switzerland. It was built from the start as an electric line in 1913. Experience from this pioneer electrified line influenced other European railways when they changed to electric traction. The company only has about 40 locomotives, but it handles a lot of traffic on its scenic mountain route.

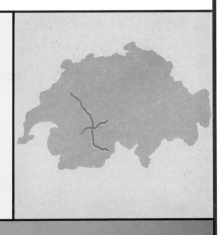

## N Gauge

⊖ Arnold, Re4/4 class, 🔌, 2414, >92mm<, 💡, Price: M

⊖ Arnold, 1st class coach, 3712, >139mm<, Price: D **Similar models:** green – 3711

**Also available**
**BLS coaches**
⊖ Arnold, 2nd class coach, 3722, >139mm<, Price: D **Similar models:** green – 3721

## HO/OO Gauge

◎ Lima, 2nd class coach, 309121, >265mm<, Price: Z

◎ Lima, 2nd class coach, 309190, >266mm<, Price: Z

◎ Roco, baggage coach, 4240A, >210mm<, Price: D

**Also available**
**BLS coaches**
◎ Lima, 1st class coach, 309114, >265mm<, Price: Z
◎ Lima, baggage car, 309338, >212mm<, Price: Z
◎ Roco, 1st class coach, 4239A, >272mm<, Price: D **Similar models:** green livery – 4239B
◎ Roco, 2nd class coach, 4238A, >264mm<, Price: D **Similar models:** green livery – 4238B

# Switzerland

## Schweizerische Bundesbahnen/ Chemins de Fer Federaux Suisses

Because Switzerland is tri-lingual (German, French, Italian) there are three names for the same railway – abbreviated SBB/CFF/FFS. Because there are still many privately-owned lines in Switzerland, the SBB is one of the smallest state-owned systems in Europe – only 4,722 route kilometres (2,934 route miles). All routes have been electrified since 1965, and the SBB operates all the trunk routes except the BLS (see page 188).

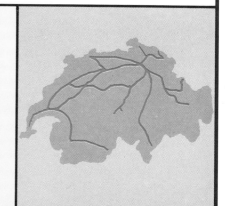

### Z Gauge

⊞ Märklin, Be6/8 'Crocodile' class, =, 8856, >91mm<, ⚡, Price:Z

### N Gauge

⊖ Arnold, Re4/4 class, ⚡, 2413, >92mm<, ⚡, Price:K **Similar models:** Re4/4 II, TEE red and cream livery – 2412

⊖ Arnold Ce6/8II 'Crocodile' class, ⚡, 2465, >121mm<, Price:L **Similar model:** original brown livery – 2468

⊖ Lima, RBe4/4 class, ⚏, 220204G, >150mm<, Price:Z

⊖ Minitrix, Re4/4 class, ⚡, 2976, >94mm<, ⚡, Price:K

⊖ Minitrix, Be6/8 'Crocodile', ⚡, 2926, >125mm<, ⚡, Price:L **Similar models:** brown livery – 2956

⊖ Minitrix, Re4/4 class, ⚡, 2071, >93mm<, ⚡, Price:J **Similar models:** ems-fitted – 2171 (Price:L)

⊖ Arnold, 1st class coach, 3710, >139mm<, Price:D

⊖ Arnold, 2nd class coach, 3720, >139mm<, Price:D

⊖ Arnold, baggage car, 3750, >139mm<, Price:D

⊖ Arnold, 1st class Eurofirma coach, 3772, >163mm<, Price:D

⊖ Arnold, 2nd class Eurofirma coach, 3773, >163mm<, Price:D

⊖ Fleischmann, sleeping coach, TEN livery, 8117, >165mm<, Price:D

⊖ Lima, 1st class coach, 320308, >145mm<, Price:Z

⊖ Lima, 1st class coach, 320334, >138mm<, Price:Z

# Switzerland (SBB)

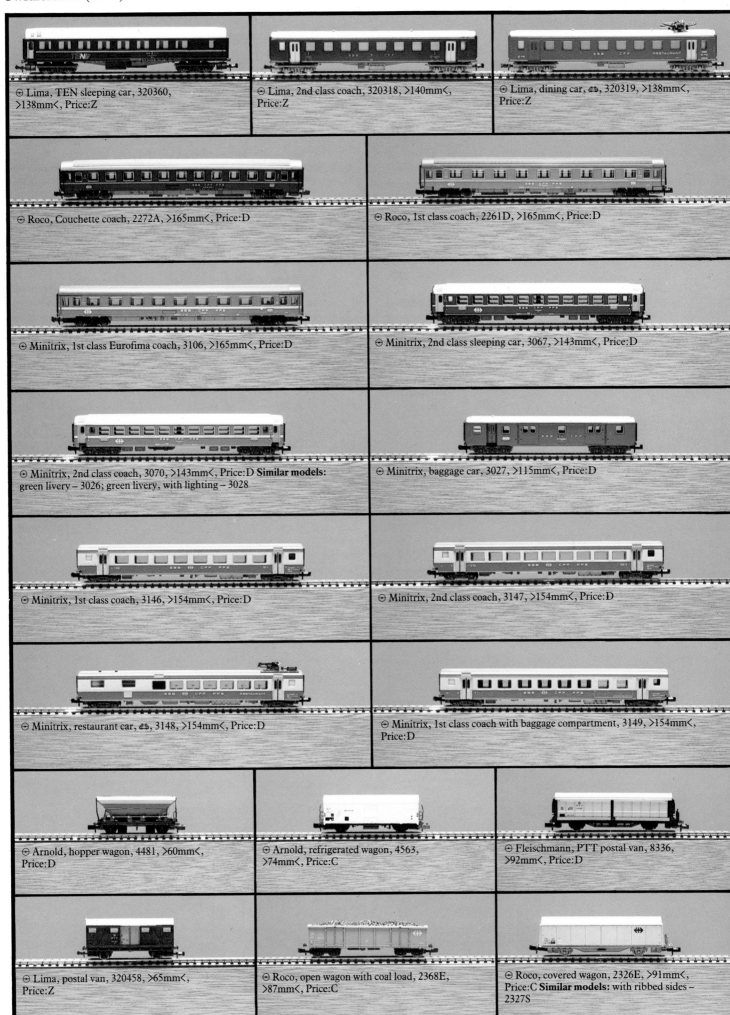

⊖ Lima, TEN sleeping car, 320360, >138mm<, Price:Z

⊖ Lima, 2nd class coach, 320318, >140mm<, Price:Z

⊖ Lima, dining car, ⏣, 320319, >138mm<, Price:Z

⊖ Roco, Couchette coach, 2272A, >165mm<, Price:D

⊖ Roco, 1st class coach, 2261D, >165mm<, Price:D

⊖ Minitrix, 1st class Eurofima coach, 3106, >165mm<, Price:D

⊖ Minitrix, 2nd class sleeping car, 3067, >143mm<, Price:D

⊖ Minitrix, 2nd class coach, 3070, >143mm<, Price:D **Similar models:** green livery – 3026; green livery, with lighting – 3028

⊖ Minitrix, baggage car, 3027, >115mm<, Price:D

⊖ Minitrix, 1st class coach, 3146, >154mm<, Price:D

⊖ Minitrix, 2nd class coach, 3147, >154mm<, Price:D

⊖ Minitrix, restaurant car, ⏣, 3148, >154mm<, Price:D

⊖ Minitrix, 1st class coach with baggage compartment, 3149, >154mm<, Price:D

⊖ Arnold, hopper wagon, 4481, >60mm<, Price:D

⊖ Arnold, refrigerated wagon, 4563, >74mm<, Price:C

⊖ Fleischmann, PTT postal van, 8336, >92mm<, Price:D

⊖ Lima, postal van, 320458, >65mm<, Price:Z

⊖ Roco, open wagon with coal load, 2368E, >87mm<, Price:C

⊖ Roco, covered wagon, 2326E, >91mm<, Price:C **Similar models:** with ribbed sides – 2327S

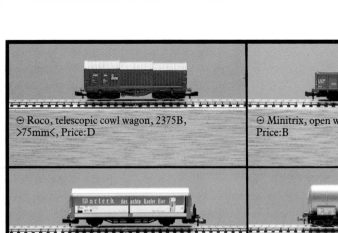

⊖ Roco, telescopic cowl wagon, 2375B, >75mm<, Price:D

⊖ Minitrix, open wagon, 3585, >56mm<, Price:B

⊖ Arnold, Felsenau refrigerated wagon, 4565, >74mm<, Price:C **Similar models:** Löwenbräu – 4566; Feldschlössen – 4567

⊖ Fleischmann, Warteck covered wagon, 8337, >92mm<, Price:D

⊖ Lima, Uetikon bogie tank wagon, 320624, >65mm<, Price:Z

⊖ Lima, Ovomaltine covered wagon, 320461, >70mm<, Price:Z

⊖ Lima, Feldschlosschen-Bier refrigerated wagon, 320470, >75mm<, Price:Z **Similar models:** Vivi-Cola – 320473; Cardinal – 320478

⊖ Roco, Ovomaltine covered wagon, 2326A, >91mm<, Price:C **Similar models:** Warteck – 2326F; Migros – 2326J; Usego – 2326K

## Also available
### SBB electric locomotives
⊖ Lima, Re4/4 class, ⊜, 220293G, Price:Z **Similar models:** green livery – 220294G
⊖ Minitrix, Ae6/6 class, ☎, 2936, >115mm<, ⚲, Price:K **Similar models:** alternative body decoration – 2939
### SBB coaches
⊖ Arnold, dining car, ⊜, 3740,>139mm<, Price:D
⊖ Lima, 2nd class coach, 320879, Price:Z

### SBB coaches
⊖ Roco, TEN sleeping car, 2278C, >165mm<, Price:D
### SBB wagons
⊖ Lima, high-sided wagon, 320642, Price:Z

## HO/OO Gauge

◎ Roco, C5/6 class, 4111A, >221mm<, ⚲, Price:L **Similar models:** ≊ – 14111A

◙ Fleischmann, Re4/4 class, ☎, 4340, >181mm<, ⚲, Price:L **Similar models:** red and cream TEE livery – 4341

◎ Lima, Ae3/6 class, ⊜, 208117LG, >164mm<, Price:Z **Similar models:** ☎ – 208117LGP; red livery, ⊜ – 208118LG; red livery, ☎ – 208118LGP

◎ Lima, Ae6/6 class, ⊜, 208046LG, >205mm<, Price:Z **Similar models:** red and white livery – 208048LG; dark green livery – 208147

191

# Switzerland (SBB)

◎ Lima, Re6/6 class, 🚃, 208051LG, >216mm<, Price:Z

◎ Lima, Re4/4 class, 🚃, 208066LG, >170mm<, Price:Z **Similar models:** green livery – 208067LG

◎ Märklin, Ae6/6 class, ≤, 🔧, 3050, >200mm<, 💡, Price:Z

◎ Märklin, Ae3/6 class, ≤, 🔧, 3151, >160mm<, 💡, Price:Z **Similar models:** green livery – 3167

◎ Märklin, Be6/8 'Crocodile' class, ≤, 🔧, 3356, >228mm<, 💡, Price:Z

◎ Roco, Ae6/6 class, 🔧, 4195S, >212mm<, 💡, Price:K

◎ Roco, Be4/6 class, 🔧, 4191A, >187mm<, 💡, Price:L **Similar models:** ≤, 14191A; red livery, DC – 4191B; red livery, ≤ – 1491B

◎ Lima, 1407-1483 class, 208031LG, >260mm<, Price:Z

◎ Lima, Bm4/4 class, 208144G, Price:Z

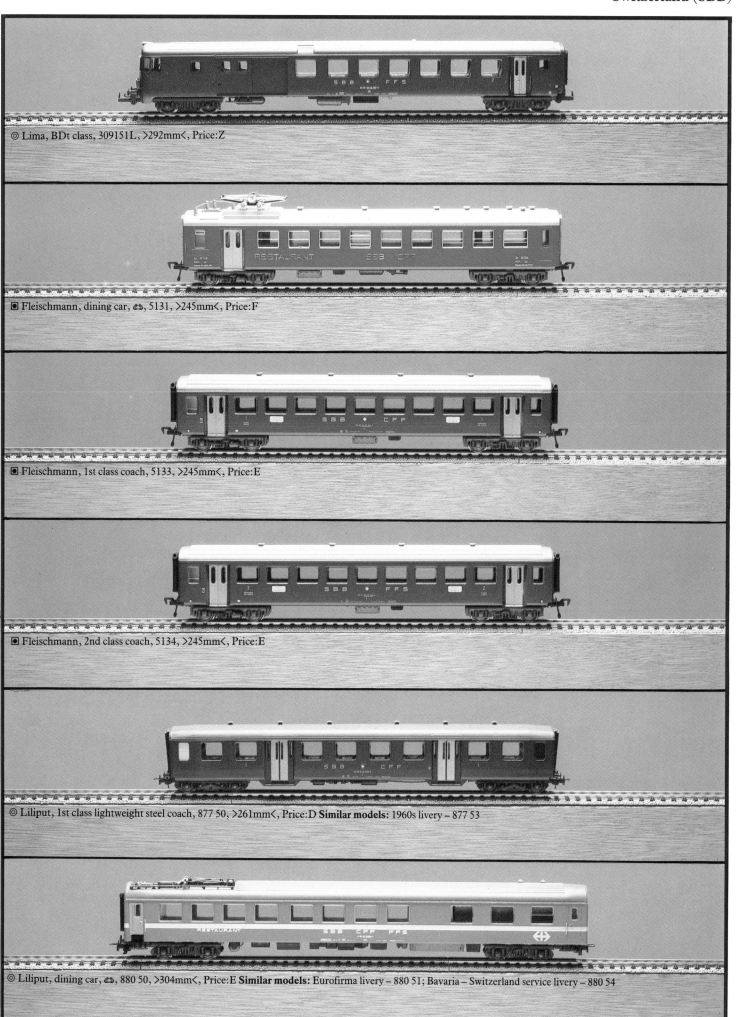

◎ Lima, BDt class, 309151L, >292mm<, Price:Z

◉ Fleischmann, dining car, 🍴, 5131, >245mm<, Price:F

◉ Fleischmann, 1st class coach, 5133, >245mm<, Price:E

◉ Fleischmann, 2nd class coach, 5134, >245mm<, Price:E

◎ Liliput, 1st class lightweight steel coach, 877 50, >261mm<, Price:D **Similar models:** 1960s livery – 877 53

◎ Liliput, dining car, 🍴, 880 50, >304mm<, Price:E **Similar models:** Eurofirma livery – 880 51; Bavaria – Switzerland service livery – 880 54

# Switzerland (SBB)

◎ Liliput, 1st class coach, 881 50, >304mm<, Price:E

◎ Liliput, 2nd class coach, 882 50, >304mm<, Price:E **Similar models:** modern (orange and white) livery – 882 54; couchette coach (green) – 883 50; couchette coach in modern (blue) livery – 883 54

◎ Lima, baggage car, 309334, Price:Z

◎ Lima, self-service restaurant car, ⛓, 309245, >268mm<, Price:Z

◎ Lima, control coach, 309161, >233mm<, Price:Z

◎ Lima, 1st class coach, 309112, >265mm<, Price:Z

◎ Lima, 2nd class coach, 309120, >265mm<, Price:Z

◎ Lima, 2nd class coach, 309159, >233mm<, Price:Z

◎ Lima, buffet car, 309175, >268mm<, Price:Z

◎ Lima, dining car, 🍴, 309211, >265mm<, Price:Z

◎ Lima, TEN sleeping car, 309237, >270mm<, Price:Z

◎ Lima, TEN sleeping car, 309251, >268mm<, Price:Z

◎ Lima, 2nd class couchette coach, 309259, ⟩270mm⟨, Price:Z

◎ Lima, 1st class coach, 309252, ⟩268mm⟨, Price:Z

◎ Lima, 2nd class coach, 309268, ⟩237mm⟨, Price:Z

◎ Lima, 2nd class coach, 309269, ⟩265mm⟨, Price:Z

◎ Lima, 1st class coach, 309316, ⟩265mm⟨, Price:Z

◎ Märklin, 3rd class coach, 4138, ⟩222mm⟨, Price:Z

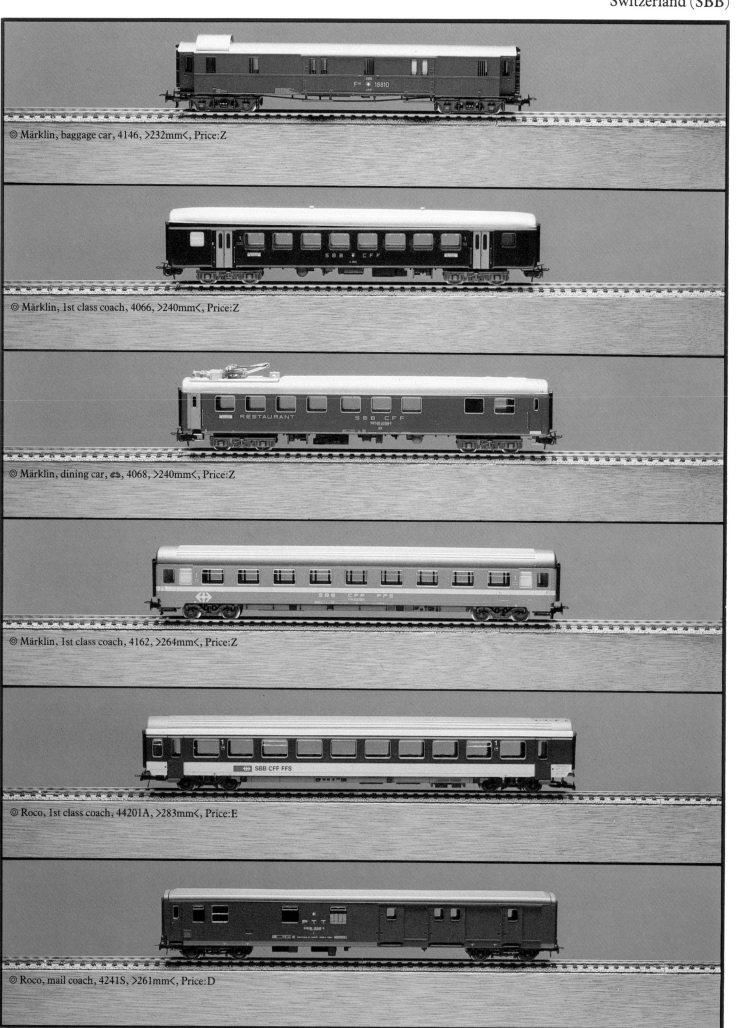

◎ Märklin, baggage car, 4146, >232mm<, Price:Z

◎ Märklin, 1st class coach, 4066, >240mm<, Price:Z

◎ Märklin, dining car, ⚏, 4068, >240mm<, Price:Z

◎ Märklin, 1st class coach, 4162, >264mm<, Price:Z

◎ Roco, 1st class coach, 44201A, >283mm<, Price:E

◎ Roco, mail coach, 4241S, >261mm<, Price:D

# Switzerland (SBB)

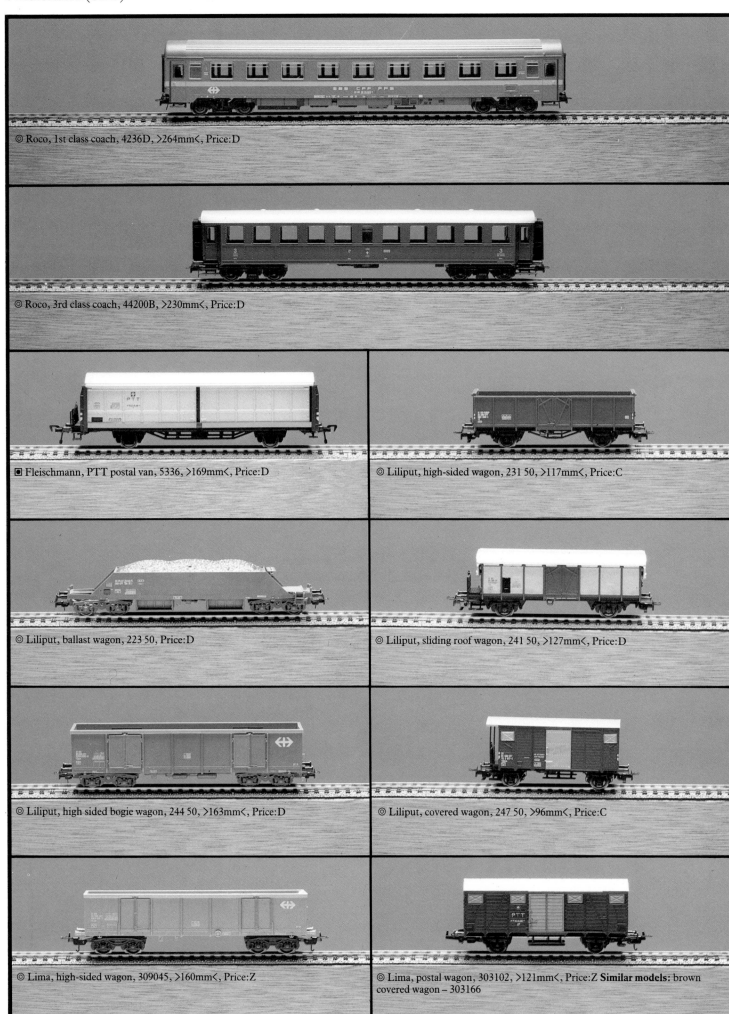

◎ Roco, 1st class coach, 4236D, >264mm<, Price:D

◎ Roco, 3rd class coach, 44200B, >230mm<, Price:D

◉ Fleischmann, PTT postal van, 5336, >169mm<, Price:D

◎ Liliput, high-sided wagon, 231 50, >117mm<, Price:C

◎ Liliput, ballast wagon, 223 50, Price:D

◎ Liliput, sliding roof wagon, 241 50, >127mm<, Price:D

◎ Liliput, high sided bogie wagon, 244 50, >163mm<, Price:D

◎ Liliput, covered wagon, 247 50, >96mm<, Price:C

◎ Lima, high-sided wagon, 309045, >160mm<, Price:Z

◎ Lima, postal wagon, 303102, >121mm<, Price:Z **Similar models:** brown covered wagon – 303166

◎ Lima, open wagon, 303177, >121mm<, Price:Z

◎ Märklin, van with brakeman's cab, 4698, >140mm<, Price:Z

◎ Roco, covered wagon, 4376S, >122mm<, Price:D

◎ Roco, telescopic cowl wagon, 4395B, >138mm<, Price:D

◎ Roco, deep well flat wagon with load, 44311D, >189mm<, Price:E

◎ Ruco, low-sided wagon with load, 1001, >90mm<, Price:Z **Similar models:** with alternative loads – 1002, 1003, 1004, 1005

◎ Ruco, low-sided wagon with brakeman's cab, 1102, >90mm<, Price:Z **Similar models:** with alternative loads – 1103, 1104, 1105

◎ Ruco, covered wagon, 2001, >90mm<, Price:Z **Similar models:** alternative livery – 2005

◎ Ruco, Enge beer wagon with brakeman's cab and canopy, 2108, >90mm<, Price:Z

▣ Fleischmann, Warteck covered wagon, 5337, >169mm<, Price:D

◎ Liliput, Shell bogie tank wagon, 225 51, >172mm<, Price:D **Similar models:** Esso – 225 52; Ermeco – 225 59 (Price:E)

◎ Liliput, Alusuisse bulk carrier wagon, 243 50, >168mm<, Price:D

# Switzerland (SBB)

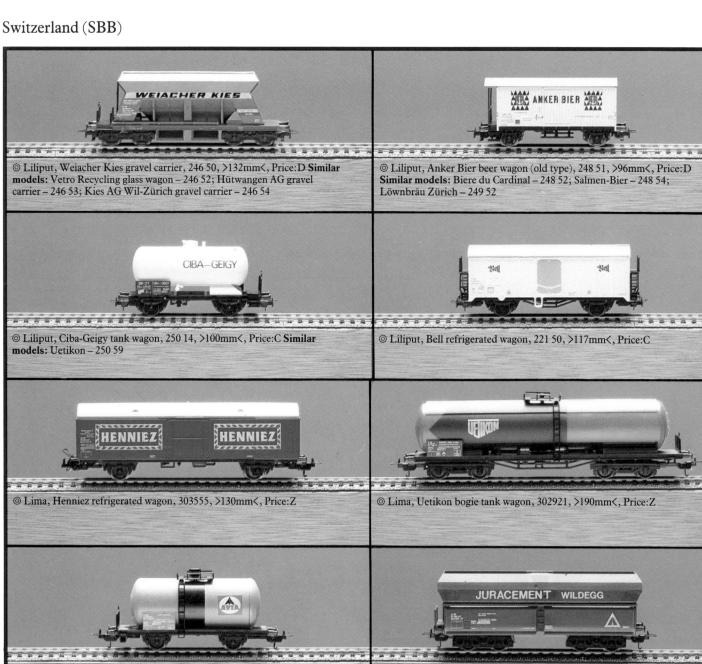

◎ Liliput, Weiacher Kies gravel carrier, 246 50, >132mm<, Price:D **Similar models:** Vetro Recycling glass wagon – 246 52; Hütwangen AG gravel carrier – 246 53; Kies AG Wil-Zürich gravel carrier – 246 54

◎ Liliput, Anker Bier beer wagon (old type), 248 51, >96mm<, Price:D **Similar models:** Biere du Cardinal – 248 52; Salmen-Bier – 248 54; Löwnbräu Zürich – 249 52

◎ Liliput, Ciba-Geigy tank wagon, 250 14, >100mm<, Price:C **Similar models:** Uetikon – 250 59

◎ Liliput, Bell refrigerated wagon, 221 50, >117mm<, Price:C

◎ Lima, Henniez refrigerated wagon, 303555, >130mm<, Price:Z

◎ Lima, Uetikon bogie tank wagon, 302921, >190mm<, Price:Z

◎ Lima, Avia tank wagon, 302722, >116mm<, Price:Z

◎ Lima, Juracement hopper wagon, 302896, >139mm<, Price:Z

◎ Lima, Ovomaltine covered wagon, 303154, >120mm<, Price:Z

◎ Lima, Cardinal covered wagon, 303152, >126mm<, Price:Z

◎ Lima, Aproz covered wagon, 303206, >242mm<, Price:Z

◎ Märklin, Eichhof beer wagon, 4420, >115mm<, Price:Z

◎ Märklin, high-capacity cement wagon, 4691, >133mm<, Price:Z

◎ Märklin, Feldschlösschen beer tank wagon, 4632, >195mm<, Price:Z

◎ Roco, Ovomaltine covered wagon, 4340, >168mm<, Price:D **Similar models:** Warteck – 4340F; Usego – 4340N

◎ Ruco, De L'aigle St. Imier beer wagon with canopy, 2301, >90mm<, Price:Z

◎ Ruco, Maggi covered wagon, 2002, >90mm<, Price:Z

◎ Liliput, tool wagon for construction train, 278 55, >168mm<, Price:D

◎ Liliput, coach owned by Feldschlössen brewery, 277 51, >168mm<, Price:D **Similar models:** blue – 277 52; green – 277 53

## Also available

### SBB steam locomotives
◎ Liliput, 3/5 600 class, ⊑,107 55, >213mm<, ♀ , Price:J
◎ Liliput, E3/3 'Tigerli' class, 33 50, >100mm<, ♀ , Price:K

### SBB electric locomotives
◎ Liliput, Ae 4/7 class, 47 50, ♀ , Price:M **Similar models:** ⊑ – 47 55

### SBB coaches
▣ Fleischmann, baggage car, 5130, >237mm<, Price:E
◎ Liliput, 2nd class coach, 269 50, >168mm<, Price:D
◎ Liliput, 3rd class coach, 278 50, >168mm<, Price:D
◎ Liliput, 2nd class lightweight steel coach, 876 50, >261mm<, Price:Z
◎ Liliput, 2nd class lightweight steel coach, with centre doors, 878 50, >261mm<, Price:D **Similar models:** 1960s livery –878 53
◎ Liliput, lightweight steel baggage car, 879 50, >234mm<, Price:D **Similar models:** 1960s livery – 879 53
◎ Liliput, 1st class Intercity coach, 884 50, >280mm<, Price:E
◎ Liliput, 2nd class Intercity coach, 885 50, >280mm<, Price:E
◎ Liliput, dining car Intercity coach, 886 50, > 280mm<, Price:E
◎ Liliput, 1st class with baggage compartment, 887 50, >280mm<, Price:E
◎ Lima, 2nd class coach, 309189, >266mm<, Price:Z
◎ Roco, 2nd class coach, 4238S, >284mm<, Price:D
◎ Roco, 1st class coach, 4439S, >272mm<, Price:D
◎ Roco, couchette coach, 4243A, >264mm<, Price:Z

### SBB coaches
◎ Roco, 2nd class coach, 44200A, >230mm<, Price:D
◎ Roco, baggage car, 4240S, >210mm<, Price:D

### SBB wagons
◎ Liliput, low-loader wagon, 200 50, >158mm<, Price:E
◎ Liliput, covered wagon, 235 50, >117mm<, Price:C
◎ Liliput, brake van, 245 50, >106mm<, Price:D **Similar models:** alternative livery – 245 54
◎ Roco, silo wagon, 44314A, >122mm<, Price:D
◎ Roco, covered wagon, 4340E, >168mm<, Price:D **Similar models:** with ribbed body – 4341S
◎ Ruco, Maggi covered wagon with brakeman's cab, 2101, >90mm<, Price:Z

### Private-owner wagons
◎ Liliput, Aproz van, 229 50, >117mm<, Price:D **Similar models:** Hülimann Bier – 235 51
◎ Liliput, Eichhof Bier beer wagon, 229 51, >117mm<, Price:D
◎ Liliput, Shell bogie tank wagon, 258 51, >172mm<, Price:D **Similar models:** Schenk – 258 50; Esso – 258 52; BP – 258 53; Avia – 258 54, Total – 258 56
◎ Lima, Carlsberg refrigerated wagon, 303552, >130mm<, Price:Z
◎ Lima, Feldschlösschen-Bier refrigerated wagon, 303195, >130mm<, Price:Z

**Miscellaneous**
◎ Liliput, workmen's coach for construction train, 269 55, >168mm<,
Price:D
◎ Liliput, former luggage van used as depot wagon, 275 55, >168mm<,
Price:D
◎ Liliput, 'Ölwehr' (fire-fighting and pollution control) tank and van, 810 50.
>206mm<, Price:D

# Switzerland

# Rhätische Bahn

The Rhätische Bahn (RhB) is a narrow-gauge line started in 1889. Steep gradients and enormous civil engineering projects were necessary, with many viaducts and tunnels. The line reaches 1,800 metres (6,000ft) by the time it reaches St Moritz. The line was electrified by 1923. There are about 60 electric locomotives now in use, and some electric railcars. Two old steam locomotives are used for special trips on the line.

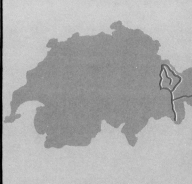

## HOe Narrow Gauge

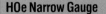

◎ Bemo, (HOe), Ge4/4 class, ⬦, 1050/5, >139mm<, Price:L **Similar models:** HOm – 1250/5. Available with alternative names: 1050/6,7,8,9,10 (HOe); 1250/6,7,8,9,10 (HOm)

◎ Bemo, (HOe), 2nd class coach, 3054, >171mm<, Price:D **Similar models:** HOm – 3254; alternative livery, HOe – 3055; alternative livery, HOm – 3255

◎ Bemo, (HOe), 1st and 2nd class coach, 3056, >171mm<, Price:D **Similar models:** HOm 3256; red livery, HOe – 3057; red livery, HOm – 3257

◎ Bemo, (HOe), covered wagon, 2050, >98mm<, Price:D **Similar models:** HOm – 2250

◎ Bemo, (HOe), high-sided wagon, 2051, >102mm<, Price:D **Similar models:** HOm – 2251

◎ Bemo, (HOe), cement wagon, 2052, >89mm<, Price:D **Similar models:** HOm – 2252; alternative livery, HOe – 2053; alternative livery HOm – 2253

**Also available**
**RhB electric locomotives**
◎ Bemo, (HOe), Ge6/6 class, ⬦, 1055, >153mm<, Price:L **Similar models:** HOm – 1255
**RhB wagons**
◎ Bemo, (HOe), open wagon, 2055, >102mm<, Price:D **Similar models:** HOm – 2255; alternative livery, HOe – 2056; alternative livery, HOm – 2256
**RhB coaches**
◎ Bemo, (HOe), 2nd class coach, 3058, >171mm<, Price:D **Similar models:** HOm – 3258

# Austria

# Österreichische Bundesbahnen

The Österreichische Bundesbahnen (ÖBB) was known as the Bundesbahn Österreich (BBÖ) until 1950. Nationalization proper started in 1880, but the ending of the Austro-Hungarian Empire in 1918 meant a new start. The current ÖBB has characteristics and routes similar to the German and Swiss railways (and some common locomotive types). Several famous Trans-Europe expresses run over ÖBB rails.

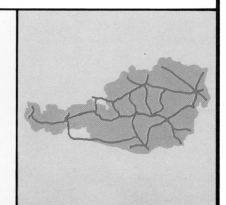

## N Gauge

⊖ Fleischmann, 0-10-0 tank locomotive, 7095, >79mm<, ♀, Price:K

⊖ Fleischmann, 4-6-0 locomotive, 7161, >122mm<, ♀, Price:K

⊖ Fleischmann, 2-10-0 locomotive, 7178, >150mm<, ♀, Price:L

⊖ Arnold, 1020 class, ♠, 2330, >118mm<, ♀, Price:K

⊖ Arnold, 1118 class, ♠, 2454, >116mm<, ♀, Price:L

⊖ Roco, 1044 class, ♠, 2158A, >100mm<, ♀, Price:J

⊖ Arnold, BVT power car, 2915, >87mm<, ♀, Price:J

⊖ Arnold, BVT driving trailer (unpowered), 2917, >87mm<, ♀, Price:E

⊖ Arnold, 1st class coach, 3311, >128mm<, Price:D

⊖ Roco, 1st class coach, 2261A, >165mm<, Price:Z

⊖ Roco, 2nd class coach, 2262A, >165mm<, Price:Z

⊖ Minitrix, ballast wagon, 3520, >76mm<, Price:D

⊖ Roco, open wagon, 2331B, >60mm<, Price:B

⊖ Roco, telescopic cowl wagon, 2375A, >75mm<, Price:D

## Also available

**ÖBB steam locomotives**
⊖ Fleischmann, 2-6-0 tank locomotive, 7031, >68mm<, ♀, Price:J
⊖ Roco, 44 class, 2106G, >141mm<, Price:L

**ÖBB diesel railcars**
⊖ Arnold, BTL intermediate coach, 2916, >87mm<, Price:D

**ÖBB coaches**
⊖ Arnold, 1st class Eurofirma coach, 3776, >163mm<, Price:D
⊖ Arnold, 2nd class coach, 3321, >128mm<, Price:D

**ÖBB coaches**
⊖ Arnold, 2nd class Eurofirma coach, 3777, >163mm<, Price:D
⊖ Roco, TEN sleeping car, 2278B, >165mm<, Price:D
⊖ Roco, 1st and 2nd class coach, 2280B, >165mm<, Price:D
⊖ Roco, restaurant car, 2281A, Price:D
⊖ Roco, 2nd class coach, 2264D, >131mm<, Price:D

# Austria (ÖBB)

**HO/OO Gauge**

◉ Fleischmann, 4-6-0 'P8' locomotive, 4161, >214mm<, ♀, Price:L  (supplied with transfers; shown here in NS livery)

◉ Fleischmann, 2-10-0 locomotive, 4178, >270mm<, ♀, Price:M

◎ Roco, 658 class, 4112B, >159mm<, ♀, Price:L

◎ Roco, 44 class, 4126G, >260mm<, ♀, Price:L

◎ Roco, 93 class, 4122C, >159mm<, ♀, Price:K

◎ Lima, 1043 class, ⛭, 208060LG, >176mm<, Price:Z

◎ Märklin, 1043 class, ≦, ☎, 3041, >175mm<, ♀, Price:Z

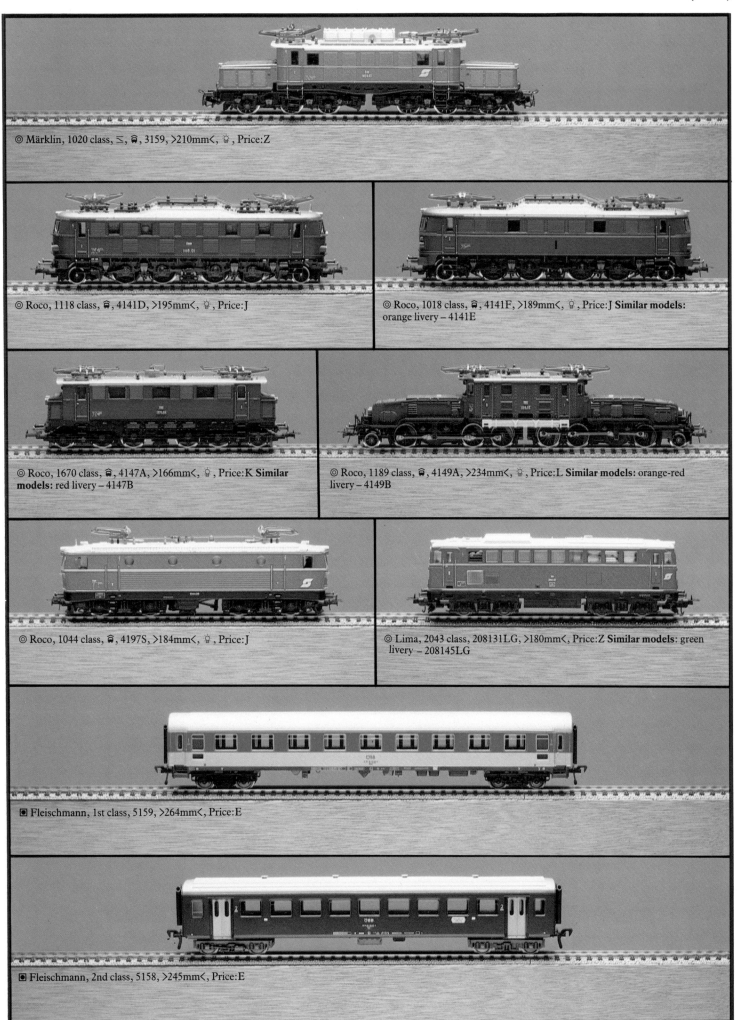

◎ Märklin, 1020 class, ⊆, 🖂, 3159, >210mm<, 💡, Price:Z

◎ Roco, 1118 class, 🖂, 4141D, >195mm<, 💡, Price:J

◎ Roco, 1018 class, 🖂, 4141F, >189mm<, 💡, Price:J **Similar models:** orange livery – 4141E

◎ Roco, 1670 class, 🖂, 4147A, >166mm<, 💡, Price:K **Similar models:** red livery – 4147B

◎ Roco, 1189 class, 🖂, 4149A, >234mm<, 💡, Price:L **Similar models:** orange-red livery – 4149B

◎ Roco, 1044 class, 🖂, 4197S, >184mm<, 💡, Price:J

◎ Lima, 2043 class, 208131LG, >180mm<, Price:Z **Similar models:** green livery – 208145LG

◉ Fleischmann, 1st class, 5159, >264mm<, Price:E

◉ Fleischmann, 2nd class, 5158, >245mm<, Price:E

◎ Märklin, 1st class Eurofirma coach, 4149, >264mm<, Price:Z

◎ Roco, 2nd class coach, 4237A, >254mm<, Price:D

◎ Roco, 1st class coach, 4236A, >264mm<, Price:D

◎ Roco, 2nd class coach, 44203A, >271mm<, Price:D **Similar models:** red and cream livery – 44203B

◎ Roco, four-wheeled 2nd class coach, 4201B, >160mm<, Price:D

◎ Roco, four-wheeled 1st class coach, 4203B, >161mm<, Price:D

◎ Roco, four-wheeled baggage coach, 4204B, >160mm<, Price:D

◎ Roco, covered wagon, 4301D, >104mm<, Price:B

◎ Roco, covered wagon, 4305F, >104mm<, Price:B

◎ Roco, bogie covered wagon, 4369B, >206mm<, Price:D

◎ Roco, ballast wagon, 4334B, >79mm<, Price:D

◎ Roco, hopper wagon with coal load, 4335B, >111mm<, Price:D

◎ Roco, telescopic cowl wagon, 4395A, >138mm<, Price:D

## Also available

### BBÖ steam locomotives
◎ Liliput, 2-8-4 type 84, 106 10, >272mm<, Price:M **Similar models:** ≲ – 106 15 (Price:M)
◎ Liliput, 2-8-4 type 214.04 ex-works grey, 106 12, >272mm<, Price:N

### BBÖ coaches
◎ Liliput, 4-wheeled mail coach, 272 10, >127mm<, Price:C
◎ Liliput, 4-wheeled coach, 273 10, >126mm<, Price:D
◎ Liliput, 4-wheeled coach, 273 12, >126mm<, Price:D
◎ Liliput, express coach, 280 10, >232mm<, Price:D
◎ Liliput, passenger coach, 295 13, >224mm<, Price:D
◎ Liliput, 3rd class express coach, 833 13, >240mm<, Price:D

### ÖBB steam locomotives
◎ Liliput, 42 class, 42 13, Price:M **Similar Models:** ≲ – 42 18
◎ Liliput, 52 class, 52 12, >268mm<, Price:M **Similar models:** ≲ – 52 17; DC, with round chimney – 52 10
◎ Liliput, 2-6-0 tank locomotive, 91 13, >120mm<, Price:L
◎ Liliput, 214 class, 106 13, >272mm<, Price:N
◎ Liliput, Class 638, 108 10, >214mm<, Price:L **Similar models:** ≲ – 108 15 (Price:K)

### ÖBB electric locomotives
▣ Fleischmann, 1043 class, 🔌, 4366, >179mm<, 💡, Price:L
◎ Liliput, 1245.500 type, 🔌, 113 11, >147mm<, Price:K **Similar models:** ≲ – 113 16; green livery, DC – 113 10; green livery, ≲ – 113 15
◎ Liliput, 1040.10 type, 🔌, 115 10, >147mm<, 💡, Price:K **Similar models:** ≲ – 115 15 (Price:L); 1040.07 type, red livery, DC – 115 11 (Price:K); 1040.07 type, red, ≲ – 115 16
◎ Liliput, 1042.500 type, 🔌, 114 11, >187mm<, 💡, Price:L **Similar models:** ≲ – 114 16; green livery, DC – 114 10; green, ≲ – 114 15
◎ Liliput, 1020, 🔌, 119 11, >212mm<, 💡, Price:L **Similar models:** ≲ – 119 16; green livery, DC – 119 10

### ÖBB coaches
◎ Liliput, express coach, 287 10, >240mm<, Price:D **Similar models:** 1st and 2nd class commuter coach – 287 70
◎ Liliput, baggage car, 289 10, >250mm<, Price:D
◎ Liliput, 'skirted' 1st class coach with UIC inscription, 831 10, >247mm<, Price:D **Similar models:** new red and beige livery – 831 14; green livery, 1st and 2nd class – 832 10; green livery, 2nd class – 833 10; red and beige livery, 2nd class – 833 14
◎ Liliput, 'skirted' mail coach, 838 10, >257mm<, Price:D
◎ Liliput, couchette coach with UIC inscription, 883 10 >304mm<, Price:D

### ÖBB wagons
◎ Liliput, low-loader wagon, 200 10, >158mm<, Price:E
◎ Liliput, wagon for use with low-loader 200 10, 204 12, >118mm<, Price:C
◎ Liliput, bogie log carrier, 201 10, >227mm<, Price:D **Similar models:** load of MAT containers – 201 11; with Coca-Cola containers – 201 16; with Eskimo containers – 201 15; with Sealand container – 202 10; with Seatrain container – 202 11; with Interfrigo container – 202 13
◎ Liliput, platform wagon, 203 00, >118mm<, Price:B **Similar models:** with load of Eskimo container – 203 15 (Price:D); with Sea-Cont container – 203 14 (Price:D); with MAT container – 203 11 (Price:D); with Coca-Cola container – 203 16 (Price:D); with Interfrigo container – 203 17 (Price:D); with Röstrand container – 203 80 (Price:D); with Volvo container – 203 81 (Price:D); with SJ container – 203 82 (Price:D)

### ÖBB wagons
◎ Liliput, low gondola wagon, 204 10, >118mm<, Price:C
◎ Liliput, gondola with stakes, 208 10, >127mm<, Price:C
◎ Liliput, timber wagon with brakeman's cab, 206 00, >127mm<, Price:C
◎ Liliput, bogie flat wagon, 212 10, 152mm, Price:C
◎ Liliput, covered van with brakeman's cab, 214 10, >106mm<, Price:C
**Similar models:** workshop wagon – 214 11
◎ Liliput, ore wagon, 220 10, >114mm<, Price:D
◎ Liliput, high-capacity van, 242 10, >166mm<, Price:D
◎ Liliput, van with UIC inscription, 254 10, >103mm<, Price:C
◎ Liliput, brake van, 259 10, >103mm<, Price:D
◎ Roco, low-sided wagon with stakes, 4306B, >124mm<, Price:C
◎ Roco, open wagon, 4314C, >94mm<, Price:C
◎ Roco, open wagon, 4309B, >104mm<, Price:B

### Private-owner wagons
◎ Liliput, NÖ milk wagon, 205 10, >127mm<, Price:Z
◎ Liliput, Rigips van, 229 10, >117mm<, Price:C
◎ Liliput, Eternit open wagon, 237 10, >117mm<, Price:C
◎ Liliput, Liliput 6-axle bulk carrier, 239 10, >158mm<, Price:D **Similar models:** yellow livery – 239 11; Ranshofen-Berndorf – 239 12
◎ Liliput, Hartsteinwerk Kitzbühel gravel wagon, 246 12, >132mm<, Price:D
◎ Liliput, Shell-Austria tank wagon, 250 01, >100mm<, Price:C **Similar models:** Esso – 250 02
◎ Liliput, Solvay high-pressure tank wagon, 251 11, >100mm<, Price:D
◎ Liliput, Esso bogie tank wagon, 258 12, >172mm<, Price:D
◎ Liliput, Intercontinentale Transportges 16-axle low-loader with transformer, 383 10, >509mm<, Price:F
◎ Liliput, Intercontinentale Transportges 16-axle low-loader with bulk container, 384 10, >293mm<, Price:F
◎ Liliput, Gösser-Bier beer wagon, 215 11, >106mm<, Price:D **Similar models:** Stiegl – 215 12

### Miscellaneous
◎ Liliput, track cleaning vehicle (as Shell tank wagon), 252 01, >118mm<, Price:D **Similar models:** Esso – 252 02; BP – 252 03; Aral – 252 04; Gasolin – 252 05
◎ Liliput, Plasser & Theurer track building vehicle OBW 10, 381 10, >112mm<, Price:D **Similar models:** motorized – 382 10 (Price:Z)
◎ Liliput, Plasser & Theurer Mainliner Duomatic 07-32″ track maintenance vehicle, (not powered), 380 10, >205mm<, Price:E

# Luxembourg

## Société Nationale des Chemins de Fer Luxembourgeois

Société Nationale des Chemins de Fer Luxembourgeois (CFL) is one of the smallest systems in Europe, with about 270 route kilometres (170 miles) of track and 50 locomotives. The company was formed in 1946 when a French-Belgian firm previously operating the line was taken over. The Luxembourg railways have remained busy because of the amount of through traffic, particularly from France and Belgium.

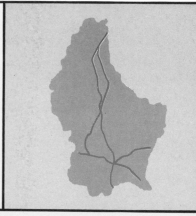

**HO/OO Gauge**

◎ Roco, 93 class, 4122D, >159mm<, ⚲ , Price:K

**Also available**
**CFL steam locomotives**
◎ Liliput, 55 class (BR 42), 42 20, >268mm<, Price:N
**CFL wagons**
◎ Liliput, goods van, 254 20, >103mm<, Price:C

# Hungary

## Magyar Államvasutak Vezérigazgatósaga

Magyar Államvasutak Vezérigazgatósaga (MÁV), the Hungarian state railway, has existed since 1869. It is one of the earliest state railways, but the first lines in the country (then Austro-Hungary) were even earlier, being laid in 1846. In 1933 MÁV became the first railway to operate an overhead AC high voltage electric mainline route in modern style. Today, apart from some electric locomotives, traction is mainly diesel.

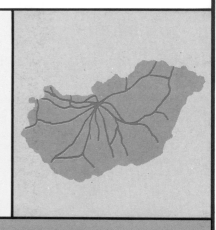

**TT Gauge**

Berliner Bahnen, M61 class, 2532, >158mm<, ⚲ , Price:Z

Berliner Bahnen, 1st class coach, 3613, >195mm<, Price:Z

Berliner Bahnen, covered wagon, 4132, >76mm<, Price:Z

Berliner Bahnen, bogie tank wagon, 5415, >104mm<, Price:Z

# USSR

## Sovietskie Zeleznye Dorogi

The Soviet railways have the greatest mileage in the world (about 138,000 kilometres or nearly 86,000 miles). Nationalization dates back to the late 19th century, with the remaining private lines being absorbed after the 1917 revolution. A gauge of 5ft is used throughout, and although steam was almost universal until the 1950s, virtually all locomotives are now diesel or electric. Passenger traffic is still very important, but the trains are slow.

**TT Gauge**

Berliner Bahnen, YM32 class, 2622, >105mm<, Price:Z

Berliner Bahnen, YC1 class, ⚙, 2313, >130mm<, ⚙, Price:Z

# Czechoslovakia

## Československé Státni Dráhy

Československé Státni Dráhy (CSD) is the Czechoslovakian state railway. On formation of the Czechoslovak state in 1918 those lines of the old Austro-Hungarian system within the new borders became part of CSD and about 160 kilometres (100 miles) of new routes were added. The system now has good diesel and electric designs. Most lines are standard gauge, but there are some narrow and broad gauge lines.

**TT Gauge**

Berliner Bahnen, T679 class, 2641, >158mm<, ⚙, Price:Z

Berliner Bahnen, T435 class, 2621, >105mm<, Price:Z

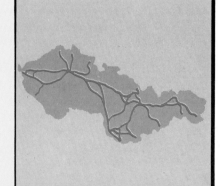

Berliner Bahnen, E499 class, ⚙, 2311, >130mm<, ⚙, Price:Z **Similar models:** green and yellow livery – 2312

Berliner Bahnen, 1st and 2nd class coach, 3611, >195mm<, Price:Z

Berliner Bahnen, dining car, 3711, >195mm<, Price:Z

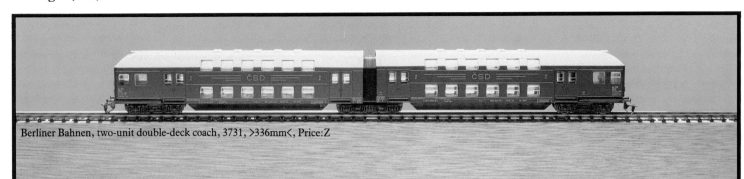

Berliner Bahnen, two-unit double-deck coach, 3731, >336mm<, Price:Z

Berliner Bahnen, covered wagon, 4131, >76mm<, Price:Z

Berliner Bahnen, bogie tank wagon, 5412, >104mm<, Price:Z

# Portugal

# Caminhos de Ferro Portugueses

The Caminhos de Ferro Portugueses (CP) is unusual because it is a private company that has gained a monopoly by absorbing its rivals over the years. It is a broad gauge railway of 5ft 6in, with a few narrow gauge lines. There are about 2,800 route kilometres (1,800 miles), centred on Lisbon with three major routes radiating from the capital. The CP remains a moderately successful operation.

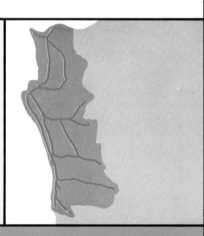

## HO/OO Gauge

© Lima, BoBo electric locomotive, 208069LG, >200mm<, Price:Z

© Lima, 1st class coach, 309160, >265mm<, Price:Z

**Also available**
**Private-owner wagons**
© Electrotren, GALP liquid fuel tank wagon, 5425, >160mm<, Price:D

# Spain

## Red Nacional de los Ferrocarriles Espanoles

The Red Nacional de los Ferrocarriles Espanoles (RENFE) was formed when Franco's government nationalized various private lines in 1939. Most trunk routes had been built to a broad gauge of 5ft 6in, but many standard and narrow gauge railways also existed. Under RENFE the railways were modernized, and fast train, such as the Talgo, were introduced. Over 3,000 kilometres (2,000 miles) are electrified.

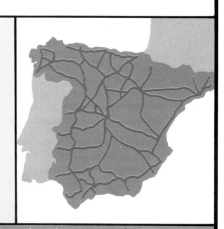

### N Gauge

⊖ Ibertren, FFA class, 013, >115mm<, Price:Z

⊖ Ibertren, Mitsubishi electric, 027, >110mm<, Price:Z **Similar models:** ≠ – 962

⊖ Ibertren, Alshom electric, 014, >124mm<, Price:Z **Similar models:** ≠ – 952; red and white livery, 2-rail – 015; red and white livery, ≠ – 953

⊖ Roco, 7630 class, ⚥, 2157B, >108mm<, ⚥, Price:J

⊖ Ibertren, Talgo 2000 class, 026, >110mm<, Price:Z **Similar models:** ≠ – 961

⊖ Ibertren, double Alco diesels, 024, >234mm<, Price:Z **Similar models:** ≠ – 959; silver and green livery, 2-rail – 025; silvery and green livery, ≠ – 960

⊖ Ibertren, single Alco diesel, 023, >115mm<, Price:Z **Similar models:** ≠ – 958; green and yellow livery, 2-rail – 022; green and yellow livery, ≠ – 957

⊖ Ibertren, Alco 2100 class, 012, >123mm<, Price:Z **Similar models:** ≠ – 951

⊖ Ibertren, BB class, 016, >117mm<, Price:Z **Similar models:** ≠ – 954

⊖ Roco, 307 class, 2152B, >91mm<, ⚥, Price:J

⊖ Ibertren, end Talgo coaches (pair), 281, Price:Z

⊖ Ibertren, 1st class coach, 201, >130mm<, Price:Z **Similar models:** 2nd class – 203; 1st class, blue livery – 202; 2nd class, blue livery – 204; 1st class, red and cream livery – 210; 2nd class, red and cream livery – 211; 1st class, green and cream livery – 213; 2nd class, green and cream livery – 214

⊖ Ibertren, luggage van, 205 >130mm<, Price:Z **Similar models:** blue livery – 206; red and cream livery – 212; green and cream livery – 215; green and grey livery – 216; alternative green and grey livery – 221; mail coach – 225

# Spain (RENFE)

⊖ Ibertren, 4-wheeled 1st class coach, 208, >87mm<, Price:Z **Similar models:** 2nd class (green) – 209

⊕ Ibertren, 3rd class coach, 226, >130mm<, Price:Z

⊖ Ibertren, sleeping coach, 207, >145mm<, Price:Z

⊖ Ibertren, sleeping coach, 227, >130mm<, Price:Z **Similar models:** blue livery – 228

⊖ Lima, 2nd class coach, 320310, >138mm<, Price:Z

⊖ Ibertren, low-sided wagon, 301, >61mm<, Price:Z **Similar models:** grey – 302; brown, with load of 2 cars – 303; grey, with load of 2 cars – 304

⊖ Ibertren, medium-sided wagon, 321, >61mm<, Price:Z **Similar models:** grey – 322; brown, with load of coal – 323

⊖ Ibertren, covered goods wagon, 341, >61mm<, Price:Z **Similar models:** dark green – 342; yellow – 343; white – 344; green – 345

⊖ Ibertren, short flat wagons (one with brake cab) and load of timber, 373, >133mm<, Price:Z **Similar models:** flat wagon only – 371; flat wagon with brake cab only – 372

⊖ Ibertren, low-sided wagon, 391, >110mm<, Price:Z **Similar models:** grey – 392; brown, with load of pipes – 393; grey, with load of pipes – 394; brown, with load of boxes – 395

⊖ Ibertren, high-sided wagon, 411, >110mm<, Price:Z **Similar models:** grey – 412; brown, with load of sand – 413; grey, with load of sand, 414

⊖ Ibertren, low-sided wagon with uprights, 431, >110mm<, Price:Z **Similar models:** grey – 432; brown, with load of tree trunks – 433; grey, with load of tree trunks – 434

⊖ Ibertren, livestock wagon, 448, >109mm<, Price:Z **Similar models:** banana wagon – 447

⊖ Ibertren, car carrier with cars, 452, >131mm<, PriceZ **Similar models:** without cars – 451

⊖ Ibertren, Campsa tank wagon, 351, >68mm<, Price:Z **Similar models:** Shell – 352; Esso – 353; STP – 354; Gulf – 355; Aral – 356; BP – 357; Fina – 358

⊕ Ibertren, Butano bogie tank wagon, 361, >110mm<, Price:Z **Similar models:** white – 362

⊖ Ibertren, Transfesa refrigerated van, 382, >69mm<, Price:Z **Similar models:** white – 381

⊖ Ibertren, Transfesa livestock wagon, 446, >109mm<, Price:Z

⊖ Ibertren, mine wagon, 461, >44mm<, Price:Z **Similar models:** green – 462; blue – 463; yellow – 464; grey – 465; orange – 466

⊖ Lima, Semat car transporter, 320791, Price:Z

**Also available**
**RENFE coaches**
⊖ Ibertren, 1st class Talgo coaches (pair), 282, Price:Z
⊖ Ibertren, 1st class Talgo coach, bar coach (pair), 284, Price:Z
⊖ Ibertren, 2nd class Talgo coaches (pair), 283, Price:Z

**HO/OO Gauge**

◎ Ibertren, 242 T.1600 locomotive, 2.106, >183mm<, Price:Z **Similar models:** INI 242 T.1600, oil-fired – 2.107

◎ Lima, 7600 class, 🔌, 208062LG, >212mm<, Price:Z

◎ Electrotren, Class 333, 2020, >236mm<, Price:K **Similar models:** ≅ – 2001

◎ Ibertren, diesel shunter, 2.101, >111mm<, Price:Z

◎ Ibertren, Alco 2100, 2.104, >225mm<, ⚲, Price:Z

◎ Ibertren, Talgo 2000, 2.108, >203mm<, Price:Z

◎ Lima, 333 class, 208125LG, >236mm<, Price:Z

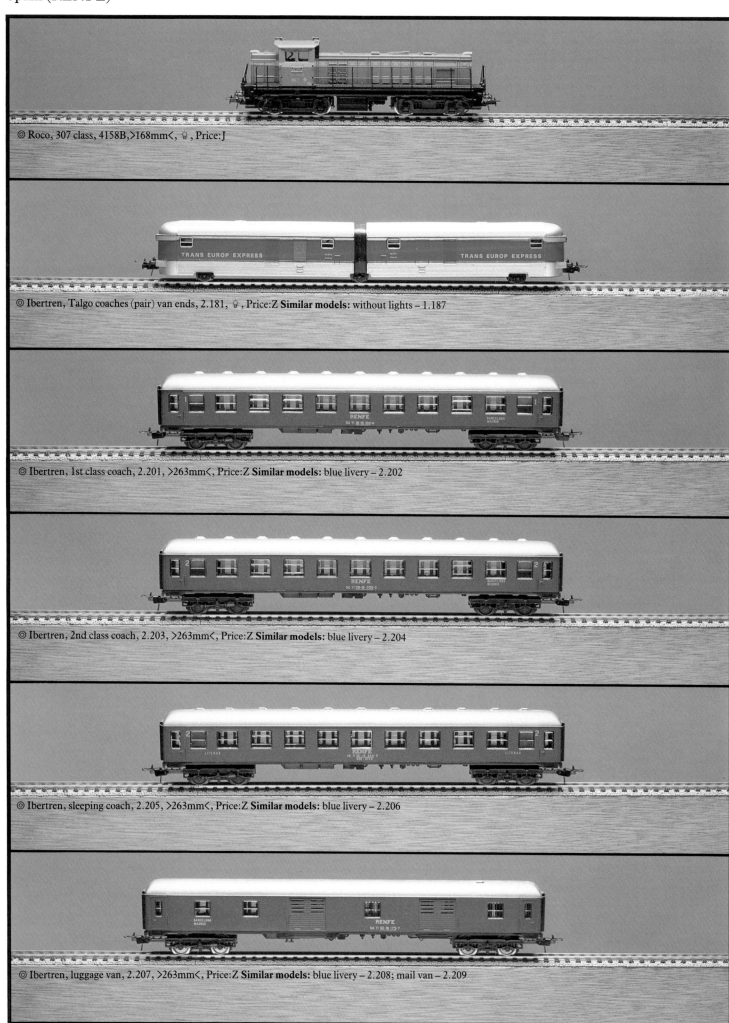

◎ Roco, 307 class, 4158B, >168mm<, ☺ , Price:J

◎ Ibertren, Talgo coaches (pair) van ends, 2.181, ☺ , Price:Z **Similar models:** without lights – 1.187

◎ Ibertren, 1st class coach, 2.201, >263mm<, Price:Z **Similar models:** blue livery – 2.202

◎ Ibertren, 2nd class coach, 2.203, >263mm<, Price:Z **Similar models:** blue livery – 2.204

◎ Ibertren, sleeping coach, 2.205, >263mm<, Price:Z **Similar models:** blue livery – 2.206

◎ Ibertren, luggage van, 2.207, >263mm<, Price:Z **Similar models:** blue livery – 2.208; mail van – 2.209

◎ Lima, 1st class coach, 309142, >268mm<, Price:Z

◎ Lima, 2nd class coach, 309143, >268mm<, Price:Z

◎ Lima, baggage car, 309165, >255mm<, Price:Z

◎ Electrotren, platform wagon, 1000, >115mm<, Price:C **Similar models:** grey livery – 1001; with load of logs – 1005; with load of bags and cover – 1006; with load of bags (no cover) – 1014 (Price:D)

◎ Electrotren, flat wagon with canvas container, 1441, >163mm<, Price:C **Similar models:** without container – 1441

◎ Electrotren, low-sided wagon, 1101, >115mm<, Price:C **Similar models:** grey livery – 1100; with load of boxes – 1103; with load of barrels – 1104; with load of drums – 1105; with load of cotton bales – 1106; with load of glass sheet packing box – 1107; with assorted load – 1108

◎ Electrotren, high-sided wagon, 1200, >115mm<, Price:C **Similar models:** grey, with load of coal – 1201

◎ Electrotren, closed van, 1300, >115mm<, Price:C **Similar models:** green livery – 1301 (Price:C); grey, with DC tail lamp – 1303 (Price:D); grey, with AC tail lamp – 1302 (Price:D)

◎ Electrotren, closed ORE van, 1308, >125mm<, Price:C **Similar models:** special ORE van (green) – 1315; ambulance van – 1311

# Spain (RENFE)

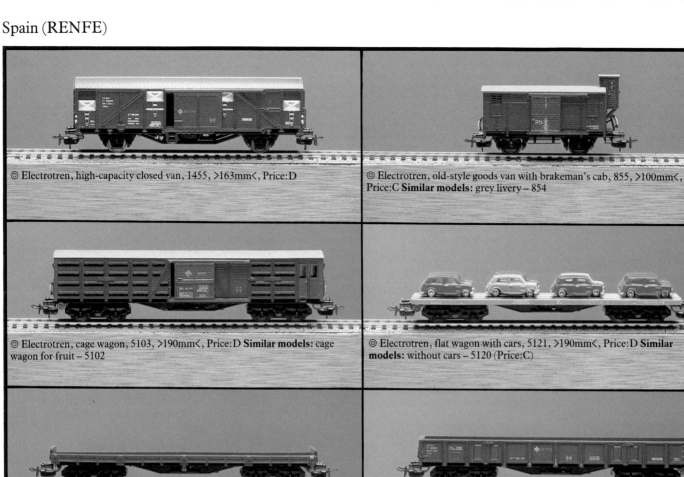

◎ Electrotren, high-capacity closed van, 1455, >163mm<, Price:D

◎ Electrotren, old-style goods van with brakeman's cab, 855, >100mm<, Price:C **Similar models:** grey livery – 854

◎ Electrotren, cage wagon, 5103, >190mm<, Price:D **Similar models:** cage wagon for fruit – 5102

◎ Electrotren, flat wagon with cars, 5121, >190mm<, Price:D **Similar models:** without cars – 5120 (Price:C)

◎ Electrotren, long low-sided wagon, 5123, >190mm<, Price:C **Similar models:** with load of logs – 5124; with load of 3 containers – 5127

◎ Electrotren, long high-sided wagon, 5151, >190mm<, Price:C **Similar models:** grey livery – 5150

◎ Electrotren, bogie liquid gas tank wagon, 5301, >190mm<, Price:D

◎ Ibertren, low-sided wagon, 2.301, >139mm<, Price:Z **Similar models:** grey – 2.302; brown, load of lorry – 2.303; grey, load of lorry – 2.304; brown, load of car and boat – 2.305; grey, load of car and lorry – 2.306; brown, with load of cable reels – 2.307; grey, load of cable reels – 2. 308

◎ Ibertren, flat wagon with uprights, 2.351, >139mm<, Price:Z **Similar models:** grey – 2.352; brown, with load of lorry – 2.353; grey, with load of lorry – 2.354; brown, with load of wood – 2.355

◎ Ibertren, long, medium-sided wagon, 2.411, >236mm<, Price:Z **Similar models:** grey – 2.412; brown, with load of coal – 2.413; grey, with load of coal – 2.414; brown, with mixed load – 2.415; grey, with mixed load – 2.416; brown, with load of phosphates – 2.417; grey, with load of phosphates – 2.418

◎ Ibertren, long, low wagon with uprights, 2.451, >236mm<, Price:Z **Similar models:** grey – 2.452; brown with tree trunk – 2.453; grey, with tree trunk – 2.454; brown, with load of wood – 2.455; grey, with load of wood – 2.456; brown, with load of lorry with trailer – 2.457; grey, with load of lorry with trailer – 2.458; brown, with load of tanker lorry – 2.459; grey, with load of tanker lorry – 2.460; brown, with pipe load – 2.461; grey, with pipe load – 2.462; brown with load of three Renfe containers – 2.463; grey, with load of three Renfe containers – 2.464

◎ Ibertren, bogie covered wagon, 2.470, >190mm<, Price:Z

◎ Lima, container wagon, 302872, >168mm<, Price:Z

◎ Electrotren, Transfesa refrigerator van, 1305, >140mm<, Price:C **Similar models:** P.C. refrigerator van – 1312

◎ Electrotren, Transfesa closed van, 1306, >145mm<, Price:C

◎ Electrotren, SEAT closed van, 1316, >125mm<, Price:C **Similar models:** Coplaca banana van – 1317

◎ Electrotren, Transfesa high-capacity closed van, 1450, >163mm<, Price:D

◎ Electrotren, Shell tank wagon, 1802, >95mm<, Price:C **Similar models:** BP – 1803

◎ Electrotren, Gonzalez Byass wine wagon, 800, >105mm<, Price:D

◎ Electrotren, Gonzalez Byass wine wagon with brakeman's cab, 801, >115mm<, Price:D

◎ Electrotren, Transfesa cement wagon, 1402, >125mm<, Price:D

◎ Electrotren, Ministerio de Agricultura cereal hopper wagon, 1400, >105mm<, Price:C

◎ Electrotren, Transfesa sheep wagon, 5100, >190mm<, Price:D **Similar models:** Foreva cattle wagon – 5101

◎ Electrotren, Antracitas de Ponferrada coal wagon, 5152, >190mm<, Price:C

# Spain (RENFE)

◎ Electrotren, Transfesa hopper wagon, 5200, >190mm<, Price:D **Similar models:** Saltra – 5201

◎ Electrotren, Esso ammonia wagon, 5300, >190mm<, Price:D

◎ Electrotren, Transfesa cement hopper wagon, 5401, >170mm<, Price:D **Similar models:** P.C.P. – 5400

◎ Electrotren, Mobil liquid phosphorus tank wagon, 5421, >160mm<, Price:D **Similar models:** Texaco – 5422; Aral liquid fuel – 5423; Shell special fuels – 5424

◎ Ibertren, Schweppes covered wagon, 2.371, >139mm<, Price:Z **Similar models:** Findus – 2.372; Tente – 2.373; Coca-Cola – 2.374; Danone – 2.375; Voll Damm – 2.376; Ford – 2.377; Tide – 2.378; Red Cross – 2.379

◎ Ibertren, Campsa tank wagon, 2.381, >139mm<, Price:Z **Similar models:** Shell – 2.382; Esso – 2.383; Repsol – 2.384; Bayer – 2.3845;2 Aral – 2.386; BP – 2.387; Fina – 2.388; Mobil – 2.389; Total – 2.390

◎ Ibertren, Martini bogie covered wagon, 2.471, >190mm<, Price:Z **Similar models:** Kodak – 2.472; Moulinex – 2.473; Carlsberg – 2.474; Tio Pepe – 2.475

◎ Electrotren, track cleaning vehicle, 1401, >115mm<, Price:D

## Also available

**RENFE diesel locomotives**
◎ Lima, Co-Co diesel locomotive, 208106LG, >205mm<, Price:Z
◎ Roco, 307 class, 4158B,>168mm<, ♀ , Price:J

**RENFE coaches**
◎ Ibertren, Talgo coaches (pair), 1st class and bar coach, 2.183, ♀ , Price:Z
**Similar models:** without lights – 2.189
◎ Ibertren, Talgo coaches (pair), 1st class, 2.182, ♀ , Price:Z **Similar models:** without lights – 2.188

**RENFE wagons**
◎ Electrotren, old-style goods van, 805, >95mm<, Price:C **Similar models:** grey livery – 804

**Private-owner wagons**
◎ Electrotren, Esso tank wagon with brakeman's cab, 1901, >105mm<, Price:C **Similar models:** Campsa – 1900
◎ Electrotren, Fina tank wagon, 1711, >125mm<, Price:C **Similar models:** Campsa – 1710; Repsol – 1712; Aral – 1713
◎ Electrotren, Semat car carrier, 6003, >305mm<, Price:D **Similar models:** without cars – 6001

# Spain

## Madrid-Zaragoza-Alicante

The Madrid-Zaragoza-Alicante (MZA) railway was the largest of the privately capitalized lines in Spain before nationalization in 1939. It operated the two most important routes in Spain – from Madrid to Barcelona and Madrid to Seville. The MZA suffered badly from damage and disruption during the Spanish Civil War (1936-39), and this was a major factor leading to nationalization.

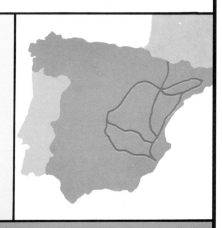

### N Gauge

⊖ Ibertren, 2nd class coach, 222, >117mm<, Price:Z

⊖ Ibertren, luggage van, 223, >55mm<, Price:Z **Similar models:** green livery – 224

### HO/OO Gauge

◎ Ibertren, 242 T.1600 class, 2.105, >183mm<, Price:Z

◎ Electrotren, 2-4-0 tank locomotive, 4001, >96mm<, Price:G **Similar models:** ⊴ – 4000 (Price:J); ⊴, green livery – 4002 (Price:J); 12V DC, green livery – 4003 (G)

◎ Electrotren, mail van, 856, >98mm<, Price:D **Similar models:** green livery – 857

◎ Electrotren, coach, 1500, >118mm<, Price:C **Similar models:** with DC interior lights – 1504 (Price:D); with AC lights – 1502 (Price:D); green livery, no lights – 1501 (Price:C); green with DC lights – 1505 (Price:D); green with AC lights – 1503 (Price:D)

◎ Electrotren, coach used for Catalonian service, 5000, >213mm<, Price:D **Similar models:** with AC interior lighting – 5002; with DC interior lighting – 5004; green livery, without lighting – 5001; green, with AC lighting – 5003; green, with DC lighting – 5005

◎ Electrotren, coach used on Catalonian service (with roof vents), 5006, >213mm<, Price:D **Similar models:** with AC interior lighting – 5007; with DC lighting – 5008

# Italy

## Ferrovie dello Stato

The Ferrovie dello Stato (FS) was formed in 1905 to link up all the major private lines that had been built in the 19th century. Electrification started as long ago as 1900, and diesel traction came before 1940. Steam lingered until recent times, although now modern diesel and electric trains give the FS a good reputation for style and comfort over its 16,000 route kilometres (10,000 miles).

⊕ Arnold, 0-8-0 locomotive, 2516, >118m<, ♀, Price:K

⊖ Fleischmann, 0-10-0 tank locomotive, 7095, >79mm<, ♀, Price:K

⊖ Lima, E424 class, ⇌, 220202G, >95mm<, Price:Z

⊖ Lima, E444 class, ⇌, 220206G, >104mm<, Price:Z

⊕ Arnold, 1st class Eurofirma coach, 3780, >163mm<, Price:D

⊖ Arnold, 2nd class Eurofirma coach, 3781, >163mm<, Price:D

⊕ Lima, mail coach, 320302, >138mm<, Price:Z

⊖ Lima, 1st class TEE coach, 320337, >138mm<, Price:Z

⊕ Roco, 1st class coach, 2261E, >165mm<, Price:D

⊕ Lima, flat wagon (pair) with load, 320482, >136mm<, Price:Z **Similar models:** load of timber – 320483

⊕ Lima, container wagon, 320486, >120mm<, Price:Z

⊖ Lima, car transporter, 320481, >134mm<, Price:Z

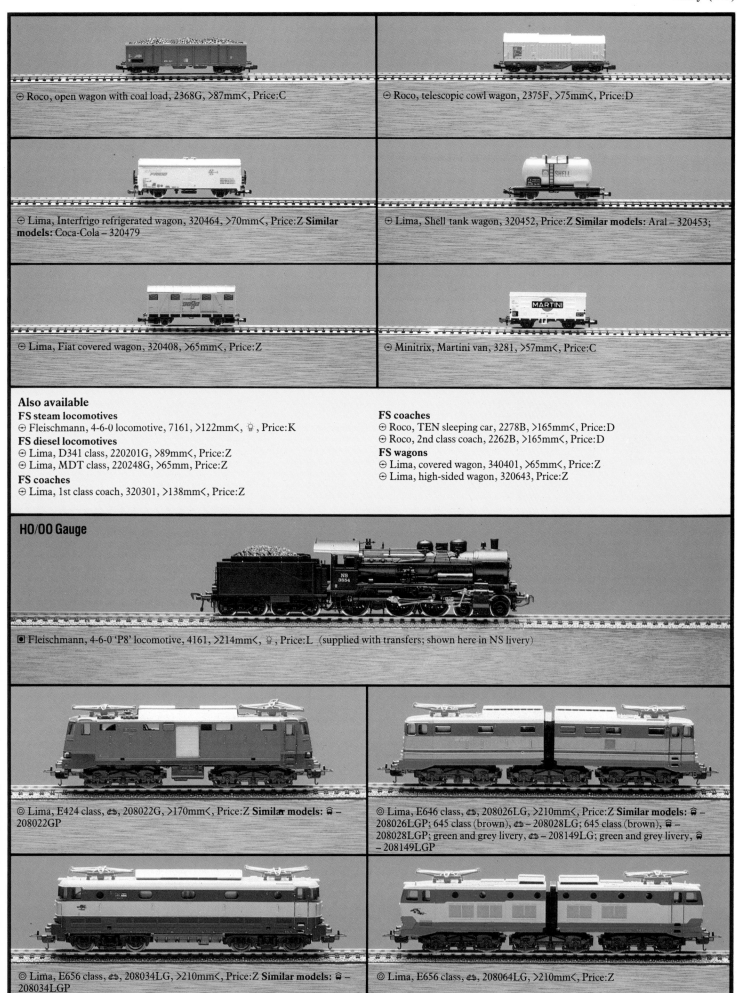

⊖ Roco, open wagon with coal load, 2368G, >87mm<, Price:C

⊖ Roco, telescopic cowl wagon, 2375F, >75mm<, Price:D

⊖ Lima, Interfrigo refrigerated wagon, 320464, >70mm<, Price:Z **Similar models:** Coca-Cola – 320479

⊖ Lima, Shell tank wagon, 320452, Price:Z **Similar models:** Aral – 320453;

⊖ Lima, Fiat covered wagon, 320408, >65mm<, Price:Z

⊖ Minitrix, Martini van, 3281, >57mm<, Price:C

## Also available

**FS steam locomotives**
⊖ Fleischmann, 4-6-0 locomotive, 7161, >122mm<, ☺, Price:K

**FS diesel locomotives**
⊖ Lima, D341 class, 220201G, >89mm<, Price:Z
⊖ Lima, MDT class, 220248G, >65mm, Price:Z

**FS coaches**
⊖ Lima, 1st class coach, 320301, >138mm<, Price:Z

**FS coaches**
⊖ Roco, TEN sleeping car, 2278B, >165mm<, Price:D
⊖ Roco, 2nd class coach, 2262B, >165mm<, Price:D

**FS wagons**
⊖ Lima, covered wagon, 340401, >65mm<, Price:Z
⊖ Lima, high-sided wagon, 320643, Price:Z

## HO/OO Gauge

▣ Fleischmann, 4-6-0 'P8' locomotive, 4161, >214mm<, ☺, Price:L  (supplied with transfers; shown here in NS livery)

◎ Lima, E424 class, ⇔, 208022G, >170mm<, Price:Z **Similar models:** ⌂ – 208022GP

◎ Lima, E646 class, ⇔, 208026LG, >210mm<, Price:Z **Similar models:** ⌂ – 208026LGP; 645 class (brown), ⇔ – 208028LG; 645 class (brown), ⌂ – 208028LGP; green and grey livery, ⇔ – 208149LG; green and grey livery, ⌂ – 208149LGP

◎ Lima, E656 class, ⇔, 208034LG, >210mm<, Price:Z **Similar models:** ⌂ – 208034LGP

◎ Lima, E656 class, ⇔, 208064LG, >210mm<, Price:Z

# Italy (FS)

◎ Märklin, E424 class, ⊵, 🔌, 3035, >175mm<, 🔧, Price:Z

◎ Roco, E626 class, 🔌, 4187A, >173mm<, 🔧, Price:J **Similar models:** different body detail – 4187C

◎ Lima, D342.4 class, 208068LG, >165mm<, Price:Z

◎ Lima, 1st class coach, 309115, >268mm<, Price:Z

◎ Lima, 2nd class coach, 309116, >268mm<, Price:Z

◎ Lima, suburban coach, 309118, >270mm<, Price:Z

◎ Lima, 1st class TEE coach, 309133, >268mm<, Price:Z **Similar models:** Grand Confort livery – 309138

◎ Lima, 2nd class coach, 309136, >270mm<, Price: Z

◎ Lima, 2nd class suburban coach, 309137, >270mm<, Price: Z

◎ Lima, self-service restaurant car, 309236, >268mm<, Price: Z

◎ Lima, mail coach, 309304, >255mm<, Price: Z

◎ Lima, baggage car, 309315, >255mm<, Price: Z **Similar models:** Grand Confort livery – 309317; orange and white livery – 309348

◎ Lima, 1st class coach, 309329, >268mm<, Price: Z

◎ Märklin, TEN 1st and 2nd class sleeping coach, 4152, >270mm<, Price:Z

◎ Roco, 1st class coach, 4236E, >264mm<, Price:D

◎ Roco, 2nd class coach, 4237B, >264mm<, Price:D

◎ Lima, low-sided wagon with brakeman's cab and container, 302830, >116mm<, Price:Z **Similar models:** with three Löwenbräu containers – 302819

◎ Lima, covered wagon, 303161, >121mm<, Price:Z

◎ Lima, open wagon, 303171, >121mm<, Price:Z

◎ Lima, flat wagon with brakeman's cab (load of pipes), 302811, >116mm<, Price:Z

◎ Lima, covered wagon, 303200, >240mm<, Price:Z

◎ Lima, covered wagon, 303209, >250mm<, Price:Z

◎ Roco, covered wagon, 4300S, >124mm<, Price:B

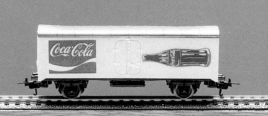

◎ Electrotren, 1470, Transfesa refrigerator van, >163mm<, Price:D

◎ Liliput, Migros refrigerated van, 234 34, >117mm<, Price:D

◎ Lima, Coca-Cola refrigerated wagon, 303113, >126mm<, Price:Z

◎ Lima, Fiat covered wagon, 302867, >227mm<, Price:Z

◎ Lima, Mobiloil bogie tank wagon, 302903, >190mm<, Price:Z

◎ Lima, Fiat covered wagon, 303163, >121mm<, Price:Z

◎ Lima, S.I.T.F.A. car transporter, 309050, >290mm<, Price:Z

**Also available**

**FS steam locomotives**
▣ Fleischmann, 0-10-0 tank locomotive, 4095, >145mm<, ♀. Price:I.

**FS electric locomotives**
◎ Lima, E663 class, ⚫, 208136LG, Price:Z **Similar models:** ☗ – 208136LGP

**FS diesel locomotives**
◎ Lima, D445 class, 208152LG, Price:Z **Similar models:** green livery – 208151LG

**FS coaches**
◎ Lima, 2nd class coach, 309119, >270mm<, Price:Z
◎ Lima, TEN couchette coach, 309233, >268mm<, Price:Z
◎ Lima, 2nd class driving coach, 309273, >303mm<, Price:Z

**FS coaches**
◎ Lima, 2nd class coach, 309272, >303mm<, Price:Z
◎ Lima, 2nd class coach, 309271, >303mm<, Price:Z
◎ Lima, 2nd class double-deck coach, 309228, >274mm<, Price:Z
◎ Lima, 2nd class double-deck end coach, 309229, >274mm<, Price:Z

**FS wagons**
◎ Lima, flat wagons (pair) with load of pipes, 309039, >215mm<, Price:Z
◎ Lima, coal wagon, 303174, >121mm<, Price:Z
◎ Roco, telescopic cowl wagon, 4395G, >138mm<, Price:D
◎ Roco, deep well flat wagon with load, 44311C, >189mm<, Price:E

# South Africa

## South African Railways

South African Railways (SAR) is mainly narrow gauge (3ft 6in), though there are some 2ft gauge minor lines. Because coal is more plentiful than oil, steam locomotives have continued to play a significant role even into the 1980s. The most famous South African train is the electrically-hauled Blue Train, which links Pretoria and Cape Town, and it is one of the few remaining luxury trains in service.

**HO/OO Gauge**

◎ Lima, suburban units, 🚃, 149746GP, >920mm<, Price:Z. Also available as separate items

◎ Lima, covered wagon, 309040, >142mm<, Price:Z

◎ Lima, hopper wagon, 302895, Price:Z

◎ Lima, open wagon with coal load, 303520, >121mm<, Price:Z

◎ Lima, open wagon with cover, 303521, >121mm<, Price:Z

◎ Lima, open wagon, 309041, >130mm<, Price:Z

◎ Lima, covered wagon, 309046, >142mm<, Price:Z

◎ Lima, bogie tank wagon, 302917, >158mm<, Price:Z

◎ Lima, tarpaulin-covered wagon, 309070, >142mm<, Price:Z

◎ Lima, covered hopper wagon, 309071, >170mm<, Price:Z

◎ Lima, covered hopper wagon, 309072, >135mm<, Price:Z

**Also available**
**SAR diesel locomotives**
◎ Lima, 34 class, 208134LG, Price:Z **Similar models**: blue livery – 208153LG

# Australia

## Victorian Government Railways

More recently called Vicrail, this is a 5ft 3in gauge system. It serves the state of Victoria and is centred on Melbourne. A notable surviving line is the narrow-gauge branch line from Belgrave to Menzies Creek near Melbourne. It still runs with some steam locomotives, popularly known as 'Puffing Billies'. These engines survived the breaker's yard and together with the old coaches were returned to service in the 1960s.

**HO/OO Gauge**

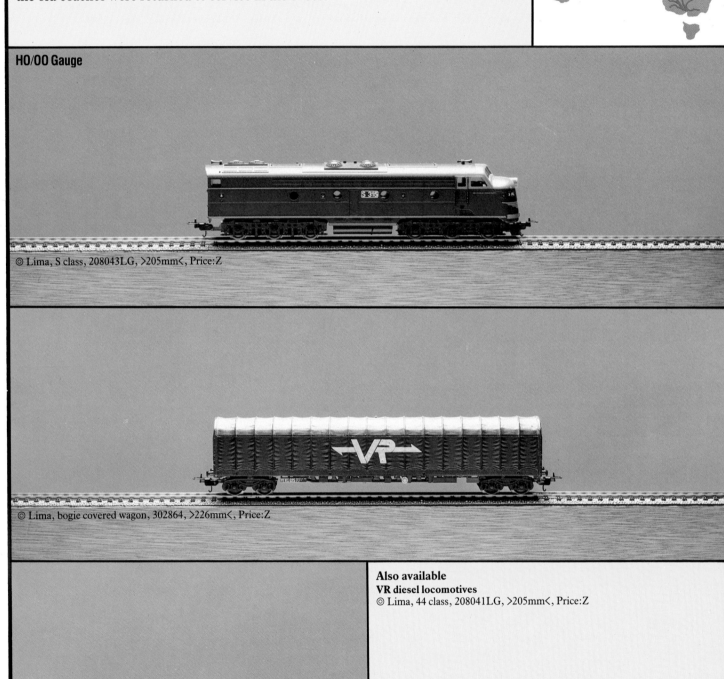

◎ Lima, S class, 208043LG, >205mm<, Price:Z

◎ Lima, bogie covered wagon, 302864, >226mm<, Price:Z

**Also available**
**VR diesel locomotives**
◎ Lima, 44 class, 208041LG, >205mm<, Price:Z

◎ Lima, open wagon, 309036, Price:Z

# Australia

## South Australian State Railways

The South Australian State Railways (SAR) served the state of South Australia, having both narrow gauge (3ft 6in) and broad gauge track. Since 1978 the country (but not suburban) lines have been transferred to the Australian National Railways system. The Overland Limited was a notable prestige express of SAR, and it still runs within the Australian National Railways system. Diesels provide the only motive power.

**HO/OO Gauge**

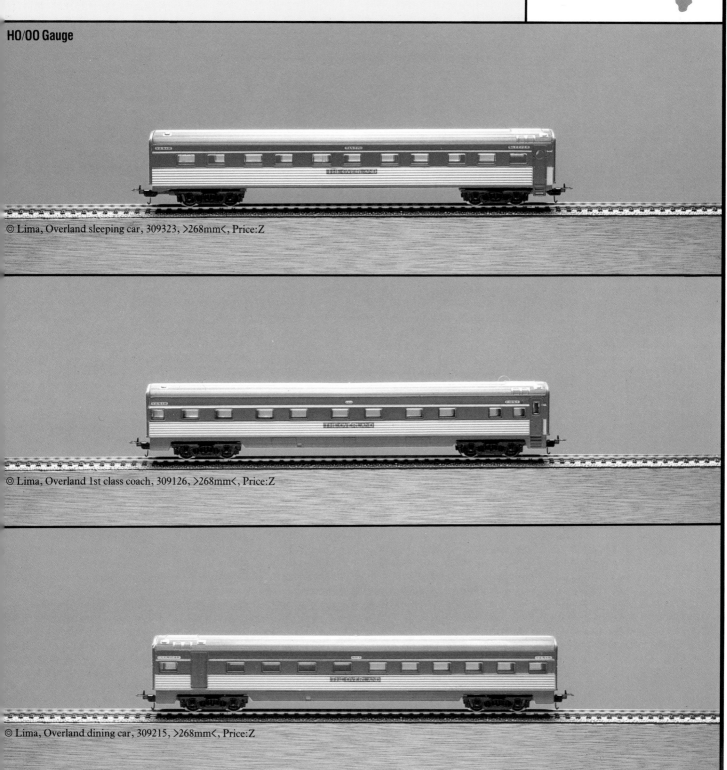

© Lima, Overland sleeping car, 309323, >268mm<, Price:Z

© Lima, Overland 1st class coach, 309126, >268mm<, Price:Z

© Lima, Overland dining car, 309215, >268mm<, Price:Z

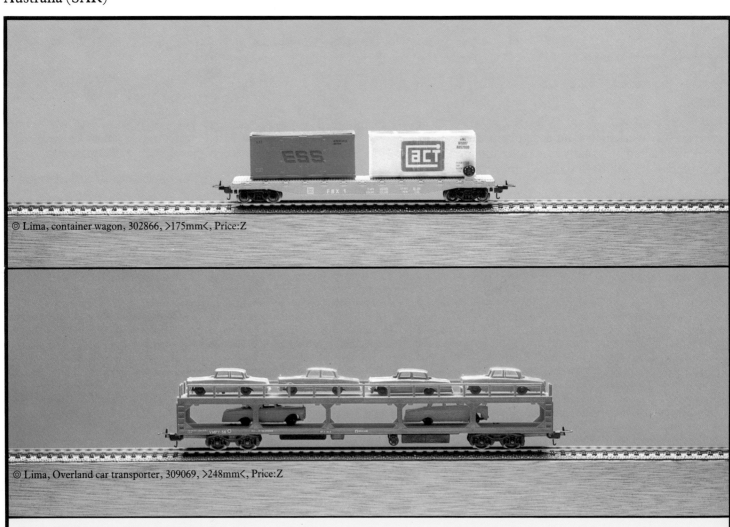

◎ Lima, container wagon, 302866, >175mm<, Price:Z

◎ Lima, Overland car transporter, 309069, >248mm<, Price:Z

**Also available**
**SAR coaches**
◎ Overland power car, 309258, Price:Z

# North America

This section of the book has been arranged to reflect the way rolling stock has traditionally been purchased for real-life American and Canadian railroads. Unlike most European railways, where each company usually has its own railway workshops and designs, railroads in the USA and Canada normally buy from outside manufacturers and have them painted, and possibly modified, to suit their own company. Although only one livery is illustrated, you will find a full list of all the railroad liveries available for that model coded under **Railroads**.

The abbreviations adopted are not necessarily those used by the actual railroad on its rolling stock, but if you look up in the key below those lines that interest you most, you will find them easy to commit to memory.

## The abbreviations used

AA = Ann Arbor Railroad
ACL = Atlantic Coast Line
ADN = Ashley, Drew & Northern
AL = Algoma Central
ALKA = Alaska Railroad
AM = Amtrak
AP = Atlantic & Union Pacific Line
ASA = Atlanta & St. Andrews
AT&SF = Atchison, Topeka & Santa Fe Railway (Santa Fe)
AWP = Atlanta & West Point Railroad
B&M = Boston & Maine Railroad
B&O = Baltimore & Ohio Railroad
BN = Burlington Northern
CANP = Canadian Pacific (Canada)
CB = Cotton Belt
CBQ = Chicago, Burlington, Quincy Railroad (Burlington Route)
CH = Chattanooga Traction
CIM = Chicago & Illinois Midland
C&O = Chesapeake & Ohio Railway
C&P = Clarendon & Pittsford
CNA = Canadian National (Canada)
CNJ = Central Railroad of New Jersey (Jersey Central Lines)
CNW = Chicago & North Western Railway
COB = Chicago Outer Belt
CON = Conrail
CPA = Central Pacific
CR = Clinchfield Railroad
D&H = Delaware & Hudson Railroad Corporation
DLW = Delaware, Lackawanna & Western
DTI = Detroit, Toledo & Ironton
DSSA = Duluth South Shore & Atlantic
EL = Erie & Lackawanna
ERIE = Erie Railroad
FEC = Florida East Coast
FR = Frisco (St. Louis – San Francisco)
GMO = Gulf, Mobile & Ohio
GN = Great Northern Railway
GTW = Grand Trunk Western Railway System
G&W = Genesee & Wyoming
IC = Illinois Central Railroad Company

IT = Illinois Terminal Railroad Company
L&N = Louisville & Nashville Railroad
LNA = Louisville, New Albany & Corydon
LV = Lehigh Valley Railroad
MC = Maine Central
MILW = Milwaukee Road (Chicago, Milwaukee, St. Paul & Pacific)
MKT = Missouri-Kansas-Texas Railroad Company (Katy Railroad)
M&P = Maryland & Pennsylvania
MP = Missouri Pacific Railroad Company
MSL = Minneapolis & St. Louis
MTW = Marinette, Tomahawk & Western
NH = New Haven (New York, New Haven & Hartford Railroad
NKP = New York, Chicago & St. Louis Railroad (Nickel Plate Road)
NP = Northern Pacific Railway Company
NYC = New York Central System
N&W = Norfolk & Western Railway Company
ON = Oregon & Northwestern
ONNO = Ontario Northland (Canada)
OPE = Oregon, Pacific & Eastern
PAEL = Pacific Electric
PC = Penn Central
PE = Pittsburgh & Lake Erie
PEAB = Peabody Short Line
PHD = Port Huron & Detroit
PR = Pennsylvania Railroad Company
PSR = Petaluma & Santa Rosa Railroad
RDG = Reading
RFP = Richmond, Fredericksburg & Potomac
RI = Rock Island (Chicago, Rock Island & Pacific Railroad)
RIO = Rio Grande (Denver & Rio Grande Western Railroad)
RUT = Rutland
RV = Rahway Valley
SCL = Seaboard Coast Line
SIR = Sierra Railroad
SOO = Minneapolis, St. Paul & Sault Ste. Marie (SOO Line)
SP = Southern Pacific Company
SPI = Spokane International Railway
SPS = Spokane, Portland & Seattle
SR = Southern Railroad/Railway System
SRN = Sabine River & Northern
SUS = Susquehanna
TEXP = Texas & Pacific
THB = Toronto, Hamilton & Buffalo (Canada)
TPW = Toledo, Peoria & Western (Rocket)
UP = Union Pacific Railroad Company
USRA = United States Railroad Administration
VMC = Vermont Central
VR = Virginian Railway
VT = Virginia & Truckee Railway
W&A = Western & Atlantic
WAB = Wabash Railroad
WM = Western Maryland Railway
WP = Western Pacific

# North America

## Burlington Northern

The Burlington Northern (BN) was the product of the first of the big mergers of recent years. It was formed in 1970 from the Northern Pacific, Great Northern, and Chicago, Burlington & Quincy. Recently it took over St Louis and San Francisco Railroad, known as the Frisco. The BN operates west and north-west from Chicago, taking in the Pacific North West coast. It has the biggest route mileage in the USA.

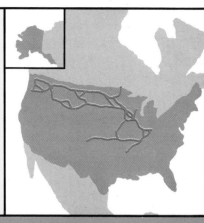

**N Gauge**

⊕ Bachmann, Northern 4-8-4, >235mm<, ♀, Price:J **Railroads:** AT&SF (51-580-02), CBQ (51-580-16), RDG (51-580-10)

⊕ Bachmann, 0-4-0 shifter, >100mm<, Price:E **Railroads:** AT&SF (51-547-02), PR (51-547-14)

⊕ Bachmann, Consolidation 2-8-0, >140mm<, ♀, Price:G **Railroads:** AT&SF (51-530-02), GN (51-530-11), RDG (51-530-10)

⊕ Bachmann, USRA 0-6-0 switcher, >120mm<, Price:F **Railroads:** AT&SF (51-505-02), PR (51-505-14)

⊕ Bachmann, old-time 4-4-0, Price:G **Railroads:** CPA (51-510-24), UP (with modifications, 51-510-01)

⊖ Bachmann, 0-4-0 switcher, >55mm<, Price:E **Railroads:** AT&SF (51-526-02), B&O (51-526-12)

⊖ Minitrix, 'old-timer' Western 0-6-0, >136mm<, ♀, Price:J **Railroads:** UP (2080)

⊖ Bachmann, Plymouth 0-6-0 switcher, >55mm<, ♀, Price:D **Railroads:** AT&SF (51-600-02), CBQ (51-600-16)

⊖ Bachmann, EMD GP40 class, >110mm<, ♀, Price:E **Railroads:** AT&SF (51-635-02), BN (51-635-03), CBQ (51-635-16), SP (51-635-07)

⊖ Bachmann, EMD F9 class, >98mm<, ♀, Price:E **Railroads:** AM (51-615-05), AT&SF (51-615-02; dummy, Price:C, 51-617-02), C&O (51-615-09), PR (51-615-14)

⊖ Bachmann, U36B class, >105mm<, ♀, Price:E **Railroads:** AT&SF (51-640-02), C&O (51-640-09), RI (51-640-08), SP (51-640-07)

⊖ Bachmann, 65ft standard combine, >110mm<, ♀, Price:C **Railroads:** AT&SF (53-1041-02), PR (53-1041-14)

⊖ Bachmann, 65ft standard coach, >110mm<, ♀, Price:C **Railroads:** AT&SF (53-1042-02), PR (53-1042-14)

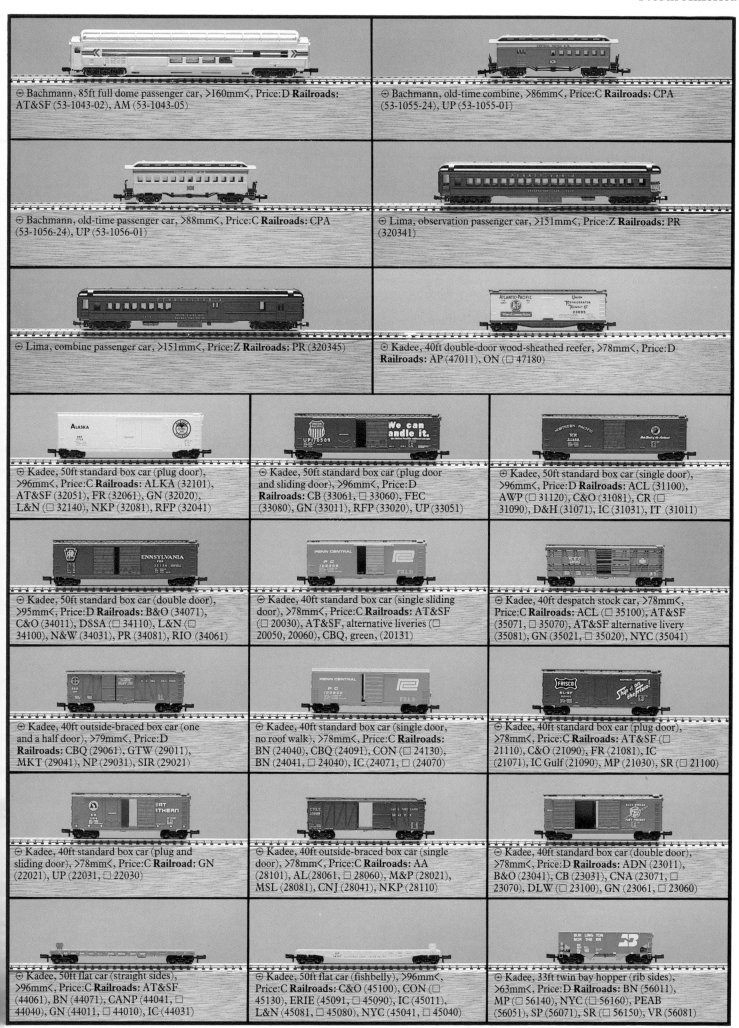

⊖ Bachmann, 85ft full dome passenger car, >160mm<, Price:D **Railroads:** AT&SF (53-1043-02), AM (53-1043-05)

⊖ Bachmann, old-time combine, >86mm<, Price:C **Railroads:** CPA (53-1055-24), UP (53-1055-01)

⊖ Bachmann, old-time passenger car, >88mm<, Price:C **Railroads:** CPA (53-1056-24), UP (53-1056-01)

⊖ Lima, observation passenger car, >151mm<, Price:Z **Railroads:** PR (320341)

⊖ Lima, combine passenger car, >151mm<, Price:Z **Railroads:** PR (320345)

⊖ Kadee, 40ft double-door wood-sheathed reefer, >78mm<, Price:D **Railroads:** AP (47011), ON (☐ 47180)

⊖ Kadee, 50ft standard box car (plug door), >96mm<, Price:C **Railroads:** ALKA (32101), AT&SF (32051), FR (32061), GN (32020), L&N (☐ 32140), NKP (32081), RFP (32041)

⊖ Kadee, 50ft standard box car (plug door and sliding door), >96mm<, Price:D **Railroads:** CB (33061, ☐ 33060), FEC (33080), GN (33011), RFP (33020), UP (33051)

⊖ Kadee, 50ft standard box car (single door), >96mm<, Price:D **Railroads:** ACL (31100), AWP (☐ 31120), C&O (31081), CR (☐ 31090), D&H (31071), IC (31031), IT (31011)

⊖ Kadee, 50ft standard box car (double door), >95mm<, Price:D **Railroads:** B&O (34071), C&O (34011), DSSA (☐ 34110), L&N (☐ 34100), N&W (34031), PR (34081), RIO (34061)

⊖ Kadee, 40ft standard box car (single sliding door), >78mm<, Price:C **Railroads:** AT&SF (☐ 20030), AT&SF, alternative liveries (☐ 20050, 20060), CBQ, green, (20131)

⊖ Kadee, 40ft despatch stock car, >78mm<, Price:C **Railroads:** ACL (☐ 35100), AT&SF (35071, ☐ 35070), AT&SF alternative livery (35081), GN (35021, ☐ 35020), NYC (35041)

⊖ Kadee, 40ft outside-braced box car (one and a half door), >79mm<, Price:D **Railroads:** CBQ (29061), GTW (29011), MKT (29041), NP (29031), SIR (29021)

⊖ Kadee, 40ft standard box car (single door, no roof walk), >78mm<, Price:C **Railroads:** BN (24040), CBQ (24091), CON (☐ 24130), BN (24041, ☐ 24040), IC (24071, ☐ 24070)

⊖ Kadee, 40ft standard box car (plug door), >78mm<, Price:C **Railroads:** AT&SF (☐ 21110), C&O (21090), FR (21081), IC (21071), IC Gulf (21090), MP (21030), SR (☐ 21100)

⊖ Kadee, 40ft standard box car (plug and sliding door), >78mm<, Price:C **Railroad:** GN (22021), UP (22031, ☐ 22030)

⊖ Kadee, 40ft outside-braced box car (single door), >78mm<, Price:C **Railroads:** AA (28101), AL(28061, ☐ 28060), M&P (28021), MSL (28081), CNJ (28041), NKP (28110)

⊖ Kadee, 40ft standard box car (double door), >78mm<, Price:D **Railroads:** ADN (23011), B&O (23041), CB (23031), CNA (23071, ☐ 23070), DLW (☐ 23100), GN (23061, ☐ 23060)

⊖ Kadee, 50ft flat car (straight sides), >96mm<, Price:C **Railroads:** AT&SF (44061), BN (44071), CANP (44041, ☐ 44040), GN (44011, ☐ 44010), IC (44031)

⊖ Kadee, 50ft flat car (fishbelly), >96mm<, Price:C **Railroads:** C&O (45100), CON (☐ 45130), ERIE (45091, ☐ 45090), IC (45011), L&N (45081, ☐ 45080), NYC (45041, ☐ 45040)

⊖ Kadee, 33ft twin bay hopper (rib sides), >63mm<, Price:D **Railroads:** BN (56011), MP (☐ 56140), NYC (☐ 56160), PEAB (56051), SP (56071), SR (☐ 56150), VR (56081)

# North America

## Canadian National Railways

Canada's railway network is dominated by two major companies – Canadian Pacific, and the state-owned Canadian National Railways (CNR). The CNR was formed in 1923 by combining several lines already owned by the government. CNR pioneered main-line diesel operation as long ago as 1928, though some steam remained until 1960. Both CNR and CP passenger services have been operated by Via Rail Canada since 1978.

⊖ Kadee, 33ft twin bay hopper (offset side), >63mm<, Price:D **Railroads:** AT&SF (55011, □ 55010), CANP (55150), CNW (□ 55110), C&O (55031), D&H (□ 55170)

⊖ Kadee, 33ft twin bay hopper (composite side), >64mm<, Price:D **Railroads:** AT&SF (57011), CBQ (57021), C&O (57071), LV (57031), NKP (57051), SR (57041), WAB (57061)

⊖ Kadee, 34ft wood-sheath caboose, >64mm<, Price:D **Railroads:** AT&SF (50041), B&M (□ 50140), BN (50051), CBQ (50081), GN (50091), IC (50031, □ 50030)

⊖ Kadee, 50ft rib side box car (single door), >97mm<, Price:D **Railroads:** ASA (□ 25070), C&P (□ 25060), MTW (25051, □ 25050), RV (□ 25090), SRN (□ 25100), VMC (25080)

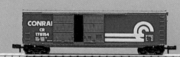

⊖ Kadee, 50ft standard box car (double door, roofwalk), >96mm<, Price:C **Railroads:** CON (37010)

⊖ Lima, stock car, >90mm<, Price:Z **Railroads:** MKT (320427)

⊖ Lima, caboose, >74mm<, Price:Z **Railroads:** AT&SF (320763)

⊖ Lima, box car, >90mm<, Price:Z **Railroad:** IC (320495)

⊖ Lima, container wagon, >120mm<, Price:Z (320796)

⊖ Lima, flat wagon with container, >88mm<, Price:Z (320760)

⊖ Lima, flat wagon with two cars, Price:Z (320772)

⊖ Kadee, 40ft double-door wood-sheathed reefer (vertical brake wheel), >78mm<, Price:D **Private-owner:** Scatena Bros. (49070, □ 49071)

⊖ Kadee, 40ft double-sheathed wood box car (single and one and a half doors), >79mm<, Price:D **Private-owner:** Ball Glass (42031), Domino Sugar (42021), Hills Bros (42101),

⊖ Kadee, bogie tank wagon, >74mm<, Price:D **Private-owner:** General Electric (65081), Phillips (65131), Sinclair (65141), Texaco (65070), Transcontinental Oil (□ 65050)

⊖ Bachmann, 41ft mechanical steel reefer, >80mm<, Price:B **Railroads:** LV, UP (models not numbered)

⊖ Bachmann, 41ft steel box car, >78mm<, Price:B **Railroads:** BN, NYC, RI, RIO (models not numbered)

⊖ Bachmann, 41ft wood side box car, >80mm<, Price:B **Railroads:** CIM, GN, WAB (models not numbered)

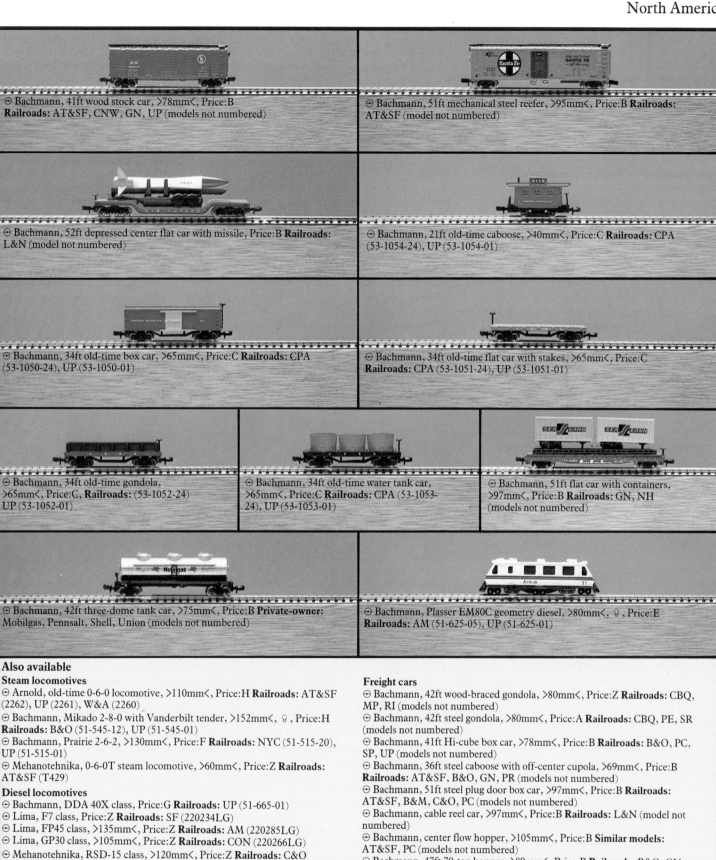

⊕ Bachmann, 41ft wood stock car, >78mm<, Price:B **Railroads:** AT&SF, CNW, GN, UP (models not numbered)

⊕ Bachmann, 51ft mechanical steel reefer, >95mm<, Price:B **Railroads:** AT&SF (model not numbered)

⊕ Bachmann, 52ft depressed center flat car with missile, Price:B **Railroads:** L&N (model not numbered)

⊕ Bachmann, 21ft old-time caboose, >40mm<, Price:C **Railroads:** CPA (53-1054-24), UP (53-1054-01)

⊕ Bachmann, 34ft old-time box car, >65mm<, Price:C **Railroads:** CPA (53-1050-24), UP (53-1050-01)

⊕ Bachmann, 34ft old-time flat car with stakes, >65mm<, Price:C **Railroads:** CPA (53-1051-24), UP (53-1051-01)

⊕ Bachmann, 34ft old-time gondola, >65mm<, Price:C, **Railroads:** (53-1052-24) UP (53-1052-01)

⊕ Bachmann, 34ft old-time water tank car, >65mm<, Price:C **Railroads:** CPA (53-1053-24), UP (53-1053-01)

⊕ Bachmann, 51ft flat car with containers, >97mm<, Price:B **Railroads:** GN, NH (models not numbered)

⊕ Bachmann, 42ft three-dome tank car, >75mm<, Price:B **Private-owner:** Mobilgas, Pennsalt, Shell, Union (models not numbered)

⊕ Bachmann, Plasser EM80C geometry diesel, >80mm<, ♀, Price:E **Railroads:** AM (51-625-05), UP (51-625-01)

## Also available

### Steam locomotives
⊕ Arnold, old-time 0-6-0 locomotive, >110mm<, Price:H **Railroads:** AT&SF (2262), UP (2261), W&A (2260)
⊕ Bachmann, Mikado 2-8-0 with Vanderbilt tender, >152mm<, ♀, Price:H **Railroads:** B&O (51-545-12), UP (51-545-01)
⊕ Bachmann, Prairie 2-6-2, >130mm<, Price:F **Railroads:** NYC (51-515-20), UP (51-515-01)
⊕ Mehanotehnika, 0-6-0T steam locomotive, >60mm<, Price:Z **Railroads:** AT&SF (T429)

### Diesel locomotives
⊕ Bachmann, DDA 40X class, Price:G **Railroads:** UP (51-665-01)
⊕ Lima, F7 class, Price:Z **Railroads:** SF (220234LG)
⊕ Lima, FP45 class, >135mm<, Price:Z **Railroads:** AM (220285LG)
⊕ Lima, GP30 class, >105mm<, Price:Z **Railroads:** CON (220266LG)
⊕ Mehanotehnika, RSD-15 class, >120mm<, Price:Z **Railroads:** C&O (T421/420)
⊕ Mehanotehnika, FA-1 class, >101mm<, Price:Z **Railroads::** C&O (T422)
⊕ Mehanotehnika, SD-45 class, >118mm<, Price:Z **Railroads:** C&O (T437)
⊕ Mehanotehnika, F-40PH class, >108mm<, Price:Z **Railroads:** AM (T442)
⊕ Mehanotehnika, WDT class, >55mm<, Price:Z **Railroads:** CBQ (T439)

### Passenger cars
⊕ Arnold, old-time passenger car with brake compartment, >90mm<, Price:D **Railroads:** UP (3613), W&A (3611)
⊕ Arnold, old-time passenger car, >90mm<, Price:D **Railroads:** UP (3614), W&A (3612)

### Freight cars
⊕ Bachmann, open quad offset hopper, Price:A **Railroads:** MSL, PEAB, PR, RI (models not numbered)

### Freight cars
⊕ Bachmann, 42ft wood-braced gondola, >80mm<, Price:Z **Railroads:** CBQ, MP, RI (models not numbered)
⊕ Bachmann, 42ft steel gondola, >80mm<, Price:A **Railroads:** CBQ, PE, SR (models not numbered)
⊕ Bachmann, 41ft Hi-cube box car, >78mm<, Price:B **Railroads:** B&O, PC, SP, UP (models not numbered)
⊕ Bachmann, 36ft steel caboose with off-center cupola, >69mm<, Price:B **Railroads:** AT&SF, B&O, GN, PR (models not numbered)
⊕ Bachmann, 51ft steel plug door box car, >97mm<, Price:B **Railroads:** AT&SF, B&M, C&O, PC (models not numbered)
⊕ Bachmann, cable reel car, >97mm<, Price:B **Railroads:** L&N (model not numbered)
⊕ Bachmann, center flow hopper, >105mm<, Price:B **Similar models:** AT&SF, PC (models not numbered)
⊕ Bachmann, 47ft 70-ton hopper, >89mm<, Price:B **Railroads:** B&O, GN (models not numbered)
⊕ Bachmann, 36ft wide-vision caboose, >69mm<, Price:B **Railroads:** AT&SF, C&O, RI, UP (models not numbered)
⊕ Bachmann, 41ft Hi-cube outside braced box car, >97mm<, Price:B **Railroads:** B&O, PC, SCL, SP (models not numbered)
⊕ Kadee, 50ft gondola (straight sides, drop ends), >97mm<, Price:D **Railroads:** AT&SF (48060), B&O (48020), DLW (48070), IT (48050), PR (48010), SP (48031), □ 48030)
⊕ Kadee, bogie tank wagon, >76mm<, Price:D **Railroads:** B&O (□ 65020)
⊕ Kadee, 40ft double-sheathed wood box car (single door), >78mm<, Price:D **Railroads:** C&O (42121), GN (42081, □ 42080), RUT (42111)
⊕ Lima, gondola, >90mm<, Price:Z **Railroads:** SR (320418)

# North America

## Canadian Pacific Railways

The Canadian Pacific Railway (CP) – now often referred to as CP Rail – dates back to 1875. It is a corporate organization which also has interests in shipping and industry as well. It did not start dieselization until 1948, as it had it famous fleet of massive steam locomotives for trans-continental work. The passenger services of the CP and CNR have been operated by the government-sponsored Via Rail Canada since 1978.

**HO/OO Gauge**

⊚ Bachmann, Texas 2-10-4 with 52ft tender, >416mm<, ♀, ⊞, Price:L **Railroads:** C&O (41-560-22), TEXP (41-560-21). Also with electronic 'chug' and steam whistle: AT&SF (41-562-02), PR (41-562-14)

⊚ Bachmann, Mikado 2-8-2 with Vandebilt tender, >295mm<, ♀, ⊞, Price:J **Railroads:** B&O (41-545-12), UP (41-545-01). Also available with electronic steam whistle (Price:L): B&O (41-546-12), UP (41-546-01)

⊚ Bachmann, USRA 0-6-0, >220mm<, ♀, Price:G **Railroads:** AT&SF (41-506-02), PR (41-506-14)

◉ Bachmann, Prairie 2-6-2, ❯230mm❮, ♀ , Price:H **Railroads:** NYC (41-515-20), UP (41-515-01)

◉ Bowser, K-4 Pacific, Price:M **Railroads:** PR (500500)

◉ Bowser, E-6 Atlantic, Price:M **Railroads:** PR (500600)

◉ Bowser, L-1 Mikado, Price:M **Railroads:** PR (500800)

# North America

## Chicago & North Western Railroad

The Chicago & North Western (CNW) runs from Chicago north and west to Omaha, Duluth and Minneapolis. At Omaha it provides an exchange with the Union Pacific. It is now an all-freight line except for double-deck commuter trains which it operates for the Chicago Regional Transportation Authority. It is one of the few American companies that runs on the left-hand side of double tracks, like the British.

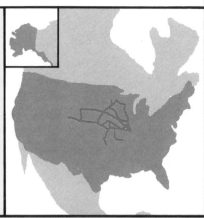

◎ Lima, Mikado type locomotive, >276mm<, Price:Z **Railroads:** MP (203009LG)

◎ Lima, 0-4-0 locomotive, >206mm<, Price:Z **Railroads:** B&O (203008LG)

◎ Lima, 0-4-0 locomotive, Price:Z **Railroads:** CNA (203007DLG)

⊚ Tyco, 2-8-0 locomotive, >285mm<, �21, ⚲, Price:H **Railroads:** B&O (245-02)

⊚ Tyco, 0-8-0 locomotive, >285mm<, �21, ⚲, Price:H **Railroads:** CH (256-15)

⊚ Tyco, 0-6-0 locomotive, >215mm<, �21, ⚲, Price:F **Railroads:** SR (257-76), WM (257-77)

⊚ Bachmann, E60CP class, �21, >240mm<, ⚲, Price:G **Railroads:** AM (41-655-05)

# North America

# Missouri-Kansas-Texas Railroad

The MKT, or 'Katy' as it is popularly called, is typical of many small railroad companies in the USA. It is centred in the industrially rich state of Texas, and remains well managed and profitable, though it has come close to failure in the past. Coal, grain, cars, and lumber are moved by the railroad, using unit trains where possible. The company is now part of Katy Industries, which has interests outside railroads.

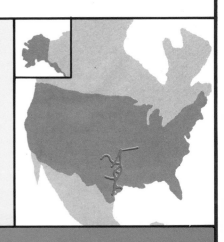

⊙ Bachmann, DD40X class, >330mm<, ⚲, Price:G **Railroads:** UP (41-665-01; with diesel horn sound (Price:J) 41-666-01)

⊙ Bachmann, EMD F9 class, >175mm<, ⚲, Price:E **Railroads:** AM (41-615-05), AT&SF (41-615-02), C&O (41-615-09)

⊙ Bachmann, EMD GP30 class, >193mm<, ⚲, Price:E **Railroads:** AT&SF (41-630-02), BN (41-630-03), C&O (41-630-09), SR (41-630-04)

◉ Bachmann, U36B class, >200mm<, Price:E **Railroads:** AT&SF (41-640-02), C&O (41-640-09), RI (41-640-08), SP (41-640-07)

◉ Bachmann, EMD F40PH class, >190mm<, ♀, Price:E **Railroads:** AM (41-645-05)

◉ Bachmann, BQ23-7 class, >200mm<, ♀, Price:F **Railroads:** C&O (41-650-09), SCL (41-650-23)

◎ Lima, MDT class, >119mm<, Price:Z **Railroads:** AT&SF (201654LG)

◎ Märklin, F7 class, ≦, >175mm<, ♀, Price:Z **Railroads:** RIO (3062, dummy end 4062), AT&SF (3060, dummy end 4060)

# North America

## Amtrak

Amtrak is the name used by the American Rail Passenger Corporation. In the 1950s and 1960s, passenger traffic fell off disastrously in the USA in the face of competition from aircraft and cars. Companies abandoned passenger services rapidly except where legal requirements forced them to be maintained. Amtrak was formed in 1972 to take over passenger operation on inter-city and trunk routes. It has been relatively successful but operates at a loss.

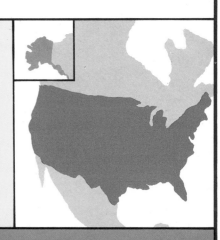

⊙ Mehanotehnika, DDT class, >112mm<, Price:Z
**Railroads:** AT&SF (T133)

⊙ Tyco, GP-20 class, >195mm<, ⚲ , Price:F **Railraods:** AT&SF (228-21), BN (228-17)

⊙ Tyco, Alco 430 class, >210mm<, ⚲ , Price:F **Railroads:** VR (235-79)

⊙ Tyco, SD-24 class, >205mm<, ⚲ , Price:F **Railroads:** RIO (239-74)

⊙ Tyco, shunter, >115mm<, 💡 , Price:F **Railroads:** AT&SF (241-21)

⊙ Tyco, E-7 class, >240mm<, 💡 , Price:F **Railroads:** MILW (255-62)

⊙ Bachmann, Budd Amfleet passenger car, >290mm<, 💡 , Price:D **Railroads:** AM (43-1022-05)

⊙ Bachmann, 47ft passenger car, >160mm<, Price:C **Railroads:** CPA (43-1029-24), UP (43-1029-01)

⊙ Bachmann, 47ft combine car, >165mm<, Price:C **Railroads:** CPA (43-1028-24), UP (43-1028-01)

# North America

## New York Central

The New York Central (NYC) was one of the most prestigious of companies, and operated the legendary 'Twentieth Century Limited' from Chicago to New York. The NYC also owned the legendary Grand Central Station in New York. Like the Pennsylvania Railroad, the NYC was in trouble financially in the 1960s and merged with PRR to become Penn Central. That bankrupt company formed a major constituent of Conrail in 1976.

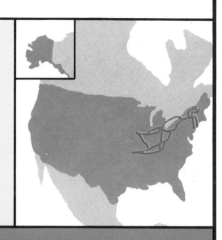

⦿ Herkimer, passenger car, >213mm<, Price:D
**Railroads:** Transfers for AT&SF, NYC, PR (model 131)

⦿ Herkimer, Astradome car, >213mm<, Price:E
**Railroads:** Transfers for AT&SF, NYC, PR (model 132)

⦿ Herkimer, observation car, >213mm<, Price:E
**Railroads:** Transfers for AT&SF, NYC, PR (model 133)

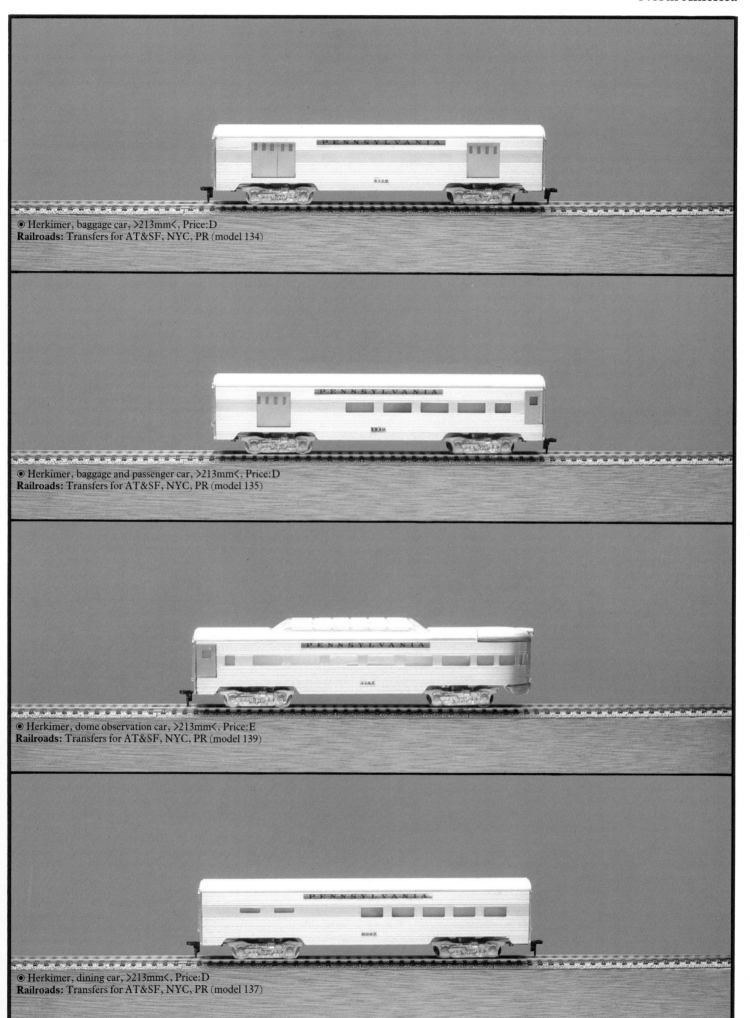

⊙ Herkimer, baggage car, >213mm<, Price:D
**Railroads:** Transfers for AT&SF, NYC, PR (model 134)

⊙ Herkimer, baggage and passenger car, >213mm<, Price:D
**Railroads:** Transfers for AT&SF, NYC, PR (model 135)

⊙ Herkimer, dome observation car, >213mm<, Price:E
**Railroads:** Transfers for AT&SF, NYC, PR (model 139)

⊙ Herkimer, dining car, >213mm<, Price:D
**Railroads:** Transfers for AT&SF, NYC, PR (model 137)

# North America

## Pennsylvania Railroad

The Pennsylvania Railroad (the 'Pennsy') was, in its day, a prestigious railroad, and one of the largest in the USA. It was big enough to build its own designs of locomotives rather than buy from outside builders. The decline of passenger traffic and the rise of trucking, helped put the Pennsy into bankruptcy after a short-lived amalgamation with New York Central (as Penn Central). In 1976 it became part of Conrail.

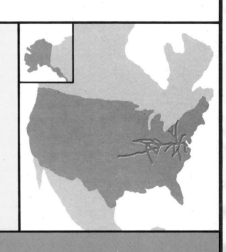

⊚ Herkimer, postal and baggage car, ≻213mm≺, Price: D
**Railroads:** Transfers for AT&SF, NYC, PR (model 138)

⊚ Herkimer, sleeping car, ≻213mm≺, Price:D
**Railroads:** Transfers for AT&SF, NYC, PR (model 136)

◎ Lima, dining car (VIA livery), ≻268mm≺, Price:Z (303606)

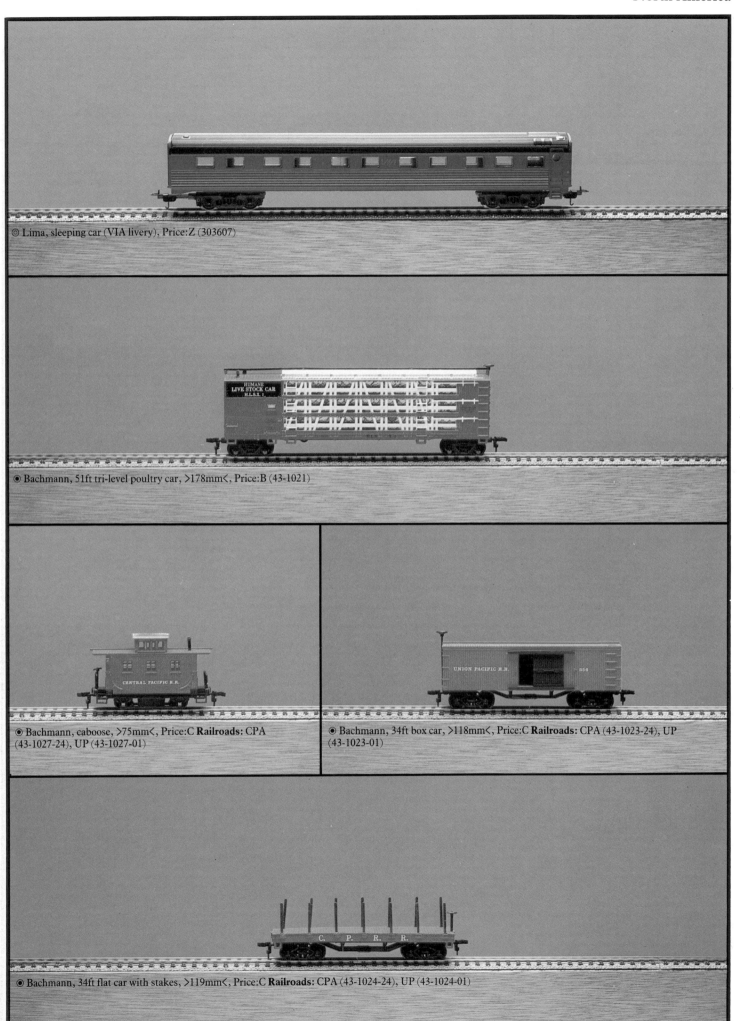

◎ Lima, sleeping car (VIA livery), Price:Z (303607)

◉ Bachmann, 51ft tri-level poultry car, >178mm<, Price:B (43-1021)

◉ Bachmann, caboose, >75mm<, Price:C **Railroads:** CPA (43-1027-24), UP (43-1027-01)

◉ Bachmann, 34ft box car, >118mm<, Price:C **Railroads:** CPA (43-1023-24), UP (43-1023-01)

◉ Bachmann, 34ft flat car with stakes, >119mm<, Price:C **Railroads:** CPA (43-1024-24), UP (43-1024-01)

# North America

## Santa Fe

The Santa Fe (or Aitchison, Topeka, & Santa Fe to give it its full title), is one of the key systems in the USA. It dates back to the 1870s and runs to the West Coast – San Francisco, Los Angeles via the SW route, and reaches east to Chicago. Before the days of Amtrak it used to operate the sleek 'Chief', 'Super Chief', and 'El Capitan' expresses, but it is now an all-freight system of about 19,000 kilometres (12,000 miles).

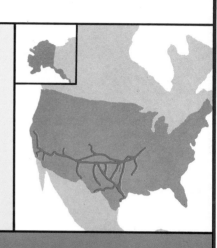

⊛ Bachmann, 34ft gondola, >118mm<, Price:C **Railroads:** CPA (43-1025-24), UP (43-1025-01)

⊛ Bachmann, 34ft water tank car, >118mm<, Price:C **Railroads:** CPA (43-1026-24), UP (43-1026-01)

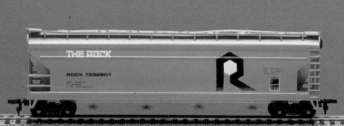

⊛ Bachmann, 56ft center flow hopper, >190mm<, Price:B **Railroads:** RI (model not numbered)

⊛ Bachmann, 41ft Hi-cube box car, >140mm<, Price:B **Railroads:** CBQ, NYC, RIO, UP (models not numbered)

◉ Bachmann, 41ft steel box car, >140mm<, Price:A **Railroads:** AT&SF, C&O, RI, UP (models not numbered)

◉ Bachmann, 42ft open quad offset hopper, >245mm<, Price:A **Railroads:** BN, MSL, RI, UP (models not numbered)

◉ Bachmann, 36ft wide-vision caboose, >120mm<, Price:B **Railroads:** AT&SF, BN, C&O, CON (models not numbered)

◉ Bachmann, 51ft mechanical steel reefer, >175mm<, Price:A **Railroads:** AT&SF, BN (models not numbered)

◉ Bachmann, 41ft wood stock car, >140mm<, Price:A **Railroads:** AT&SF, CNW, GN, UP (models not numbered)

# North America

## Southern Pacific

Another of the great names in railway history, the Southern Pacific (SP) runs trains along the Pacific coast (it took over the rival Central Pacific in 1955) and across the southern part of the USA to New Orleans. At one time it had routes across the Mexican border too. The Louisiana & South Western Railroad (The Cotton Belt) is a subsidiary whose stock carries the SP colour scheme but different lettering.

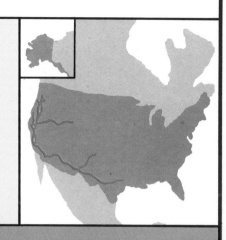

⦿ Bachmann, 48ft flat with logs, >110mm<, Price:B **Railroads:** GN, L&N (models not numbered)

⦿ Bachmann, 56ft all doors box car, >208mm<, Price:B **Railroads:** AT&SF, SP, SR (models not numbered)

⦿ Bachmann, 57ft covered steel coil car, >197mm<, Price:B **Railroads:** B&LE, PE (models not numbered)

◉ Bachmann, 51ft pulpwood rack car with logs, >175mm<, Price:B **Railroads:** AT&SF, PC (models not numbered)

◎ Märklin, 50ft box car, >184mm<, Price:Z **Railroads:** WP (4571)

◎ Märklin, gondola, >170mm<, Price:Z **Railroads:** L&N (4575)

◉ Mehanotehnika, box car, >177mm<, Price:Z **Railroads:** PC (T081) (model is shown here in GTW livery, no longer available)

# North America

## Union Pacific

One of the great names in railroad history, the Union Pacific (UP) opened up the transcontinental link across America in the 1860s. It went in for a 'big engine' policy and was famous for the Big Boy and other huge steam locomotives. It had big diesels and turbines too. It is now an all-freight line and has recently formed a Pacific Rail combine with Missouri Pacific and Western Pacific (each retaining its separate identity).

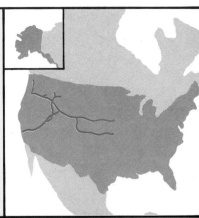

◉ Tyco, 50ft box car, >175mm<, Price:A **Railroads:** BN (339E)

◉ Tyco, gondola with culvert pipes, >140mm<, Price:A **Railroads:** BN (341G)

◉ Tyco, skid flat with culvert pipes, >140mm<, Price:A **Railroads:** GN (342D)

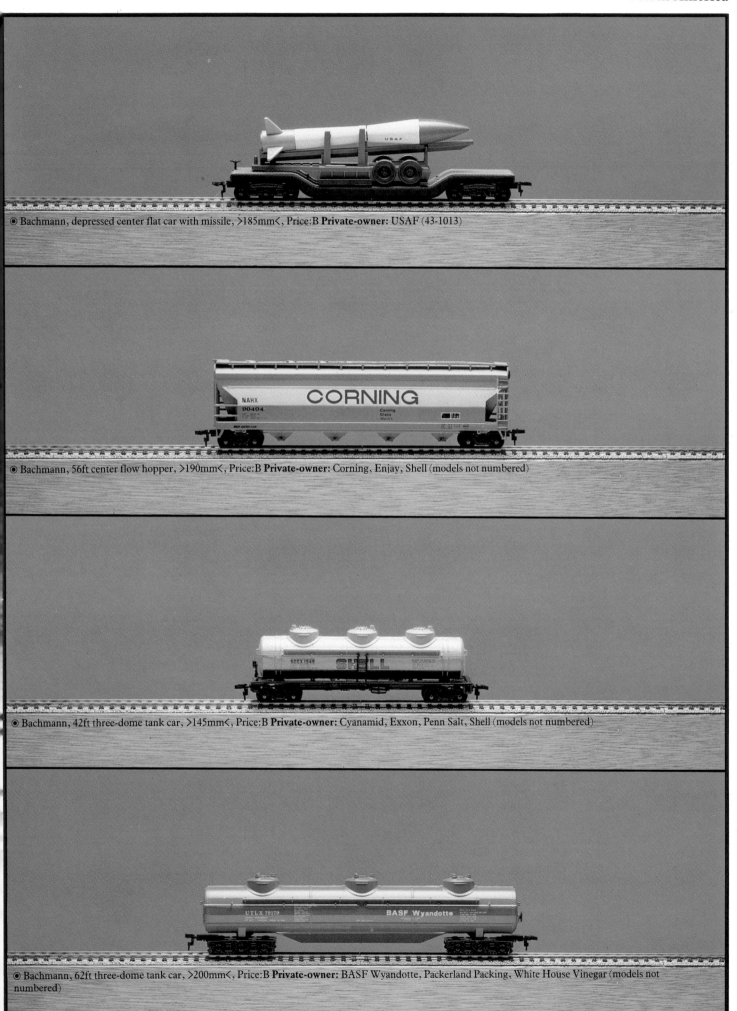

◉ Bachmann, depressed center flat car with missile, >185mm<, Price:B **Private-owner:** USAF (43-1013)

◉ Bachmann, 56ft center flow hopper, >190mm<, Price:B **Private-owner:** Corning, Enjay, Shell (models not numbered)

◉ Bachmann, 42ft three-dome tank car, >145mm<, Price:B **Private-owner:** Cyanamid, Exxon, Penn Salt, Shell (models not numbered)

◉ Bachmann, 62ft three-dome tank car, >200mm<, Price:B **Private-owner:** BASF Wyandotte, Packerland Packing, White House Vinegar (models not numbered)

# North America

## Also available

### Steam locomotives
◎ Bowser, I-1 Decapod, Price:M **Railroads:** PR (500700)

◎ Bowser, H-9 Consolidation, Price:M **Railroads:** PR (500900)

◎ Bachmann, Northern, 4-8-4 with 52ft tender, >394mm<, ⚲, ⚙, Price:K **Railroads:** AT&SF (41-580-02), CBQ (41-580-16). Also with electronic 'chug-chug' and steam whistle (Price:L) AT&SF (41-582-02), CBQ (41-582-16). Overland 4-8-4, ⚲, ⚙ (Price:K): UP (41-535-01)

◎ Bachmann, Daylight GS4 4-8-4 with 48ft tender, >394mm<, ⚲, Price:K **Railroads:** C&O (41-550-09), SP (41-550-07)

◎ Bachmann, 4-4-0 tender locomotive, >182mm<, ⚲, Price:H **Railroads:** CPA (41-510-24), UP (minor variations, 41-510-01)

◎ Bachmann, Consolidation 2-8-0, >279mm<, ⚲, ⚙, Price:J **Railroads:** AT&SF (41-530-02), GN (41-530-11), RDG (41-530-10)

◎ Bachmann, Niagra 4-8-4 with 52ft tender, ⚲, ⚙, Price:K **Railroads:** NYC (41-540-20)

◎ Bachmann, 4-6-0 with Vanderbilt tender, >270mm<, ⚲, ⚙, Price:H **Railroads:** CNW (41-520-31), SP (41-520-01)

◎ Mehanotehnika, 0-4-0 locomotive, >172mm<, ⚙, Price:Z **Railroad:** PR (T005), B&O (without smoke, T005) (state version when ordering)

◎ Mehanotehnika, USRA 4-6-2 locomotive, >287mm<, ⚙, Price:Z **Railroad:** AT&SF (without smoke, T006), SP (T006) (state version when ordering)

◎ Mehanotehnika, 2-8-2 locomotive, >285mm<, Price:Z **Railroads:** C&O (T007), SR (without smoke, T007) (state version when ordering)

### Diesel locomotives
◎ Bachmann, EMD GP40 class, >203mm<, ⚲, Price:E **Railroads:** AT&SF (41-635-02), BN (41-635-03), CON (41-635-06), UP (41-635-01)

◎ Bachmann, 0-6-0 switcher, >132mm<, ⚲, Price:E **Railroads:** AT&SF (41-600-02), CBQ (41-600-16)

◎ Bachmann, SD40-2 class, ⚲, Price:F **Railroads:** AT&SF (41-670-02), BN (41-670-03), SCL (41-670-23), UP (41-670-01)

◎ Lima, FP45 class, >250mm<, Price:Z **Railroads:** AM (208075LG; dummy 209605), CNA (288077LG), AT&SF (208071LG; dummy 209600)

◎ Lima, C420 ALCO SP class, >200mm<, Price:Z **Railroads:** SP (208089LG; dummy 209628)

◎ Mehanotehnika, FP-45 class, >250mm<, Price:Z **Railroads:** SF (T012)

◎ Mehanotehnika, C-628 class, >234mm<, Price:Z **Railroads:** SCL (T015)

◎ Mehanotehnika, SD-40 class, >229mm<, Price:Z **Railroads:** UP (T019

◎ Mehanotehnika, FM class, >191mm<, Price:Z **Railroads:** AT&SF (T021)

◎ Mehanotehnika, FM class (with dummy end), Price:Z **Railroads:** AT&SF (T036)

◎ Mehanotehnika, GE-35 class, >108mm<, Price:Z **Railroads:** CON (T132)

◎ Mehanotehnika, MDT class, >112mm<, Price:Z **Railroads:** B&O (T136)

◎ Mehanotehnika, FA-1 class, >183mm<, Price:Z **Railroads:** AT&SF (T130)

◎ Mehanotehnika, HP-1000, >155mm<, Price:Z **Railroads:** IC (T131)

◎ Mehanotehnika, ALCO 415 class, >174mm<, Price:Z **Railroads:** BN (T154)

◎ Mehanotehnika, SW-1 class, >157mm<, Price:Z **Railroads:** CANP (T126)

◎ Mehanotehnika, F-9 class, >174mm<, Price:Z **Railroads:** CANP (T138)

◎ Mehanotehnika, ALCO RS-11 class, >187mm<, Price:Z **Railroads:** CNA (T156)

◎ Tyco, GG-1 class, >260mm<, ⚲, Price:F **Railroads:** PR (251-01)

◎ Tyco, Baldwin Shark Nose class, >210mm<, ⚲, Price:F **Railroads:** RI (222-10)

◎ Tyco, F-9 class, >200mm<, ⚲, Price:F **Railroads:** CH (224-03)

◎ Tyco, Alco Super 630 class, >250mm<, ⚲, Price:F **Railroads:** AT&SF (250-21)

### Passenger cars
◎ Bachmann, dome passenger car, Price:D **Railroads:** AM (43-1017-05)

◎ Lima, Amtrak passenger car, >268mm<, Price:Z **Railroads:** AM (303600)

### Freight cars
◎ Bachmann, 51ft steel plug door box car, >178mm<, Price:A **Railroads:** C&O, PC, RI, UP (models not numbered)

◎ Bachmann, 36ft caboose, >120mm<, Price:B **Railroads:** CBQ, CNW, NYC, SCL (models not numbered)

◎ Bachmann, 42ft steel gondola, >240mm<, Price:A **Railroads:** BN, CBQ, SR, UP (models not numbered)

◎ Lima, caboose, >140mm<, Price:Z **Railroads:** SP (303611)

◎ Lima, gondola, >176mm<, Price:Z **Railroads:** SOO (303651)

◎ Mehanotehnika, 50ft gondola, >177mm<, Price:Z **Railroads:** RDG (T073)

◎ Mehanotehnika, stock car, >177mm<, Price:Z **Railroad:** CANP (T072)

◎ Mehanotehnika, hopper car, >176mm<, Price:Z **Railroads:** CANP (T077)

◎ Tyco, hopper car, >160mm<, Price:A **Railroads:** UP (344E)

### Private-owner freight cars
◎ Bachmann, 51ft box car, >178mm<, Price:B **Private-owner:** Chef Boyardee, Flying Eagle, Graffiti, Old West Line, Redball Express, Smuckers (models not numbered)

◎ Bachmann, 51ft mechanical steel reefer, >175mm<, Price:A **Railroads:** Pacific Fruit, Swifts (models not numbered)

### Private-owner freight cars
◎ Lima, reefer, >140mm<, Price:Z **Private-owner:** Pacific Fruit Express (303226)

◎ Lima, 40ft bogie tank car, >148mm<, Price:Z **Private-owner:** Exxon (303625), BP (303626)

◎ Mehanotehnika, 40ft reefer, >142mm<, Price:Z **Private-owner:** State of Maine Potatoes (T071)

◎ Mehanotehnika, bogie tank car, >176mm<, Price:Z **Private-owner:** Jack Frost (T079)

◎ Mehanotehnika, box car, >177mm<, Price:Z **Private-owner:** Tropicana (T088)

◎ Tyco, billboard reefer car, >160mm<, Price:A **Private-owner:** Baby Ruth (355C)

◎ Tyco, reefer wagon, >145mm<, Price:A **Private-owner:** Swift (329A)

◎ Tyco, cattle wagon, >145mm<, Price:A **Private-owner:** Laramie (312H)

◎ Tyco, single-dome bogie tank wagon, >140mm<, Price:A **Private-owner:** Coca-Cola (315L), Texaco (315A)

### Miscellaneous
◎ Bachmann, Plasser EM80C geometry diesel (track cleaning vehicle), >147mm<, Price:E **Railroads:** AM (41-625-05), UP (41-625-01)

# Useful Addresses

How easily you can buy the models illustrated in this book will depend on where you live. Manufacturers quite naturally tend to have the best distribution in their own country, and the lower-priced mass-market items will be more widely available than the higher-priced more specialist models. Do not expect to find most of the models in this book in your local model shop – there are so many items that it would be impossible for retailers to stock every manufacturer's range. But do not give up either – you should be able to buy most of the models without too much difficulty if you set about it in the right way.

You can easily find out which ranges your local hobby shop stocks, and if they are unable to help, buy a few model railway magazines. If you are new to the hobby, glance at a few on the bookshelves to see which have the most advertisements. They may not necessarily be the best magazines from an editorial viewpoint, but you will find that some have a huge advertising section, while in others it is more scanty.

You are likely to see someone offering the range that you are interested in – although unless you are lucky you will probably have to send off for your models by mail order. If prices are not mentioned in the advertisement, phone and check both price and availability (you will find that both can vary considerably).

If these steps do not produce the model that you want, then write to the manufacturer. Some will supply direct, others will only deal through agents, but all should be willing to put you in touch with someone that can supply the model. You may be given the name and address of the agent in your country, and he will in turn be able to tell you the nearest stockist (he probably won't be willing to supply direct). Enclose a self-addressed envelope and an international reply coupon when you write to a manufacturer. If you enclose three or four international reply coupons (five or six if you want an airmail reply), manufacturers may be prepared to send you a catalogue direct.

The list of manufacturers' names and addresses given below include all those whose products have been mentioned in this book, plus some others that we were unable to include for various reasons. We have also indicated the countries in which the manufacturers have told us they normally distribute, and any countries to which they are unable to supply models.

Remember also that models are not always in production and if stocks have run out you may have to wait for your model.

**Ade**
Ade-Modelleisenbahnen GmbH,
Postfach 4246,
D-7042 Filderstadt 4,
West Germany.

**Arnold**
K. Arnold GmbH,
PO Box 1046,
D-8500 Nürnberg,
West Germany.

**Athearn**
Athearn,
19010 Laurel Park Road,
Compton,
CA 90222,
USA.

**Bachmann**
Bachmann Industries Inc.,
1400 E. Erie Avenue,
Philadelphia,
Pennsylvania 19124,
USA.
Distribute in Canada, France, Germany, Italy, USA. Unable to export direct to modellers in other countries.

**Bemo**
Bemo Modelleisenbahnen GmbH,
Stuttgarter Strasse 59,
D-7336 Uhingen,
Postfach 1213,
West Germany.

**Berliner Bahnen**
VEB Berliner TT-Bahnen,
Demusa,
Charlottenstrasse 46,
DDR-1080 Berlin,
East Germany.
Distribute in Belgium, Denmark, Finland, France, Germany, Great Britain, Holland, Sweden. Unable to export direct to modellers in other countries.

**Bowser**
Bowser Manufacturing Co. Inc.,
21 Howard Street,
PO Box 322,
Montoursville,
PA 17754,
USA.
Will accept orders direct from any country.

**Electrotren**
Electrotren,
Juan Pradillo, 9,
E-Madrid 20,
Spain.
Distribute in Andorra, Argentina, Australia, Austria, Belgium, Canada, Denmark, France, Germany, Great Britain, Holland, Italy, Mexico, New Zealand, Portugal, South Africa, Spain, Sweden, Switzerland, USA, Venezuela. Unable to export direct to modellers in other countries.

**Ellmar**
Ellmar Products Ltd.,
117 Maybank Road,
South Woodford,
London,
E18 1EJ.

**Farish** see **Graham Farish**

**Fleischmann**
Gebr. Fleischmann KG,
Postfach 910148,
Kirchenweg 13,
D-8500 Nürnberg 91,
West Germany.
Distribute in Andorra, Argentina, Australia, Austria, Belgium, Canada, Colombia, Denmark, Eire, Finland, France, Germany, Great Britain, Holland, Hong Kong, Italy, Japan, Kuwait, Luxembourg, Mexico, New Zealand, Norway, Phillipines, Portugal, Saudi Arabia, Singapore, South Africa, Spain, Sweden, Switzerland, USA, Venezuela. Unable to export direct to modellers in other countries.

**Fulgurex**
Fulgurex SA,
33 Avenue de Rumine,
CH-1005 Lausanne,
Switzerland.
Distribute in Austria, Belgium, France, Germany, Great Britain, Holland, Italy, Spain, Switzerland. Will export direct to modellers in other countries.

**Graham Farish**
Grafar Ltd.,
Romany Works,
Wareham Road,
Holton Heath,
Poole,
Dorset,
BH16 6JL.
Distribute in Australia, Canada, France, Germany, Holland, New Zealand, South Africa, USA. Will export direct to modellers in other countries in cases of difficulty.

**HAG**
HAG Modelleisenbahnen,
Parketteriestrasse 15,
CH-9016 St. Gallen,
Switzerland.
Distribute in Australia, Austria, Belgium, Canada, Germany, Great Britain, Holland, Italy, Japan, New Zealand, Spain, Sweden, USA. Unable to export direct to modellers in other countries.

**Herkimer**
Herkimer Tool and Model Works, Inc.,
PO Box 191,
Herkimer,
New York 13350,
USA.

**Hornby**
Hornby Hobbies Ltd.,
Westwood,
Margate,
Kent,
CT9 4JX.
Distribute in Australia, Canada, Great Britain, South Africa, all European countries. Unable to export direct to modellers in other countries.

**Ibertren**
Model-Iber,
Sociedad Anonima,
Roger de Flor, 86,
E-Barcelona 13, Spain.
Distribute in Belgium, Canada, Denmark, France, Germany, Italy, Japan, Spain, Switzerland, USA. Unable to export direct to modellers in other countries.

**Jouef**
Jouef SA,
72 rue des Archives,
Paris,
F-75003,
France.

**Kadee**
Kadee Quality Products Co.,
720 South Grape Street,
Medford,
Oregon 97501,
USA.
Distribute in Australia, Austria, France, Germany, Great Britain, New Zealand, Saudi Arabia, South Africa, South and Central America, Switzerland, USA. Will supply direct to modellers in other countries.

**LGB**
Ernst Paul Lehmann Patentwerk,
Postfach 3048,
Nürnberg 1,
D-8500,
West Germany.
Distribute in most countries (but not Soviet bloc). Unable to export direct to modellers.

**Life-Like**
Life-Like Products Inc.,
1600 Union Avenue,
Baltimore,
Maryland 21211,
USA.
Distribute in Australia, Canada, Great Britain, New Zealand, South Africa, USA. Unable to export direct to modellers in other countries.

**Lionel**
Fundimensions,
General Mills Toy Group,
26750, 23 Mile Road,
Mount Clemens,
MI 48043,
USA.

**Liliput**
Liliput Spielwarenfabrik Gesellschaft mbH.,
Walter Bücherl,
Kalvarienberggasse 22,
Postfach 8,
A-1172 Wien,
Austria.
Distribute in Austria, Belgium, France, Germany, Great Britain, Italy, Sweden, Switzerland, USA. Unable to export direct to modellers in other countries.

**Liliput (UK)**
Liliput Model Railways (U.K.) Ltd.,
1 and 4 Station Yard,
Industrial Estate,
Bala,
Gwynedd,
North Wales.
Distributes in Great Britain. Will export direct to modellers in other countries, where not represented.

**Lima**
Lima SpA,
Via G Impriali 77,
I-36100 Vicenza,
Italy.

# Addresses/Index

**Mainline**
Mainline Railways,
The Palitoy Company,
Owen Street,
Coalville,
Leicestershire,
LE6 2DE.
Distribute in Australia and New Zealand (by Toltoys), and UK.
Unable to export direct to modellers in other countries.

**Märklin**
Gebr. Märklin & Cie. GmbH,
Postfach 860/880,
Holzheimer Strasse 8,
D-7320 Göppingen,
West Germany.
Distribute in about 40 countries. Unable to export direct to modellers.

**Mehanotehnika**
Mehanotehnika,
YU-66310 Izola,
Yugoslavia.
Products exported to about 50 countries (sometimes produced for other companies). Unable to export direct to modellers, and models cannot be supplied to agents or retailers in South Africa.

**Metropolitan**
Metropolitan SA,
Route du grand mont,
Le Mont,
Lausanne,
CH-1052,
Switzerland.
Mainly brass models.

**Model Power**
Model Power,
200 5th Avenue,
New York,
NY 10010,
USA.
American type models made exclusively for Model Power by Mehanotehnika, Roco, Trix, and other contractors, under Model Power direction and tooling.

**Peco**
Pritchard Patent Products Co. Ltd.,
Underleys,
Beer,
Seaton,
Devon,
EX12 3NA.
Distribute to Andorra, Australia, Belgium, Canada, Denmark, France, Germany, Great Britain, Italy, Japan, New Zealand, Norway, South Africa, Spain, Sweden, Switzerland, USA. Will export direct to modellers in other countries (but not Soviet bloc countries).

**Piko**
Demusa,
Charlottenstrasse 46,
DDR-1080 Berlin,
East Germany.

**Rivarossi**
Rivarossi,
Via P10 X1 157-159,
Como 22100,
Italy.
Distribute in Argentina, Australia, Austria, Belgium, Canada, Denmark, Finland, France, Germany, Great Britain, Holland, Italy, Japan, Mexico, New Zealand, Norway, Portugal, Spain, South Africa, Sweden, Switzerland, USA. Unable to export direct to modellers in other countries.

**Roco**
Roco Modellspielwaren,
Jakob-Auer-Strasse 8,
Saltzburg,
A-5033,
Austria.

**Roundhouse**
Model Die Casting Inc.,
3811-15 W. Rosecrans,
Box 926,
Hawthorne,
California 90250,
USA.
Distribute in Australia, Great Britain, USA. Unable to export direct to modellers in other countries.

**Ruco**
Walter Waibel AG.,
Konradstrasse 20,
CH-8005 Zürich,
Switzerland.

**Swisstoys**
Walter Waibel AG.,
(address as Ruco)

**Trix**
Trix Mangold GmbH.,
Kreulstrasse 40,
D-8500,
Nürnberg 10,
West Germany.
Distribute in all countries either through importers/distributors, agents, or retail exporters. Unable to export direct to modellers.

**Tyco**
Tyco Industries Inc.,
540 Glen Avenue,
Moorestown,
New Jersey 08057,
USA.

**Wrenn**
G & R Wrenn Ltd.,
7-11 Bowlers Croft,
Basildon,
Essex,
SS14 3DU.

# Index